Cerdà 150

Years of modernity

Francesc Magrinyà
Fernando Marzá

CERDÀ 150 YEARS OF MODERNITY

Some authors date the advent of modernity, the end of the classical mentality, as the moment when Gödel's incompleteness theorems and the Heisenberg uncertainty principle transformed all suppositions of certain truth. Cerdà formed an inseparable part of that group of people who, with their science, introduced us into the modern era. Modernity means the continuity of a project, its impact and its influence on the future.

Cerdà is more relevant than ever today. The basic principles that formed the ideological foundation of his work, according to leading geographer Joan Tort, are: the citizen as a point of reference; an integrative approach; the territory as the sum of city and country; universality; anticipation; complexity; coherence; the relation of different scales; justice and equity.

Cerdà set out his thinking in Teoría general de la urbanización [General theory of Urbanization] and was forgotten, rescued from oblivion and once more forgotten, though his work is part of everyday life in Barcelona. This is because Cerdà was an awkward figure who extolled the classical values of the enlightenment and deductive rationalism, with a universalistic conception of the world that contrasts with violent or exclusive approaches.

The key to the celebration of the 150th anniversary of the initial approval of the "project for the remodelling and extension of Barcelona" is a forward-looking approach, looking to the future in an attempt to transform society so that, as the citizens at the centre of everything, we work to improve the living conditions of the generations that follow. Cerdà worked for the present that is ours today, which in his day was the future.

One of the basic lessons that Cerdà taught was a passion for study, finding pleasure in work, and conviction in defending, spreading and communicating ideas, involving those in public office as necessary.

With his ideas, Cerdà proved to be a precursor who was far ahead of his time. He worked with pleasure, passion and dedication to make them reality, despite the obstacles he found in his way.

The aim of marking this 150th anniversary is to debate ideas and to use this celebration as an excuse to talk about models of city and, accordingly, models of society.

Ildefons Cerdà was a civil engineer, a profession that involves hard work, abnegation, dedication, a vocation to serve the public and, most of all, study as a means to knowledge in the materialization of the project. Cerdà studied in depth the living conditions of the working class and every other aspect related to his plan, technically and scientifically, as no one had done before. His professionalism was key to the success of the new city extension.

Professionalism calls for across-the-board knowledge. All professional activity and therefore all companies related to science, technology and engineering have to recruit, coordinate and integrate all the know-how available.

Times have changed, and today the example of Cerdà, in professional terms, requires complicity between public administration and private venture. Private venture has to contribute technological value, promote universities, expand internationally and have recourse to a network of professionals capable of solving any problem in their field of speciality, anywhere.

The exercise of professionalism bestows authority, which means pre-eminence, prestige, dignity, public and private leadership, and particularly the capacity to influence events by means of decision-making, knowledge, courage and quality, and should never be associated with arrogance, money, obtuseness or the consciousness of being at the top of a hierarchy. This was the authority that Cerdà wielded and the path that we have to follow.

In late 2005, Albert Serratosa proposed that I should found and be president of the FUTIC (www.ildefonscerda.org), the Fundació Urbs i Territori, Ildefons Cerdà [Ildefons Cerdà Urbs and Territory Foundation]. It was initially made up of professionals who have gradually been joined by government agencies, professional associations and the private sector. The FUTIC is based on and inspired by the work of this illustrious urbanist, not just for his historical value but also as a reference for future planning.

The FUTIC has worked very hard—though not as hard as Cerdà—to acquaint the public with the undeniable modernity of the man's work. This exhibition is an example of the work carried out in his time by the illustrious civil engineer who set an example of professionalism and universality, with broad-based, ambitious objectives, which is an example to be followed.

The FUTIC has been a productive coming together of individual professionals, government bodies (local, autonomous and central), professional associations, the university world and the private sector. There are still many issues to be addressed by this association of bodies, which, with broad-based social backing, can find solutions to a series of problems. The design of the territory of the future is at stake; we have to prepare for the 21st century in the same way that Cerdà worked to prepare what is our present day.

Cerdà left us a great legacy, and it is our job to continue it. He created a new science that we have to extend by means of a combined professional effort, by means of a global approach, study and reflection, taking the necessary time to make the right decisions. But they have to be made.

Cerdà was undeniably modern. The principles and concepts developed by our fellow professional must show us the way. We will overcome the obstacles that exist and move forward to forge the society of the 21st century. All the Cerdàs, all over the world—and there are many more than it might initially seem—are already working on this task.

Angel Simón Grimaldos
President of the FUTIC

GRAN
HOTEL
HAVANA

O M M

HOTEL

Cerdà[150]

Years of modernity

The exhibition "Cerdà, 150 Years of Modernity" marks the 150th anniversary of the initial approval of the Projecte de Reforma i Eixample de Barcelona [Project for the Remodelling and Extension of Barcelona] of 1859. Other exhibitions have been held about Cerdà's project. The most outstanding past shows include an exhibition to mark the centenary of the Eixample Project in 1859, coinciding with the first Urbanism Congress in 1959; the exhibition "Ildefons Cerdà. 1876-1976", held in 1976 on the occasion of the centenary of the death of Ildefons Cerdà, centring on analysis of the Eixample layout and the grid tradition; and the exhibition "Mostra Cerdà. Urbs i territori" [The Cerdà Exhibition. Urbs and Territory] held in 1994 after the discovery of new documents relating to Cerdà in 1988, particularly about the development of his 1859 Eixample project. The latter exhibition was based on three phases of development of Cerdà's project: the Avantprojecte d'Eixample de Barcelona [Preliminary Project for the Extension of Barcelona] of 1855, the Projecte de Reforma i Eixample de Barcelona [Project for the Remodelling and Extension of Barcelona] of 1859, and a reworking of the 1859 project in the Avantprojecte de Docks de Barcelona [Preliminary Docks Project for Barcelona] of 1863.

The motive for the present-day exhibition is the celebration of 150 years of Cerdà's Eixample. One of the aims of the exhibition is to take a closer look at the values of the Eixample extension that has been built up over the last 150 years. Another is to propose an exercise in understanding the elements used in its construction, and in passing, to offer reflection on the process of planning, designing and constructing a city. In order to facilitate an understanding of its contents, with the aim of communicating with the public, the exhibition separates the city's constituent elements so that visitors can reflect on the possibility of planning different elements and, when they leave the exhibition, see the city through different eyes.

The exhibition space is divided into three parts. The first includes the elements that represent the construction of the Eixample: housing, the grid, the street, the chamfered corners and the sewerage system. The next section takes the grid as its basis and analyses the various configurations of city blocks associated with housing, industry, facilities and green spaces. It explores the city extension that we know as Cerdà's Eixample, as opposed to the more central Eixample that has traditionally showcased Modernista architecture. The aim is to highlight the way the grid has accommodated a series of fabrics: residential, mixed housing and industry, primarily industrial and even precarious, with shanty constructions.

Another purpose of the exhibition is to illustrate a planned approach to equipping the city with activities and facilities and the way project becomes reality. Finally, the exhibition seeks to analyse the growth of the Eixample with the various means of transport acting as generators of different types of urban form, in keeping with Cerdà's principle that each form of transport generates a form of urbanization.

The materials chosen for the exhibition are, as far as possible, original plans, supplemented by photographs that are, in most cases, little known, along with models to offer a clear explanation of the concepts presented and panels showing how Cerdà planned the different elements of the city.

We would particularly like to thank the archives and the people who have spent many years cataloguing documents that are vital for the reconstruction of historical memory and the urban history of the city and of the Eixample in particular. This exhibition represents a concerted effort to extend the field of knowledge to the whole of Cerdà's Eixample plan.

We regard the material exhibited here, much of which is little known, as a solid basis for a future museum of public works and architecture in Barcelona.

Finally, we would like to express our particular thanks to the people who have placed their trust in us, particularly the Fundació Urbs i Territori. Ildefons Cerdà (FUTIC) and, most especially, Albert Serratosa and Salvador Tarragó, who trusted in us throughout the organization of this exhibition.

Fernando Marzá and **Francesc Magrinyà**

introduction_

A chronology of Cerdà _

1815 Born at Mas Cerdà, Centelles (Osona).

1828 Ildefons and Miquel Cerdà studied Latin grammar in Centelles.

1830 Ildefons studied philosophy at the Episcopal School in Vic.

1831 Studied mathematics in Barcelona.

1832 Studied nautical science, architecture and technical drawing at the Board of Trade School in Barcelona.

1835 Moved to Madrid to study at the School of Civil Engineering.

1841 Qualified as an engineer.

1841-1848 Worked as a civil engineer at the Directorate General of Public Works of the Spanish Ministry of Public Works.

1844 Travelled to Nimes and saw the railway for the first time.
Worked at the optical telegraph office in Catalonia.

1842 Designed the Barcelona-Sarrià road.

1843 Carried out fieldwork for the left-hand canal of the river Llobregat.

1844 Worked on the piping of drinking water in the city of Valencia.

1848 First railway line in the Iberian Peninsula: Barcelona-Mataró.
Married Clotilde Bosch.
Inherited the family estate.

1849 Gave up the post of civil engineer to study urbanization.

1851 Elected member of the Cortes parliament.

1851-1854 Worked on the construction of the Barcelona-Granollers railway line.

1854 Civil engineer for the Treasury, starting work on his study of the extension, or Eixample, of Barcelona.
Commander of sappers in the National Militia.

1854-1856 Member of Barcelona City Council

1854 Drew up the topographical survey maps of the environs of Barcelona.
Drafted his preliminary extension project.
Commissioner in Madrid dealing with the conflict of the general strike.

1855 In Madrid, commissioned by the Council, he negotiated the concession of the Barcelona extension according to the principles of his preliminary project.
Started work on a study of the mine railway from Granollers to Sant Joan de les Abadesses.
Moved to Paris, making visits to Barcelona to promote the Sant Joan railway line project.
Wrote the *Monografía estadística de la Clase Obrera* [Statistical Monograph of the Working Class].

1856 Travelled to Paris, where he remained until 1858.

1858 The Spanish Ministry of Public Works acquired the competence for city extensions (9 December)

1859 Applied to the Ministry of Public Works for authorization to carry out studies for the extension of Barcelona (12 January). Royal Order authorizing Cerdà to draw up studies for the Remodelling and Extension of Barcelona (2 February). In Madrid he presented his Project for the Remodelling and Extension of Barcelona, dated March (18 April). Royal Order approving the Project for the Remodelling and Extension = Teoría de la Construcción de las ciudades aplicadas al proyecto de reforma y ensanche de Barcelona [Theory of city construction applied to the project for the remodelling and extension of Barcelona] (7 June). A Council Commission travelled to Madrid with an exposition to prevent the application of the Royal Order of 7 June (27 July). Royal Order ratifying the Order of 7 June approving the project for the remodelling and extension of Barcelona (31 July). Council circular outlining the conditions for the appointment of the Examining Board of projects submitted to tender (2 September).

1860 Royal Decree (31 May) authorizing the Extension according to Cerdà's project.

Appointed director of the Civil Government for the control and indication of reparcelling of land and street planning, until 1865, when he resigned.

1861 Presented the Remodelling Project for Madrid = *Teoría de la Viabilidad Urbana y Reforma de la de Madrid* [Theory of urban viability and remodelling of that of Madrid].

1863 Drafted the project for connecting sea and land routes = *Teoría del enlace del movimiento de las vías marítimas y terrestres, con aplicación al puerto de Barcelona* [Theory of connection of movement of sea and land routes, with application to the port of Barcelona] (unpublished).

Appointed director of the property company "El Fomento del Ensanche de Barcelona", until 1865.

Member of Barcelona City Council until 1866.

1864 Prepared the publication of the *Teoría General de la Urbanización* [General theory of urbanization].

1865 He went to live in the Eixample, in Carrer de Bruc.

1866 Refused to disclose the detail plans for the construction of the Eixample.

1867 Published the *Teoría General de la Urbanización, y aplicación de sus principios y doctrinas a la Reforma y Ensanche de Barcelona* [General theory of urbanization and application of its principles and doctrines to the remodelling and extension of Barcelona].

1868 Drew up the project for the rerouting of the Riera de Malla watercourse (unpublished).

1870 In response to the yellow fever epidemic in Barcelona, he took his daughters to the family home, Mas Cerdà.

1871 Death of his brother and collaborator Miquel.

Representative for the district of Centelles on the Barcelona Provincial Council.

1872 Formed part of a special commission to study the implementation of the interior remodelling of Barcelona.

He was President of the Judicial Division Project Commission of the Province of Barcelona.

1873 Acting President of Barcelona Provincial Council and Vice-President of the Provincial Commission until January 1874.

Produced the project for provincial division into 10 regional confederations of municipalities.

1874 Participated in the Remodelling Commission for the construction of Carrer de Bilbao (Via Laietana).

1875 He left Barcelona and settled in Madrid in an attempt to collect payment for his work.

Worked on the theory of colonization of the territory.

1876 Died in the spa at Caldas de Besaya (Cantabria).

Fig. 1_ ***Memoria del Anteproyecto del Ensanche de Barcelona* [Description of the Preliminary Project for the Extension of Barcelona]. 1855.** Author: Ildefons Cerdà. Source: Government Archives. Section of the Ministry of Education and Science

Fig. 2_ ***Monografía estadística de la clase obrera de Barcelona en 1856* [Statistical Monograph of the Working Class in 1856]. 1868.** Author: Ildefons Cerdà. Source: Biblioteca Pública Episcopal del Seminari de Barcelona.

Fig. 3_ ***Teoría de la Construcción de las Ciudades* [Theory of City Construction]. 1859.** Author: Ildefons Cerdà. Source: Government Archives. Section of the Ministry of Education and Science.

Fig. 4_ ***Ordenanzas municipales de construcción para la ciudad de Barcelona y pueblos comprendidos en su Ensanche* [Municipal construction bylaws for the city of Barcelona and the villages contained in its Extension]. 1859.** Author: Ildefons Cerdà. Source: Government Archives. Section of the Ministry of Education and Science.

Fig. 5_ ***Reforma y Ensanche de Barcelona. Plan económico* [Remodelling and Extension of Barcelona. Economic Plan]. 1860.** Author: Ildefons Cerdà. Source: Library of the Ateneu Barcelonès.

Fig. 6_ ***Cuatro palabras sobre el Ensanche* [A few words about the Extension]. 1861.** Author: Ildefons Cerdà. Source: CRAI- Philosophy, Geography and History Library. University of Barcelona.

Fig. 7_ ***Fomento del Ensanche de Barcelona.* 1863.** Author: Ildefons Cerdà. Source: Arxiu Històric de la Ciutat de Barcelona.

Fig. 8_ ***Teoría General de la Urbanización* [General theory of urbanization]. 1867 (vol. I).** Author: Ildefons Cerdà. Source: Fernando Marzá - Neus Moyano Collection.

Fig. 9_ ***Teoría General de la Urbanización* [General theory of urbanization]. 1867 (vol. II).** Author: Ildefons Cerdà. Source: Library of the Col·legi d'Arquitectes de Catalunya

ENSANCHE DE LA CIUDAD DE BARCELONA

MEMORIA DESCRIPTIVA

de los trabajos facultativos y estudios estadísticos

HECHOS DE ÓRDEN DEL GOBIERNO,

y consideraciones que se han tenido presentes

EN LA FORMACION DEL

ANTE-PROYECTO

PARA

EL EMPLAZAMIENTO Y DISTRIBUCION

del

NUEVO CASERIO.

Fig. 1

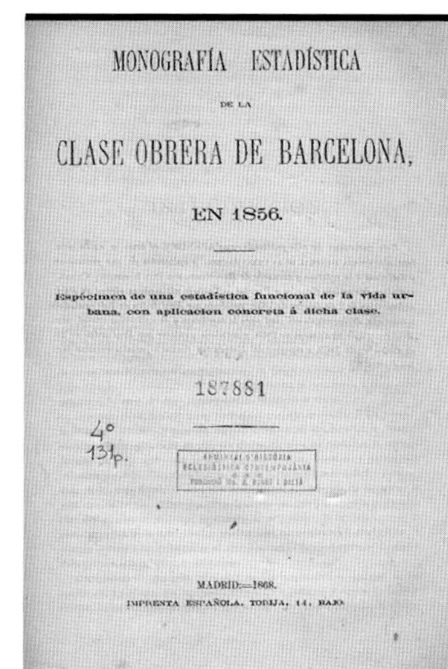

MONOGRAFÍA ESTADÍSTICA

DE LA

CLASE OBRERA DE BARCELONA,

EN 1856.

Espécimen de una estadística funcional de la vida urbana, con aplicacion concreta á dicha clase.

MADRID.—1868.

IMPRENTA ESPAÑOLA, TORIJA, 14, BAJO.

Fig. 2

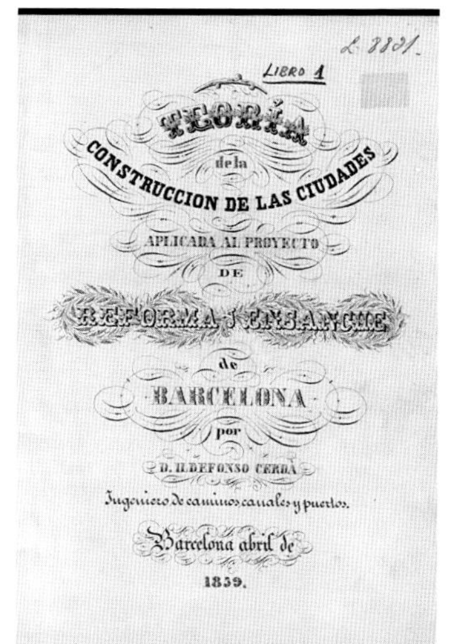

TEORÍA de la CONSTRUCCION DE LAS CIUDADES

APLICADA AL PROYECTO DE

REFORMA Y ENSANCHE

de

BARCELONA

por

D. ILDEFONSO CERDÁ

Ingeniero de caminos canales y puertos.

Barcelona abril de 1859.

Fig. 3

ORDENANZAS MUNICIPALES DE CONSTRUCCION

para

LA CIUDAD

de

BARCELONA

y

PUEBLOS COMPRENDIDOS

en su

ENSANCHE.

Setiembre de 1859.

Fig. 4

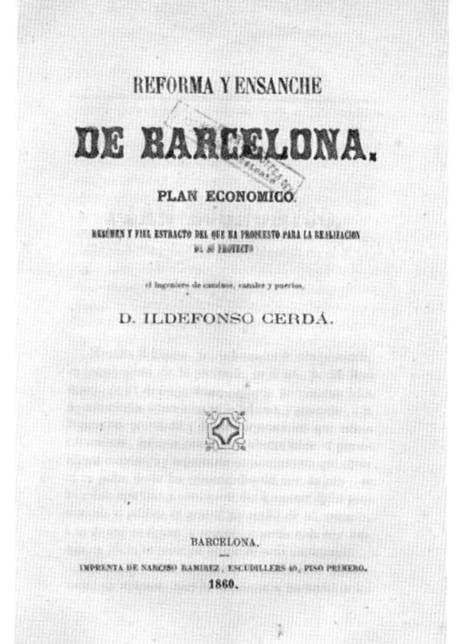

REFORMA Y ENSANCHE

DE BARCELONA.

PLAN ECONOMICO.

RESÚMEN Y FIEL EXTRACTO DEL QUE HA PROPUESTO PARA LA REALIZACION DE SU PROYECTO

el Ingeniero de caminos, canales y puertos,

D. ILDEFONSO CERDÁ.

BARCELONA.

IMPRENTA DE NARCISO RAMIREZ, ESCUDILLERS 40, PISO PRIMERO.

1860.

Fig. 5

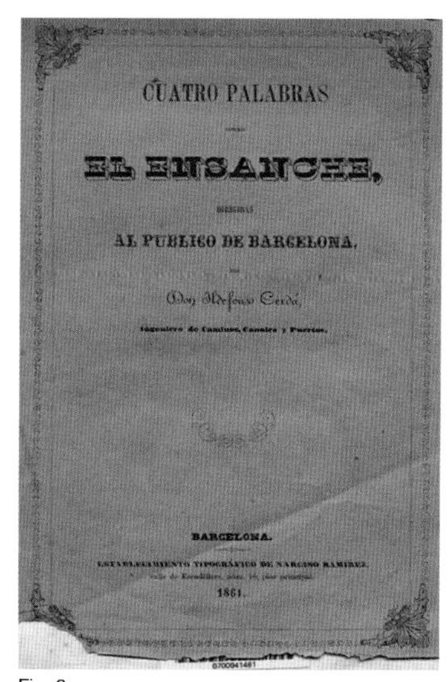

CUATRO PALABRAS

SOBRE

EL ENSANCHE,

DIRIGIDAS

AL PUBLICO DE BARCELONA,

POR

Don Ildefonso Cerdá,

Ingeniero de Caminos, Canales y Puertos.

BARCELONA.

ESTABLECIMIENTO TIPOGRÁFICO DE NARCISO RAMIREZ,

1861.

Fig. 6

FOMENTO

DEL ENSANCHE DE BARCELONA.

RAZON SOCIAL.

PUIG, VIDAL, BABOT Y COMPAÑÍA.

JUNTA CONSULTIVA.

D. RAMON BONAPLATA, hacendado.
» BARTOLOMÉ VIDAL, hacendado y del comercio.
» HERMENEGILDO MATARÓ, propietario y del comercio.
» RAMON ESTRUCH, hacendado y del comercio.
» JOSÉ ANTONIO de MAGAROLA, hacendado.
» EUSEBIO CORONAS, propietario y del comercio.
D. LUIS VILLAVECCHIA, propietario y del comercio.
» FEDERICO MARESCH, propietario y del comercio.
» FRANCISCO PARELLADA y RIBAS, propietario y del comercio.
» JUAN MUMBRU, propietario.
» NARCISO de FOXA, hacendado.
» ANTONIO MARQUÉS, propietario.
» JOSÉ CERDA y SOLER, hacendado.
» JUAN PLA y BROQUETAS, propietario.

Director Facultativo: D. ILDEFONSO CERDÁ.—Secretario General: D. MANUEL ANGELON.

Oficinas de la Sociedad; calle de la Ciudad, n.º 5, piso principal.

BARCELONA.

ESTABLECIMIENTO TIPOGRÁFICO DE NARCISO RAMIREZ, pasaje de Escudillers, núm. 4.

1863.

Fig. 7

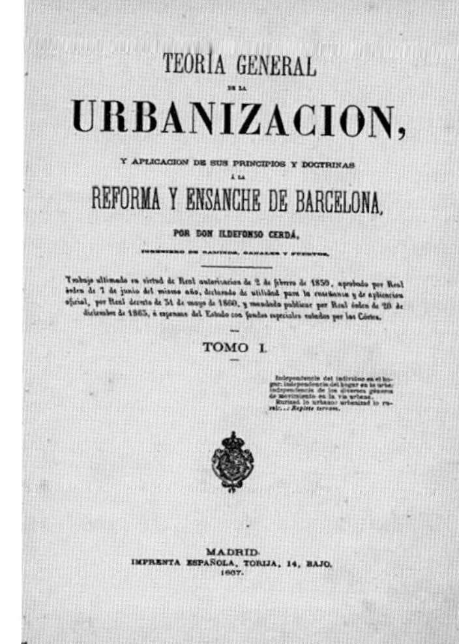

TEORÍA GENERAL

DE LA

URBANIZACION,

Y APLICACION DE SUS PRINCIPIOS Y DOCTRINAS

Á LA

REFORMA Y ENSANCHE DE BARCELONA,

POR DON ILDEFONSO CERDÁ,

INGENIERO DE CAMINOS, CANALES Y PUERTOS.

Trabajo ultimado en virtud de Real autorizacion de 2 de febrero de 1859, aprobado por Real órden de 7 de junio del mismo año, declarado de utilidad para la enseñanza y de aplicacion oficial, por Real decreto de 31 de mayo de 1860, y mandado publicar por Real órden de 20 de diciembre de 1865, á expensas del Estado con fondos especiales votados por las Córtes.

TOMO I.

MADRID.

IMPRENTA ESPAÑOLA, TORIJA, 14, BAJO.

1867.

Fig. 8

TEORÍA GENERAL

DE LA

URBANIZACION,

Y APLICACION DE SUS PRINCIPIOS Y DOCTRINAS

Á LA

REFORMA Y ENSANCHE DE BARCELONA,

POR DON ILDEFONSO CERDÁ,

INGENIERO DE CAMINOS, CANALES Y PUERTOS.

Trabajo ultimado en virtud de Real autorizacion de 2 de febrero de 1859, aprobado por Real órden de 7 de junio del mismo año, declarado de utilidad para la enseñanza y de aplicacion oficial, por Real decreto de 31 de mayo de 1860, y mandado publicar por Real órden de 20 de diciembre de 1865, á expensas del Estado con fondos especiales votados por las Córtes.

TOMO II.

LA URBANIZACION CONSIDERADA COMO UN HECHO CONCRETO.

ESTADÍSTICA URBANA DE BARCELONA.

MADRID.

IMPRENTA ESPAÑOLA, TORIJA, 14, BAJO.

1867.

Fig. 9

Influences

"Before, however, making a decision, I wanted to gauge the extent of the work I was about to take on. I saw that, to develop it in due form, it was necessary to learn everything written about architecture from Vitruvius to Léonce Reynaud; with everything said in matters of law from Solon to Bentham; everything that has been said about societal studies from Plato to Proudhon; everything that has been said about hygiene from Hippocrates to the present day; everything that has been written about statistics from Moses to the present day; in geography from ... to ...; in Administration from.... to....; in politics from ... to...; in moral or religion from ... to ...; in philosophy from ... to ...; etcetera."

(Ildefons Cerdà, *Indice Cronológico* [Chronological Index], 1875).

Fig. 1_ ***Saint-Simon, son premier écrit: lettres d'un habitant de Genève à ses contemporains, 1809: sa Parabole politique, 1819: le Nouveau Christianisme*. 1825.** Published by Olinde Rodrigues, 1832. Source: CRAI-Economics Library. University of Barcelona

Fig. 2_ ***Principios de legislación y de codificación, estractados de las obras del filósofo inglés Jeremías Bentham por Francisco Ferrer y Valls* [Principles of legislation and codification, extracted from the works of English philosopher Jeremy Bentham by Francisco Ferrer y Valls]. 1834.** Author: Jeremy Bentham, jurist. Source: Socials Sciences Library. Autonomous University of Barcelona (UAB).

Fig. 3_ ***Économie politique.* 1804.** Author: Jean-Baptiste Say, economist. Source: Historical Science and Technology Holdings. Library of the ETSEIB. Polytechnic University of Catalonia (UPC).

Fig. 4_ ***Teoría de la contribución* [The theory of taxation]. 1862 (1st edition 1861).** Author: Pierre-Joseph Proudhon, politician. Source: CRAI-Economics Library. University of Barcelona.

Fig. 5_ ***I Dieci libri dell'architettura* [Ten books on architecture]. 1567.** Author: Marcus Vitruvius Pollio, architect. Source: Library of the Col·legi d'Arquitectes de Catalunya.

Fig. 6_ ***Traité d'architecture contenant des notions générales sur les principes de la construction et sur l'histoire de l'art* [Treatise on architecture containing general notions on the principles of construction and the history of art]. 1850.** Author: Léonce Reynaud. Source: Library of the ETSEIB. Polytechnic University of Catalonia (UPC).

Fig. 7_ ***Diccionario geográfico-estadístico-histórico de España y sus posesiones de ultramar* [Dictionary of geography, statistics and history of Spain and its overseas possessions]. 1846. Volume I.** Author: Pascual Madoz, politician. Source: Socials Sciences Library. Autonomous University of Barcelona (UAB).

Fig. 8._ ***Estadística de Barcelona* [Statistics of Barcelona]. 1962 (facsimile of the 1849 original).** Author: Laureà Figuerola, economist and politician. Source: Institut d'Estadística de Catalunya.

Fig. 9_ ***Elementos de higiene pública ó arte de conservar la salud de los pueblos* [Elements of public hygiene or the art of conserving the people's health]. 1862 (1st edition 1846).** Author: Pere Felip Monlau, hygienic doctor. Source: Historical Science and Technology Holdings. Library of the ETSEIB. Polytechnic University of Catalonia (UPC)

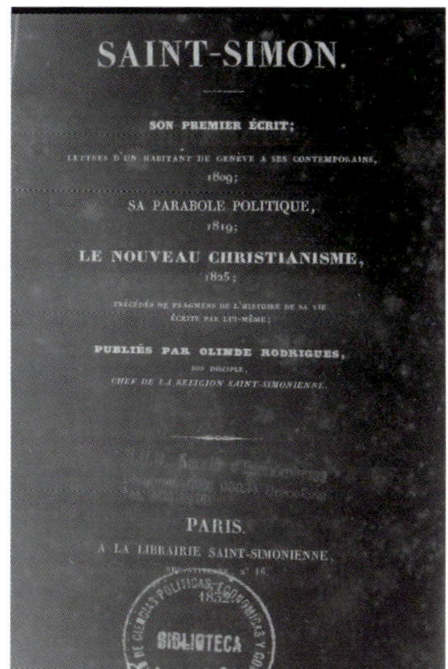
SAINT-SIMON.

SON PREMIER ÉCRIT;

LETTRES D'UN HABITANT DE GENÈVE A SES CONTEMPORAINS,

1803;

SA PARABOLE POLITIQUE,

1819;

LE NOUVEAU CHRISTIANISME,

1825;

PRÉCÉDÉS DE FRAGMENS DE L'HISTOIRE DE SA VIE ÉCRITE PAR LUI-MÊME;

PUBLIÉS PAR OLINDE RODRIGUES,

SON DISCIPLE,

CHEF DE LA RELIGION SAINT-SIMONIENNE.

PARIS,

A LA LIBRAIRIE SAINT-SIMONIENNE,

1832.

Fig. 10

PRINCIPIOS

DE

LEGISLACION Y DE CODIFICACION,

ESTRACTADOS

DE LAS OBRAS DEL FILOSOFO INGLES

JEREMÍAS BENTHAM,

POR

Francisco Ferrer y Valls.

TOMO I.

MADRID:

IMPRENTA DE D. TOMAS JORDAN.

MARZO DE 1834.

Fig. 11

H. BAUDRILLART

J.-B. SAY

ÉCONOMIE POLITIQUE

PARIS. — GUILLAUMIN et Cie, 14, rue Richelieu

Fig. 12

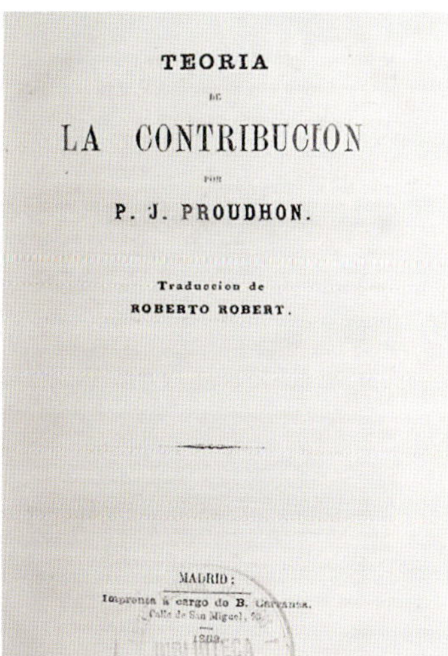
TEORIA

DE

LA CONTRIBUCION

POR

P. J. PROUDHON.

Traduccion de

ROBERTO ROBERT.

MADRID:

Imprenta á cargo de B. Carranza,

Calle de San Miguel,

Fig. 13

I DIECI LIBRI

DELL'ARCHITETTVRA

DI M. VITRVVIO,

Tradotti & commentati da Monsr. Daniel Barbaro eletto Patriarca d'Aquileia, da lui riueduti & ampliati; & hora in più commoda forma ridotti.

IN VENETIA,

Appresso Francesco de' Franceschi Senese, & Giouanni Chrieger Alemano Compagni.

M D LXVII.

Fig. 14

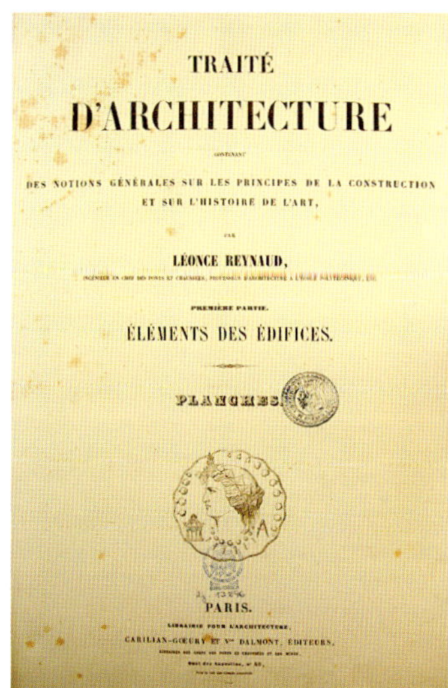
TRAITÉ

D'ARCHITECTURE

CONTENANT

DES NOTIONS GÉNÉRALES SUR LES PRINCIPES DE LA CONSTRUCTION ET SUR L'HISTOIRE DE L'ART,

PAR

LÉONCE REYNAUD,

PREMIÈRE PARTIE.

ÉLÉMENTS DES ÉDIFICES.

PLANCHES.

PARIS.

LIBRAIRIE POUR L'ARCHITECTURE,

CARILIAN-GOEURY ET Vor DALMONT, ÉDITEURS,

Fig. 15

DICCIONARIO

GEOGRAFICO-ESTADISTICO-HISTORICO

DE

ESPAÑA

Y SUS POSESIONES DE ULTRAMAR.

POR PASCUAL MADOZ.

TOMO I.

SEGUNDA EDICION.

MADRID.

1846.

Fig. 16

ESTADÍSTICA

DE

BARCELONA

EN

1849.

PUBLÍCALA

DON LAUREANO FIGUEROLA,

profesor de Economía política, derecho público y administracion en la Universidad literaria de Barcelona, individuo de la sociedad Económica barcelonesa de Amigos del pais en la clase de estadística, de la Academia de buenas letras etc.

BARCELONA.

IMPRENTA Y LIBRERÍA POLITÉCNICA DE TOMAS GORCHS,

calle del Cármen, junto á la Universidad.

Diciembre de 1849.

Fig. 17

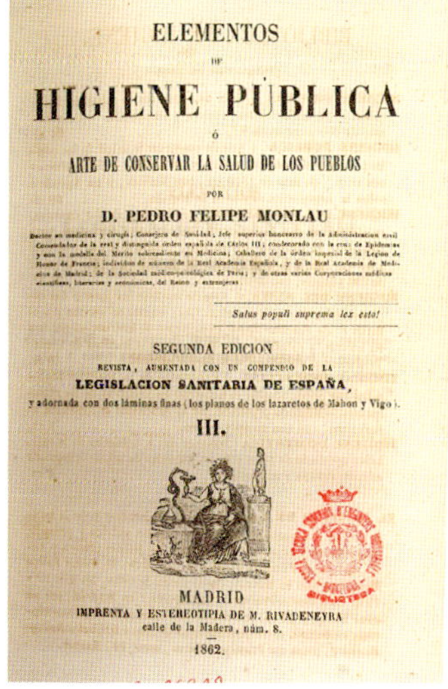
ELEMENTOS

DE

HIGIENE PÚBLICA

Ó

ARTE DE CONSERVAR LA SALUD DE LOS PUEBLOS

POR

D. PEDRO FELIPE MONLAU

Salus populi suprema lex esto!

SEGUNDA EDICION

REVISTA, AUMENTADA CON UN COMPENDIO DE LA

LEGISLACION SANITARIA DE ESPAÑA,

y adornada con dos láminas finas (los planos de los lazaretos de Mahon y Vigo).

III.

MADRID

IMPRENTA Y ESTEREOTIPIA DE M. RIVADENEYRA

calle de la Madera, núm. 8.

1862.

Fig. 18

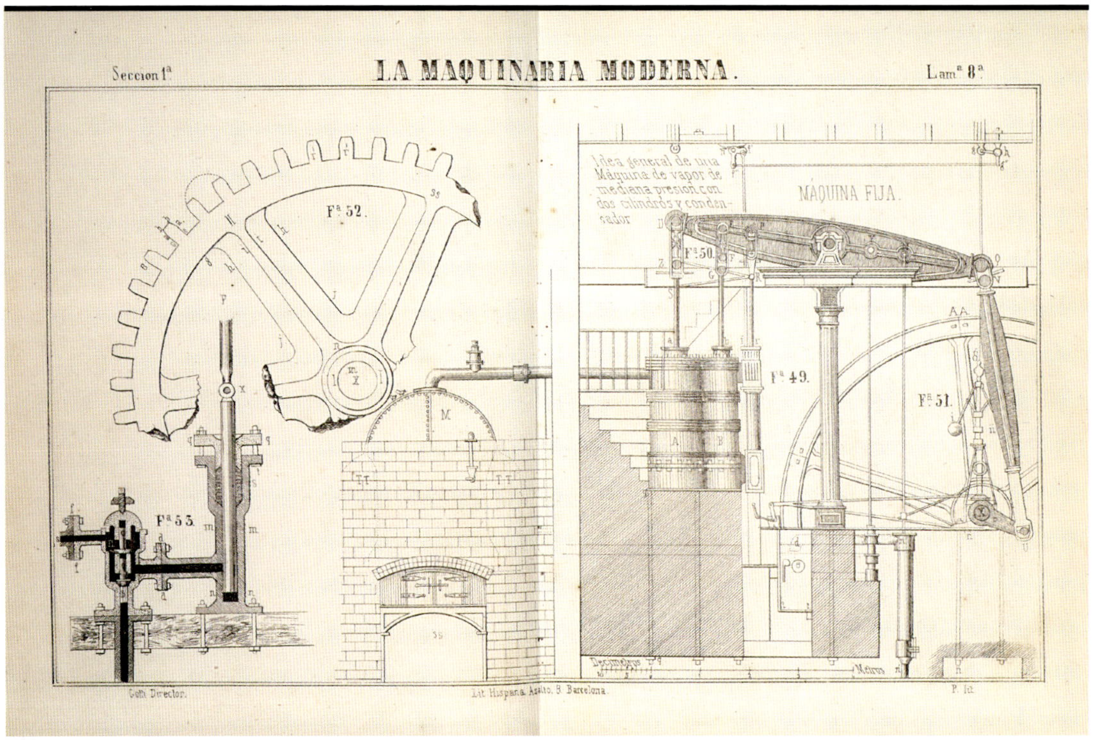

The Barcelona of Cerdà

1821	Yellow fever epidemic on Barcelona
1832	Founding in Barcelona of El Vapor factory
	Cholera epidemic in Paris and London
1833	Death of Ferdinand VII. Regency of Maria Cristina
	First Carlist War
1834	Cholera epidemic in Barcelona
	Founding in Barcelona of El Vulcano ship building plant
1835	The confiscation of Mendizábal
	Burning of Barcelona's convents
1841	Publication of the pamphlet *Abajo las murallas* [Down with the walls]
1845	Approval of the Property Tax Act
1848	Creation of the Barcelona Provincial Statistics Commission
	Creation of the Industrial Institute of Catalonia
	First railway in the Iberian Peninsula: Barcelona-Mataró
1849	Publication of *Estadística de Barcelona* [Barcelona's Statistics] by Laureà Figuerola
1851	First parcelling survey of the city of Barcelona by Joan Soler Mestres
1858	The Ministry of Public Works acquired jurisdiction for city extensions (9 December)
1859	Monturiol's first tests with the submarine Ictíneo
	Opening of the Suez Canal

Plate 8. *La maquinària moderna* [Modern machinery] (1859). Author: José Gotti. Source: Arxiu Històric de la Ciutat de Barcelona

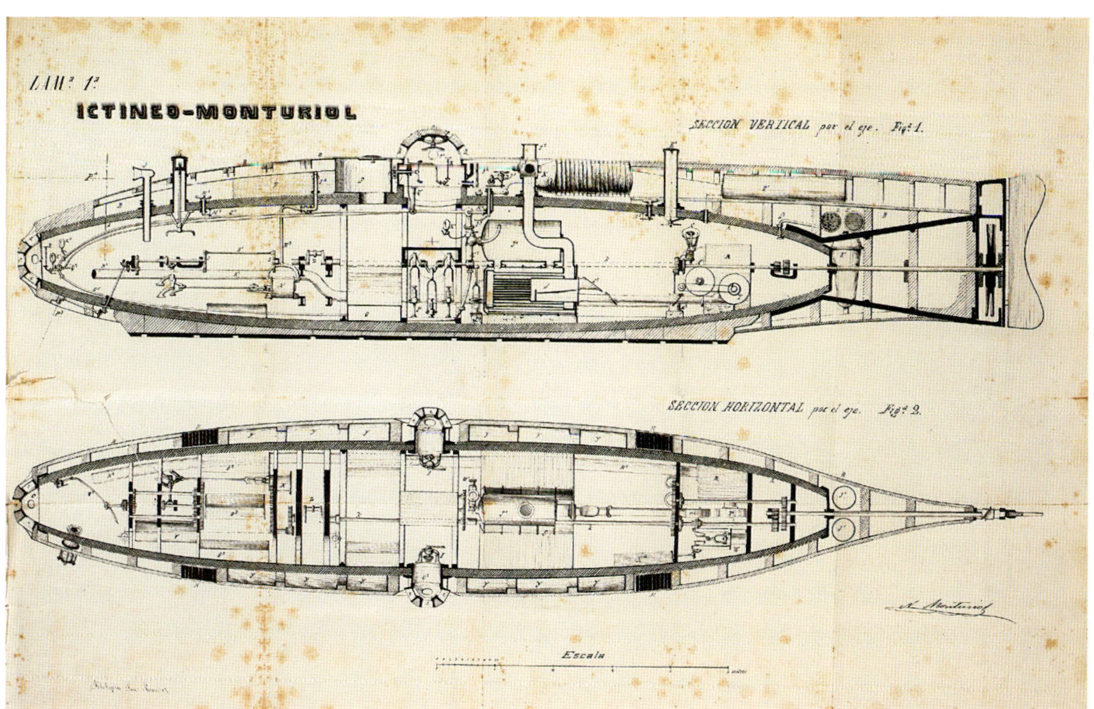

***Ensayo sobre el arte de navegar por debajo del agua* [Essay on the art of underwater navigation] (1891).** Author: Narcís Monturiol, inventor and politician. Source: Fernando Marzá - Neus Moyano Collection

Ictineo-Monturiol. Plate 1. *Ensayo sobre el arte de navegar por debajo del agua* [Essay on the art of underwater navigation]. 1860. Author: Narcís Monturiol, inventor and politician. Source: Fernando Marzá - Neus Moyano Collection

Sert Hermanos y Solá textile factory: interior of the spinning mill (undated). Draughtsman: Antoni Rigalt
Source: Arxiu Històric de la Ciutat de Barcelona

From the walled city of Barcelona to the Eixample extension

The walled city became increasingly densely populated with the advent of the industrial revolution. The need for labour for the factories attracted immigration, and the poor hygienic conditions of workers' homes led to epidemics. The city had to be adapted to new conditions of hygiene and transport. The solution was to demolish the walls and construct a city extension.

The initial proposals were provided by the military, which wanted to demolish part of the town walls and extend the walled enclosure. Gradually, however, the idea of the unlimited city, or city without walls, took shape. The topographical survey maps produced by the Military Engineering Brigade are an example of this initial phase.

The Property Tax Act of 1845 proposed the collection of taxes according to the returns of each plot of land. This called for the compilation of statistics and plot surveys about the territory. In 1849, Laureà Figuerola produced his Estadística de Barcelona [Barcelona Statistics] and, in 1855, Pascual Madoz wrote the Diccionari Estadístic [Statistical Dictionary]. Plot plans were also drawn up, such as the one by Joan Soler Mestres for the municipality of Barcelona in 1851.

This was the context for debate about the Eixample, and Ildefons Cerdà was commissioned to draw up the Topographical Map of the environs of Barcelona in 1855. With this plan and his description, Cerdà began his reflection on the urbanization of cities, and used Barcelona and its remodelling and extension as the basis for analysis and proposals.

La Maquinista Terrestre y Maritima. Historical figure (1855-1955). Author: Alberto del Castillo. 1955. Source: Fernando Marzá - Neus Moyano Collection

View of the Rambla and the Barcelona Plain from the Church of El Pi (1855-1860). Photograph: unknown author. Source: Historical Archive of the Col·legi d'Arquitectes de Catalunya

Demolition of the city wall (1880-1889). Photograph: unknown author. Source: Arxiu Fotogràfic de Barcelona

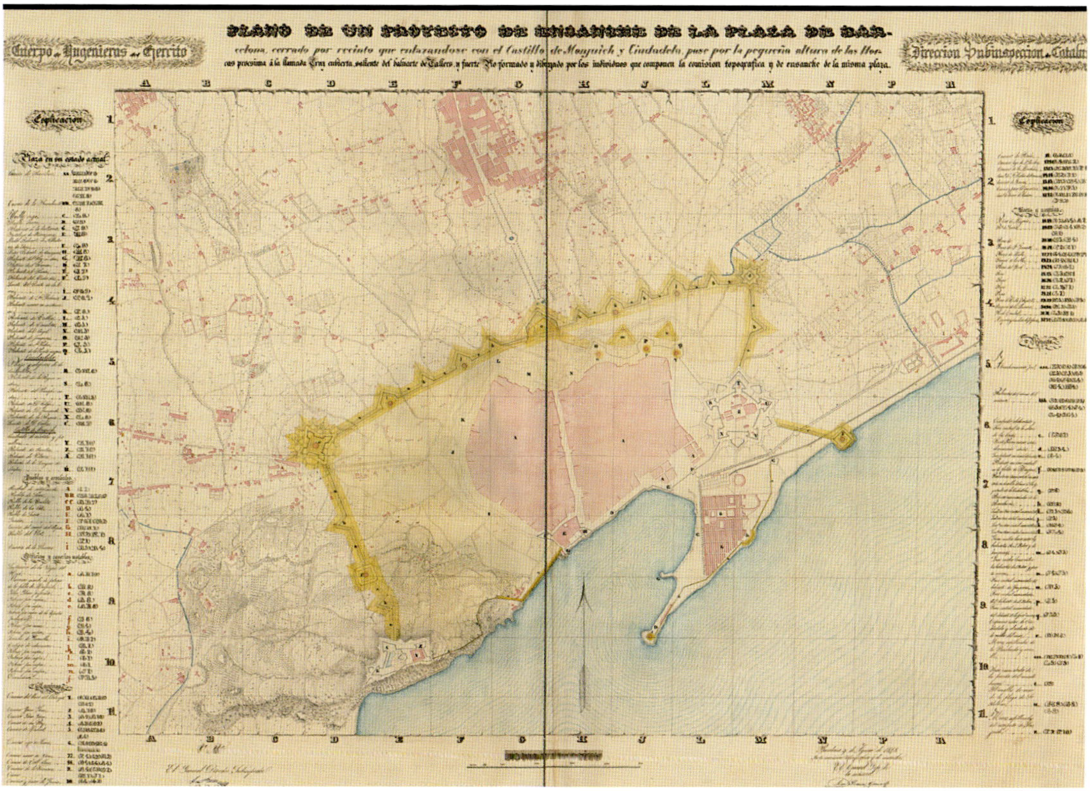

Project for a limited extension for new fortifications as far as Montjuïc (1848). Author: Manuel Ramón García. Topographic and Extension Commission of the Military Engineering Corps. Source: Archivo General Militar de Madrid

Geometric map of the jurisdictional area of the city of Barcelona separated from the municipality of the Town of Gracia, which were previously joined (1851). Author: Joan Soler i Mestres. Source: Arxiu Històric de la Ciutat de Barcelona

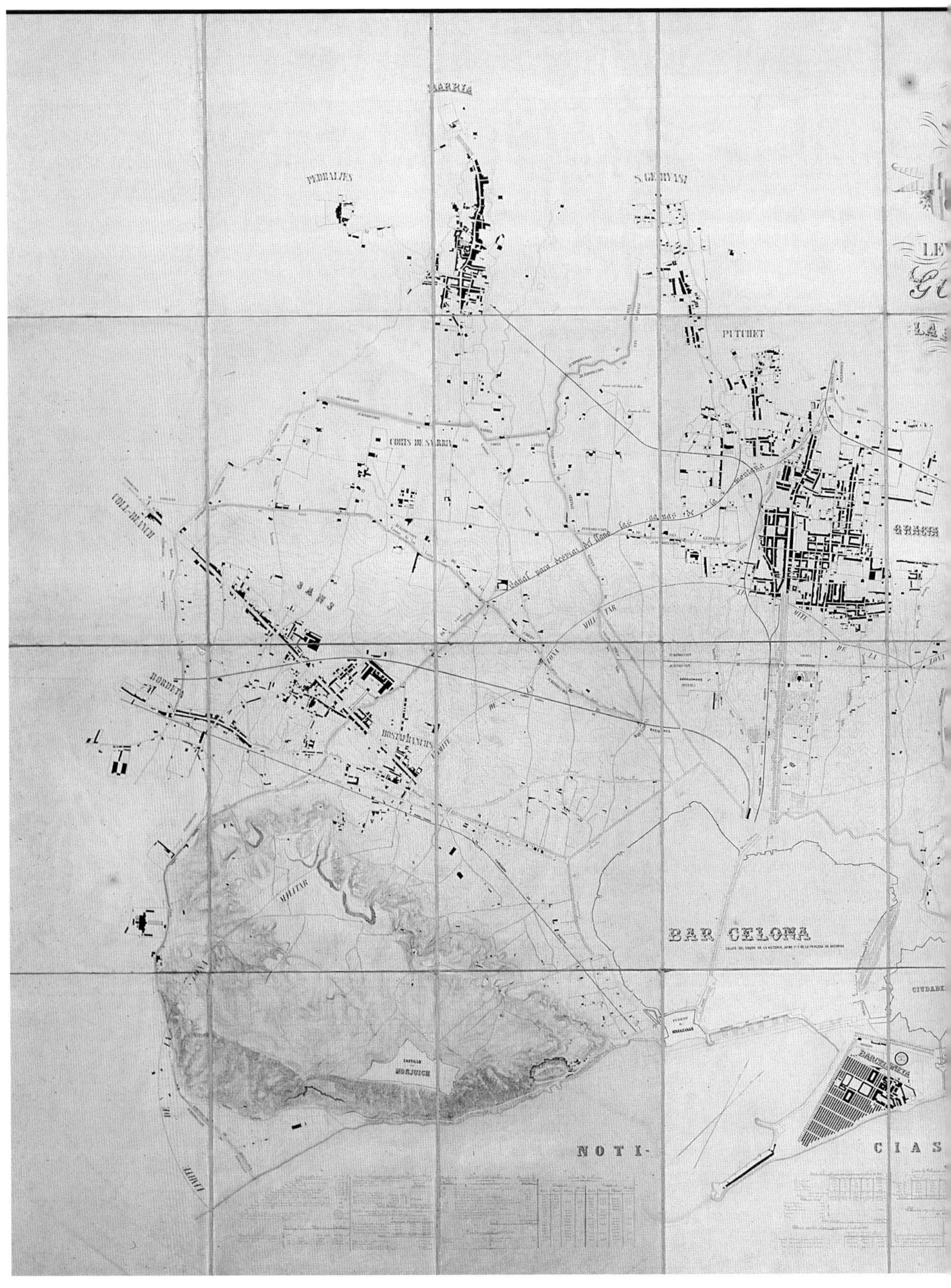
SARRIA
PEDRALVES
S. GERVASI
PUTCHET
CORTS DE SARRIA
COLL-BLANCH
SANS
GRACIA
BORDETA
HOSTAFRANCHS
BAR CELONA
CASTILLO DE MONJUICH
NOTI-
CIAS
CIUDADE

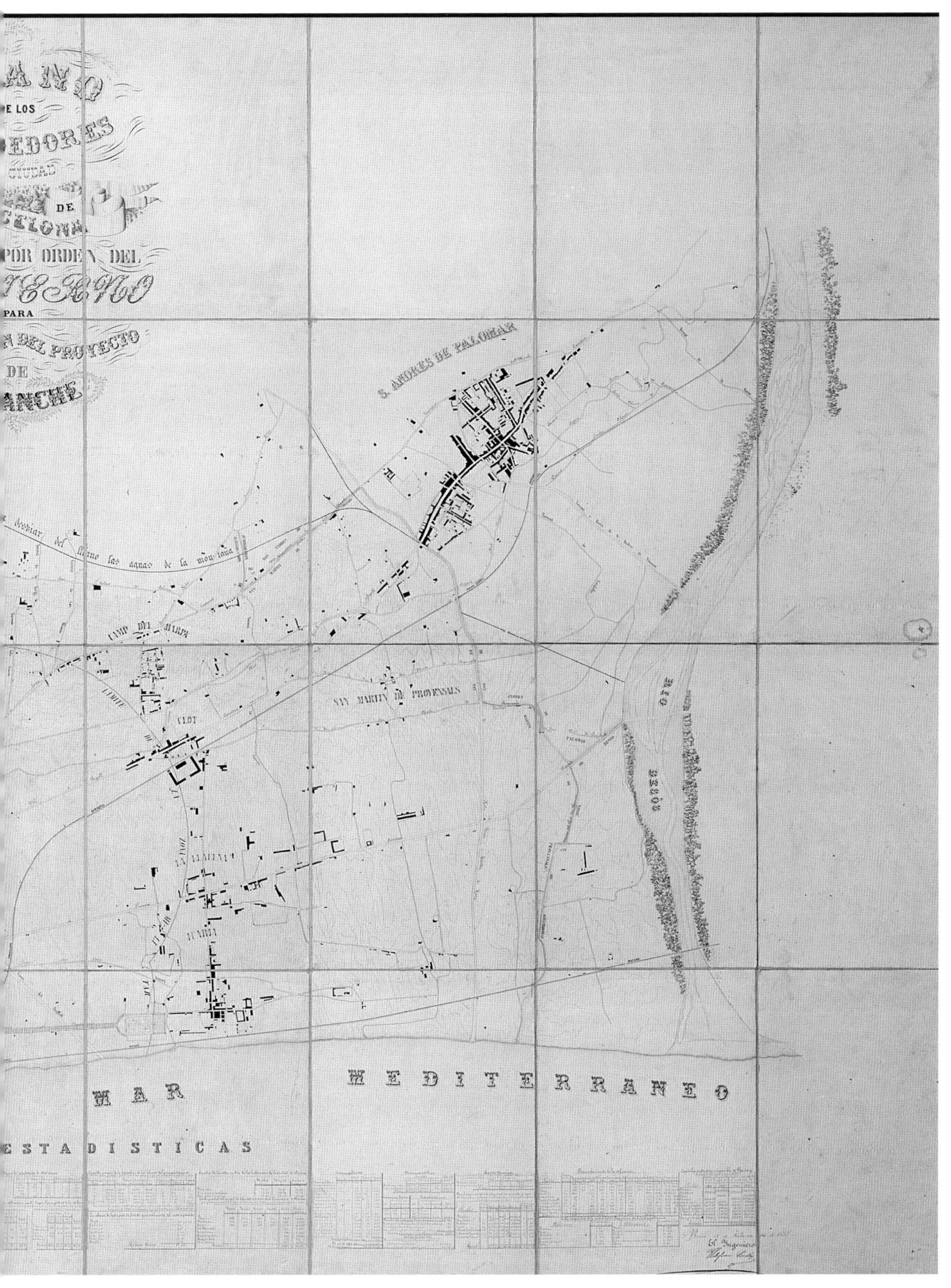

Topographic survey map of the environs of Barcelona (1855). Author: Ildefons Cerdà. Source: Temporary holdings of the Patronat del Castell de Montjüic - Museu Militar.

housing_

“The first condition that cities have to meet is free-standing constructions.”

(I. Cerdà, *Teoría de la Construcción de las Ciudades*, 1859)

Cerdà's apartment building models: a justification of the shift from the detached house to the freestanding block containing apartment buildings with party walls, and reflection on the minimum housing unit

Cerdà wrote that "The first condition that cities have to meet is free-standing constructions. [...] a system of street blocks open on two sides is a transition from the present-day system towards one of detached buildings set in their own gardens, which is, strictly speaking, the only admissible system" (I. Cerdà, *Teoría de la Construcción de Ciudades* [Theory of City Construction], 1859).

To implement this principle, Cerdà moved from the ideal 20x20 m detached house (the first order middle-class home) to a 20x20 m building between party walls comprising a ground floor plus three upper storeys (fourth order middle-class home), which gave way to the model of the rental building, commissioned by an owner who used the piano nobile as a dwelling and the ground floor for business, and rented out the upper floors.

In his analysis of residential models for workers, Cerdà also introduced the concept of the "minimum housing unit" and applied it to a family home that displays some similarities with the model envisaged many years later by modern rationalism, represented by Le Corbusier's *unité d'habitation.*

The evolution of dwellings in Barcelona's Eixample: from Cerdà to the present day

The model of fourth order middle-class home produced by the rental building has readily evolved to adapt to the different needs and changing uses of the city of Barcelona in the last 150 years. The evolution of the rental building can be divided into four main periods:

1_The residential city and the appearance of the rental building model

2_The residential + commercial city, with the division of the ground floor and the appearance of the mezzanine and basement

3_The residential + commercial + industrial city, with occupation of the courtyard at the centre of the city block

4_The residential + commercial + industrial + service city that is recovering the courtyard at the centre of the city block

[1] See fig. page 35 and 37 I [2] See fig. page 39

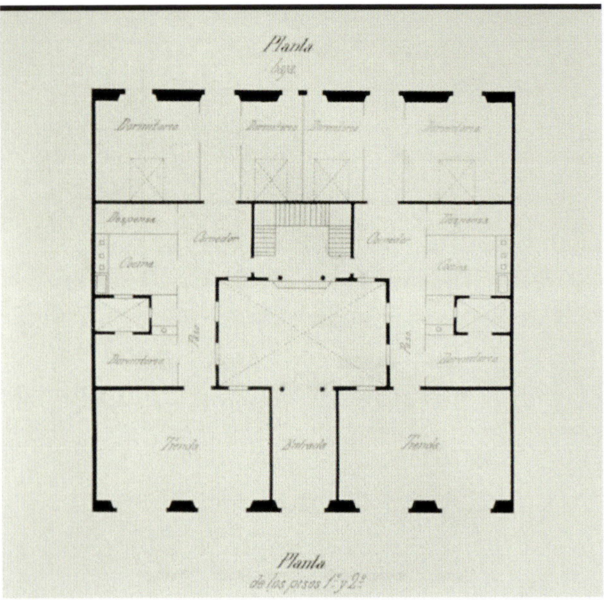

Fig. 1

Fig. 2

Increasing density of housing saw buildings with a ground floor plus three upper floors give way to a model comprising a ground floor plus five upper floors, which was consolidated in the late 19th century, and buildings with a ground floor plus six upper floors, and a further two penthouse floors at the time of highest occupation of the Eixample, before returning to the regulatory ground floor plus five upper floors with the approval of the 1976 Pla General Metropolità de Barcelona [Barcelona Master Plan].

In spite of this, maintaining an invariable maximum depth of grouped buildings allowed the formation of a unitary courtyard at the centre of the city block, guaranteeing highly favourable conditions of hygiene and sunlighting.

Within this evolution, the ground floors with a mezzanine have provided business premises with an area (750-2200 m2) large enough to accommodate shops and, later, industrial workshops, to coexist with the residential function. The result is a compact, complex, diverse city that is a referent for sustainable models today.

[3] See fig. 2 I [4] See fig. page 46 I [5] See fig. page 43, 44 and 45

Fig. 1 Fourth-order middle-class home. Ildefons Cerdà. Teoría de la Construcción de las Ciudades [Theory of City Construction]. 1859.
Fig. 2 Comparison of a building comprising ground floor with five storeys and a building of ground floor with six storeys plus two penthouse floors.

Housing in the Barcelona of Cerdà's time did not meet minimum conditions

Cerdà analysed housing in Barcelona and discovered, among other things, that:

–"The population of Barcelona is excessively condensed, with just 12 m² corresponding to each individual, when science prescribes 40 m² per individual"

–"Mortality in Barcelona is twice what it is in London"

–"The cost of a cubic metre of breathable air is 34% higher on fourth floors than on the piano nobile"

(I. Cerdà, *Monografia estadística de la classe obrera* [Statistical Monograph of the Working Class], 1856)

The problem of the lack of independence of the individual at home in the dwellings

Cerdà reviewed the houses being built in Barcelona and analysed the conditions of the working class who were unable to afford to rent a dwelling with conditions of hygiene that met the following criteria:

–Hygienic: "providing each person with the sufficient quantity of breathable air"

–Social: "each house should accommodate a single family"

–Economic: "creating decent basic housing without increasing the cost of rents"

–Political: "increasing the number of owners and, therefore, the guarantees of urban tranquillity and public order"

(Ildefons Cerdà, *Teoria de Construcció de Ciutats* [Theory of City Construction], 1859)

He then used his Memòria de l'Avantprojecte d'Eixample de Barcelona [Description of the Preliminary Barcelona Extension Project], of 1855, to draw up a systematic body of reflection on housing and to design a series of four models of middle-class homes and four models of homes for workers.

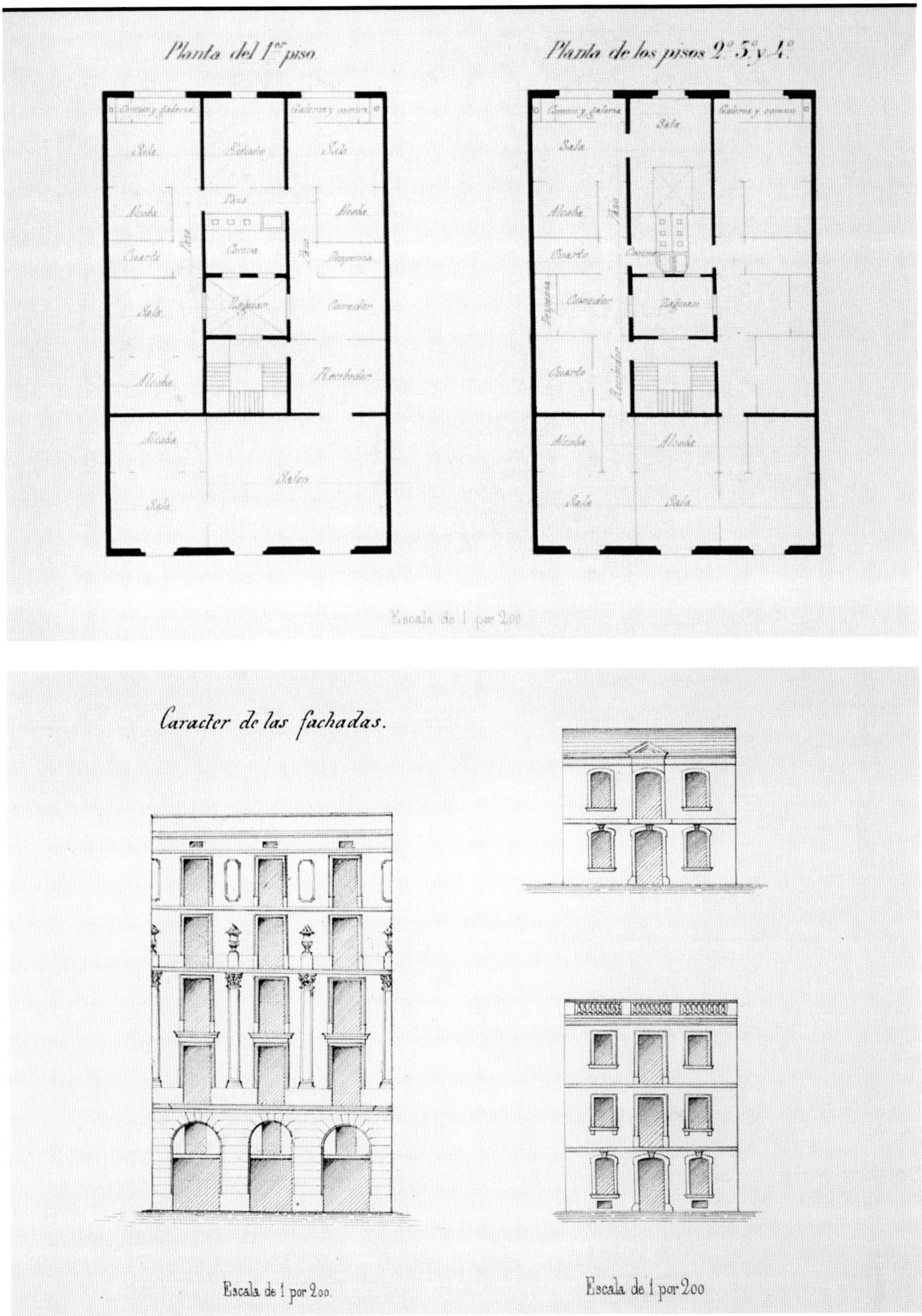

Layout of the homes generally constructed in Barcelona. Detail of the minimum housing unit for a family (third order) and for single people (fourth order). Ildefons Cerdà. *Memoria del Anteproyecto del Ensanche de Barcelona* [Description of the Preliminary Project for the Extension of Barcelona], 1855 Government Archives. Section of the Ministry of Education and Science.

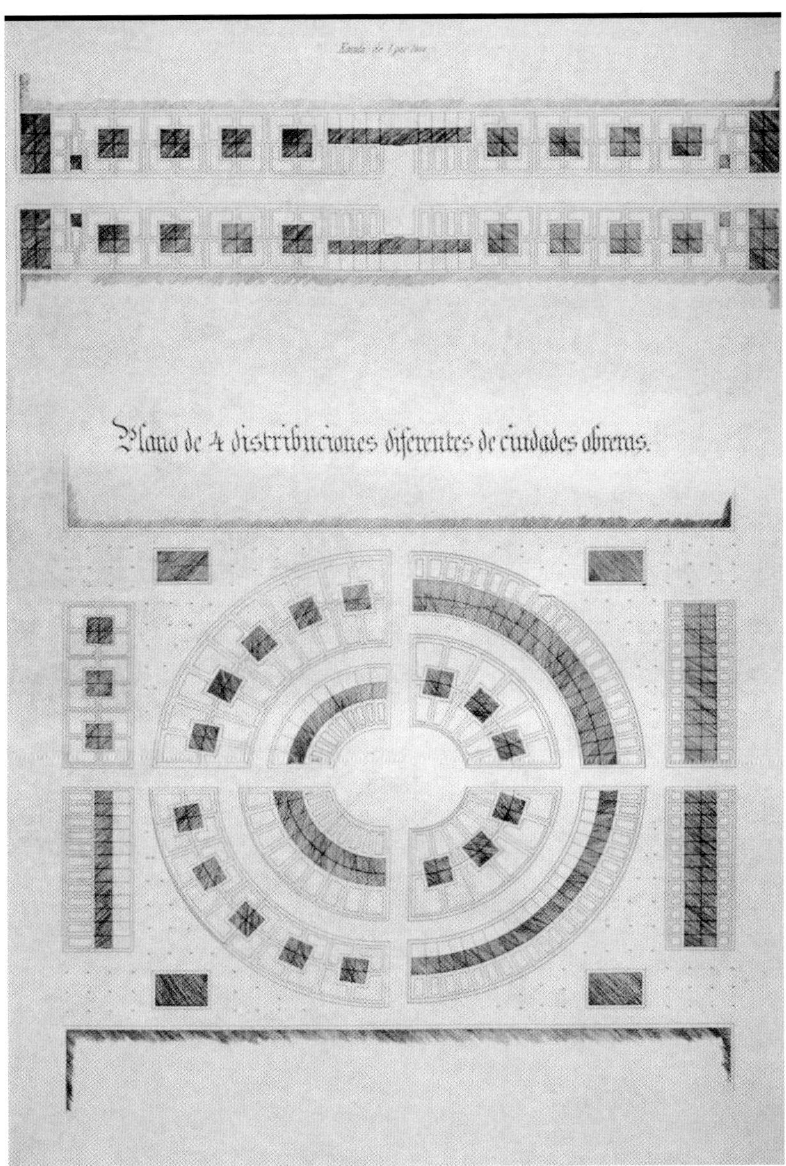

Cerdà's worker housing: reflection on the minimum housing unit

The first half of the 19th century had seen models of workers' cities proposed in Lille, Mulhouse and Paris, which Cerdà took into account when designing his models of worker housing with shared services.

Some of these models propose the "minimum housing unit", which was similar to the model designed many years later by modern rationalism.

Cité de Paris approved and subsidized by the State. Ildefons Cerdà. *Teoría de la Construcción de las Ciudades* [Theory of City Construction]. 1859. Source: Government Archives, Section of the Ministry of Education and Science.

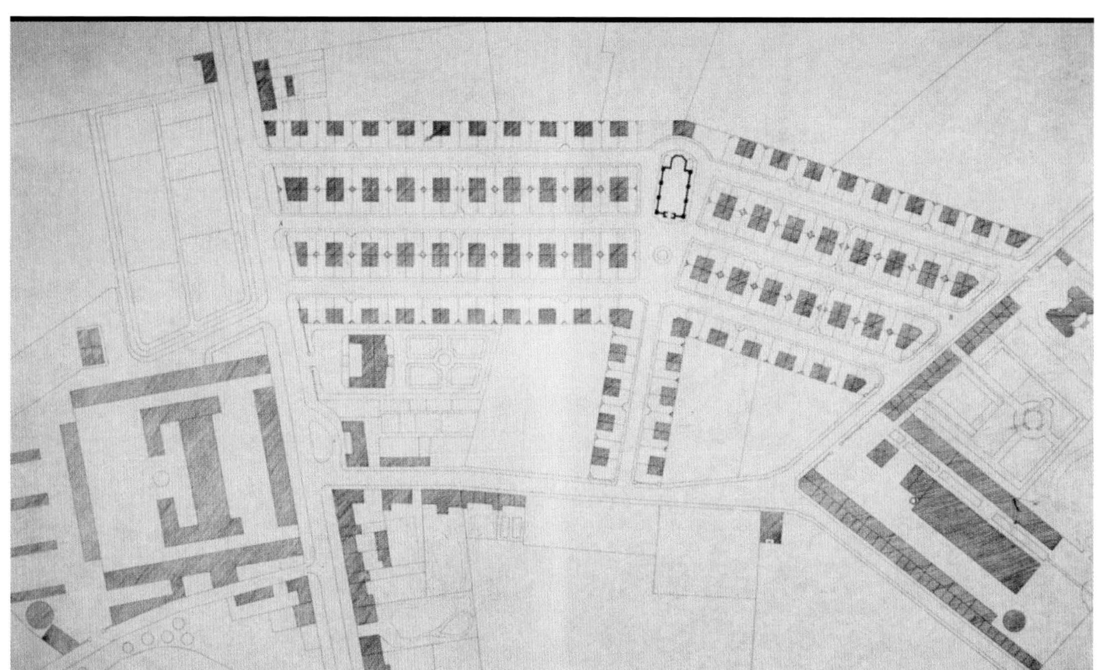

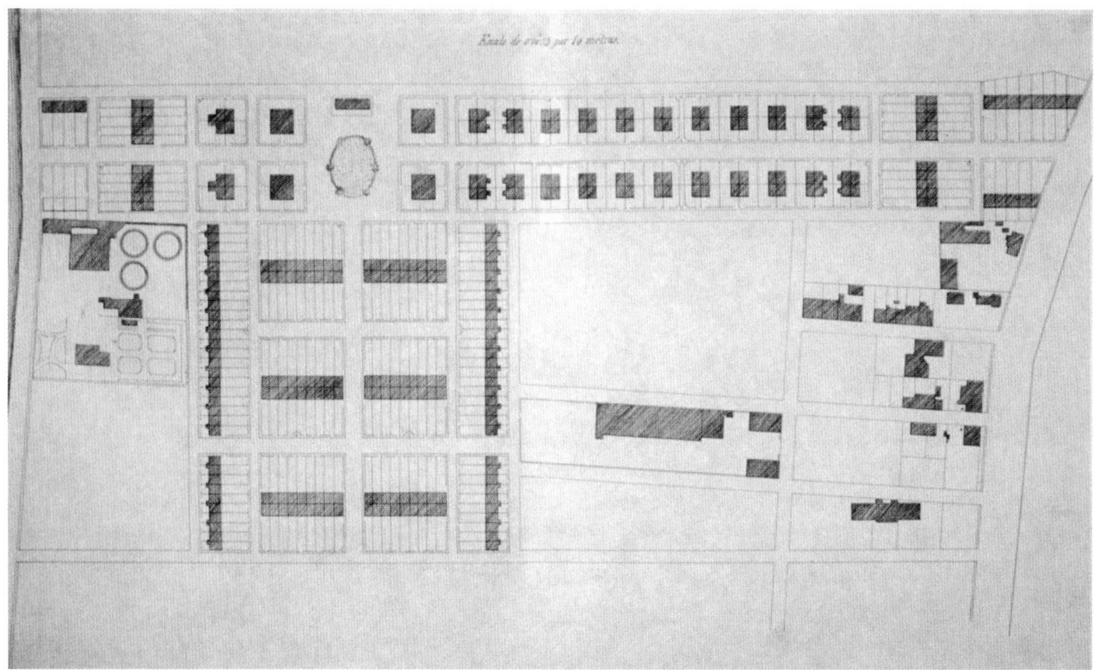

Marcq i Marquette's Cité Ouvrière near Lille.
Mulhouse's Cité Ouvrière.
Ildefons Cerdà. *Teoría de la Construcción de las Ciudades* [Theory of City Construction]. 1859. Source: Government Archives, Section of the Ministry of Education and Science.

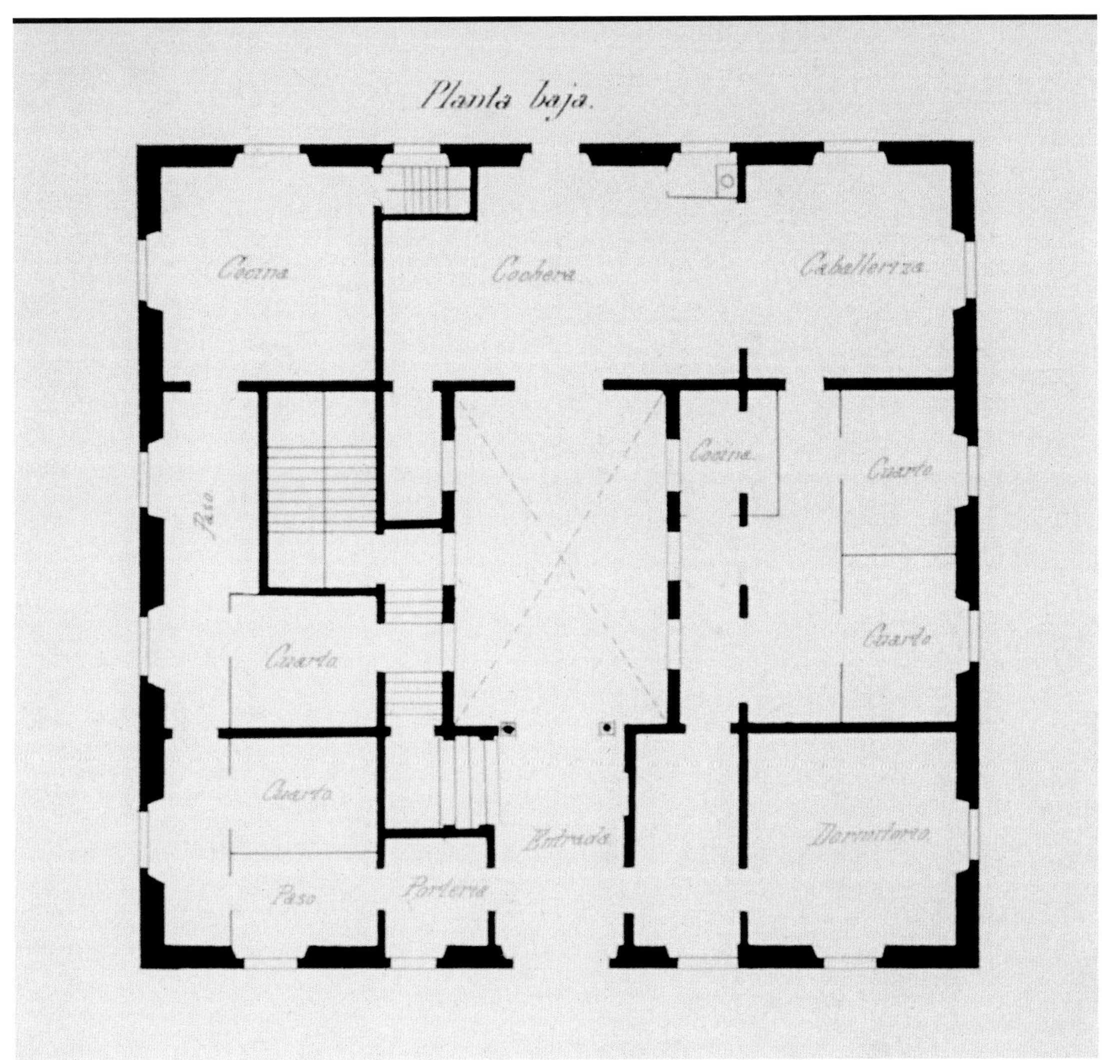

Models of the bourgeois house

Cerdà seeks the ideal house which is the first order bourgeois house. Of the four bourgeois house models that are proposed, the "fourth order bourgeois house" is the one that would become the working model for rental housing in the Eixample in which the owner would construct the building and use the second floor as a residence, the ground floor for business, and the upper floors for rental flats.

First order bourgeois house. Ildefons Cerdà. *Memoria del Anteproyecto del Ensanche de Barcelona* [Description of the Preliminary Project for the Extension of Barcelona]1855. Source: Government Archives, Section of the Ministry of Education and Science.

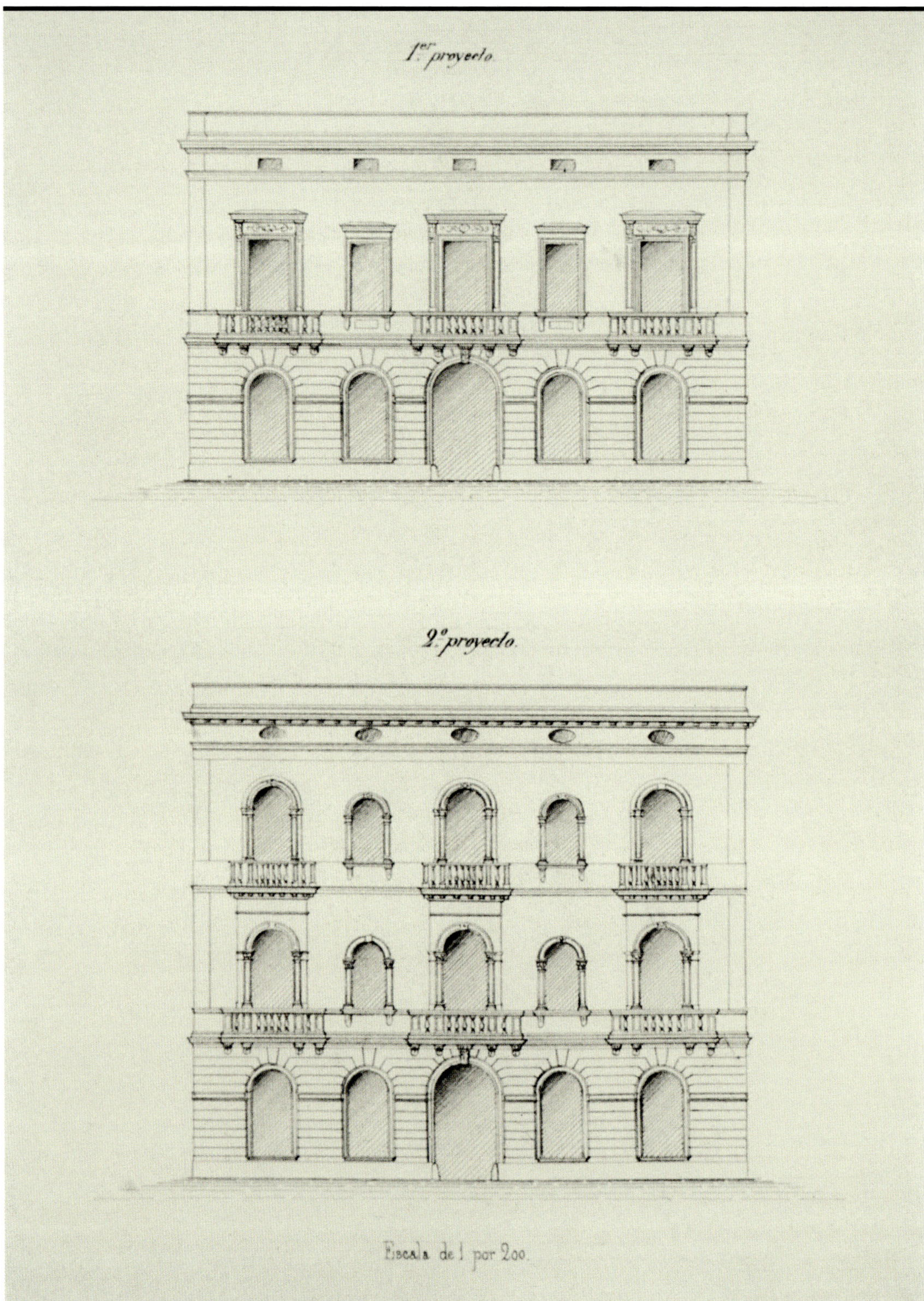

Facades of a first order, one or two floor bourgeois house. Ildefons Cerdà. *Teoría de la Construcción de las Ciudades* [Theory of City Construction]. 1859. Source: Government Archives, Section of the Ministry of Education and Science.

Model of a fourth-order middle-class home by Ildefons Cerdà (1855). Conception: Francesc Magrinyà, Fernando Marzá. Realization: ETSAV-UPC model workshop. 2009.

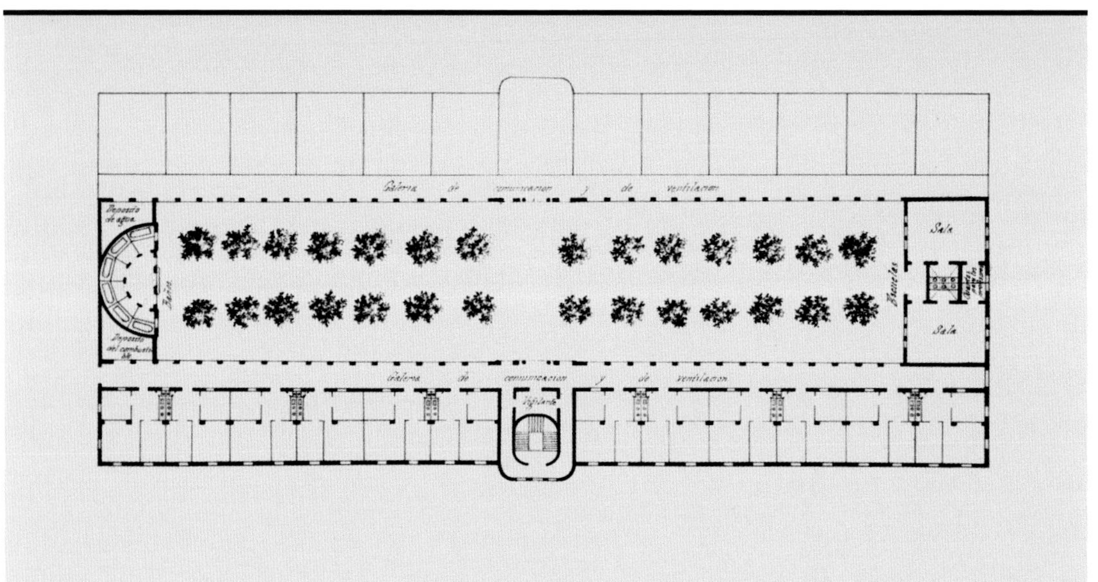

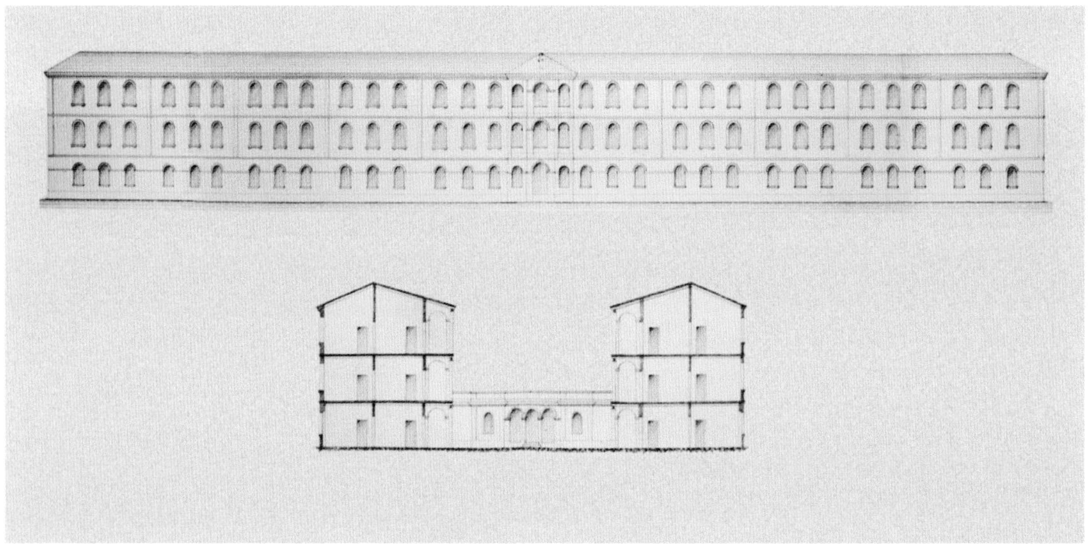

Models of the working class house

Third and fourth order house models offer "the minimum housing unit" which resembles the modern rationalist model developed much later.

Fourth-order middle-class home. Ildefons Cerdà. *Memoria del Anteproyecto del Ensanche de Barcelona.* [Description of the Preliminary Project for the Extension of Barcelona]1855. Source: Government Archives, Section of the Ministry of Education and Science.

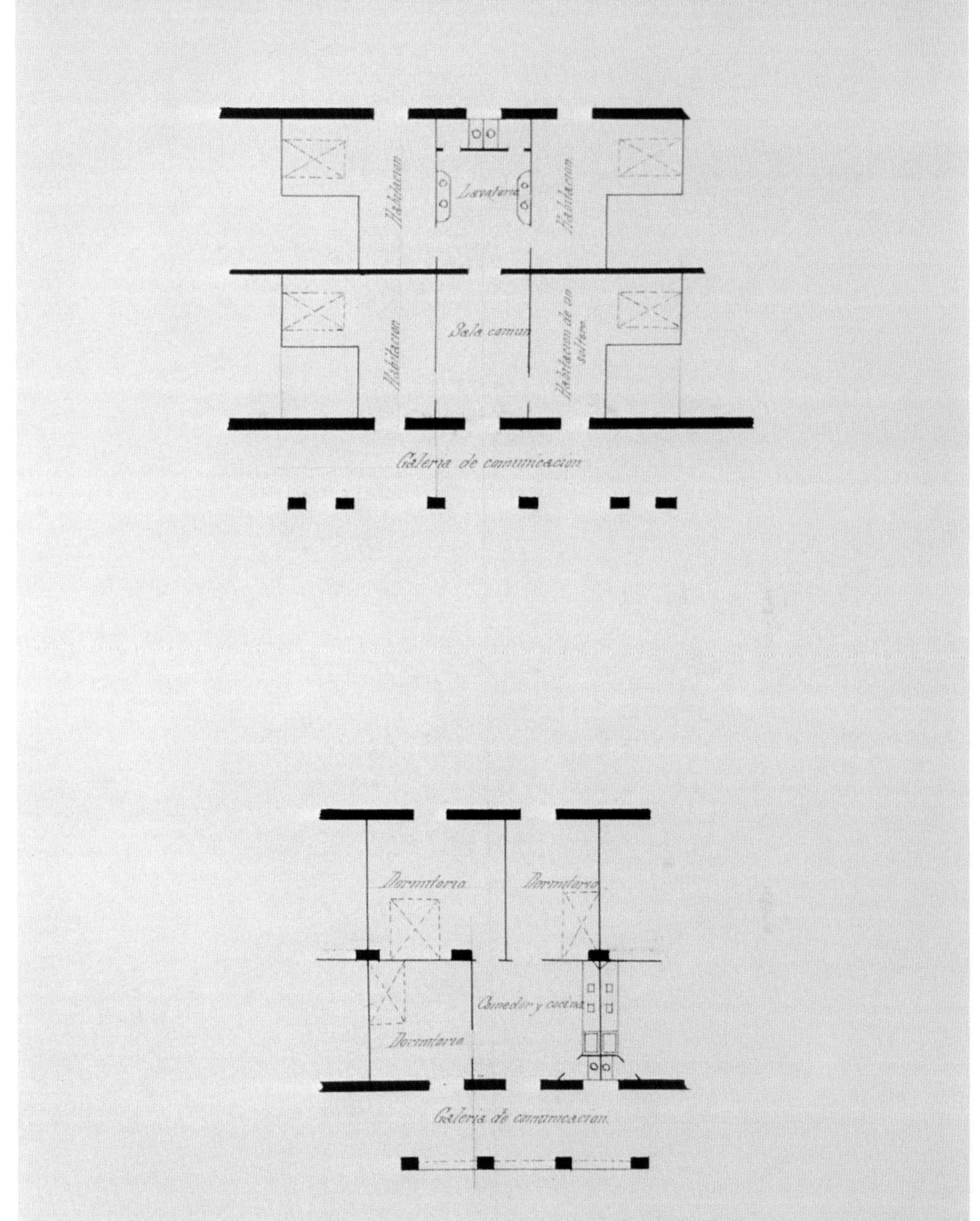

Detail of the minimum housing unit for a family (third order) and for single persons (fourth order).
Ildefons Cerdà. *Memoria del Anteproyecto del Ensanche de Barcelona.* [Description of the Preliminary Project for the Extension of Barcelona]1855. Source: Government Archives, Section of the Ministry of Education and Science.

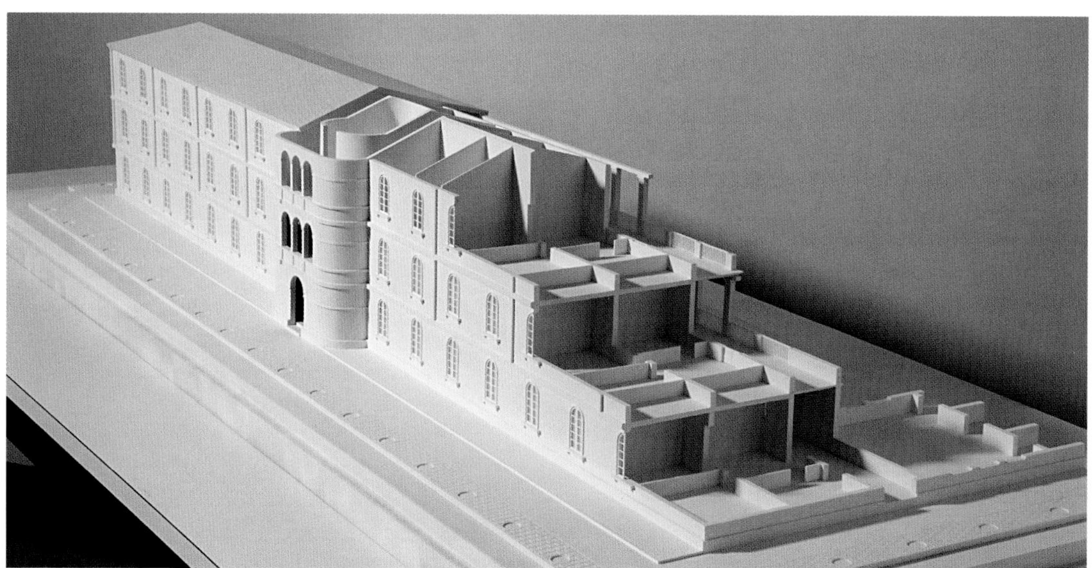

Models of third-order worker homes by Ildefons Cerdà (1855). Conception: Francesc Magrinyà, Fernando Marzá. Model: ETSAV-UPC model workshop. 2009

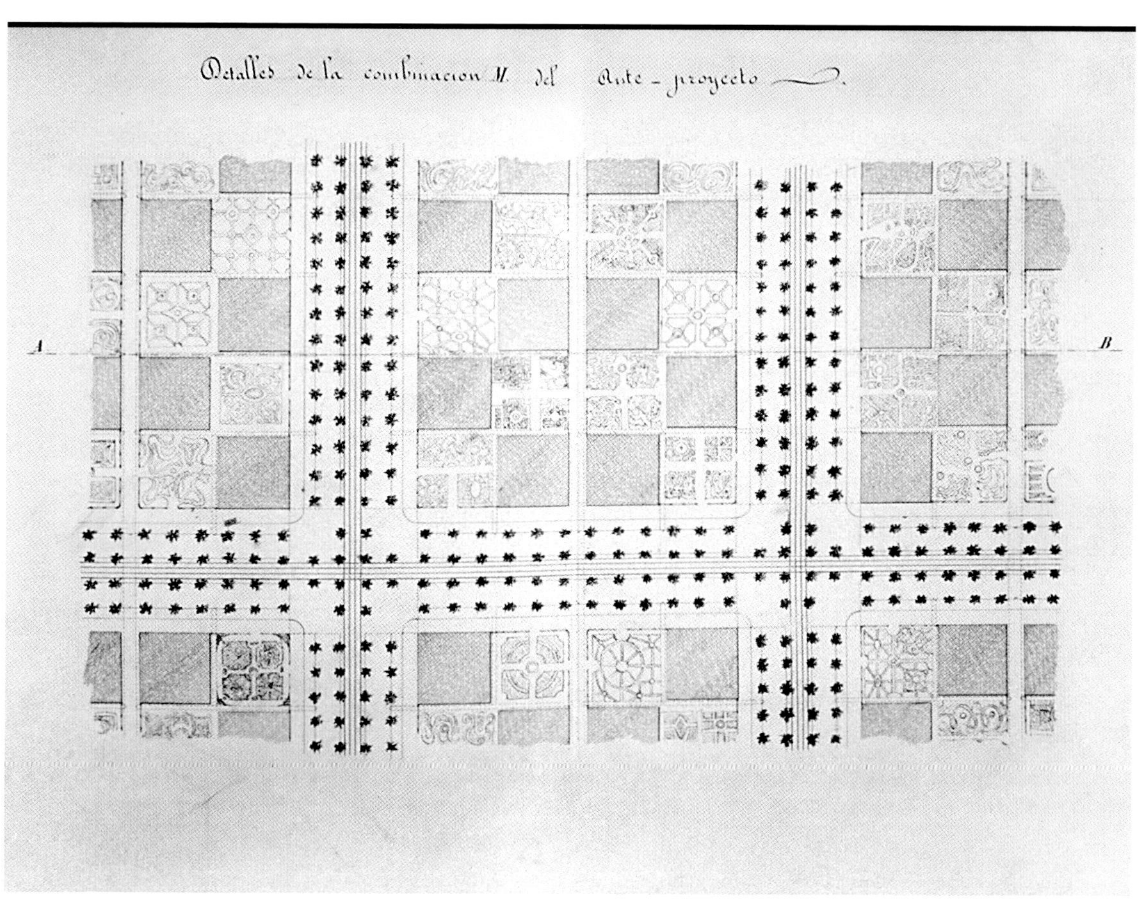

From the isolated house to the isolated building

"The first condition that cities must comply with is the isolation of buildings [....] a system of islands open on two sides is a transition from the current system toward houses that are completely isolated and surrounded by gardens which is, strictly speaking, the only acceptable system". (I. Cerdà, *Theory of City Construction*, 1859).

Detail of the M combination corresponding to the ideal housing model with first order bourgeois houses and 35m wide streets from the *Avantprojecte* of the Eixample of 1855. Ildefons Cerdà. *Teoría de la Construcción de las Ciudades* [Theory of City Construction]. 1859. Source: Government Archives, Section of the Ministry of Education and Science.

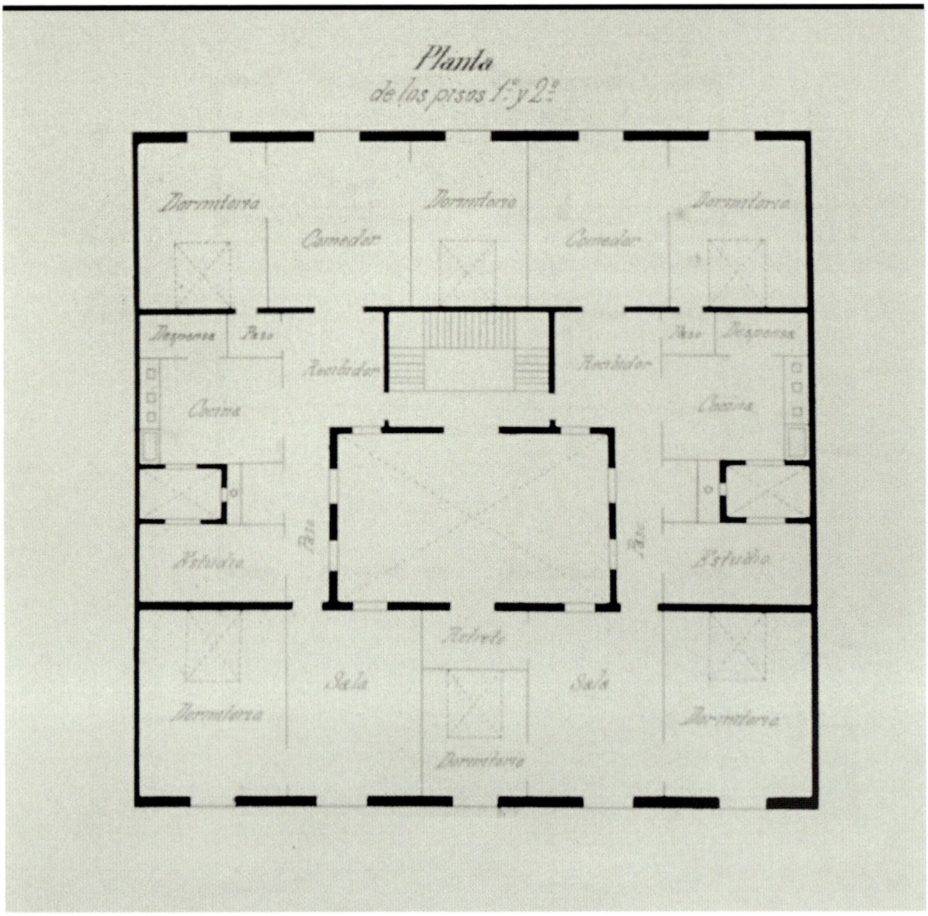

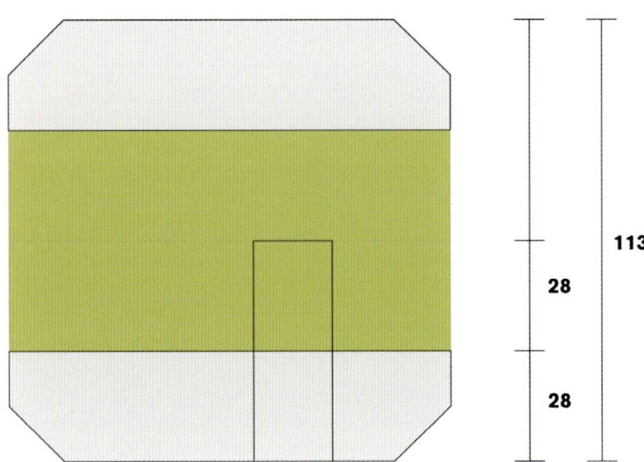

The final fourth order housing model proposed by Cerdà in 1859. Ildefons Cerdà. *Memoria del Anteproyecto del Ensanche de Barcelona.* [Description of the Preliminary Project for the Extension of Barcelona]1855. Source: Government Archives, Section of the Ministry of Education and Science.

The final fourth order housing model proposed and its relationship to the island according to Cerdà's 1859 Ordinances. Realitzation: Own.

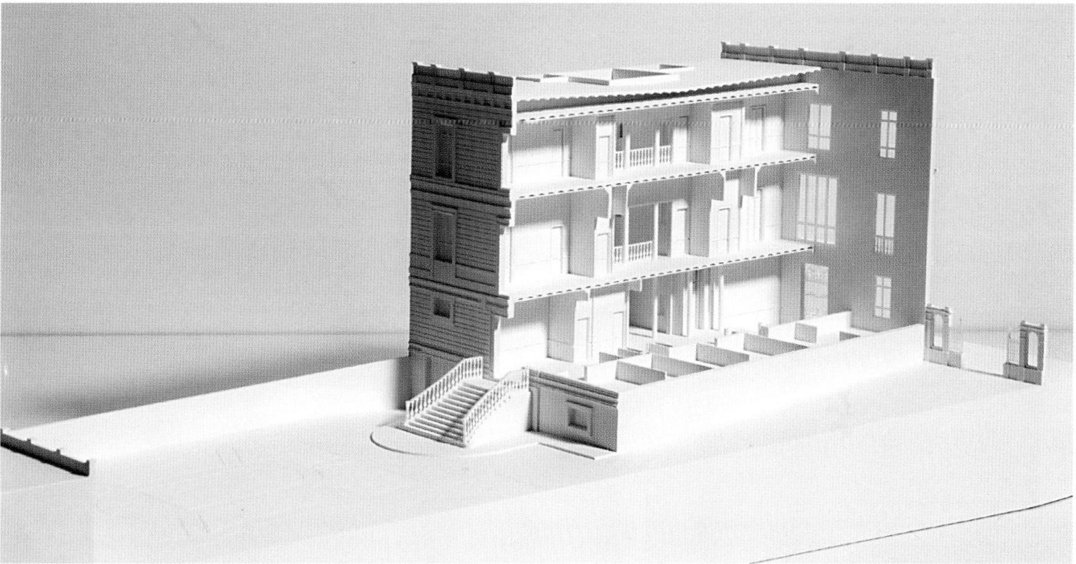

The evolution of the rental building

The rental building set in a garden was initially freestanding, later giving way first to buildings with one party wall, as shown by the model of Lorenzo Oliver House; and then with two.

Later, the ground floor was divided to create a mezzanine, especially when shops and workshops were introduced, as shown in the model of Sagnier House.

Afterwards, the penthouse was added, and the ground floor on the inside of the city block reached a peak of occupation with industry that was later replaced by services, as in the case of the Astòria building.

Single-family house of Lorenzo Oliver, Passeig de Gràcia, 13 (1869). Architect: Rafael Guastavino, Master builder: Pau Martorell. Conception: Francesc Magrinyà, Fernando Marzá. Model: ETSAV-UPC model workshop. 2009.

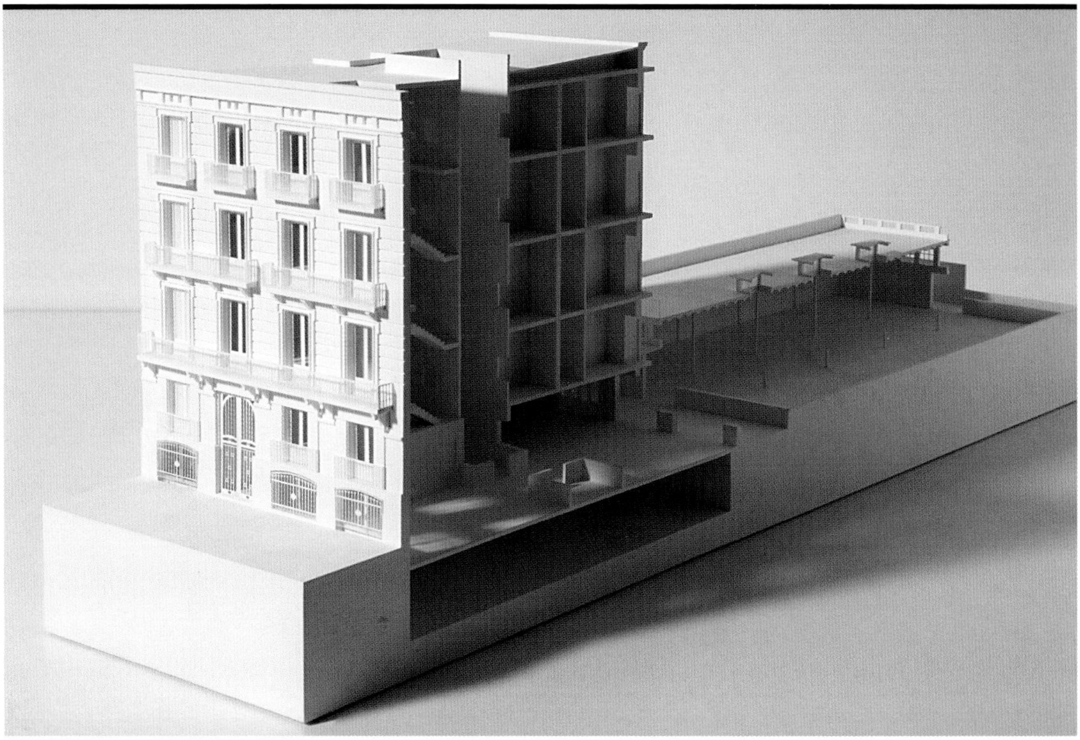

Industrial house of Anna Brugués, Carrer Consell de Cent, 288 (1904). Architect: T. Fernández. Conception: Francesc Magrinyà, Fernando Marzá. Model: ETSAV-UPC model workshop. 2009.

Astòria building, Carrer de París, 193-199 (1933-1934). Architect: Germán Rodríguez Arias. Conception: Francesc Magrinyà, Fernando Marzá. Model: ETSAV-UPC model workshop. 2009.

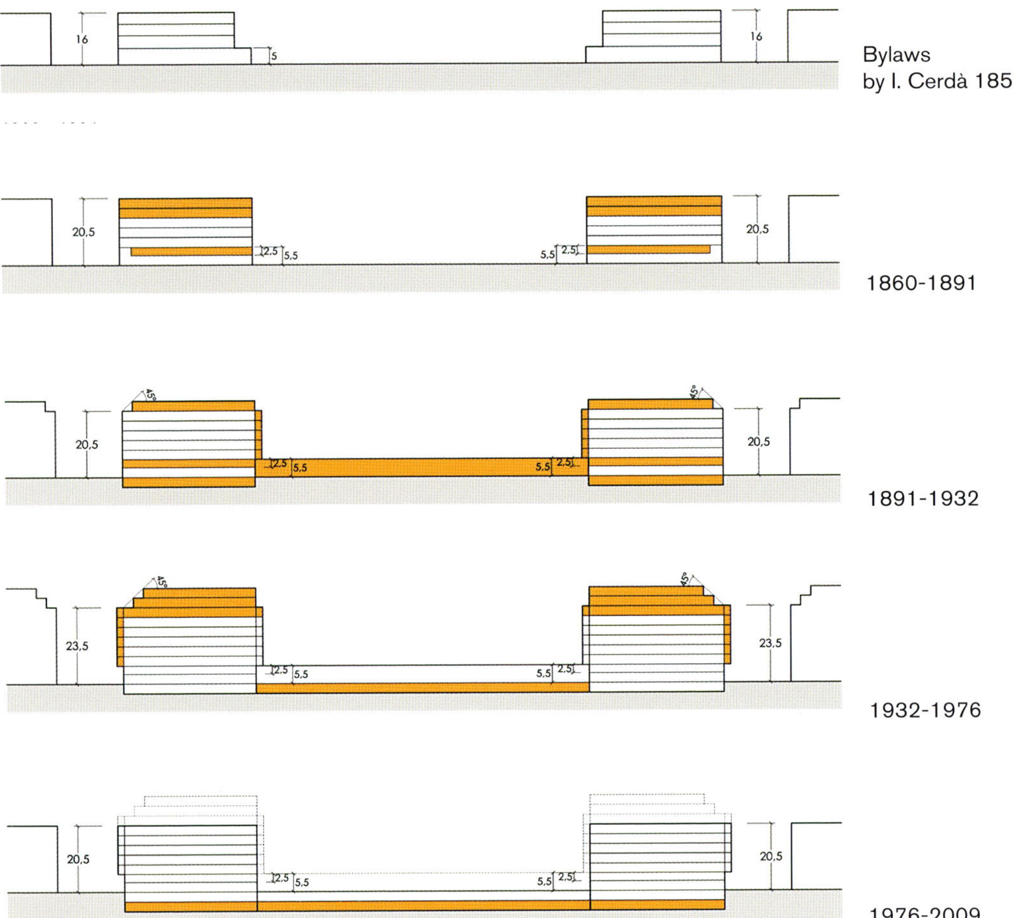

Evolution of city bylaws in the Eixample

In general, the bylaws applicable to the Eixample represent the legalization of a process under way that needs to be regularized. They can be divided into four periods:

- –1860-1891: the 1891 Bylaws represent the approval and validation of the model begun by Cerdà, giving way to a model of a city block enclosed on four sides with a maximum built depth of 28 m.
- –1892-1932: during this period, the ground floor was divided to create a mezzanine and semi-basement in the built area and the occupation of the inner courtyard up to a height of 5.5 m (ground floor + mezzanine) for industrial purposes.
- –1933-1975: this period saw increased levels of density with the appearance of a sixth storey (1932 Bylaws), a first and a second penthouse (1942 Bylaws) and the occupation of the semi-basement level in the inner courtyard (1947 Bylaws).
- –1976-2009: this was a period of recovery, particularly with the 1976 Bylaws, which marked a shift from the model of ground floor + mezzanine + six upper floors + two penthouse floors to one of ground floor + mezzanine + five upper floors.

Evolution of the Eixample Ordinances. Realitzation: Own.

Vertical extensions: 1, 2, 5, 6 i 7_carrer d'Aragó, 3_Rambla de Catalunya, 4_plaça de Tetuan, 8_Gran Via de les Corts Catalanes (2009). Fotography: Rafael Vargas.

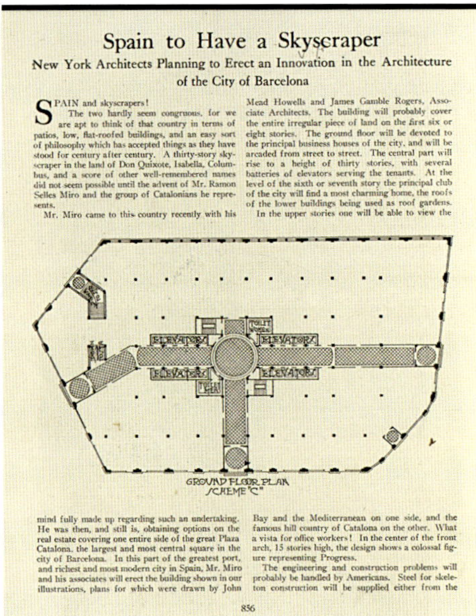

Spain to Have a Skyscraper

New York Architects Planning to Erect an Innovation in the Architecture of the City of Barcelona

SPAIN and skyscrapers!

The two hardly seem congruous, for we are apt to think of that country in terms of patios, low, flat-roofed buildings, and an easy sort of philosophy which has accepted things as they have stood for century after century. A thirty-story skyscraper in the land of Don Quixote, Isabella, Columbus, and a score of other well-remembered names did not seem possible until the advent of Mr. Ramon Selles Miro and the group of Catalonians he represents.

Mr. Miro came to this country recently with his mind fully made up regarding such an undertaking. He was then, and still is, obtaining options on the real estate covering one entire side of the great Plaza Catalona, the largest and most central square in the city of Barcelona. In this part of the greatest port, and richest and most modern city in Spain, Mr. Miro and his associates will erect the building shown in our illustrations, plans for which were drawn by John Mead Howells and James Gamble Rogers, Associate Architects. The building will probably cover the entire irregular piece of land on the first six or eight stories. The ground floor will be devoted to the principal business houses of the city, and will be arcaded from street to street. The central part will rise to a height of thirty stories, with several batteries of elevators serving the tenants. At the level of the sixth or seventh story the principal club of the city will find a most charming home, the roofs of the lower buildings being used as roof gardens.

In the upper stories one will be able to view the Bay and the Mediterranean on one side, and the famous hill country of Catalona on the other. What a vista for office workers! In the center of the front arch, 15 stories high, the design shows a colossal figure representing Progress.

The engineering and construction problems will probably be handled by Americans. Steel for skeleton construction will be supplied either from the

856

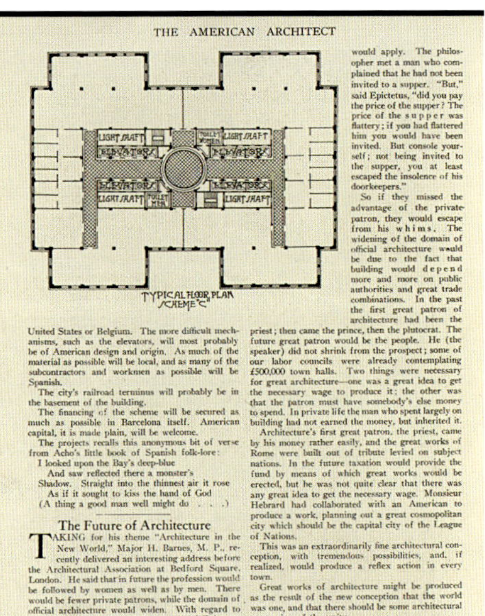

THE AMERICAN ARCHITECT

United States or Belgium. The more difficult mechanisms, such as the elevators, will most probably be of American design and origin. As much of the material as possible will be local, and as many of the subcontractors and workmen as possible will be Spanish.

The city's railroad terminus will probably be in the basement of the building.

The financing of the scheme will be secured as much as possible in Barcelona itself. American capital, it is made plain, will be welcome.

The projects recalls this anonymous bit of verse from Acho's little book of Spanish folk-lore:

I looked upon the Bay's deep-blue
And saw reflected there a monster's
Shadow. Straight into the thinnest air it rose
As if it sought to kiss the hand of God
(A thing a good man well might do . . .)

The Future of Architecture

TAKING for his theme "Architecture in the New World," Major H. Barnes, M. P., recently delivered an interesting address before the Architectural Association at Bedford Square, London. He said that in future the profession would be followed by women as well as by men. There would be fewer private patrons, while the domain of official architecture would widen. With regard to the loss of the private patron, a story of Epictetus would apply. The philosopher met a man who complained that he had not been invited to a supper. "But," said Epictetus, "did you pay the price of the supper? The price of the supper was flattery; if you had flattered him you would have been invited. But console yourself; not being invited to the supper, you at least escaped the insolence of his doorkeepers."

So if they missed the advantage of the private patron, they would escape from his whims. The widening of the domain of official architecture would be due to the fact that building would depend more and more on public authorities and great trade combinations. In the past the first great patron of architecture had been the priest; then came the prince, then the plutocrat. The future great patron would be the people. He (the speaker) did not shrink from the prospect; some of our labor councils were already contemplating £500,000 town halls. Two things were necessary for great architecture—one was a great idea to get the necessary wage to produce it; the other was that the patron must have somebody's else money to spend. In private life the man who spent largely on building had not earned the money, but inherited it.

Architecture's first great patron, the priest, came by his money rather easily, and the great works of Rome were built out of tribute levied on subject nations. In the future taxation would provide the fund by means of which great works would be erected, but he was not quite clear that there was any great idea to get the necessary wage. Monsieur Hebrard had collaborated with an American to produce a work, planning out a great cosmopolitan city which should be the capital city of the League of Nations.

This was an extraordinarily fine architectural conception, with tremendous possibilities, and, if realized, would produce a reflex action in every town.

Great works of architecture might be produced as the result of the new conception that the world was one, and that there should be some architectural expression of the unity.

858

Spain to Have a Skyscraper

New York Architects Planning to Erect an Innovation in the Architecture of the City of Barcelona

SPAIN and skyscrapers!

The two hardly seem congruous, for we are apt to think of that country in terms of patios, low, flat-roofed buildings, and an easy sort of philosophy which has accepted things as they have stood for century after century. A thirty-story skyscraper in the land of Don Quixote, Isabella, Columbus, and a score of other well-remembered names did not seem possible until the advent of Mr. Ramon Selles Miro and the group of Catalonians he represents.

Mr. Miro came to this country recently with his mind fully made up regarding such an undertaking . He was then, and still is, obtaining options on the real estate covering one entire side of the great Plaza Catalona, the largest and most central square in the city of Barcelona. In this part of the greatest port, and richest and most modern city in Spain, Mr. Miro and his associates will erect the building shown in our illustrations, plans for which were drawn by John Mead Howells and James Gamble Rogers, Associate Architects. The building will probably cover the entire irregular piece of land on the first six or eight stories. The ground floor will be devoted the principal business houses of the city, and will be arcaded from street to street. The central part will rise to a height of thirty stories, with several batteries of elevators serving the tenants. At the level of the sixth or seventh story the principal club of the city will find a most charming home, the roofs of the lower buildings being used as roof gardens.

In the upper stories one will be able to view the Bay and the Mediterranean on one side and the famous hill country of Catalona on the other. What a vista for office workers! In the center of the front arch, 15 stories high, the design shows a colossal figure representing Progress.

The engineering and construction problems will probably be handled by Americans. Steel for skeleton construction will be supplied either from the United States or Belgium. The more difficult mechanisms, such as the elevators, will most probably be of American design and origin. As much of the material as possible will be local, and as many of the subcontractors and workmen as possible will be Spanish.

The city's railroad terminus will probably be in the basement of the building.

The financing of the scheme will be secured as much as possible in Barcelona itself. American capital, it is made plain, will be welcome.

The projects recalls this anonymous bit of verse from Acho's little book of Spanish folk-lore:

I looked upon the Bay's deep-blue
And saw reflected there a monster's
Shadow. Straight into the thinnest air it rose
As if it sought to kiss the hand of God
(A thing a good man will might do...)

"Spain to have a Skyscraper", *American Architect*, 29 de desembre de 1920. Ground and upper floor in the style of the Selles-Miró building for Plaça de Catalunya. Source: New York Public Library.

THE AMERICAN ARCHITECT

OFFICE BUILDING AND HOTEL FOR BARCELONA, SPAIN

JOHN MEAD HOWELLS }
JAMES GAMBLE ROGERS } *ASSOCIATED ARCHITECTS*

857

Perspective from the Selles-Miró building toward Plaça de Catalunya (1918). Architects: John Mead Howells and James Gamble Rogers. Source: "Spain to have a Skyscraper", *American Architect*, 29 December, 1920. New York Public Library.

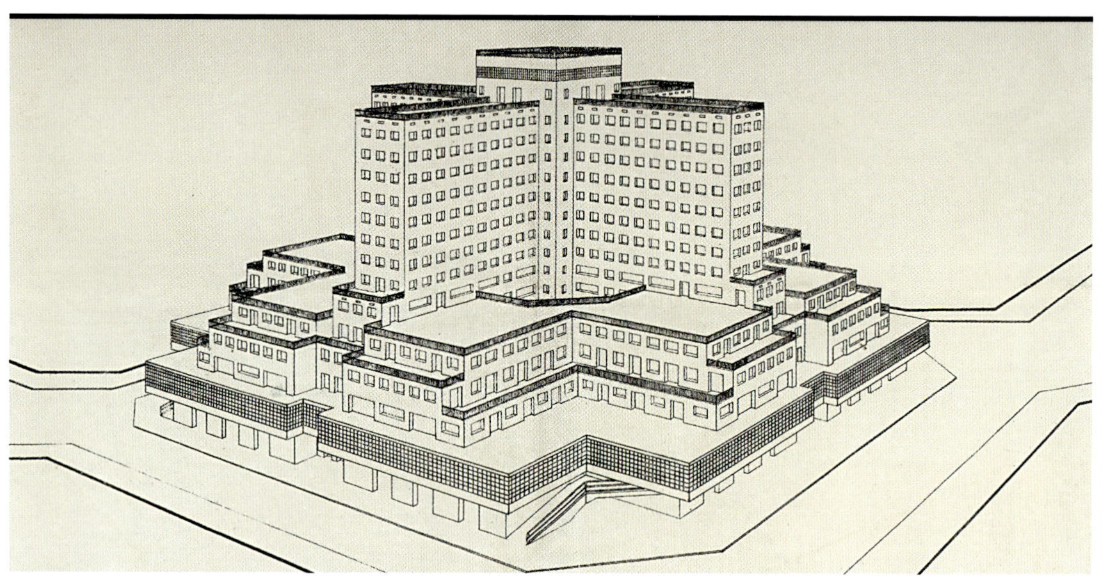

Project for a building to replace Sant Antoni Market, Carrer del Comte d'Urgell, 1, and Carrer del Comte Borrell, 56 (1930). Architect: Nicolau Maria Rubió i Tudurí. Municipal Administrative Archive. Barcelona City Council.

Urquinaona high-rise (Fàbregas building), Carrer de Jonqueres, 18 (1936-1944). Architect: Luis Gutiérrez Soto. Photograph: unknown. Institut d'Estudis Fotogràfics de Catalunya.

Banco Atlántico building, Carrer de Balmes, 168-170 (1965-1971). Architect: Francesc Mitjans. Photograph: unknown. Historical Archive of the Col·legi d'Arquitectes de Catalunya.

High-rise building at the end of Avinguda Diagonal. Photograph: Jordi Todó / TAVISA. 2008.

The evolution of worker housing

Reflection on dwellings for workers reappeared in the projects proposed by the rationalist architects in the 1930s and the progressive trends of the fifties. In the homes proposed for present-day social housing developments, this model is modified to meet new social needs.

The GATCPAC's Casa Bloc building, under construction (1932-1936). Photograph: Francesc Català-Roca. Historical Archive of the Col·legi d'Arquitectes de Catalunya.

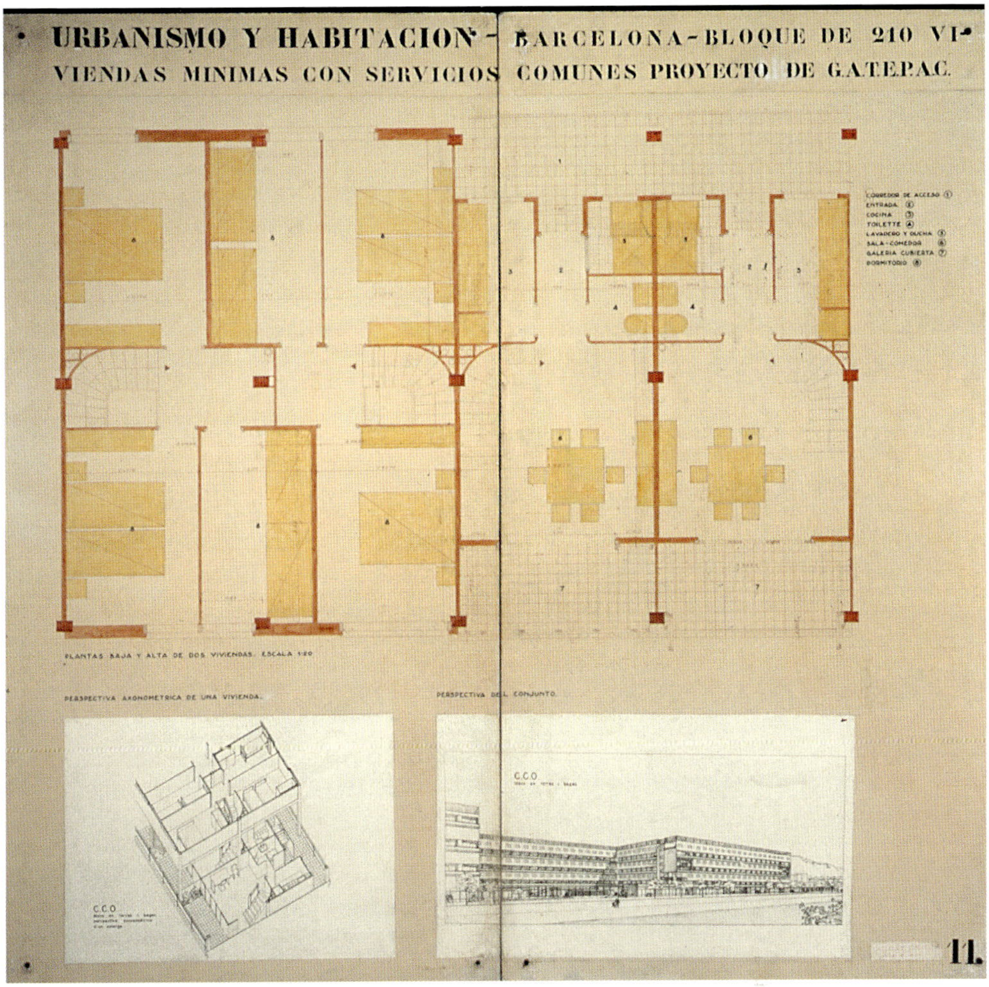

URBANISMO Y HABITACION - BARCELONA - BLOQUE DE 210 VIVIENDAS MINIMAS CON SERVICIOS COMUNES PROYECTO DE G.A.T.E.P.A.C.

11.

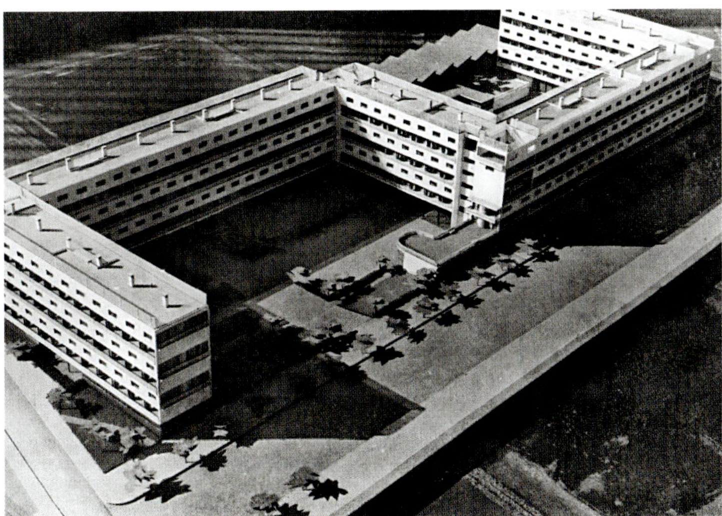

Barcelona. Block of 210 minimum dwellings with communal services, project by the "G.A.T.E.P.A.C." (1932). Panel no. 11 from the exhibition about the GATCPAC, "Urbanismo y Habitación" [Urbanism and Housing]. Historical Archive of the Col·legi d'Arquitectes de Catalunya.

Photograph of the model of Casa Bloc (1932-1936). Architects: Josep Torres Clavé, Josep Lluís Sert, Joan Baptista Subirana. Historical Archive of the Col·legi d'Arquitectes de Catalunya.

Housing block at Carrer de Pallars, 299-317 (1959). Photograph: Francesc Català-Roca. Historical Archive of the Col·legi d'Arquitectes de Catalunya.

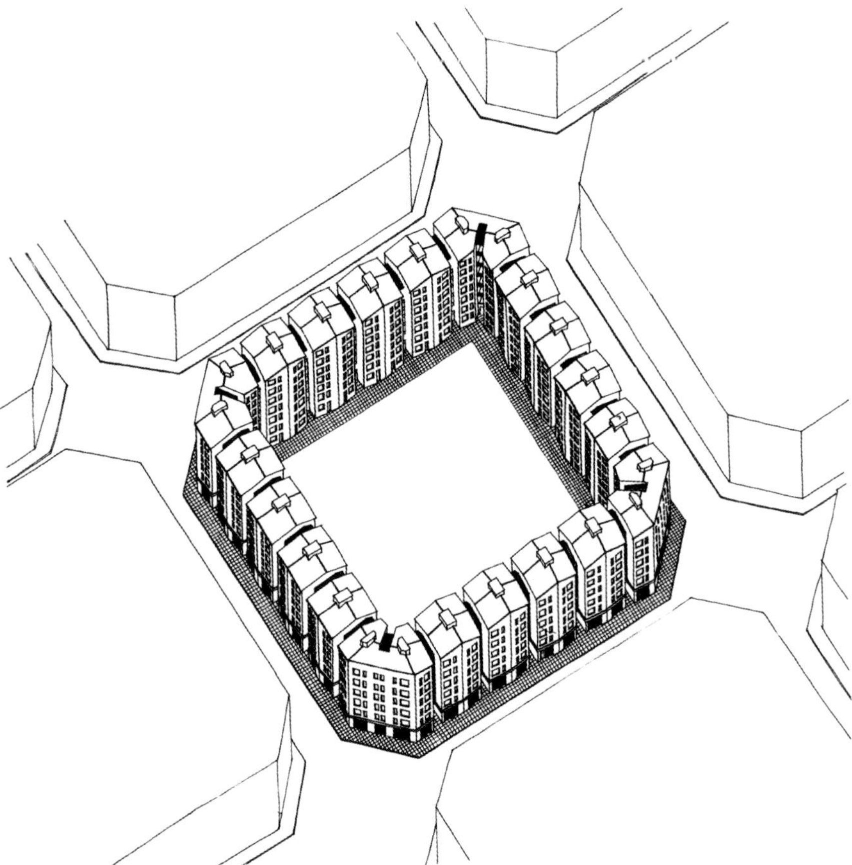

Housing block at Carrer de Pallars, 299-317 (1958). Architects: Oriol Bohigas and Josep Maria Martorell. Axonometric of the city block (unbuilt). MBM Arquitectes.

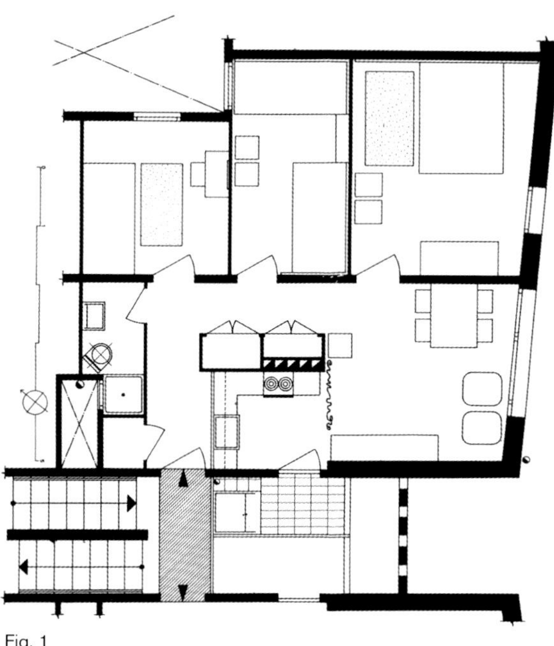

Fig. 1

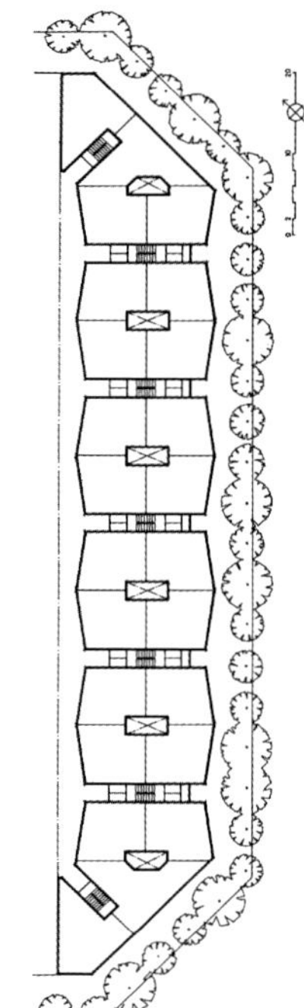

Fig. 2

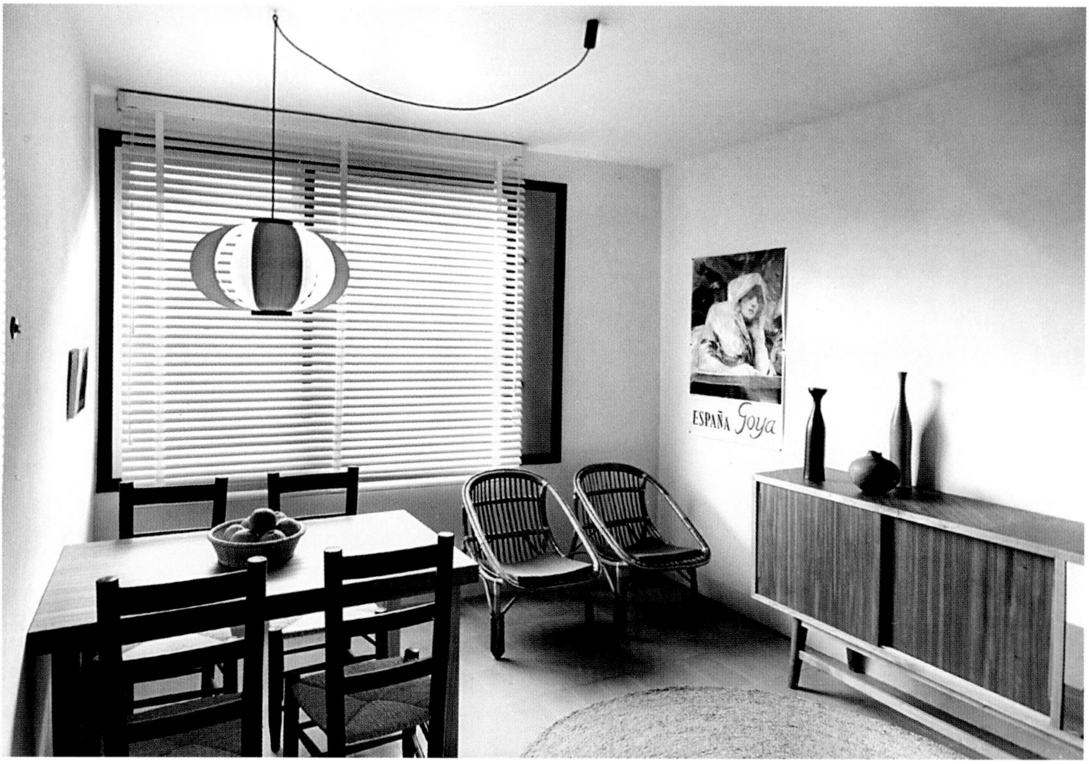

Housing block at Carrer de Pallars, 299-317 (1958). Architects: Oriol Bohigas and Josep Maria Martorell
Fig. 1 - Model floor plan of a housing unit Fig. 2 - Floor plan of the built volume. MBM Arquitectes.

Interior of an apartment in the housing block at Carrer de Pallars, 299-317 (1959).
Photograph: Francesc Català-Roca. Historical Archive of the Col·legi d'Arquitectes de Catalunya.

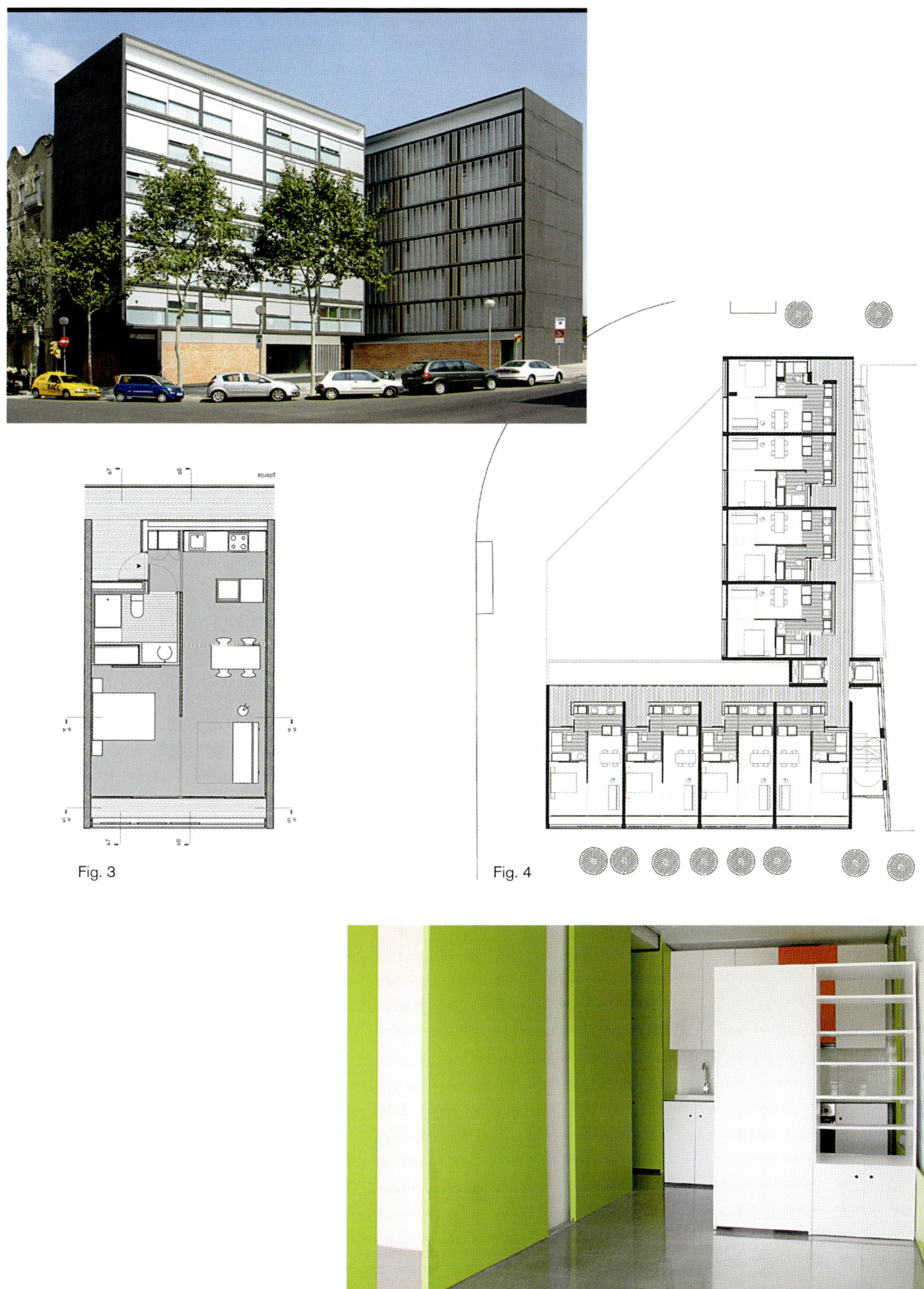

Social housing block at Carrer d'Alí Bei, 94-96 (2008). Photograph: Conxita Balcells.

Social housing block at Carrer d'Alí Bei, 94-96, with minimum units of 40 m2 (2008).
Architect: Conxita Balcells, Fig. 1 - Model floor plan, Fig. 2 - Floor plan of the built volume, Conxita Balcells associats.

the grid_

"The two essential needs of the individual are movement and rest"

(I. Cerdà, *Teoría General de la Urbanización*, 1867)

"The two essential needs of the individual are movement and rest, vies and intervies"

The bases for the construction of the new city were recognition of private property as an exchange value and the creation of adequate housing and transport conditions.

For his definition of urbanization, Cerdà took as his basis a series of dualities that identified human needs: relation and isolation, society and individual, movement and rest. The resulting urban fabric is defined by a system of *vies* and *intervies*—that is, the fabric of streets and city blocks, the latter defined as the spaces delimited by the streets[1].

Cerdà's 1861 Alignment Plan[2], separating the *vies* or streets from the *intervies* of city blocks, was the greatest exponent and remained a constant. It represented the basic order of organization in an increasingly complex urban system.

Topographic maps of Barcelona and the construction of the grid

Topographic surveys have played a vital role in the construction of Cerdà's grid, with successive maps representing a leap of scale from the Eixample to the greater territory. The first topographic survey of Cerdà's Eixample was the Geometric Map of the Barcelona Extension by Serrallach, dated 1865[3], focusing on the scope of the old municipality of Barcelona. In the framework of different attempts to annexe municipalities in the Barcelona Plain, ultimately achieved in 1897, special mention should be made of the General Map of Barcelona, its Extension and surrounding villages (1877) by Josep M. Jordán[4], and the Map of Barcelona and surroundings (1890) by Serra[5].

The 1926 Topographic Map of Barcelona, drawn up by Vicenç Martorell[6], was the basic reference for the construction of Cerdà's grid and was carried out thanks to the jurisdiction of the 1925 Municipal Statute, in the context of preparations for the 1929 International Exhibition. The city continued to be based on this topography until the preparation of the 1976 *Pla General Metropolità de Barcelona* [Barcelona Metropolitan Master Plan].

[1] See figs. pages 65-66 I [2] See fig. page 67 I [3] See fig. page 68 I [4] See fig. page 69 I [5] See fig. page 69
[6] See figs. pages 70-71 I [7] See fig. page 72

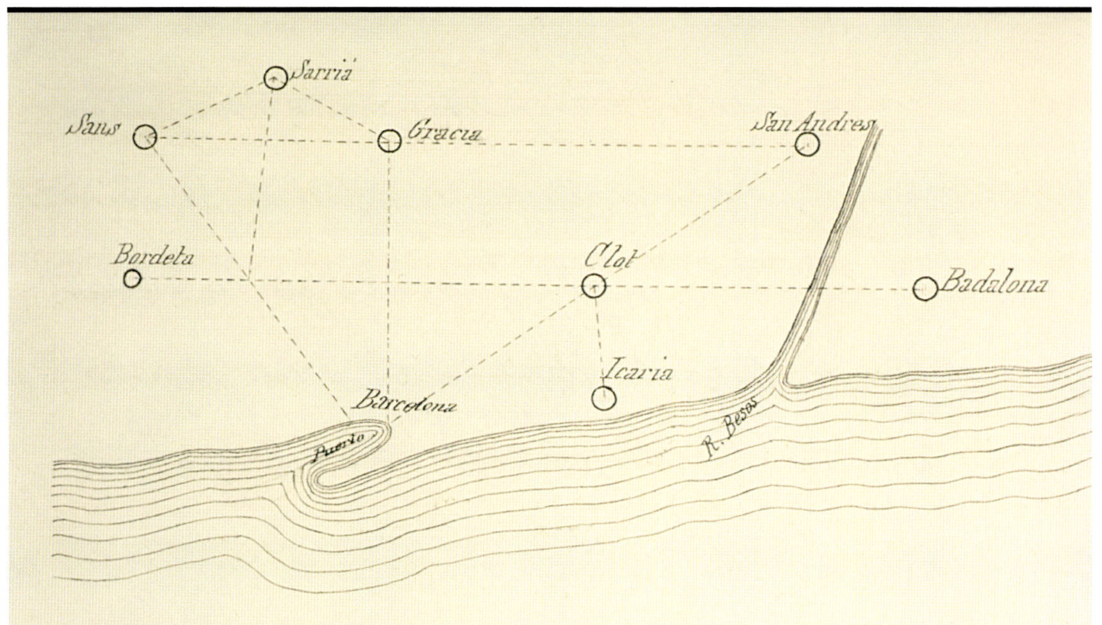

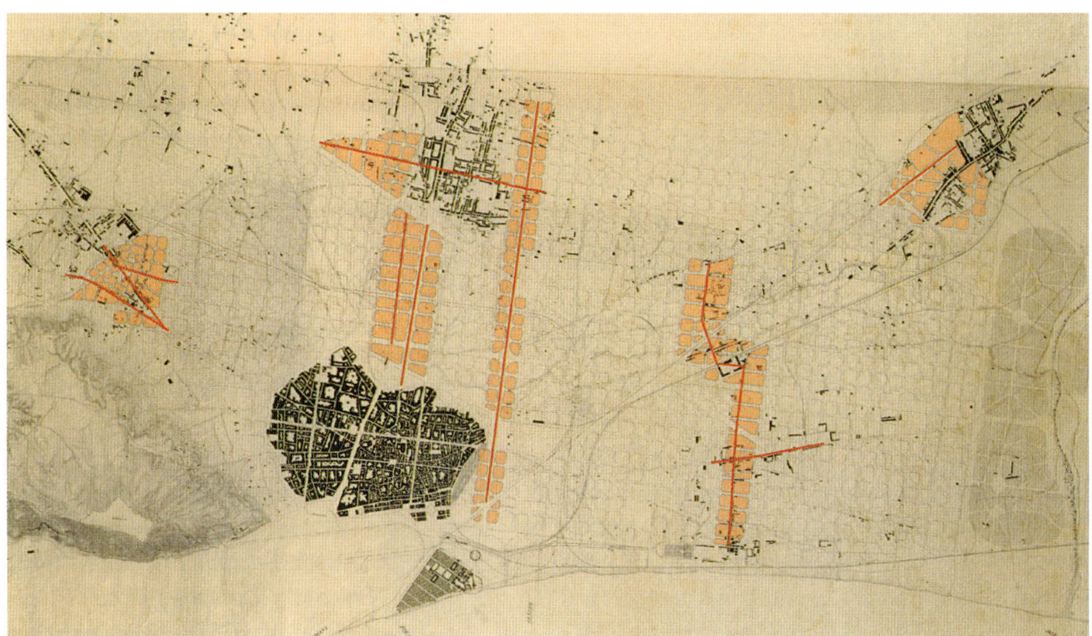

Connection of the principal streets with the municipalities in the Barcelona Plain according to Cerdà's proposal. Ildefons Cerdà. Teoría de la Construcción de las Ciudades [Theory of City Construction], 1859 Source: Government Archives. Section of the Ministry of Education and Science.

Flexibility of the Eixample layout with pre-existing streets. 2002. Conception: Francesc Magrinyà.

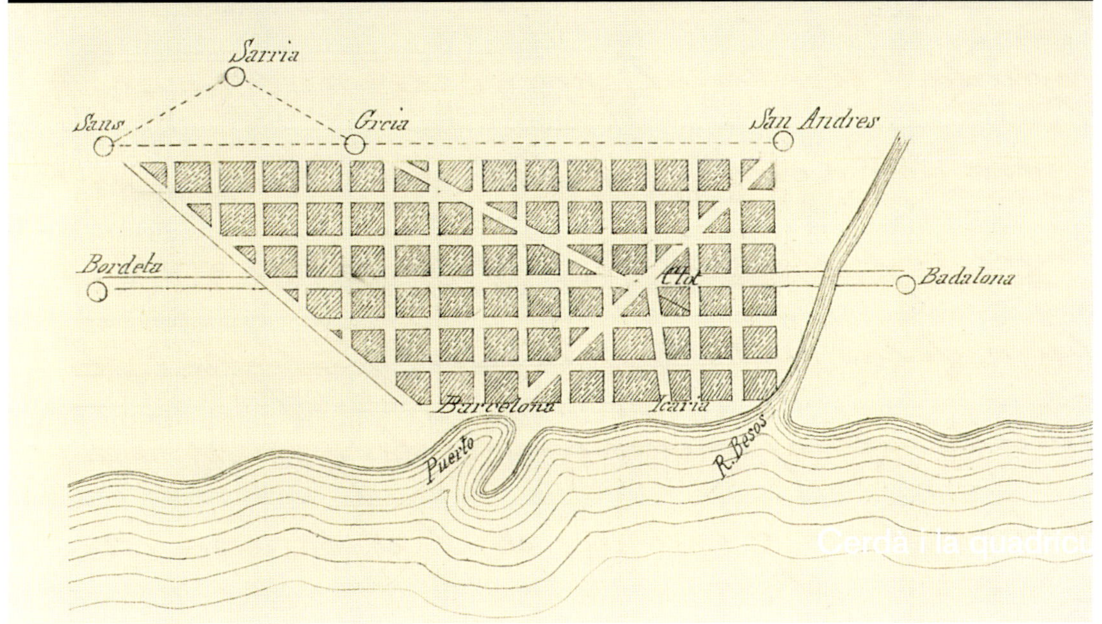

Cerdà and the grid

The use of the grid in urbanism is not new. Cerdà's grid, however, was the first to have such clearly reasoned dimensions and characteristics.

Cerdà defended the grid as a way of facilitating mobility and producing buildings that complied with acceptable conditions of density, ventilation and sunlighting.

Its characteristic parameters were:

- A street width of 20 m
- Chamfered corners creating an octagon with sides of 20 m
- Dwellings occupying 50% of the plot
- A density of 250 inhabitants per hectare

The grid was superposed onto a series of axes that connected it to the geographical territory of the Barcelona Plain. Avinguda Paral·lel, Avinguda Meridiana and Avinguda Diagonal are connected with the valleys of the rivers Llobregat and Besòs. Gran Via follows a line parallel to the coast. The grid is oriented at 45° to Meridiana and Paral·lel to ensure conditions of sunlighting for most dwellings.

Cerdà chose the grid as the optimum system of mobility and connected it to the geographical territory

Cerdà set out to design the optimum street system. After combining circular and straight streets, he found that the grid system was the only one that ensured egalitarian access.

Connection of the grid layout with the transcendent thoroughfares of Cerdà's proposal. Ildefons Cerdà. *Teoría de la Construcción de las Ciudades* [Theory of City Construction], 1859. Source: Government Archives. Section of the Ministry of Education and Science.

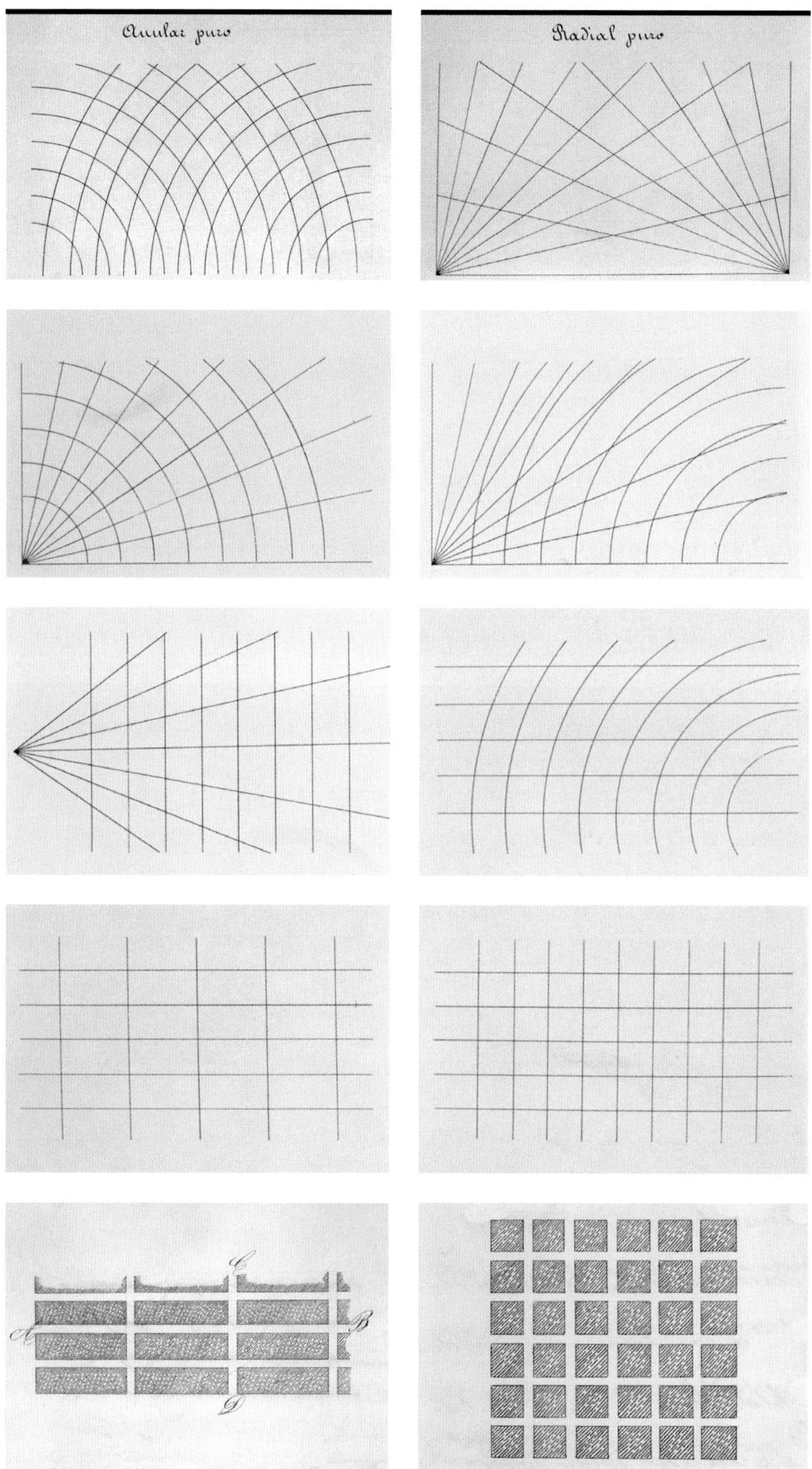

Deduction of the grid as the best system of road layout Idefons Cerdà. *Teoría de la Viabilidad Urbana* [Theory of Urban Viability], 1861. Source: Government Archives. Section of the Ministry of Education and Science.

The grid tradition and Cerdà

The grid tradition is an old one, ranging from the Greek polis (Milet) and cities colonized by the Romans (Mérida), via proposals for the cities of the Reconquista in the Iberian peninsula (Alfonso X the Wise and Eiximenis), the Latin American tradition (Philip II's Treaty of the Indies) with the example of Buenos Aires, and 18th-century military cities (Barceloneta), to US cities and the Land Ordinance of 1785 (Boston and Philadelphia).

Cerdà reviewed all of these traditions, as shown by the tables of measurements of city blocks from cities all over the world and the graphic examples of Turin, Cienfuegos, Buenos Aires, Philadelphia and Boston in the Atlas of *Teoría de la Construcción de Ciudades* ([Theory of City Construction], 1859).

Turin. Plate XXXIX. Ildefons Cerdà. *Teoría de la Construcción de las Ciudades* [Theory of City Construction], 1859. Source: Government Archives. Section of the Ministry of Education and Science.

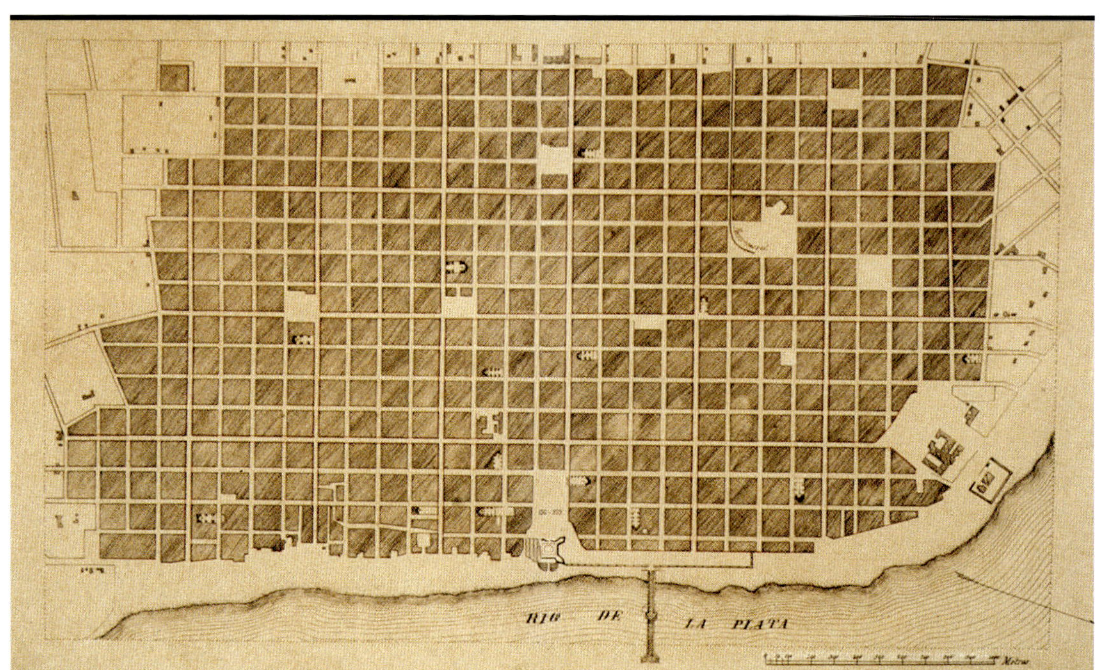

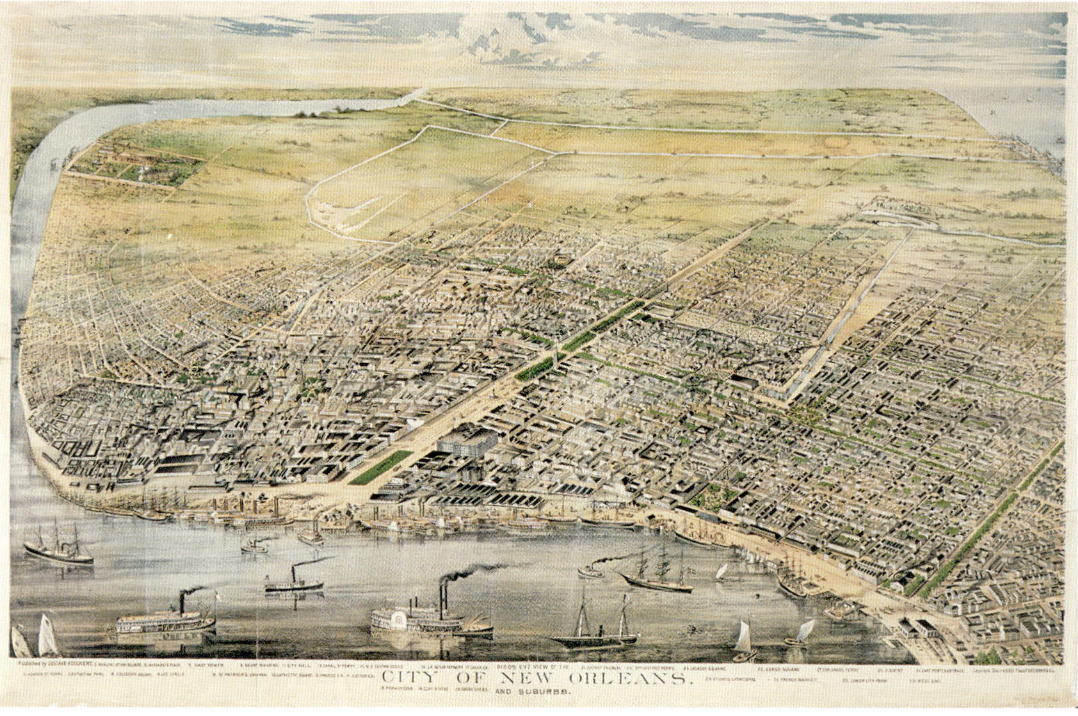

Map of Buenos Aires. Plate XLI. Ildefons Cerdà. Teoría de la Construcción de las Ciudades [Theory of City Construction], 1859. Source: Government Archives. Section of the Ministry of Education and Science.

Bird's-eye view of New Orleans and its suburbs (1883). Gustave Koeckert. Source: New York Historical Society.

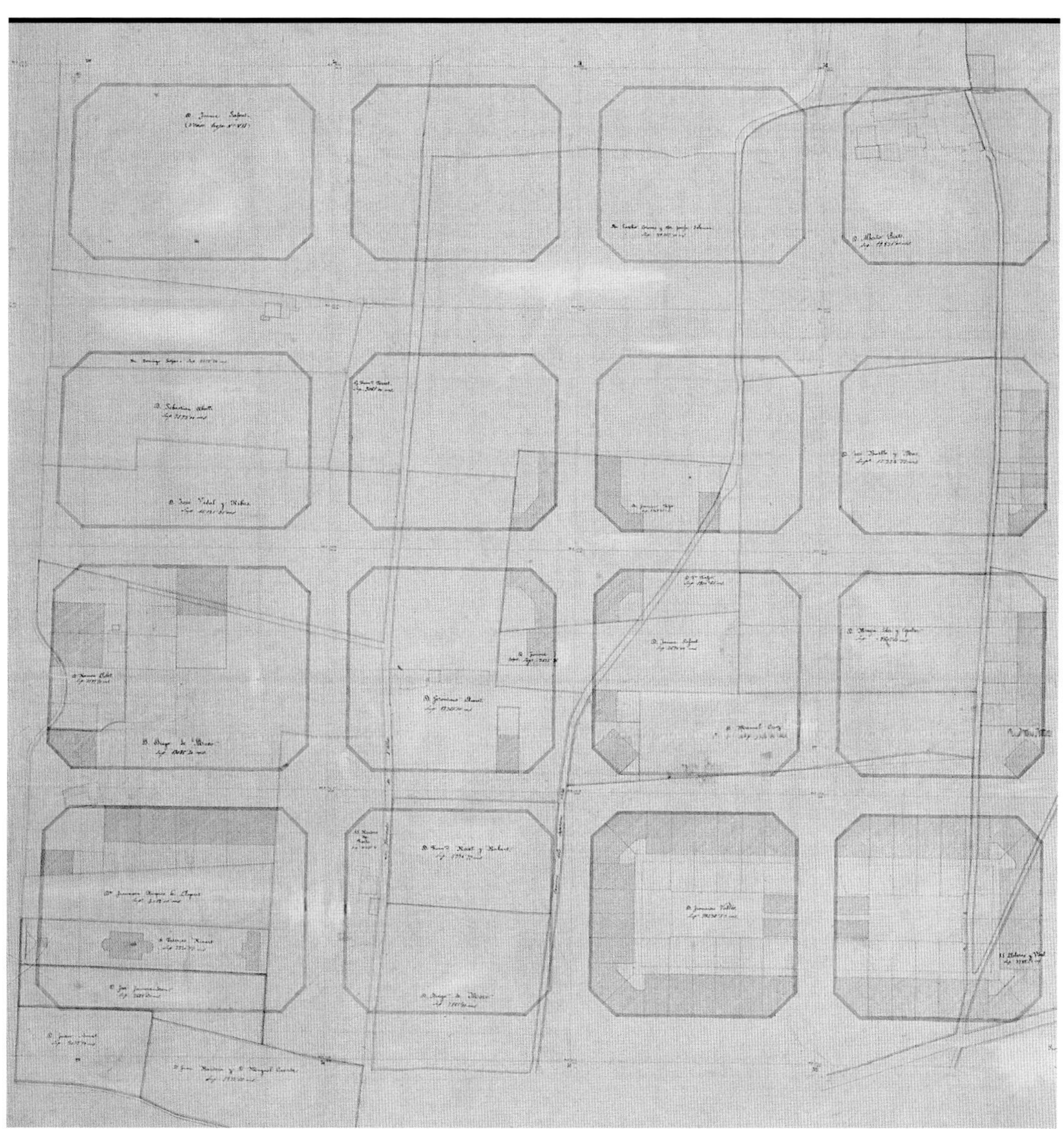

Itemized map. Sheet XII. (1860-1865). Ildefons Cerdà, Source: Cerdà Legacy. Arxiu Històric de la Ciutat de Barcelona.

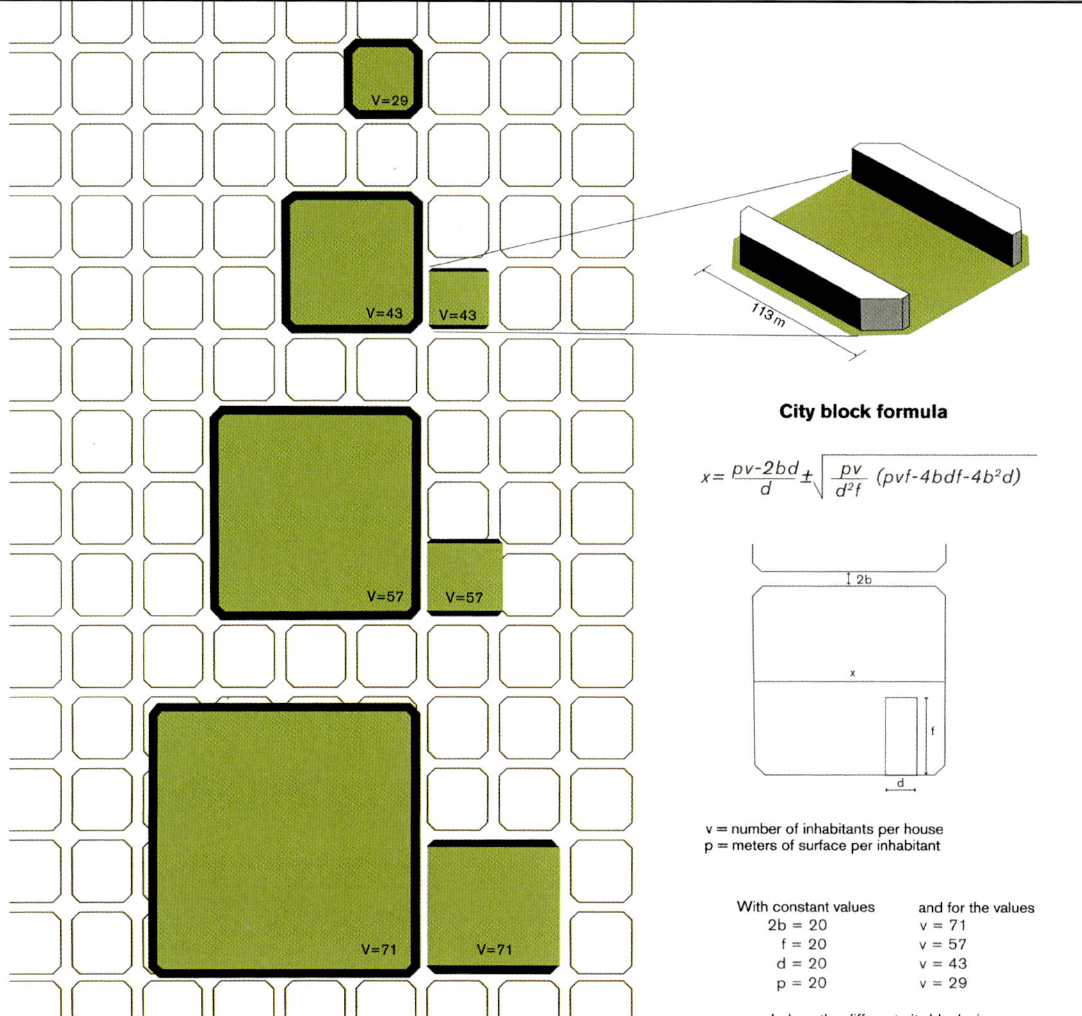

Towards the definition of the side of the city block

Having defined the criteria for using a grid made up of city blocks of equal sides, Cerdà considered various models: closed in on all four sides or open, with or without chamfered edges. Finally he decided on a typology of party wall construction with a façade and a depth of 20 m, and envisaged four types of dwelling:

- A building comprising a ground floor, for 29 inhabitants
- A building with a ground floor and one upper storey, for 43 inhabitants
- A building with a ground floor and two upper storeys, for 57 inhabitants
- A building with a ground floor and three upper storeys, for 71 inhabitants

Formula for the deduction of the dimensions of the city block (1996). Conception: Francesc Magrinyà.

Cerdà used reparcelling to impose the Alignment Plan

As administrator of the Eixample from 1860 to 1865, Cerdà was behind the implementation of his project as the Civil Government's Engineer in charge of the Eixample. In this position, he granted building permits by reparcelling and siting buildings according to the new 1861 Alignment Plan and implementing the criteria of the corresponding bylaws.

The grid was adapted to existing thoroughfares: Gràcia road (today's Passeig de Gràcia); Malla watercourse (today's Rambla Catalunya); Rambla del Poblenou and Carrer Marià Aguiló; Travessera de Gràcia.

In 1865, Cerdà also drafted and approved the Town Wall Reparcelling Project, which enabled him to adapt the initial grid of the 1859 Remodelling and Extension Project to modifications arising from reparcelling the land on which the town wall had stood, particularly with the relocation of Plaça Catalunya.

[1] See page 60

Map of alignments of the project for the extension and improvement of Barcelona (after July 1861).
Ildefons Cerdà. Source: Cerdà Legacy. Arxiu Històric de la Ciutat de Barcelona.

Geometrical map of the Eixample (1865). Leandre Serrallach. Source: Historical Archive of the Col·legi d'Arquitectes de Catalunya.

General map of Barcelona, its Extension and nearby towns (1877). Josep Maria Jordan. Source: Arxiu Històric de la Ciutat de Barcelona.

Map of Barcelona and its environs (1890). Approved by the City Council, meeting on 13 January 1891. Josep Maria Serra. Source: Institut Cartogràfic de Catalunya. Cartoteca de Catalunya.

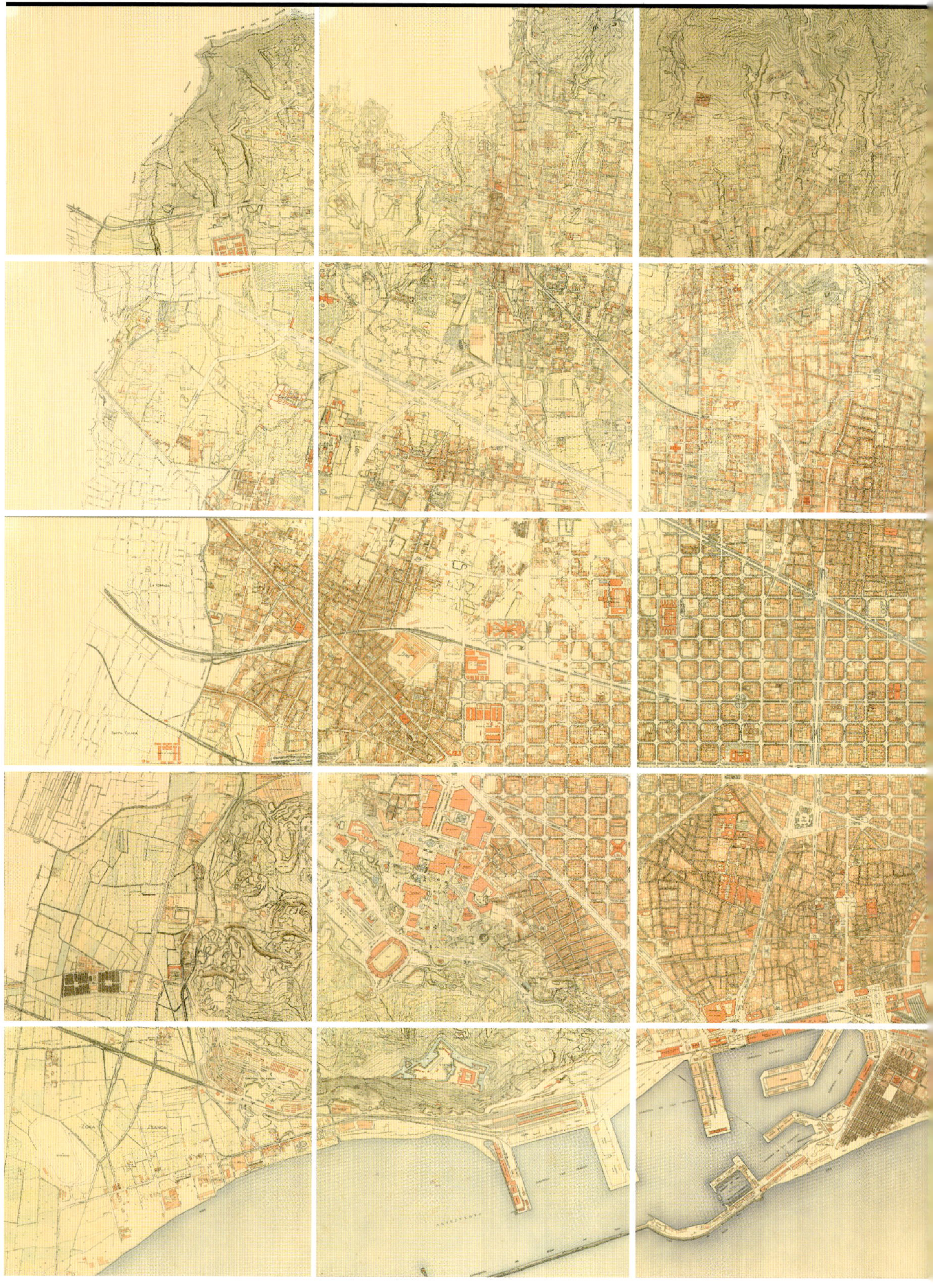

Topographical map of Barcelona (1933). Vicenç Martorell. Source: Arxiu Històric de la Ciutat de Barcelona.

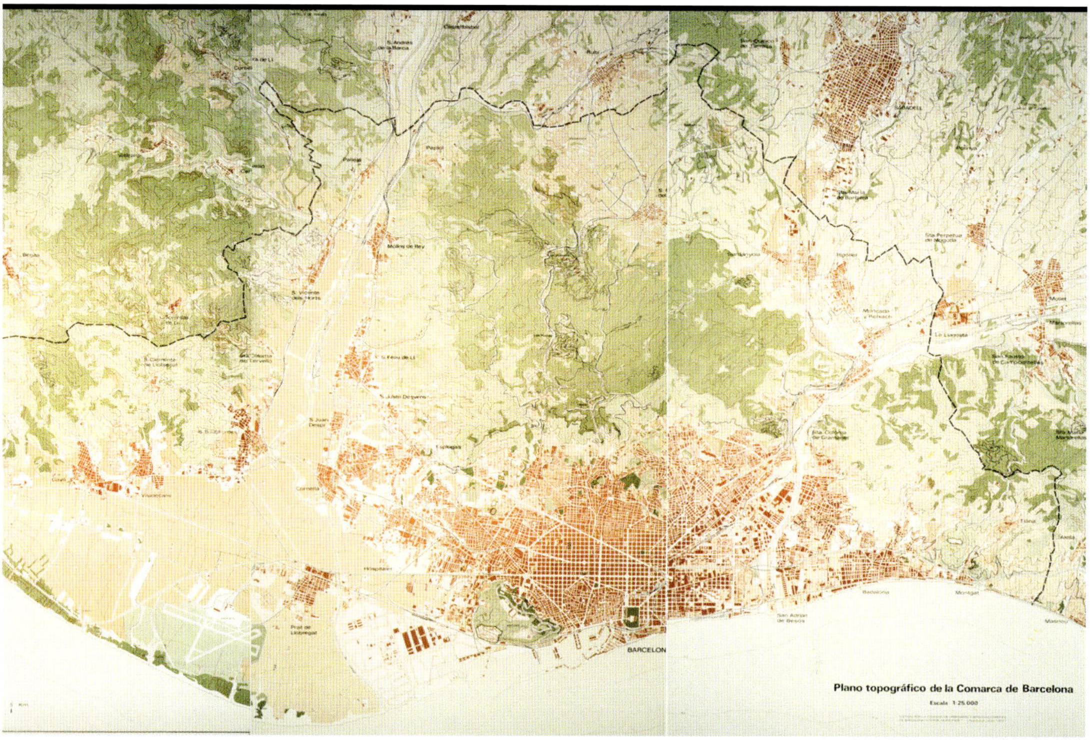

Plano topográfico de la Comarca de Barcelona

Escala 1:25.000

Topographical map of the Barcelonès county (1970). Source: Comissió d'Urbanisme i Serveis Comuns de Barcelona. Mancomunitat de Municipis.

Topographical basis of the metropolitan area, scale 1:100.000 (1996). Source: Institut d'Estudis Territorials. Department of Territorial Policy and Public Works of the Generalitat de Catalunya Autonomous Government.

Aerial view of Gran Via de les Corts Catalans, Ronda de Sant Anton and Plaça Universitat (1920-1925). Photography: Josep M. Có de Triola. Source: Centre Excursionista de Catalunya.

Aerial view of Plaça de Catalunya. Martí Cargol's first trip (20 June, 1920). Photography: Martí Cargol. Source: Centre Excursionista de Catalunya.

Aerial view of the Sagrada Família. Second journey of Martí Cargol (18 July 1920). Photograph: Martí Cargol. Source: Centre Excursionista de Catalunya.

Aerial view of Passeig de Pujades and the Parc de la Ciutadella. Second journey of Martí Cargol (18 July 1920). Photograph: Martí Cargol. Source: Centre Excursionista de Catalunya.

Aerial view of the part central of Barcelona's Eixample with Avinguda Diagonal (1920). Photograph: Martí Cargol. Source: Centre Excursionista de Catalunya.

Aerial view of Avinguda Diagonal and Passeig de Gràcia. Second journey of Martí Cargol (18 July 1920). Photograph: Martí Cargol. Source: Centre Excursionista de Catalunya.

BARCELONA

Photomap of Barcelona and its environs 1:10.000 (1947). Photograph: CETFA (Companyia Espanyola de Treballs Fotogramètrics Aeris). Source: Institut Cartogràfic de Catalunya.

Vol. 10.165, dated 1975. Source: Institut Cartogràfic de Catalunya.

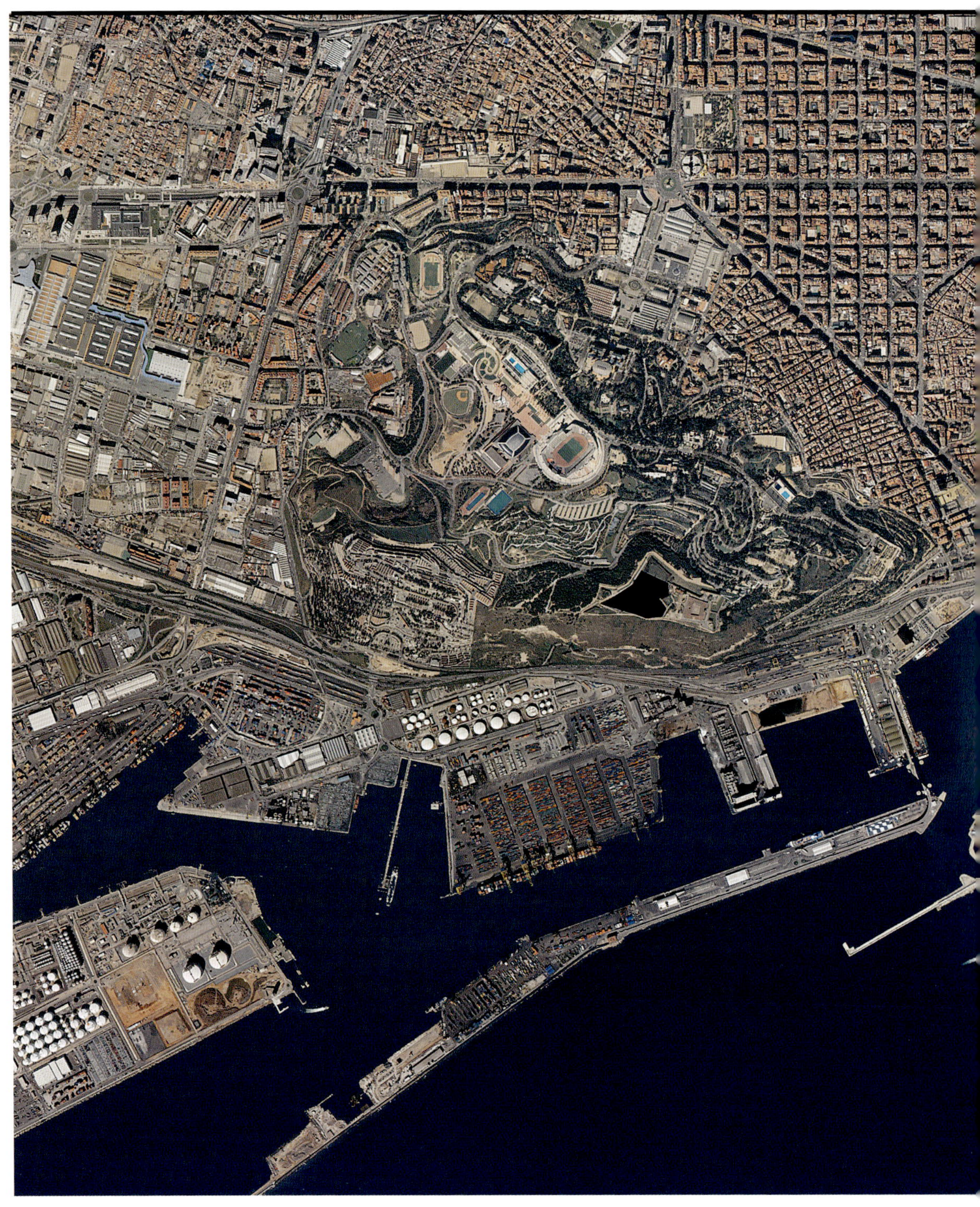

Aerial view of Barcelona's Eixample in 2008. Source: Institut Cartogràfic de Catalunya.

the street_

"The principle of independence of the different forms of movement in the urban thoroughfare"

(I. Cerdà, *Teoría General de la Urbanización*, 1867)

"The principle of independence of the different forms of movement in the urban thoroughfare"

Each form of mobility in the street, from an individual on foot to the railway, had to have its own space in the urban thoroughfare. The street had to be designed to accommodate them all, which led Cerdà to the conclusion that the street should have a minimum section of 20 m[1].

Cerdà designed the street and its chamfered corner down to the last detail, including the various forms of paving, the level crossings and the furniture, particularly the trees and the street lighting. With the passing of time, each new service and its associated furniture were superposed onto the street: water, gas, electricity, tram and car[2].

With the recent promotion of sustainable means of transport, dedicated spaces are once again being created, such as cycle and bus lanes, and pedestrian routes, marking a return to Cerdà's principle of independence of the different forms of transport in the street section (see figs 1 and 2).

The Comissió d'Eixample, a vital instrument in urbanization

The Comissió d'Eixample [City Extension Commission] played a central role in the construction of the city by deciding and promoting work on infrastructures, urbanization and facilities during the 1864-1953 period, between the 1864 City Extensions Act and the 1953 Pla Comarcal de Barcelona [Barcelona Counties Plan].

In a period, starting in 1904, the Comissió d'Eixample promoted work on the sewer system and street paving, and the construction of streets beyond the limits of the old municipality of Barcelona[3]. Initially, Cerdà controlled the application of this model in the central part of the Eixample, and it continued to be implemented in the late 19th century, as shown by the models of streets to develop the municipality of Sant Martí[4].

In 1925, the scope of the Comissió d'Eixample extended beyond the limits of Cerdà's Eixample Project, continuing to develop Avinguda Diagonal as far as the Palace of Pedralbes, and Carrer Balmes along the railway line to Sarrià, as shown by the street lighting plan of the Comissió d'Eixample of 1928.

[1] See fig. page 86 **I** [2] See fig. pages 94, 95 **I** [3] See fig. page 92 **I** [4] See fig. page 88

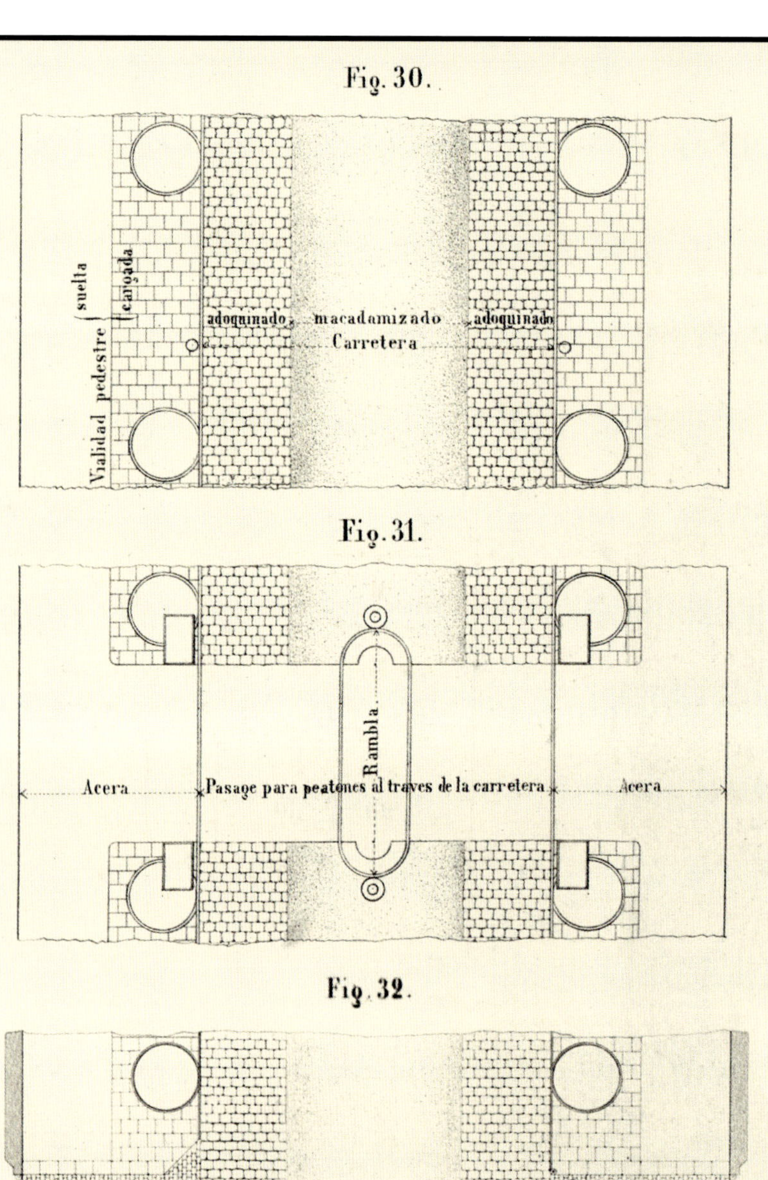

Details of street urbanization. Ildefons Cerdà. "Necesidades de la circulación. Encrucijadas en las calles de las poblaciones" [Needs of circulation. Street junctions], in Revista de Obras Públicas. 1863. Source: Biblioteca de Lletres. University of Barcelona.

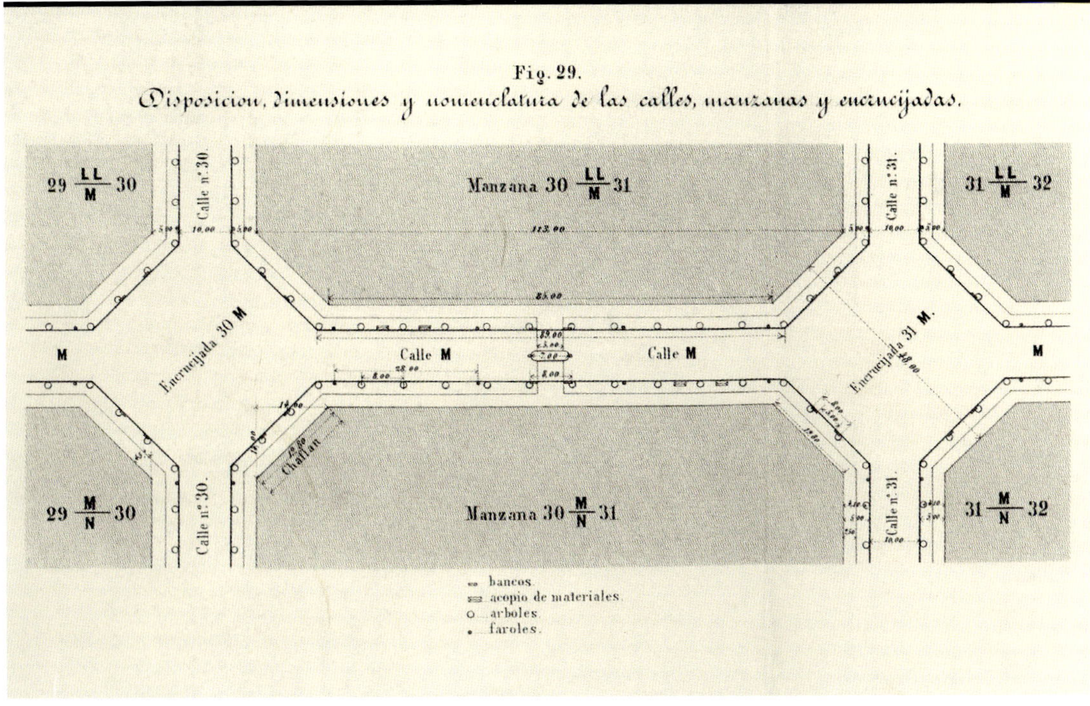

The organization of streets in the Eixample as an expression of the principle of independence of means of transport in the urban thoroughfare

In the initial proposal for the 1855 Preliminary Extension Project, Cerdà envisaged a street 35 m in width as a result of separating pedestrians, people on foot carrying goods, carts and carriages, stagecoaches and railway. The 1859 Remodelling and Extension Project included dedicated streets according to width (20, 30 and 50 m) and suggested that the railway should only circulate along those of 50 m. Later, in the 1863 Preliminary Barcelona Docks Project, Cerdà redesigned the streets of the Eixample to include some on two levels, one undergrounded for the railway and the other on the surface, for other means of transport, as in the case of Carrer Aragó.

Unity of street and squares for the construction of the Eixample with the layout, dimensions and index of streets, city blocks and crossroads. Ildefons Cerdà. **"Necesidades de la circulación. Encrucijadas en las calles de las poblaciones"** [Needs of circulation. Street junctions], in *Revista de Obras Públicas.* 1863 Source: Biblioteca de Lletres. University of Barcelona.

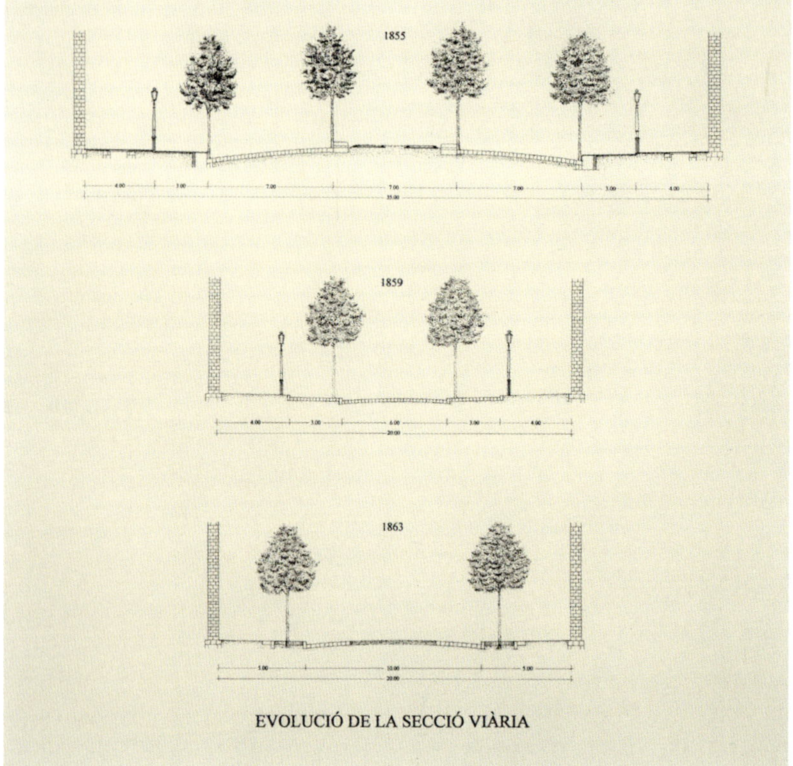

Street profile with details of paving and underground works. Plate XXXVI. Ildefons Cerdà. *Memoria del Anteproyecto del Ensanche de Barcelona* [Description of the Preliminary Project for the Extension of Barcelona], 1855. Source: Government Archives. Section of the Ministry of Education and Science.

Reworking of the street sections proposed by Cerdà for the standard street in the *Memoria del Anteproyecto del Ensanche de Barcelona* [Description of the Preliminary Project for the Extension of Barcelona] of 1855 (35 metres), the *Proyecto de Reforma y Ensanche de Barcelona* [Project for the Remodelling and extension of Barcelona] of 1859 (20 metres) and *Necesidades de la Circulación* [Needs of circulation], of 1863. Francesc Magrinyà. "Via-intervies: un nou concepte proposat per Cerdà" [Vies-intervies: a new concept proposed by Cerdà], in Cerdà Urbs i Territori. 1994.

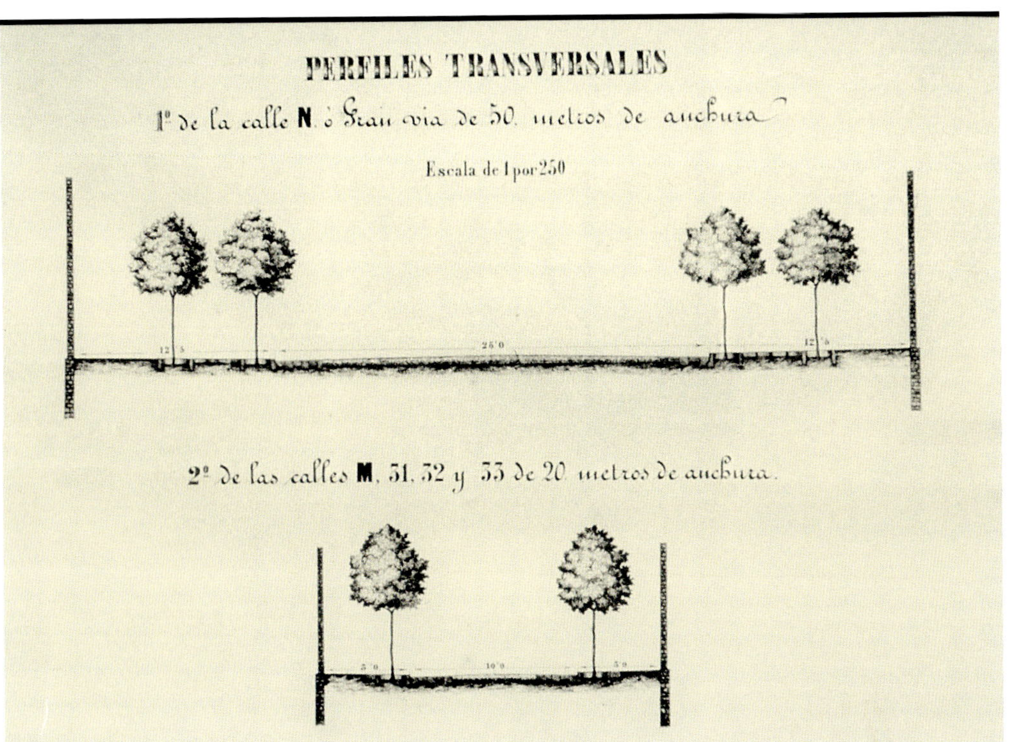

Cross sections of streets, proposed by Cerdà as technical director of the Sociedad Fomento del Ensanche property company. Ildefons Cerdà. Fomento del Ensanche de Barcelona. 1863. Source: Arxiu Històric de la Ciutat de Barcelona.

Hierarchical structure of the street in Cerdà's Eixample superposed on the grid. Production: exhibition.

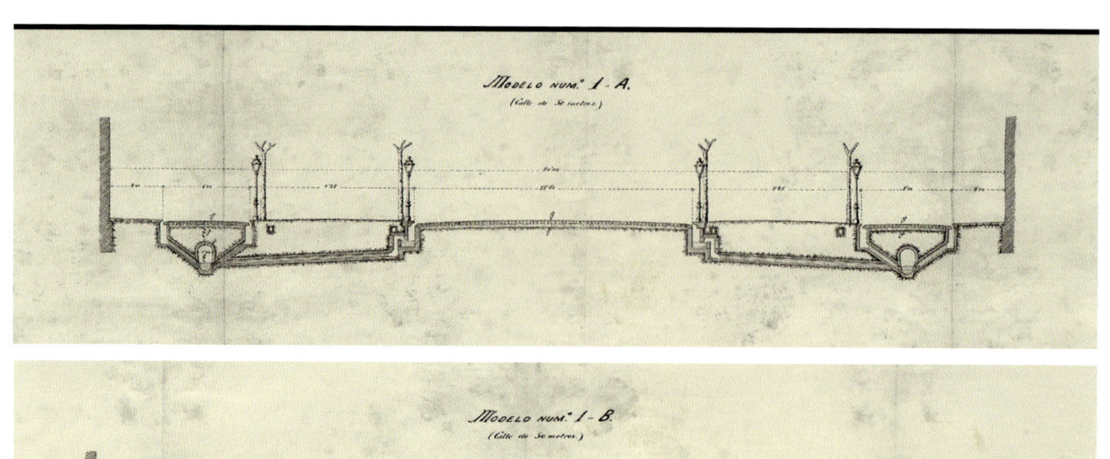

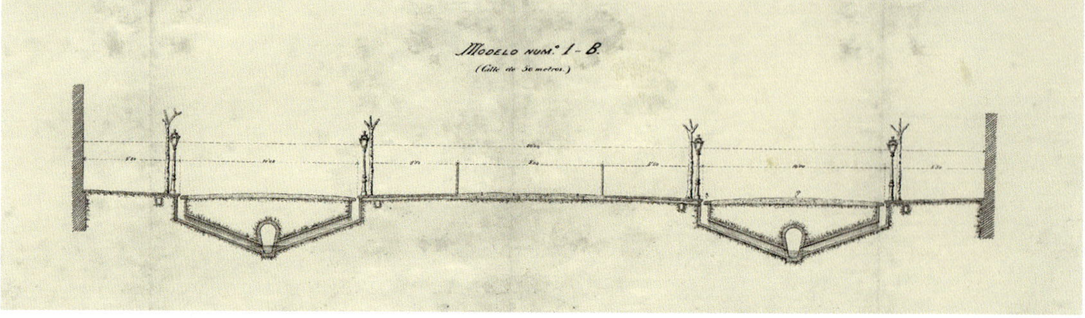

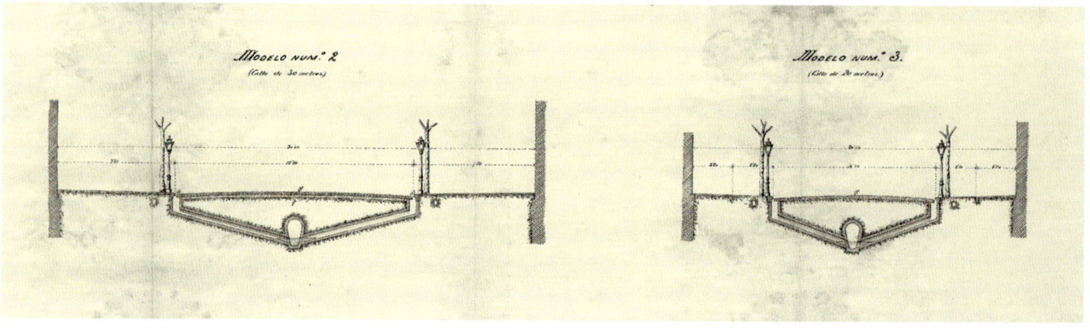

Typical sections for the general urbanization project for all the streets in to the Eixample that affect the municipality of Sant Martí de Provençals (1894). Architect: Claudi Duran Ventosa. Source: Municipal Archive of the Districte de Sant Martí.

COMISIÓN ESPECIAL DE ENSANCHE.-1927

AVENIDA DEL GENERAL PRIMO DE RIVERA

VISTA TOMADA EN PROYECCIÓN HACIA EL HOSPITAL DE SAN PABLO

COMISIÓN ESPECIAL DE ENSANCHE.-1927

AVENIDA DEL GENERAL PRIMO DE RIVERA

ASPECTO DE ESTA VÍA, DESPUÉS DE EXPLANADA

Carrer d'Espronceda. *Memoria de la Comisión de Ensanche* [Report of the City Extension Committee]. Barcelona City Council. 1927. Source: Historical Archive of the Col·legi d'Arquitectes de Catalunya.

COMISIÓN ESPECIAL
DE ENSANCHE.-1927

AVENIDA DEL GENERAL PRIMO DE RIVERA

ASPECTO DE ESTA VÍA, DESPUÉS DE EXPLANADA

COMISIÓN ESPECIAL
DE ENSANCHE.-1928

AVENIDA DE PRIMO DE RIVERA

LO QUE AYER FUÉ CAMPOS INCULTOS.

Avinguda del General Primo de Rivera (present-day Avinguda de Gaudí). *Memoria de la Comisión de Ensanche* [Report of the City Extension Committee]. Barcelona City Council. 1928. Source: Historical Archive of the Col·legi d'Arquitectes de Catalunya.

Avinguda del General Primo de Rivera (present-day Avinguda de Gaudí). *Memoria de la Comisión de Ensanche* [Report of the City Extension Committee]. Barcelona City Council. 1927. Source: Historical Archive of the Col·legi d'Arquitectes de Catalunya.

COMISIÓN ESPECIAL DE ENSANCHE.-1928

LA CALLE DE CORTES HA SIDO PROLONGADA...

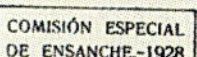

... EN DIRECCIÓN A HOSPITALET DE LLOBREGAT.

Extension of Avinguda de la Gran Via de les Corts Catalanes beyond Plaça d'Espanya. *Memoria de la Comisión de Ensanche* [Report of the City Extension Committee]. Barcelona City Council. 1928. Source: Historical Archive of the Col·legi d'Arquitectes de Catalunya.

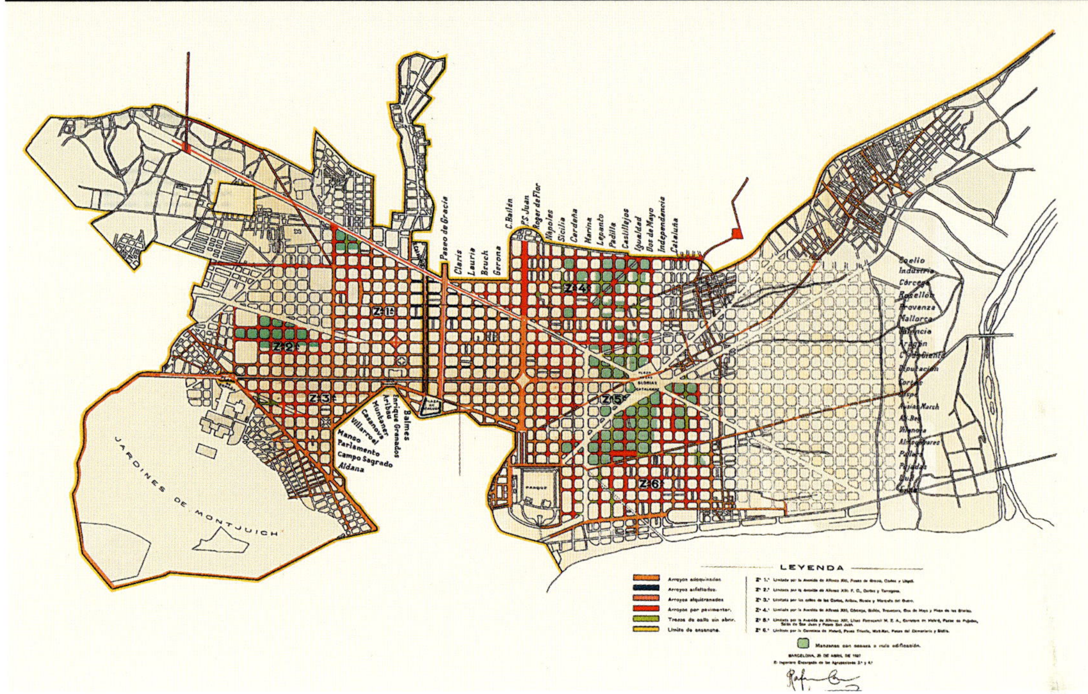

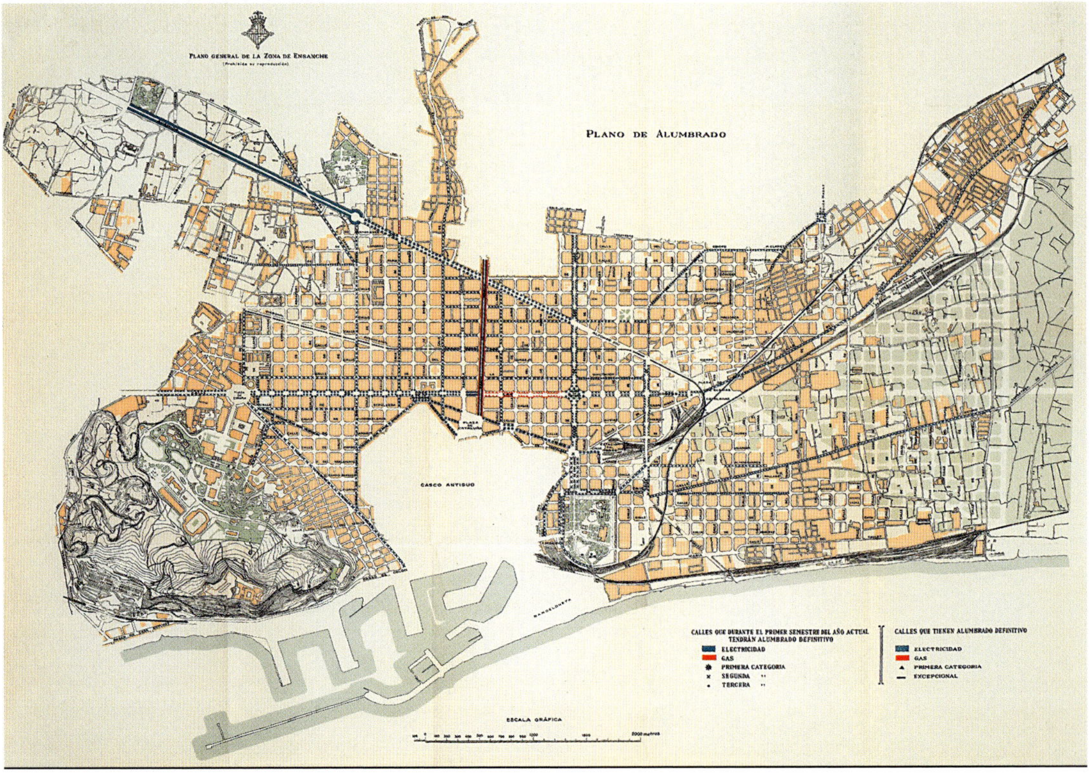

Map of street paving in the Eixample with urbanization beyond the old municipal limits of Barcelona. *Memoria de la Comisión de Ensanche* [Report of the City Extension Committee]. Barcelona City Council. 1927. Source: Historical Archive of the Col·legi d'Arquitectes de Catalunya.

Map of street lighting in the Eixample with hierarchical structure of streets. *Memoria de la Comisión de Ensanche* [Report of the City Extension Committee]. Barcelona City Council. 1928. Source: Historical Archive of the Col·legi d'Arquitectes de Catalunya.

The introduction of the various urban utilities meant a reconstruction of the street and a hierarchical organization of the streets of the Eixample

The introduction of urban utilities such as water and gas called for the construction of networks and furniture to join the existing trees and the oil street lamps.

Later, the introduction of electricity meant adding street lamps and tram lanes, and reorganizing some street sections.

The subsequent introduction of the automobile and omnibuses led to the surfacing of the main streets of the Eixample and the incorporation of their associated furniture: bus stops and petrol stations.

Differential lighting and paving of streets served to consolidate a hierarchy of streets and enhance the public space.

Surfacing of Avinguda Diagonal between Plaça de Francesc Macià and Pedralbes Palace (1925-1935).
Photograph: Josep Domínguez. Source: Arxiu Fotogràfic de Barcelona.

Urbanization of Gran Via de les Corts Catalanes, with grading, tree planting and street lighting (1873). Photograph: unknown author. Source: Mas Holdings. Fundació Institut Amatller d'Art Hispànic.

Passeig de Gràcia with details of the horse-drawn tram and pavements (1870-1879). Photograph: Joan Martí. Source: Arxiu Fotogràfic de Barcelona.

Reurbanization of Gran Via de les Corts Catalanes with setts for the introduction of electric tram rails (1906). Photograph: Frederic Ballell. Source: Arxiu Fotogràfic de Barcelona.

Reurbanization of Carrer de Balmes with asphalt surfacing on the occasion of the undergrounding of the Sarrià railway line (1929). Photograph: F. Argila. Source: Arxiu Fotogràfic de Barcelona.

Asphalting Passeig de Gràcia (1908). Photograph: Frederic Ballell. Source: Arxiu Fotogràfic de Barcelona.

Road works at the junction of Carrer de Casanova and Carrer de València (1926). Photograph: Juan Mas Guàrdia. Source: Historical Archive of the Col·legi d'Arquitectes de Catalunya.

Carrer de Balmes (1925). Photograph: Josep Domínguez. Source: Arxiu Fotogràfic de Barcelona.

Model of lamppost installed in the Saló de Sant Joan (1881). Architect: Antoni Rovira i Trias. Source: Municipal Administrative Archive. Barcelona City Council.

Model of lamppost for Passeig de Gràcia (1887). Architect: Conrad Sintas. Source: Municipal Administrative Archive. Barcelona City Council.

Design of a lamppost-clock for centres (1889). Architect: Pere Falqués. Source: Municipal Administrative Archive. Barcelona City Council.

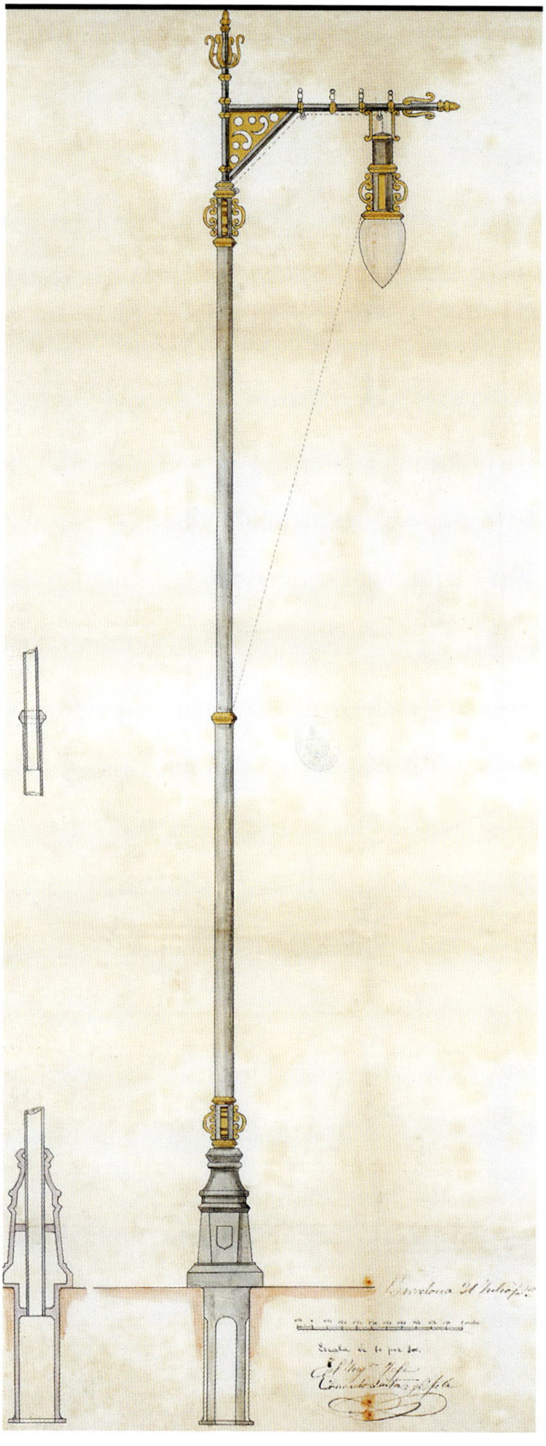

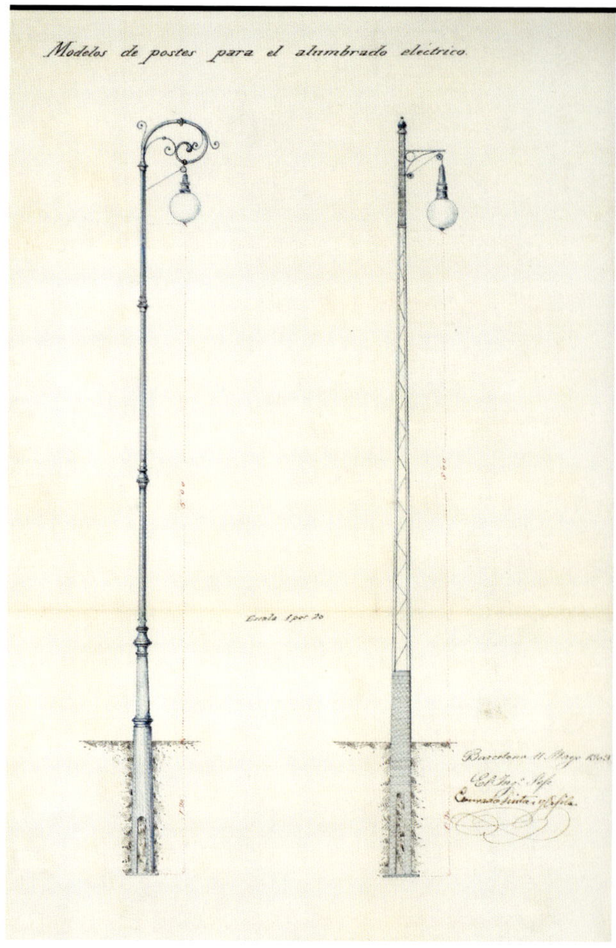

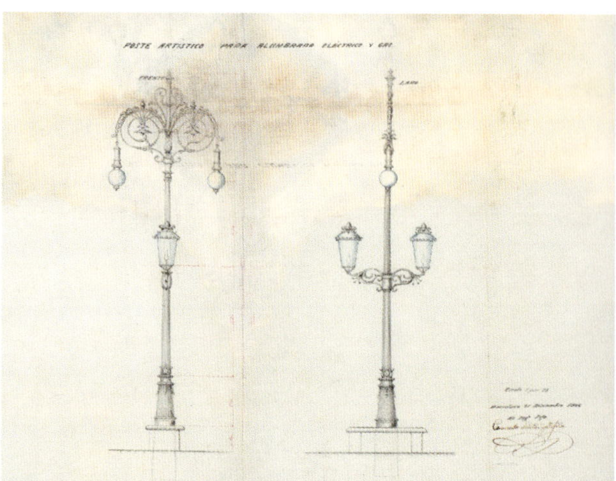

Model of lamppost for street lighting in Rambla de Catalunya (1893). Architect: Conrad Sintas. Source: Municipal Administrative Archive. Barcelona City Council.

Models of lamppost for electric street lighting (1903). Architect: Conrad Sintas. Source: Municipal Administrative Archive. Barcelona City Council.

Artistic post for electric and gas street lighting (1906). Architect: Conrad Sintas. Source: Municipal Administrative Archive. Barcelona City Council.

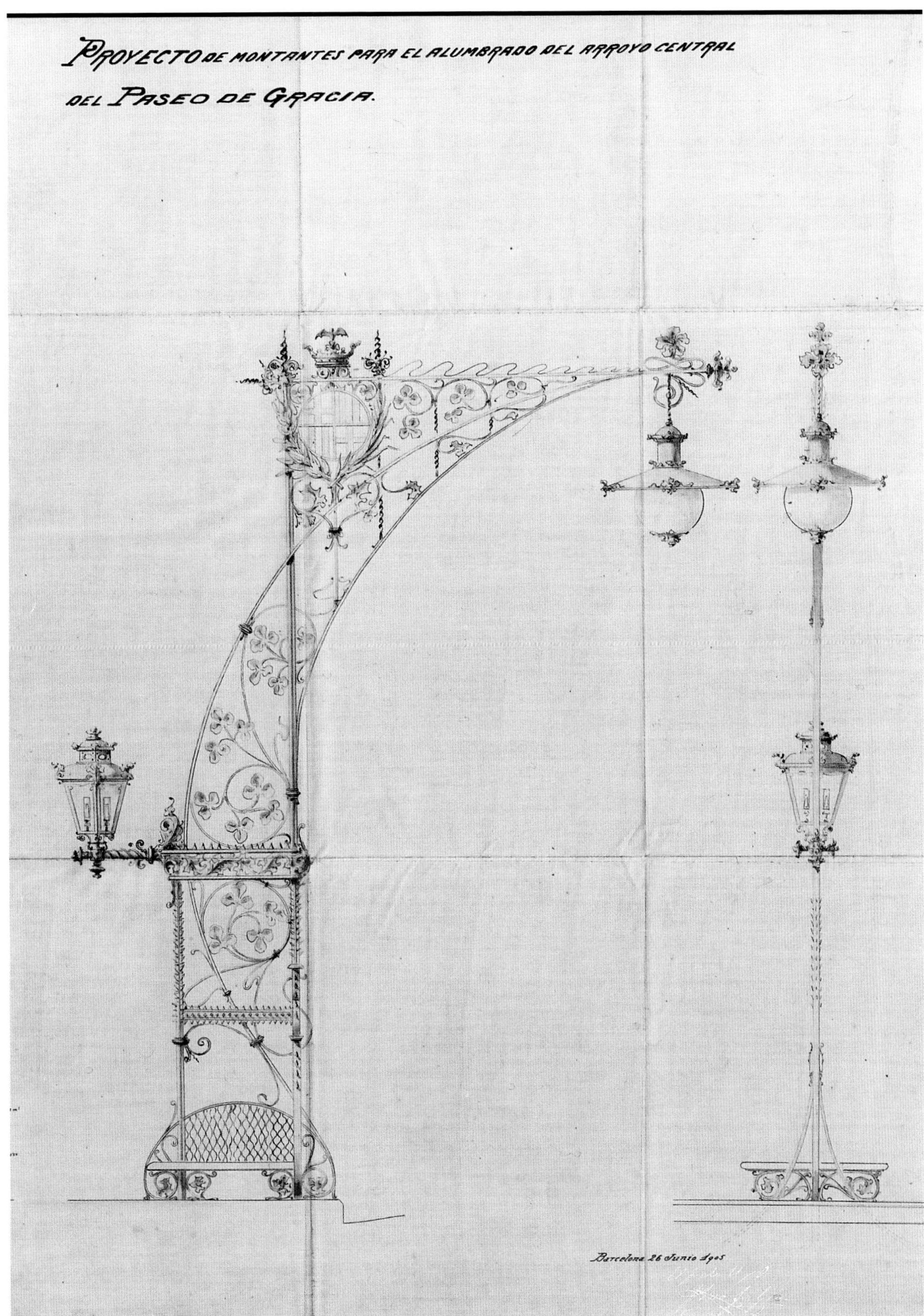

Project for street-lighting posts for the central lane of Passeig de Gràcia (1905). Architect: Pere Falqués. Source: Municipal Administrative Archive. Barcelona City Council.

HYGIENE AND CLEANLINESS

Personal
Street barbers
Servants' hairdressers (maids)
Boot- and shoeblacks

Domestic
Dustman
Whitewasher-plasterer
Mattress-maker
Chimneysweep
Floor-washer
Well-cleaner
Sandman

SALE OF GARMENTS

For personal use
Hosier
Hat-maker
Slipper-maker
Used-clothes dealer
Stick-maker
Street tinsmith

For domestic use
Haberdashery
Palencia blankets
Oilcloths for tables
Mats
Linen

UTENSILS

On sale
Brooms
Baskets
Sieves and screens
Crockery
Valencia china
Pots and pans
Mousetraps

Services
Earthenware jars and sinks
Hotplates and burners
Frying pans
Knife grinder

Buying
Rag-and-bone man

STREET INDUSTRIES AND PLACES SELLING ARTICLES OF FOOD AND DRINK, AND FOR BURNING

Food
Bread stands
Fritter stands
Wafer stands
Buns
White honey
Dried fruits and nuts
Fresh fruit
Vegetables
Dairy goods
Fresh and dried fish
Poultry
Game
Sausage seller

Drink
Water-cart men
Refreshments
Taverns and cafés, mobile and stands
Mineral waters
Vinegar
Mobile cafés

For burning
Firewood
Coal
Slack
Portable gas

MISCELLANEOUS TRADES, WITH STANDS OR MOBILE

Clothes-mender
Cobbler
Shoe-repairer
Umbrella-maker
Fan-maker
Tinsmith
Bird dealer
Cage-maker or vendor
Plaster figures
Stain removers
Chair-maker
Matchmaker
Porters
Registry office for servants, nursemaids and wet nurses
Memorial writer
Newspaper kiosks
Reading rooms
Bookstalls
Florists
Ink and miscellaneous other writing objects
Sheet music
Children's toys
Sale of dogs
Posy sellers
Cabs
Removal wagons
Carters
Itinerant jewellery makers
Street auctions
Organ-grinders and other street musicians
Monkeys and wise dogs
Street acrobats
Panoramas
Conjurers

The street is a space for interrelation and activities

In his book *Necesidades de la circulación* ([Requirements of Circulation], 1863), Cerdà listed some 90 different activities that took place in the street. He also suggested that these activities be accommodated in kiosks and allocated them a place in the street, particularly on the chamfered corners.

The last 150 years of life in the Eixample have seen a huge variety of activities. Below are some of the most characteristic of the late 19th and early 20th centuries: street selling, advertising, tree-watering, recreation, etc.

Ice for the fridges in Carrer dels Metges (1960). Photograph: Eugeni Forcano. Source: Eugeni Forcano Holdings.

Water seller (1905). Photograph: unknown author. Source: Arxiu Fotogràfic de Barcelona.

Ox drawing a cart of Champan Canónigos past La Pedrera, Passeig de Gràcia (c. 1920). Photograph: unknown author. Source: Roisin Collection. IEFC (Institut d'Estudis Fotogràfics de Catalunya).

Flea market at Sant Antoni market place (1910-1915). Photograph: unknown author. Source: Arxiu Fotogràfic de Barcelona.

Animal stalls on Rambla de Catalunya (1930). Photograph: Frederic Ballell. Source: Arxiu Fotogràfic de Barcelona.

Easter lamb fair on Passeig de Sant Joan (1907). Photograph: Frederic Ballell. Source: Arxiu Fotogràfic de Barcelona.

Christmas fair on the corner of Rambla de Catalunya and Gran Via de les Corts Catalanes, monument to Güell (undated). Photograph: Bordas. Source: Centre Excursionista de Catalunya.

First edition of Barcelona Gràfica newspaper (1930). Photograph: Josep Maria Sagarra. Source: Arxiu Fotogràfic de Barcelona.

Life on La Rambla. Watering the trees (1905-1910). Photograph: Frederic Ballell. Source: Arxiu Fotogràfic de Barcelona.

First edition of Barcelona Gràfica newspaper (1930). Photograph: Josep Maria Sagarra. Source: Arxiu Fotogràfic de Barcelona.

chamfered corner_

“The principle of continuity of movement”

(I. Cerdà: *Necesidades de la Circulación*, [Needs of Circulation], 1963)

Designing a street crossroads as a square to accommodate activities

The chamfered corner is one of the elements that best characterizes Barcelona's Eixample grid. Cerdà considered street space as a place for human relations and designed a layout of streets and squares with junctions and chamfered corners for the orderly accommodation of activities, and kiosks as their furniture[1].

The chamfered corners therefore became the chosen location for a whole range of furniture (newsstands, advertising and information points, monuments, urinals, fountains, benches, etc.) that has accumulated in the course of 150 years[2].

Cerdà designed the crossroads to provide turning space for trams[3]. In more recent years, the needs of transport have come to the fore, particularly the car, with loading bays and parking meter zones[4].

Recovering street crossroads as city squares

The octagon formed by a crossroads has a surface area equivalent to a square with a 40 m side. If we compare the 1,200 crossroads in the Eixample with the squares that currently exist in districts included in the Barcelona Plan, we see that the former are equal in size or larger[5].

These "squares" have to be recovered as places for exchange and interrelation, where pedestrians are not forced to walk around the edge. The promotion of sustainable means of transport (walking, bicycle and public transport) calls for a return to Cerdà's solution of dedicated spaces, this time for pedestrians and bicycles[6].

[1] See fig. page 114 **I** [2] See fig. page 122 to128 **I** [3] See figs. 1 & 2 page 113 **I** [5]See fig. page 115-116
[6] See fig. page 114

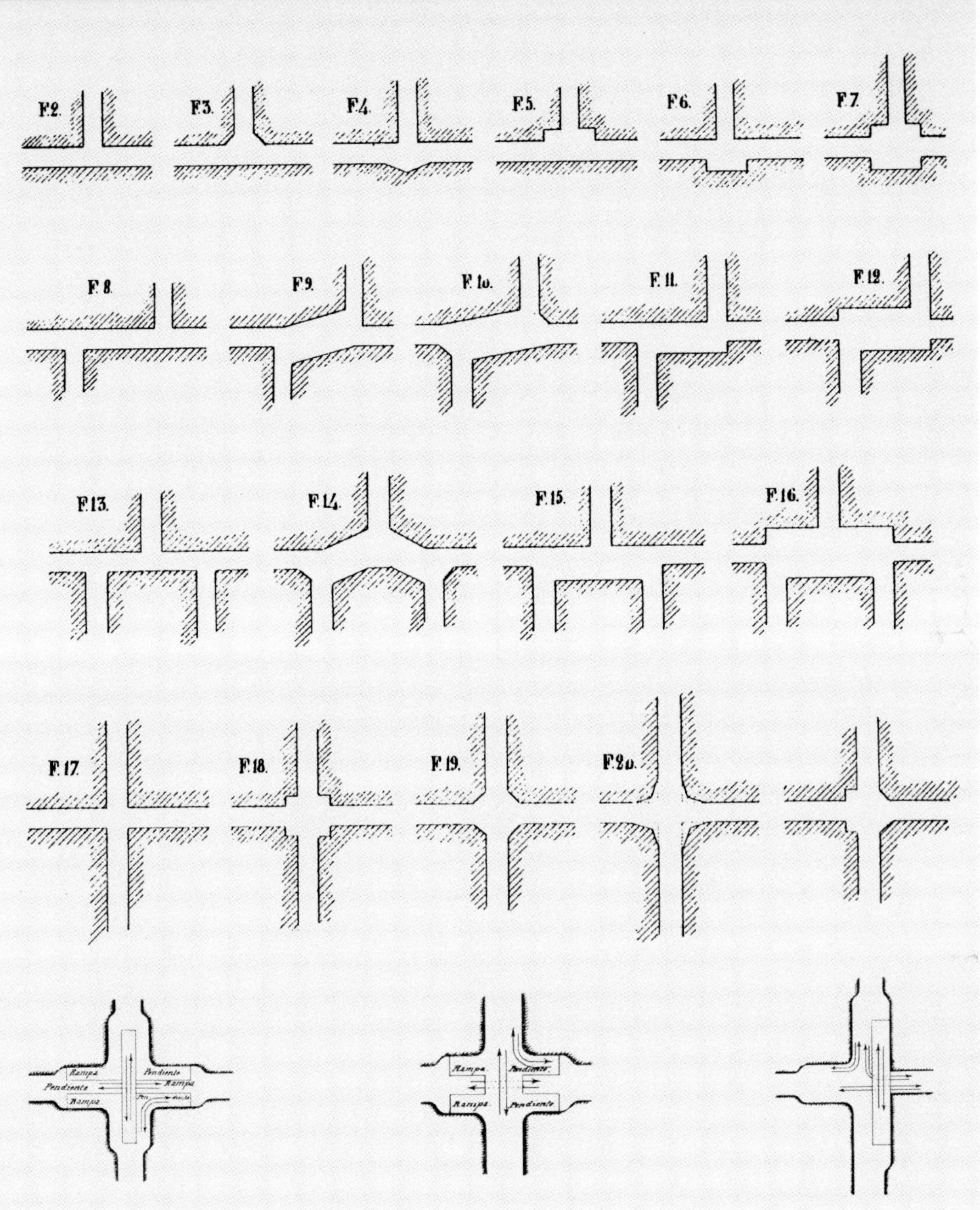

Different types of crossroads, at the same and at a different level. Ildefons Cerdà. *Teoría de la Viabilidad Urbana* [Theory of Urban Viability]. 1861. Source: Government Archives. Ministry of Culture.

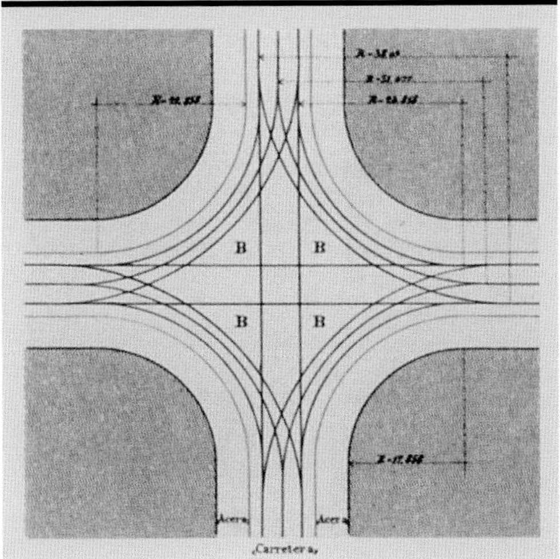

Fig. 1

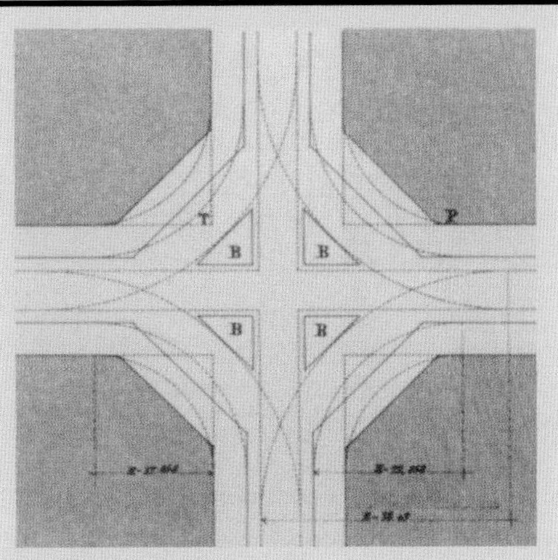

Fig. 2

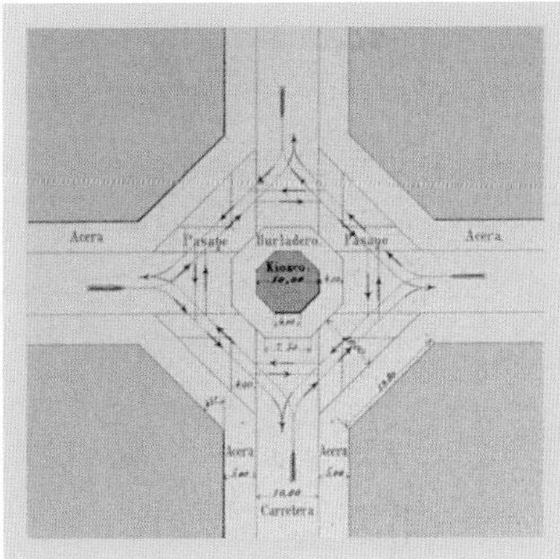

Fig. 3

The chamfered corner according to Cerdà

Cerdà started by studying the way city streets have developed through history. He reached the conclusion that the chamfered corner was a necessity and analysed the most appropriate form and dimensions.

For his design of the chamfered corner, he studied the Parisian railway of the time and its turning radius at junctions. The result was the choice of the octagon with a 20 m side as the best solution[7].

He went on to study junctions in different means of transport (pedestrians, people on foot carrying things, carriages and trains) and designed the junction to keep the number of conflicts between the different forms of circulation to a minimum. He put forward two solutions: with a kiosk at the centre or with four kiosks[8].

[7] See figs. 1 & 2 | [8] See fig. D & E page 114

Figs. 1 & 2_Crossroads. Calculating the junction to accommodate a turning radius.
Fig. 3_Crossroads. Movement with kiosk at the centre.

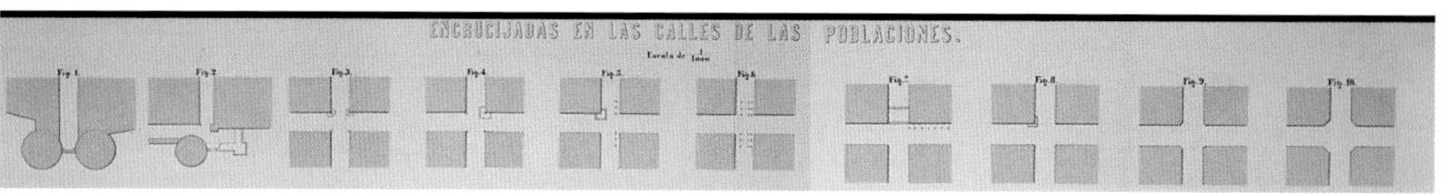

A

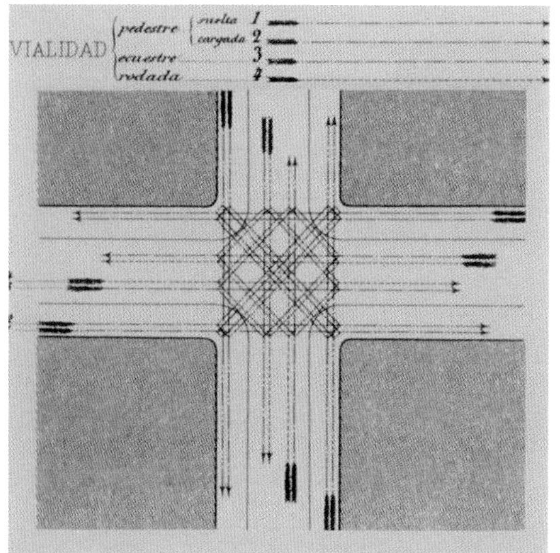

B

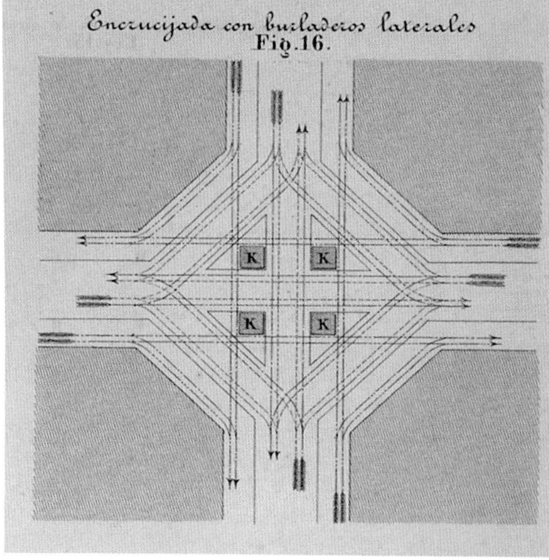

C

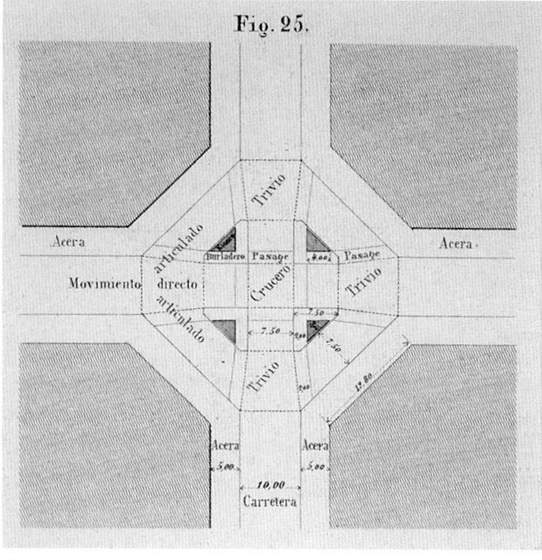

D

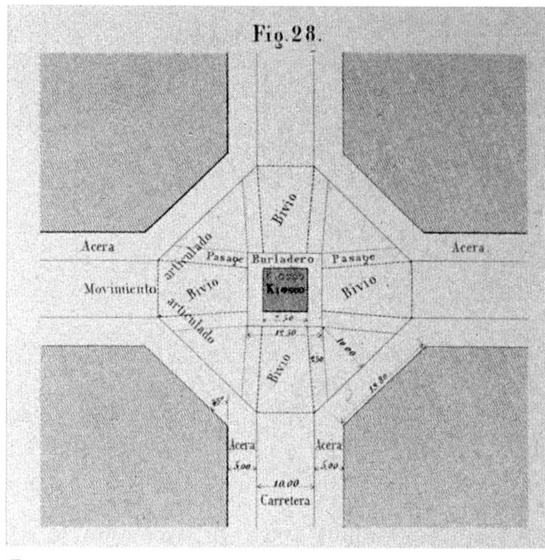

E

A_ Crossroads. Historical evolution of the crossroads
B, C._ Crossroads. Theoretical calculation of the crossroads with reorganization of movements
D._ Crossroads. Model of crossroads with pedestrian refuges at the side
E._ Crossroads. Model of crossroads with central pedestrian refuge
Ildefons Cerdà: «Necesidades de la circulación. Encrucijadas en las calles de las poblaciones» [Needs of circulation. Street junctions], *Revista de Obras Públicas* (1863). Source: Arts Library. University of Barcelona.

Solution of a chamfered corner with four kiosks. Conception: Francesc Magrinyà and Fernando Marzá. Model: ETSAV-UPC model workshop. 2009. Collection of the Fundació Urbs i Territori Ildefons Cerdà (FUTIC).

Solution of a chamfered corner with a central kiosk. Conception: Francesc Magrinyà and Fernando Marzá. Model: ETSAV-UPC model workshop. 2009. Collection of the Fundació Urbs i Territori Ildefons Cerdà (FUTIC).

Comparison between a square formed by an intersection with beveling in the Eixample and the Plaça del Comerç in Sant Andreu. Conception: Francesc Magrinyà and Fernando Marzá. Model: ETSAV-UPC model workshop. 2009. Collection of the Fundació Urbs i Territori Ildefons Cerdà (FUTIC).

Comparison between a square formed by an intersection with beveling in the Eixample and the Plaça Bacardí in Horta. Conception: Francesc Magrinyà and Fernando Marzá. Model: ETSAV-UPC model workshop. 2009. Collection of the Fundació Urbs i Territori Ildefons Cerdà (FUTIC).

Details of the crossroads in the Eixample in the itemized maps. Rambla de Catalunya and its intersections with Carrer de Pelai and Carrer de Bergara. Ildefons Cerdà. Itemized map no. XVII. 1860-1865. Source: Cerdà Legacy. Arxiu Històric de la Ciutat de Barcelona.

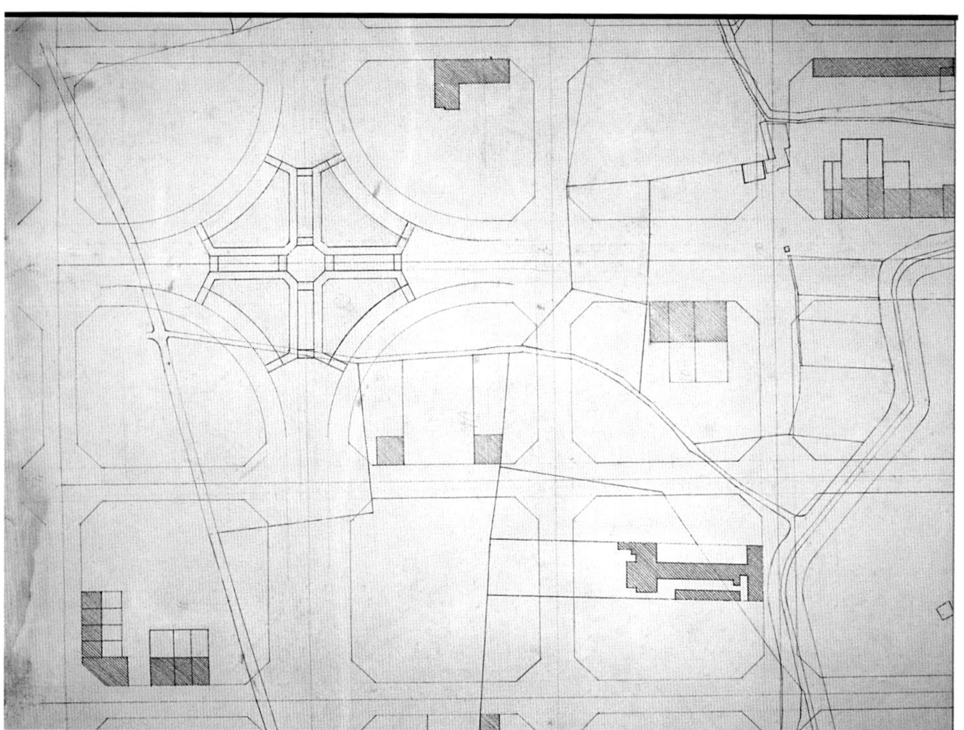

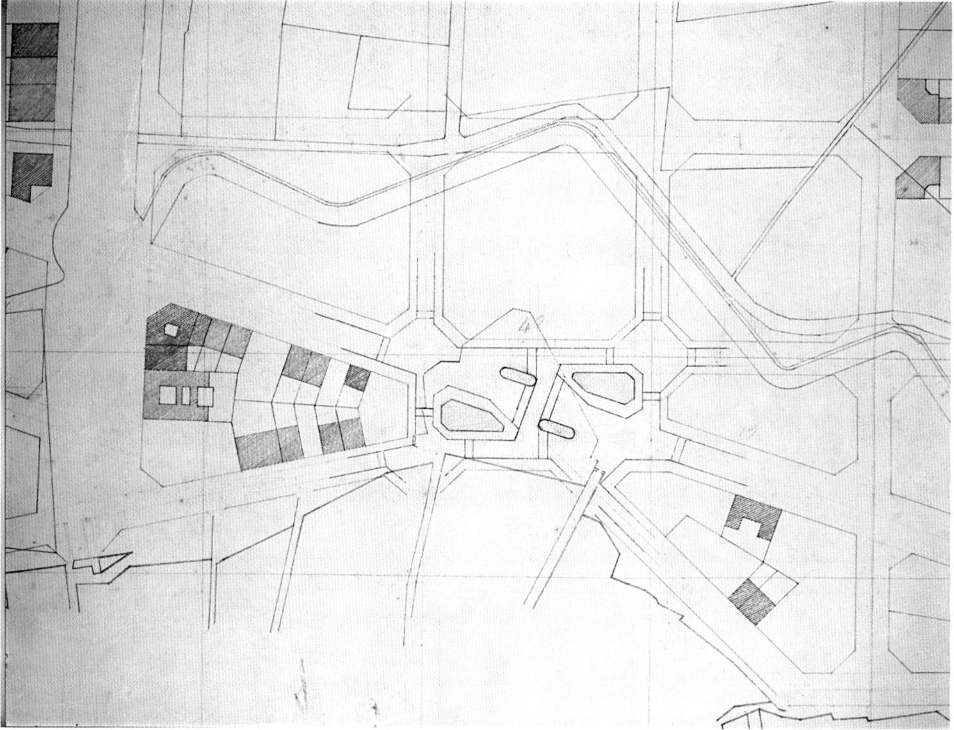

Detail of the junction of the two main orthogonal axes in the Eixample (Gran Via and Passeig de Sant Joan). Ildefons Cerdà. Topographic survey map of the construction of the Eixample. 1860-1865. Source: Cerdà Legacy. Arxiu Històric de la Ciutat de Barcelona.

Detail of the road crossings and pedestrian refuges in Plaça d'Urquinaona. Ildefons Cerdà. Topographic survey map of the construction of the Eixample. 1860-1865. Source: Cerdà Legacy. Arxiu Històric de la Ciutat de Barcelona.

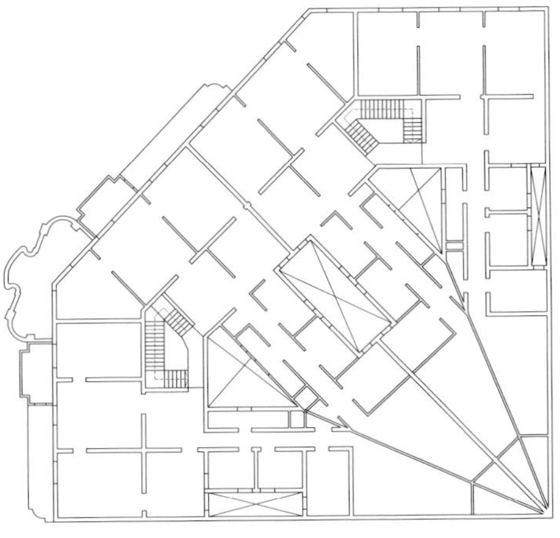

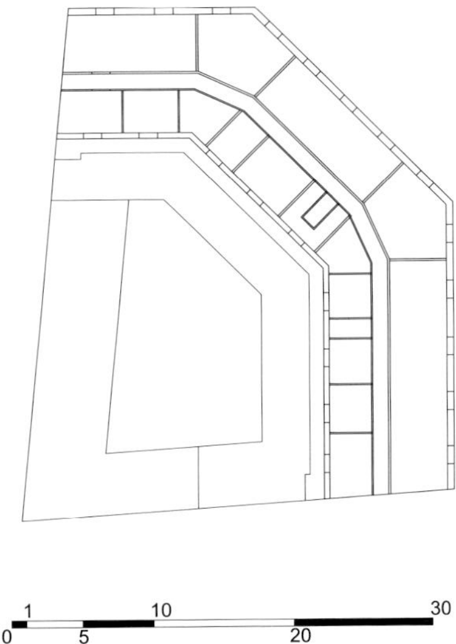

The chamfered corner is a prime position for housing

The most symbolic buildings in the first period of the Eixample were situated on the chamfered corner occupying part of the side of the city block and exploiting the greater length of façade per surface area of the property. These buildings were located in Passeig de Gràcia, Rambla de Catalunya and on the right of the Eixample.

A variety of architectural solutions were used on the chamfered corners. Some buildings chose orthogonal layouts to avoid the corner, others included elements such as bay windows to highlight the edges.

One of the buildings from this early period presents a layout with a corridor that follows the corner. Like the solution that Gaudí used in La Pedrera, the rooms give onto the corner and onto large courtyards that become interior façades.

The 1970s saw the appearance of a speculative typology with dwellings that had small ventilation shafts and highly compartmented spaces to address corner plots that had hitherto had residual uses. This solution was standardized and employed by a well-known Barcelona construction company.

Fig. 1_ Floor plan of the house for Josefa Villanueva, 1904-1909. Juli Maria Fossas. Drawing: for the exhibition.
Fig. 2_ Floor plan of the house for Josep Cerdà, 1862-1864. Antoni Valls. Drawing: for the exhibition.

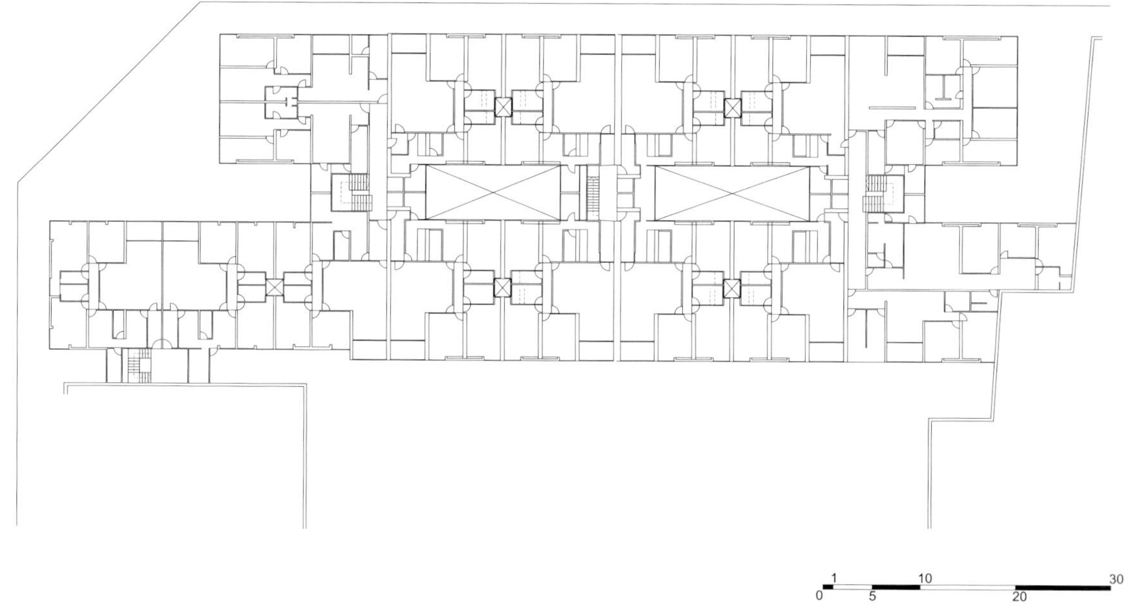

Floor plan of the Mediterrani building. 1940-1975. Antoni Bonet Castellana, Josep Puig Torné. Drawing: for the exhibition.

Façade of the house for Josep Cerdà. 1862-1864. Unknown author. Source: Historical Archive of the Col·legi d'Arquitectes de Catalunya.

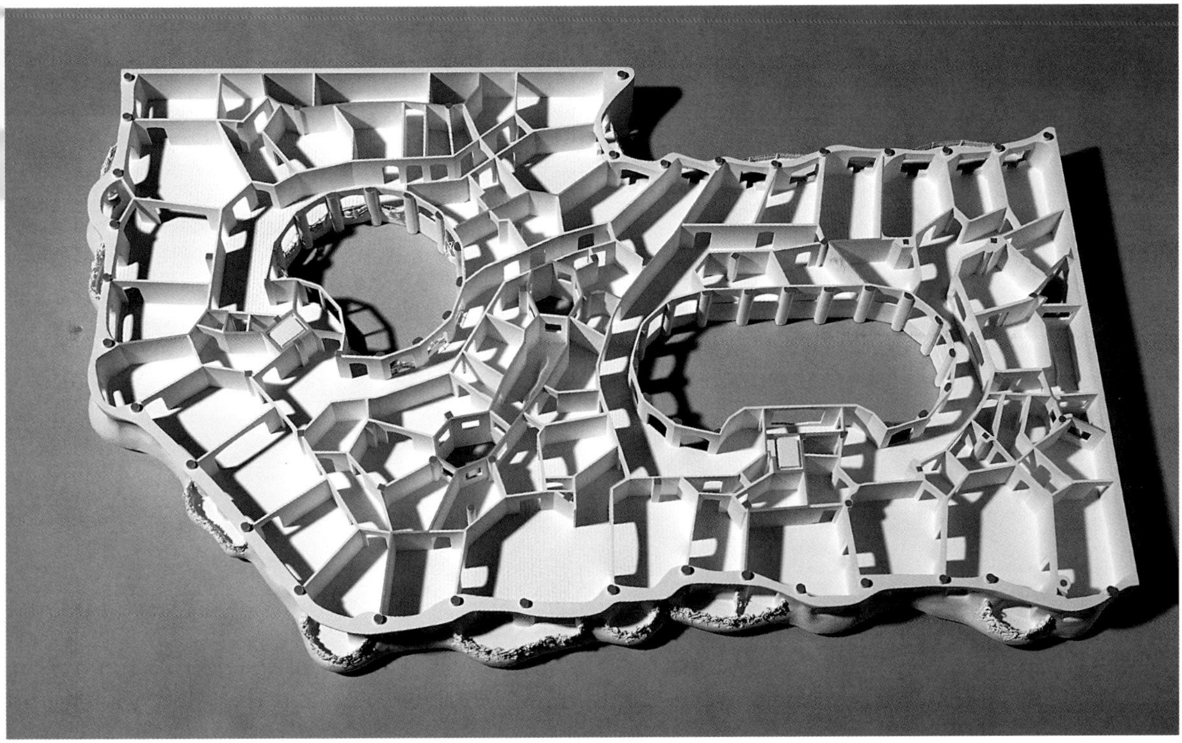

Milà House, known as La Pedrera. Passeig de Gràcia. 1910-1915. Photograph: Branguli . Source: Branguli holdings. Arxiu Nacional de Catalunya.

La Pedrera (1906-1912). Conception: Fernando Marzá and Daniel Giralt-Miracle. Model: Escola Tècnica Superior d'Arquitectura del Vallès-UPC, 1998. Source: Obra Social de Caixa Catalunya.

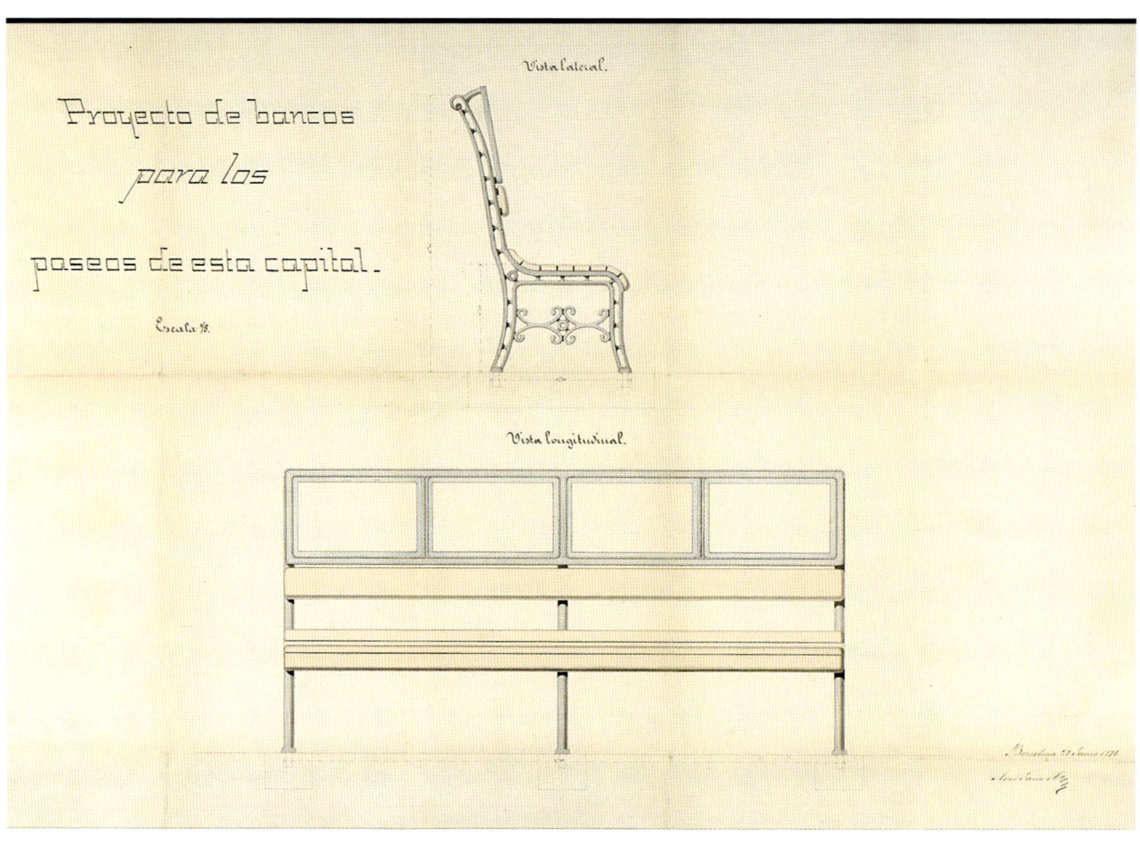

Envisioning street intersections as places that welcome activity

Cerdà defines the corner as a point of interaction and, consequently, of activities. The Eixample is a succession of stretches of street s and squares that are formed at intersections.

Consequently, we find these spaces furnished with a great variety of installations such as: newsstands, advertisers, and information booths, monuments, toilets, fountains, benches, etc., that have been accumulating over the past 150 years.

In recent years transport needs have been prioritized, especially for private vehicles, with loading zones and metered street parking. With the introduction of environmentally sustainable options such as walking, bicycling, and public transport, there will have to be a return to Cerdá's plan for direct routes for pedestrians and cyclists.

Design of benches for Barcelona's boulevards. 1876. Anet Faria. Source: Municipal Administrative Archive. Barcelona City Council.

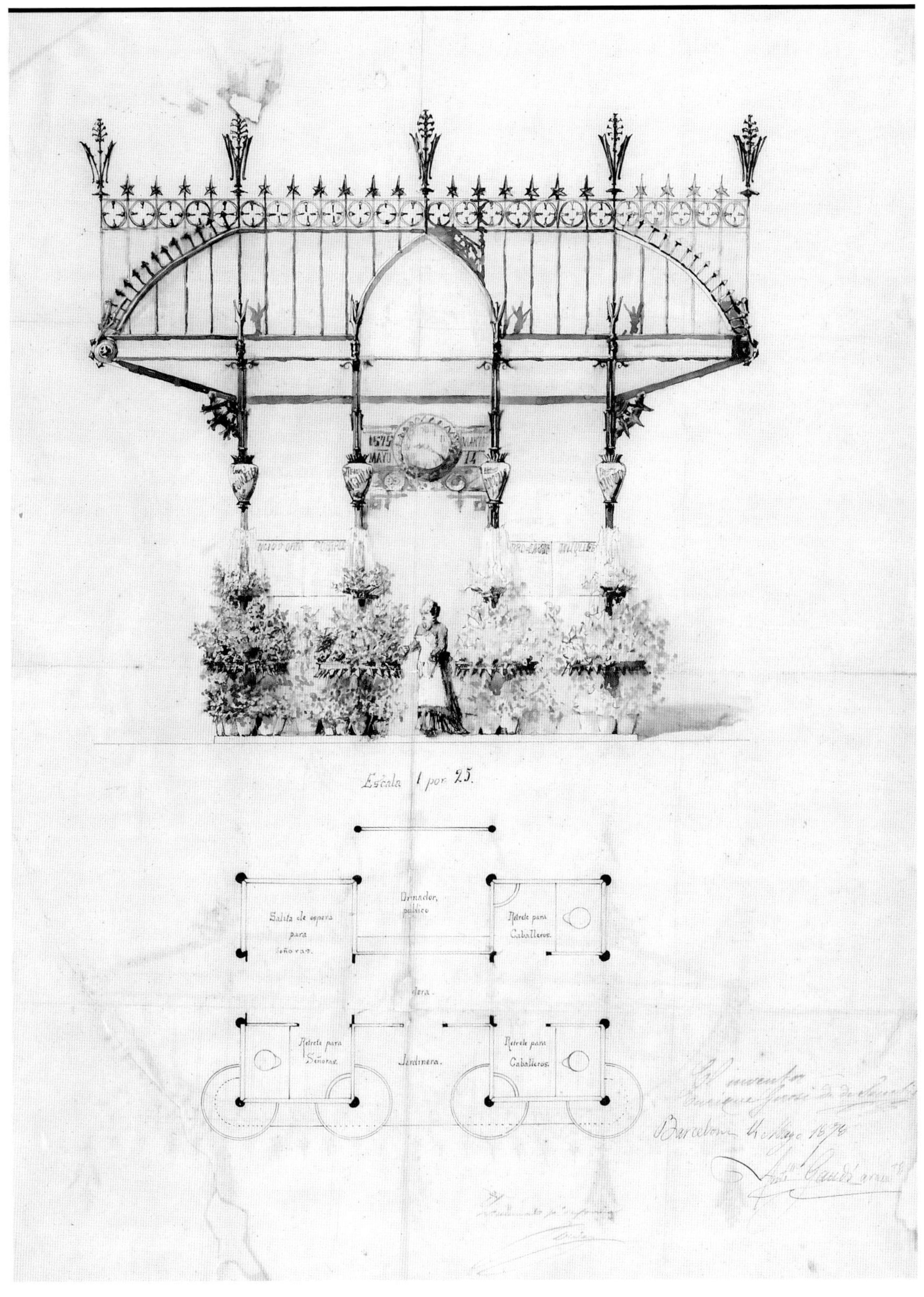

Toilet and urinal with flower stalls. 1878. Antoni Gaudí. Source: Municipal Administrative Archive. Barcelona City Council.

Design of freestanding letterboxes and floor plan of a urinal. 1857. Miquel Garriga i Roca. Source: Arxiu Històric de la Ciutat de Barcelona.

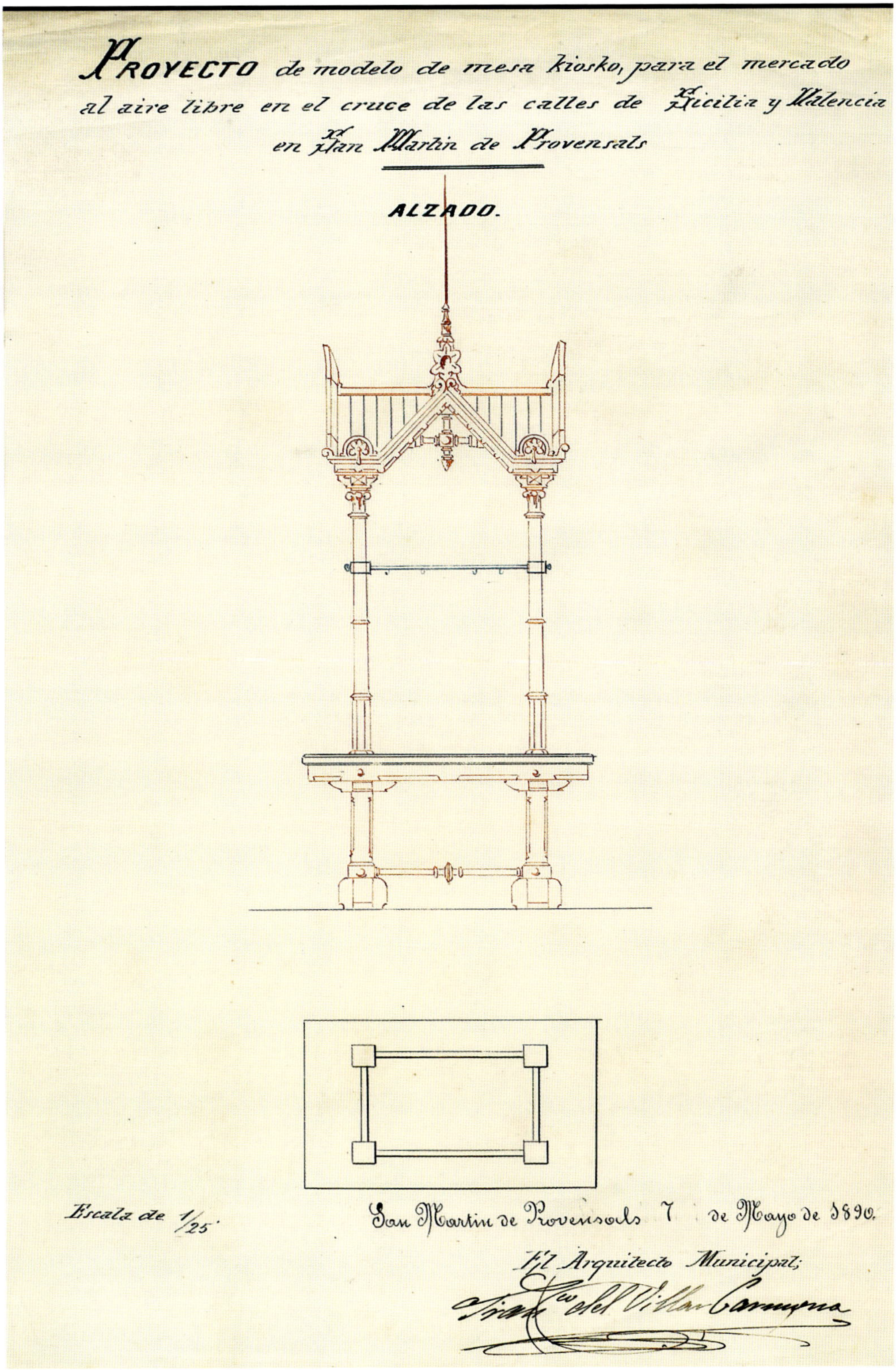

Proyecto de modelo de mesa kiosko, para el mercado al aire libre en el cruce de las calles de Sicilia y Valencia en San Martin de Provensals

ALZADO.

Escala de 1/25

San Martin de Provensals 7 de Mayo de 1890.

El Arquitecto Municipal;

Design of a stall for the open-air market at the junction of Carrer de Sicília and Carrer de València in Sant Martí de Provençals. 1890. Francisco del Villar Carmona. Source: Municipal Archive of the District of Sant Martí.

Model of an advertising panel for the public thoroughfare. 1889. Francisco Barnola. Source: Municipal Administrative Archive. Barcelona City Council.

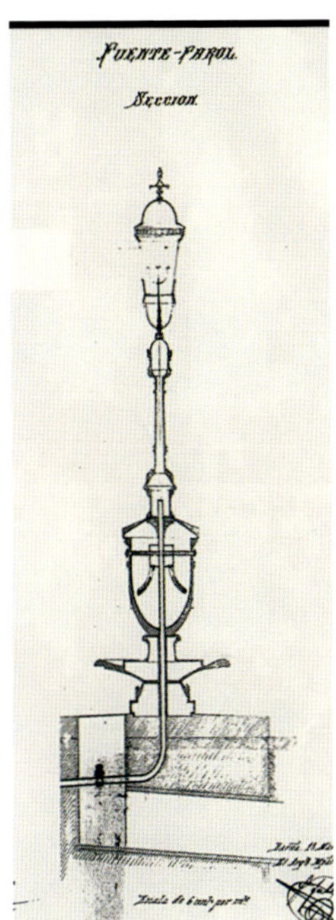

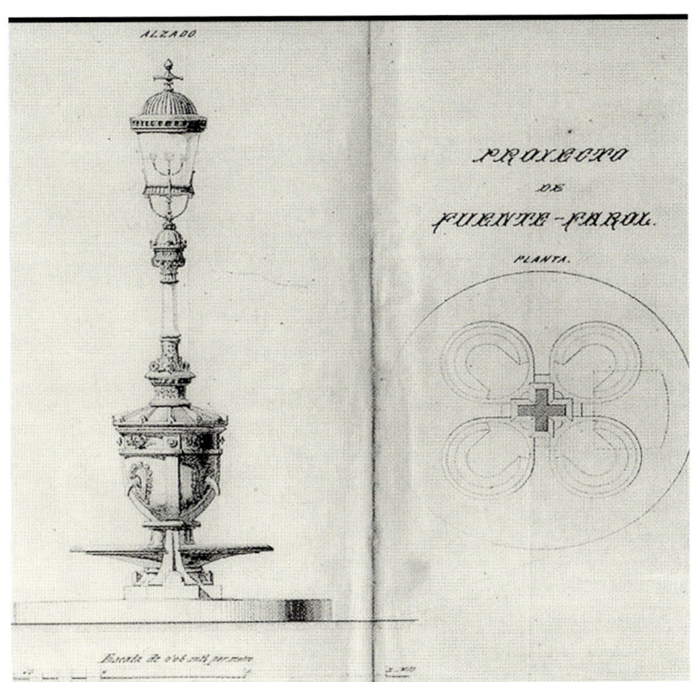

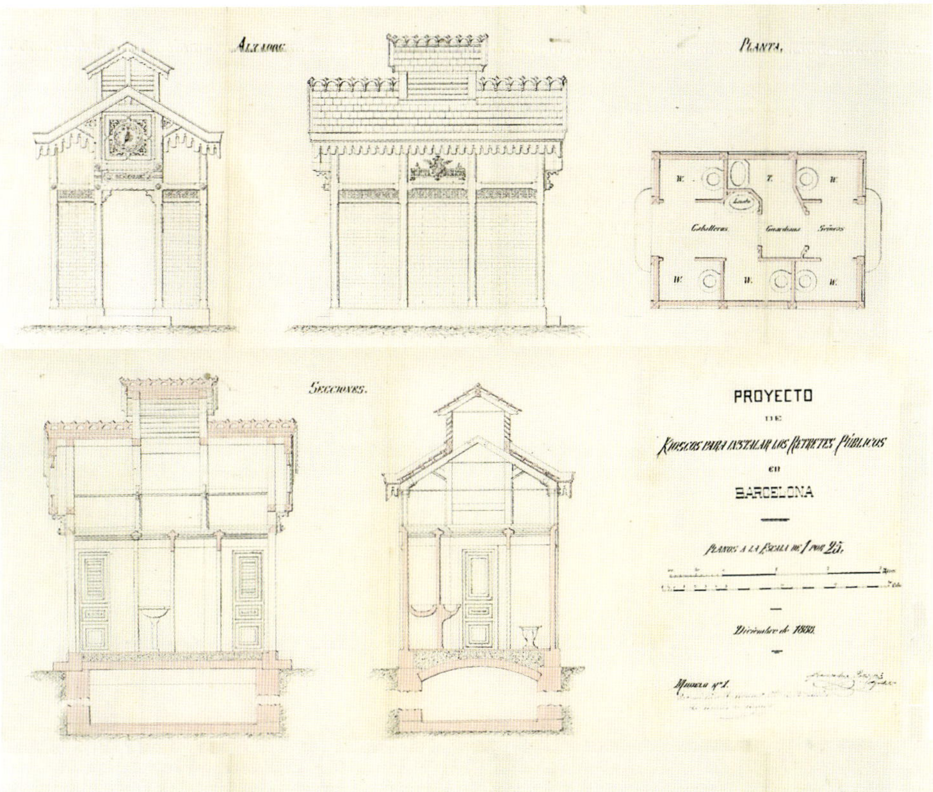

Design of a fountain-cum-lamppost. Section, floor plant and elevation. 1889. Pere Falqués. Source: Municipal Administrative Archive. Barcelona City Council.

Design of a booth for the installation of public urinals in Barcelona. 1888. Buenaventura Pollés. Source: Municipal Administrative Archive. Barcelona City Council.

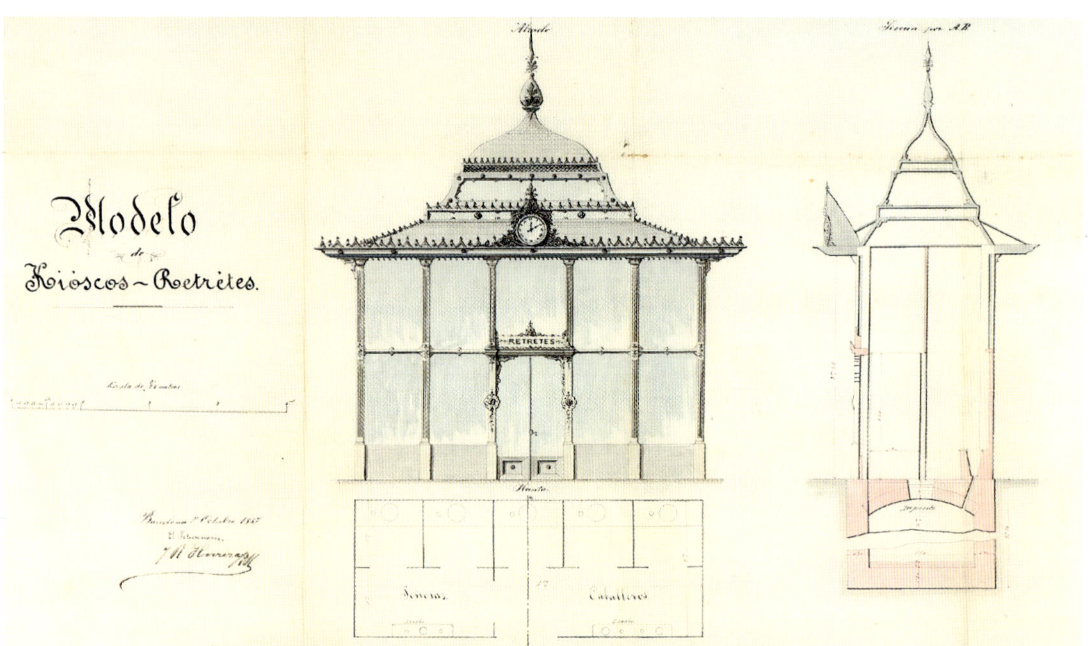

Fountain in Carrer del Parlament. 1872. Antoni Rovira i Trias. Source: Municipal Administrative Archive. Barcelona City Council.

Model of a cylindrical advertising panel for trees. 1896. Antoni Astell. Source: Municipal Administrative Archive. Barcelona City Council.

Model of a urinal booth. 1887. J.M. Herreras. Source: Municipal Administrative Archive. Barcelona City Council.

Worker on scaffolding during the construction of the towers of the Sagrada Família. 1930. Photograph: Gabriel Casas i Galobardes. Source: Gabriel Casas i Galobardes holdings. Arxiu Nacional de Catalunya.

View of a crossroads in the Eixample with chamfered corners. 1929. Photograph: Josep Gaspar i Serra. Source: Institut Cartogràfic de Catalunya. Cartoteca de Catalunya.

Circulation. 1988-1989. Photograph: Colita. Source: Arxiu Fotogràfic de Barcelona.

Municipal policeman directing the traffic. Circa 1950. Photograph: Francesc Català-Roca. Source: Historical Archive of the Col·legi d'Arquitectes de Catalunya.

sewerage_

"The networks of urban services represent the principal subterranean works of a city."

(I. Cerdà: *Teoría de la Construcción de las Ciudades*, 1859)

The background to Cerdà's proposal of a sewer system

For Cerdà, the city's conditions of hygiene, comfort and economy depended on the system of urban utility network adopted. In his Preliminary Project for the Eixample of 1855, Cerdà anticipated the integration of these networks into the overall urbanization in the form of a single gallery that included runoff drainage, water supply, gas and telegraph.[1]

On his travels between 1856 and 1858, Cerdà became familiar with the remodelling works planned by Haussmann in Paris, particularly the sewerage system proposed by Belgrand. In the case of Paris, the city's street plans and sections already included the sewerage system designed by Pierre Patte in 1769.[2] The 1859 Eixample Project continued to include septic tanks, while also introducing a new feature: septic tanks emptied by pneumatic pumps.[3]

Modernization of the drainage system by Pere Garcia Fària

Pere Garcia Fària was the other foremost reference for the city's urban utilities. In Barcelona he introduced the concept of the water cycle that Chadwick had developed in London in 1848, in which water is sourced at a distance and, once used, drained off to farmland as fertilizer,[4] thereby preventing epidemics.

Garcia Fària introduced the concept of connecting wastewater from dwellings to sewerage and also proposed a modern system of management and maintenance, and the design of a new method of urban waste collection using trucks that travelled through the sewer system.[5]

[1] See fig. page 135 | [2] See fig. 1 page 134 | [3] See fig. page 138 | [4] See fig. page 141 | [5] See fig. 2 page 134

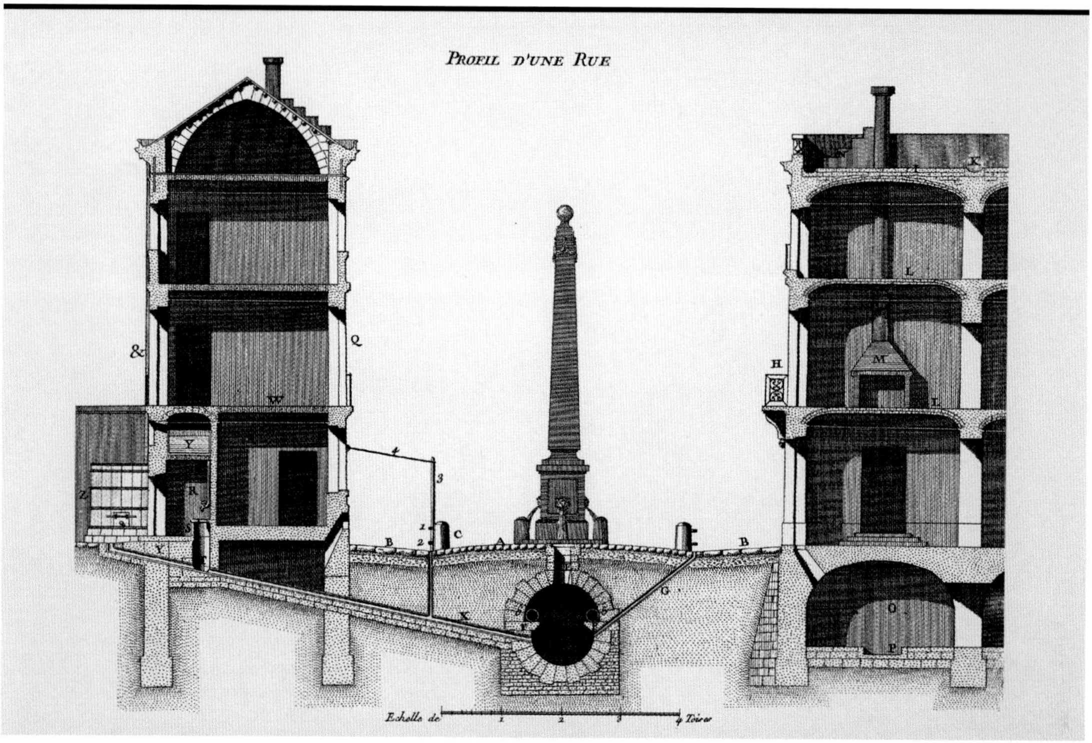

PROFIL D'UNE RUE

Echelle de 1 2 3 4 Toises

Fig. 1

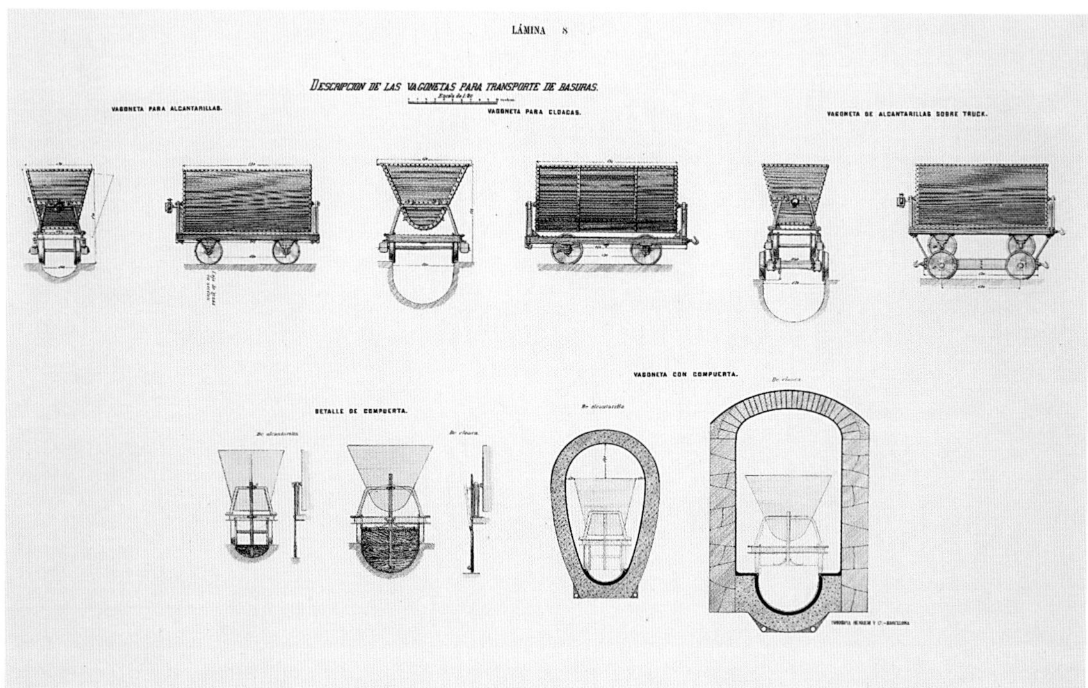

Fig. 2

Fig. 1_ Mémoires sur les objets les plus importants de l'architecture (Memoranda about the most important objects in architecture) (1973, facsimile of the 1769 original). Architect: Pierre Patte. Source: Library of the Col·legi d'Arquitectes de Catalunya.

Fig. 2_Description of trucks for waste collection. 1981. Civil engineer: Pere Garcia Fària. Source: Historical Archive of the Col·legi d'Arquitectes de Catalunya.

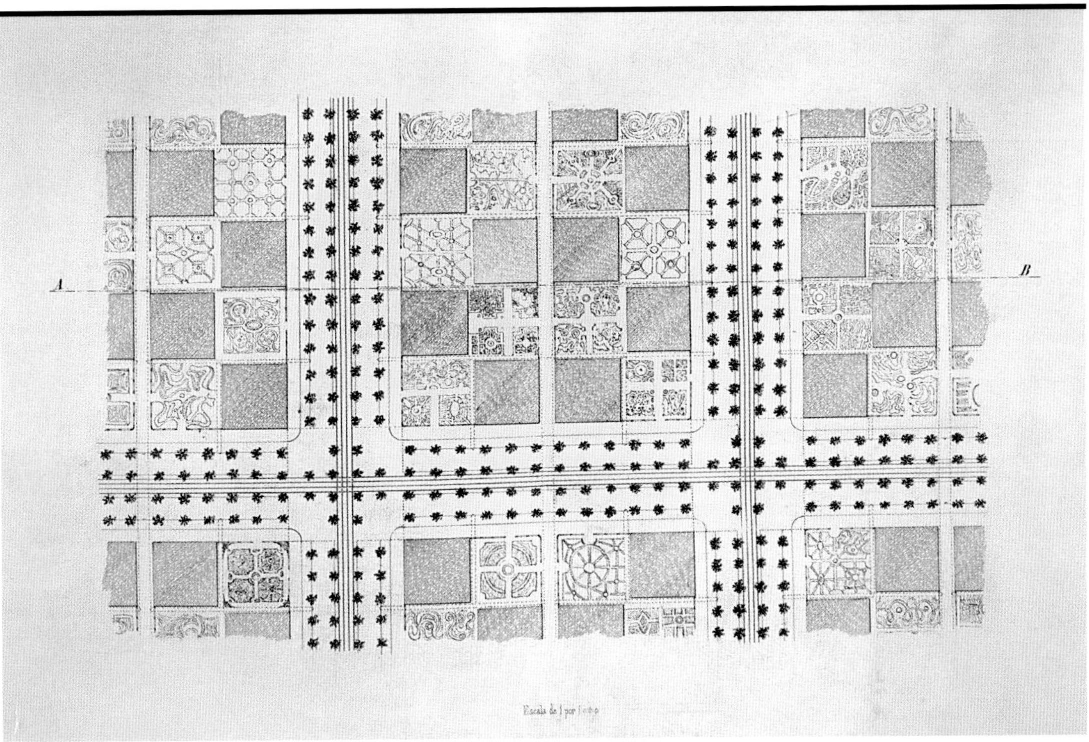

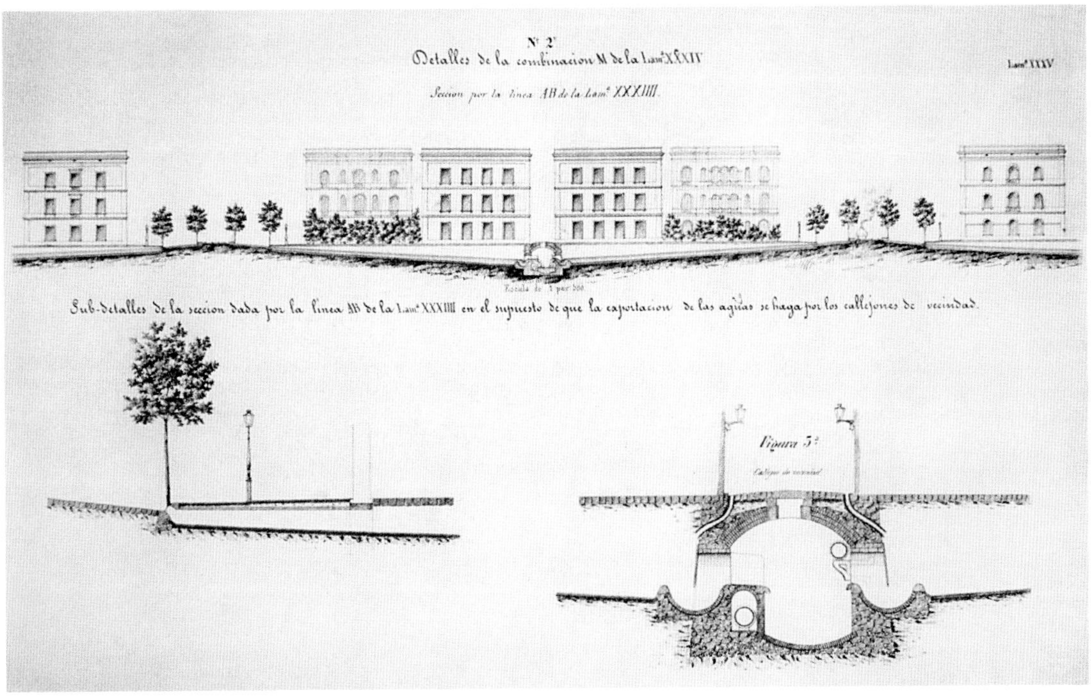

Floor plan and section of the service street with detail of the unitary gallery. Plate XXXIV, Plate XXXV. Ildefons Cerdà. *Memoria del Anteproyecto del Ensanche de Barcelona* [Description of the Preliminary Project for the Extension of Barcelona]. 1855. Source: Government Archives. Ministry of Culture.

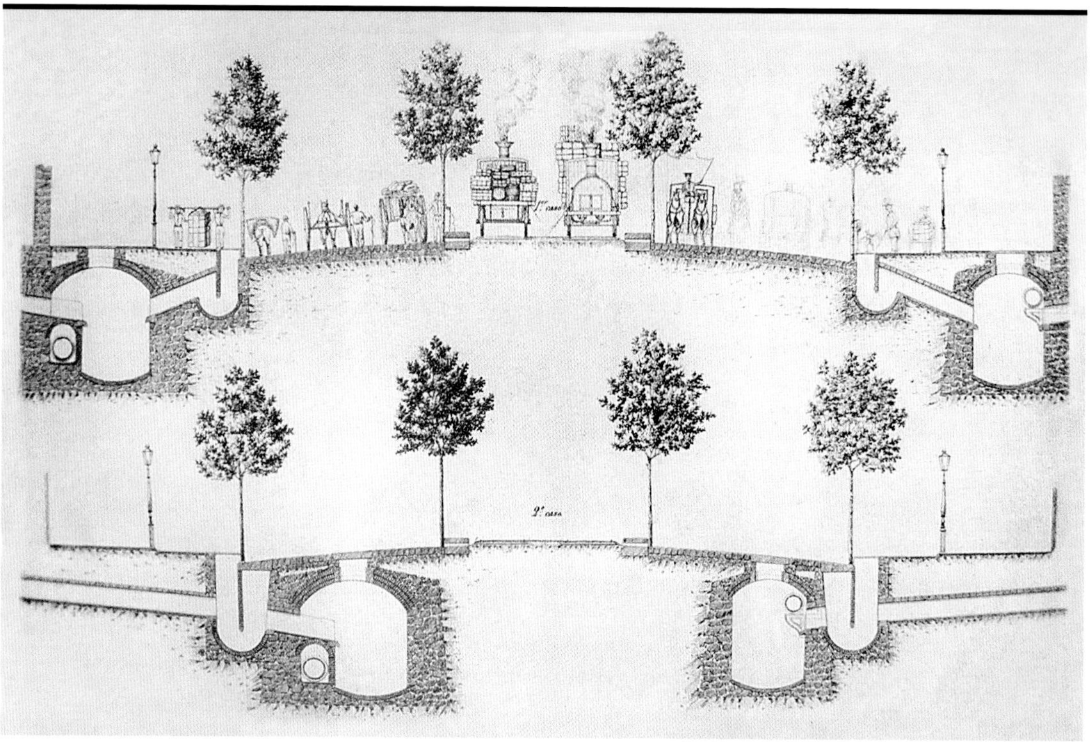

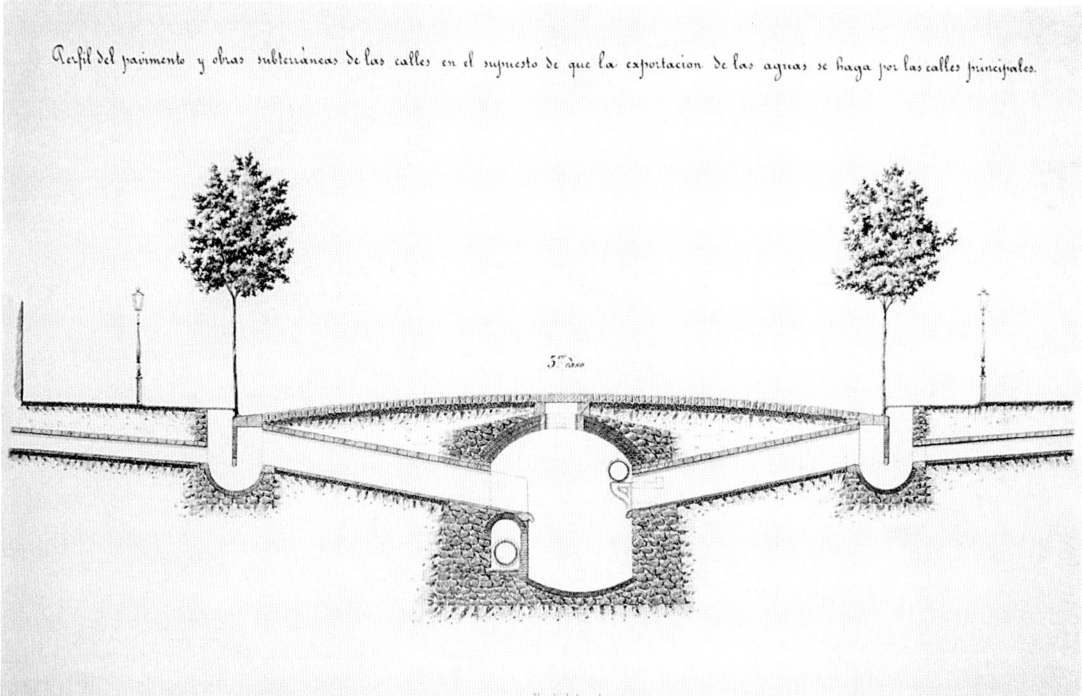
Perfil del pavimento y obras subterráneas de las calles en el supuesto de que la exportacion de las aguas se haga por las calles principales.
Escala de 1 por 100.

Street section with detail of utility networks. Plate XXXVI, Plate XXXVII. Ildefons Cerdà. *Memoria del Anteproyecto del Ensanche de Barcelona* [Description of the Preliminary Project for the Extension of Barcelona]. 1855. Source: Government Archives. Ministry of Culture.

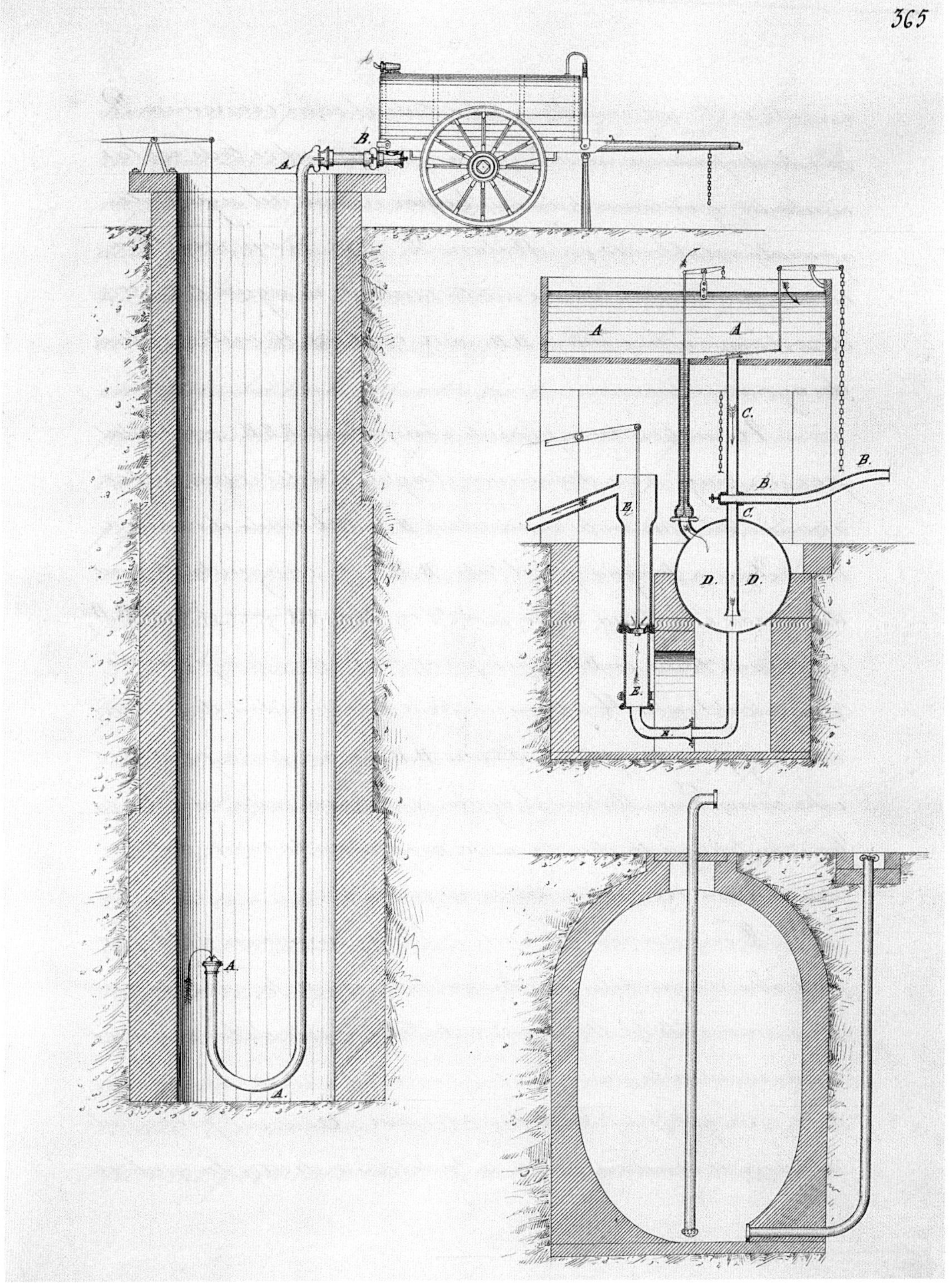

System of pneumatic pumps for emptying latrines. Ildefons Cerdà. *Teoría de la Construcción de las Ciudades* [Theory of City Construction]. 1859. Source: Government Archives. Ministry of Culture.

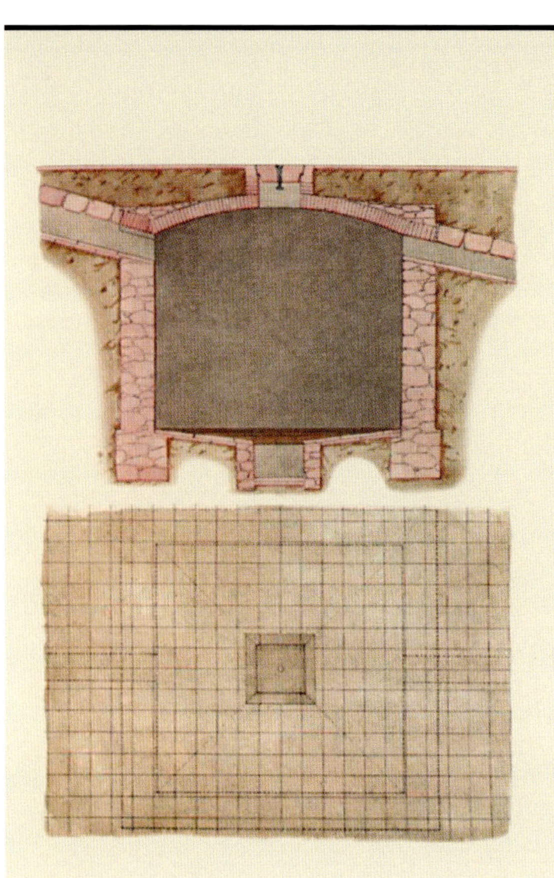

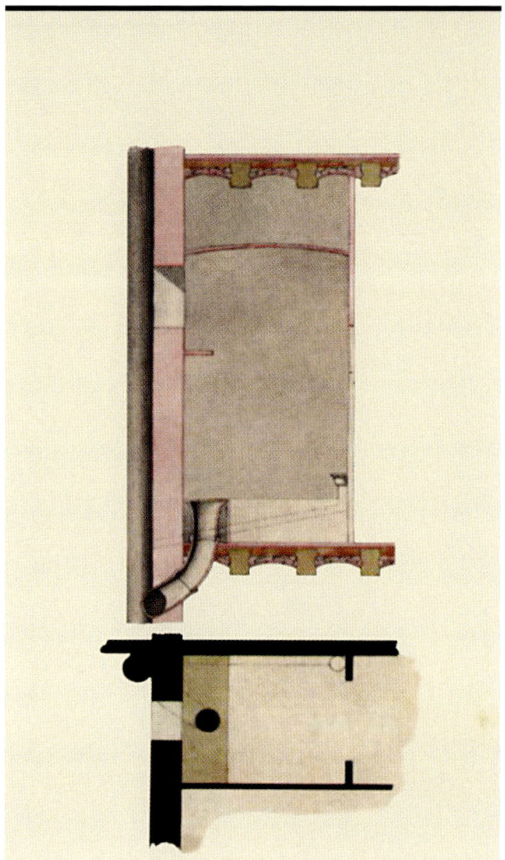

Septic tank. Plate XXXIII. Ildefons Cerdà. *Teoría de la Construcción de las Ciudades* [Theory of City Construction]. 1859. Source: Government Archives. Ministry of Culture.

Latrine connected to the septic tank. Plate XXXII. Ildefons Cerdà. *Teoría de la Construcción de las Ciudades* [Theory of City Construction]. 1859. Source: Government Archives. Ministry of Culture.

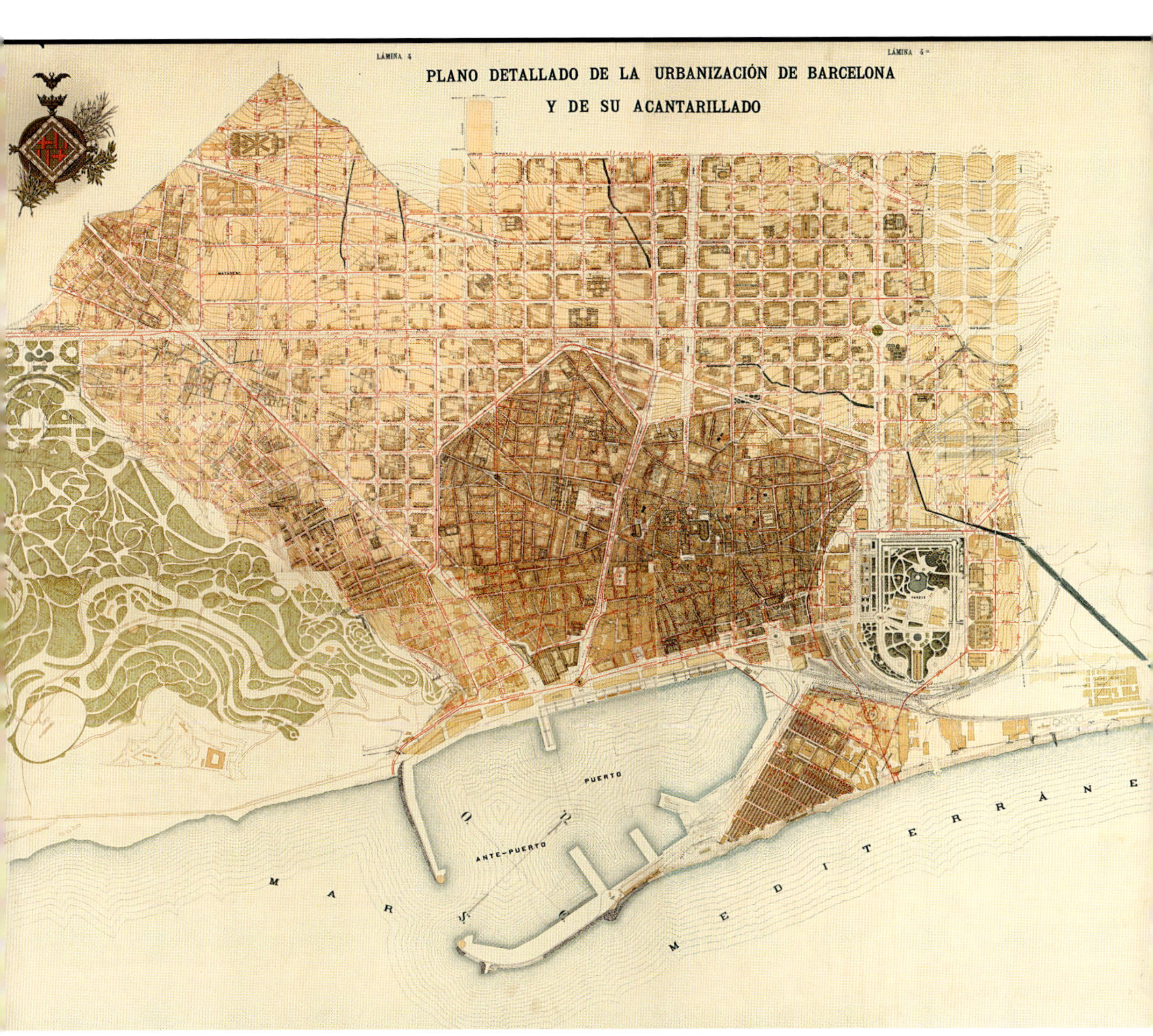

Detailed plan of the urbanization of Barcelona and its sewerage system (1891). Civil engineer: Pere Garcia Fària. Source: Historical Archive of the Col·legi d'Arquitectes de Catalunya.

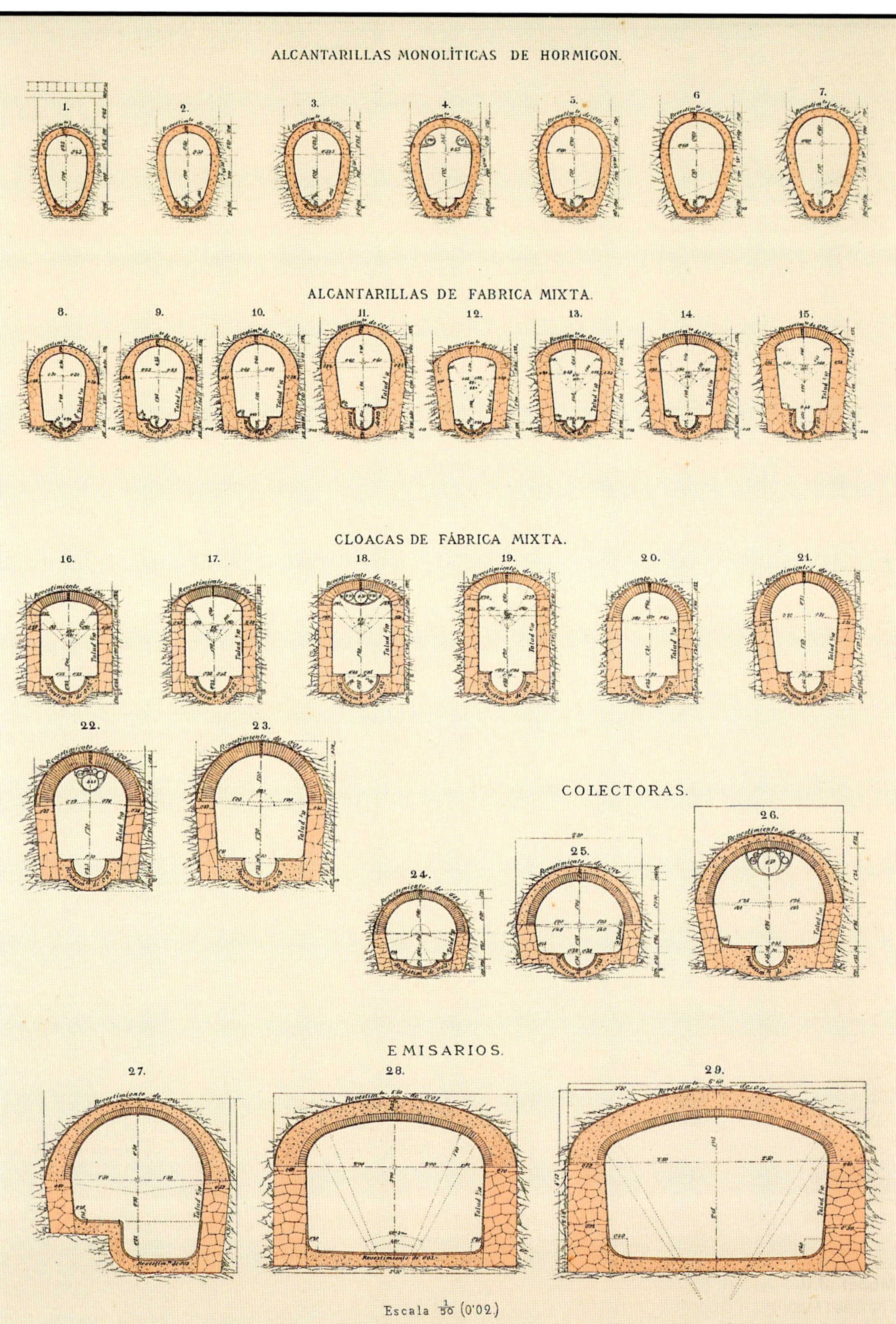

Cross-sections of the sewer galleries. Plate 5 (1891). Civil engineer: Pere Garcia Fària. Source: Historical Archive of the Col·legi d'Arquitectes de Catalunya.

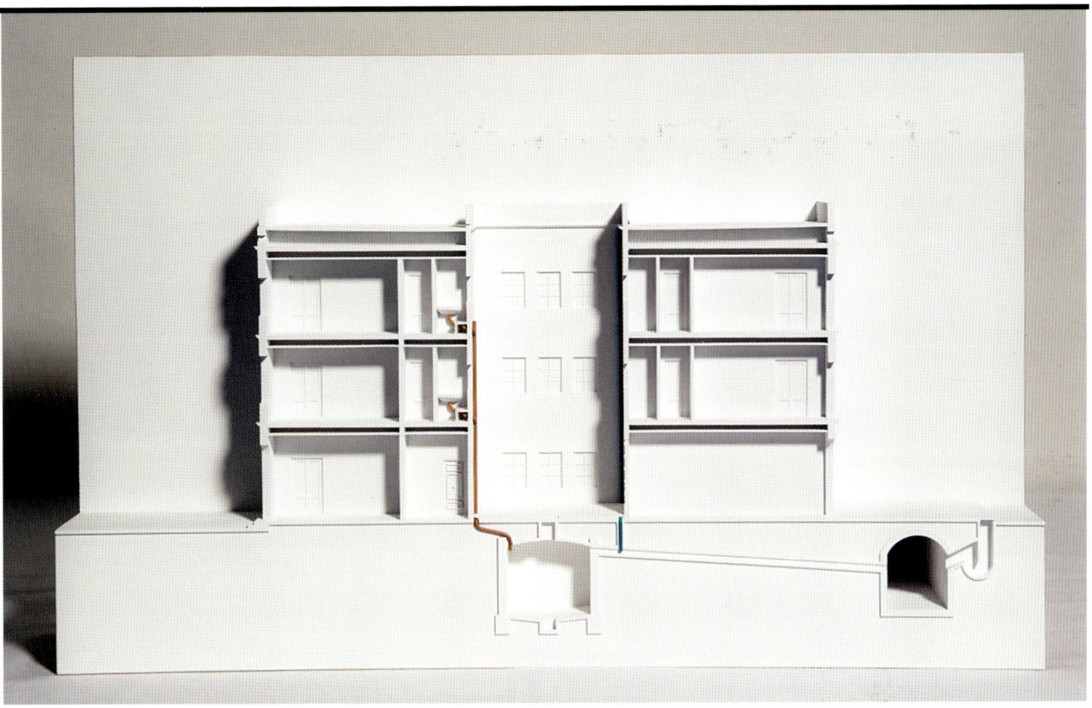

Model of the system connecting homes to the sewerage system designed by Ildefons Cerdà. Conception: Francesc Magrinyà, Fernando Marzá. Model: ETSAV-UPC model workshop. 2009. Collection of Fundació Urbs i Territori Ildefons Cerdà (FUTIC).

Model of the system connecting homes to the sewerage system designed by Pere Garcia Fària. Conception: Francesc Magrinyà, Fernando Marzá. Model: ETSAV-UPC model workshop. 2009. Collection of Fundació Urbs i Territori Ildefons Cerdà (FUTIC).

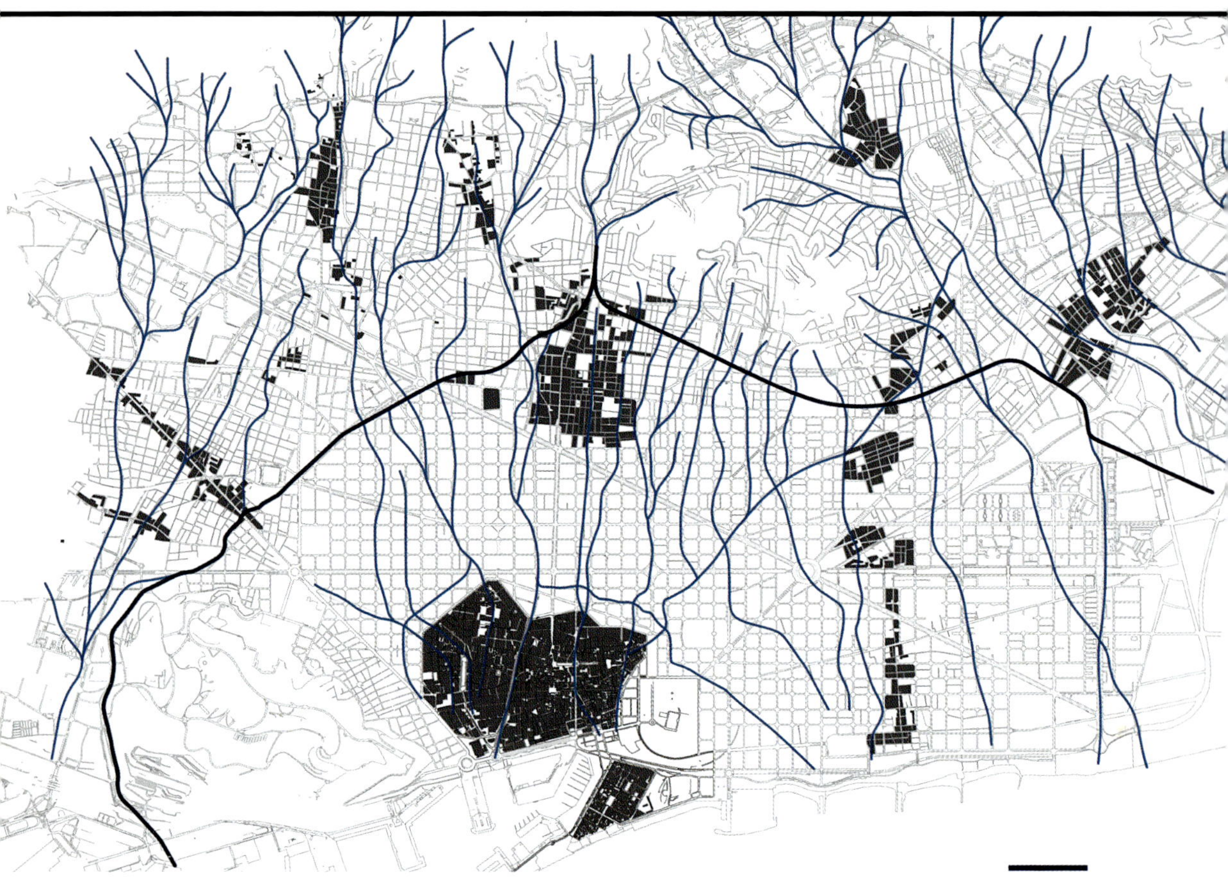

The Eixample and flooding

The fight against flooding has been a constant throughout the 150-year history of the Eixample. In his Preliminary Eixample Project of 1855, Cerdà designed a storm drain to protect the Eixample from torrential rainwater. No storm drain had been built when the old town walls were demolished, leading to a great flood in the old town in 1862. This prompted Cerdà to design the Rondes sewer, which was built in 1863 and still exists today.

The first proposal after Cerdà for a Sewerage Plan, which provided a reference until the 1936 Civil War, was designed by Pere Garcia Fària and consolidated a model that used water to transport faecal matter.

Plans drafted by Luís Jara in 1954 and Albert Vilalta in 1969 represented the sewerage systems until work began on preparing for the Olympic Games. The 1988 Special Sewerage Plan for Barcelona and the construction of collecting systems in Vila Olímpica and Poblenou put an end to flooding in these sectors.

The 2004 Integrated Sewerage Plan later constructed flood control systems to prevent flooding in Poble Sec and Carrer Urgell, and in Rambla Prim.

Watercourses in the Barcelona Plain and Cerdà's Eixample. Drawing: for the exhibition.

Map of Barcelona and its environs and the Llobregat Plain. Plate 1. (1891). |Civil engineer: Pere Garcia Fària. Source: Historical Archive of the Col·legi d'Arquitectes de Catalunya.

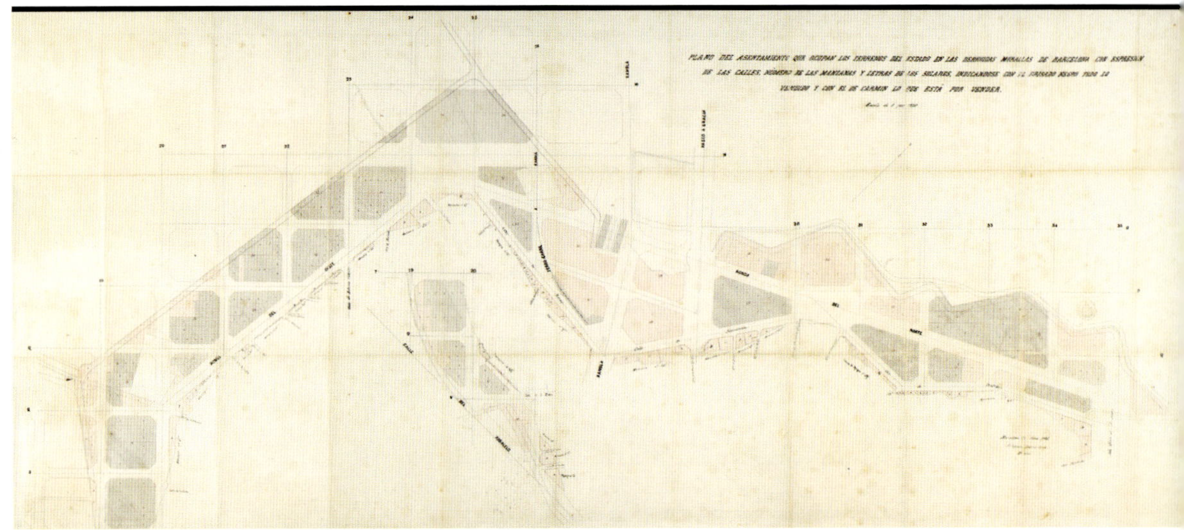

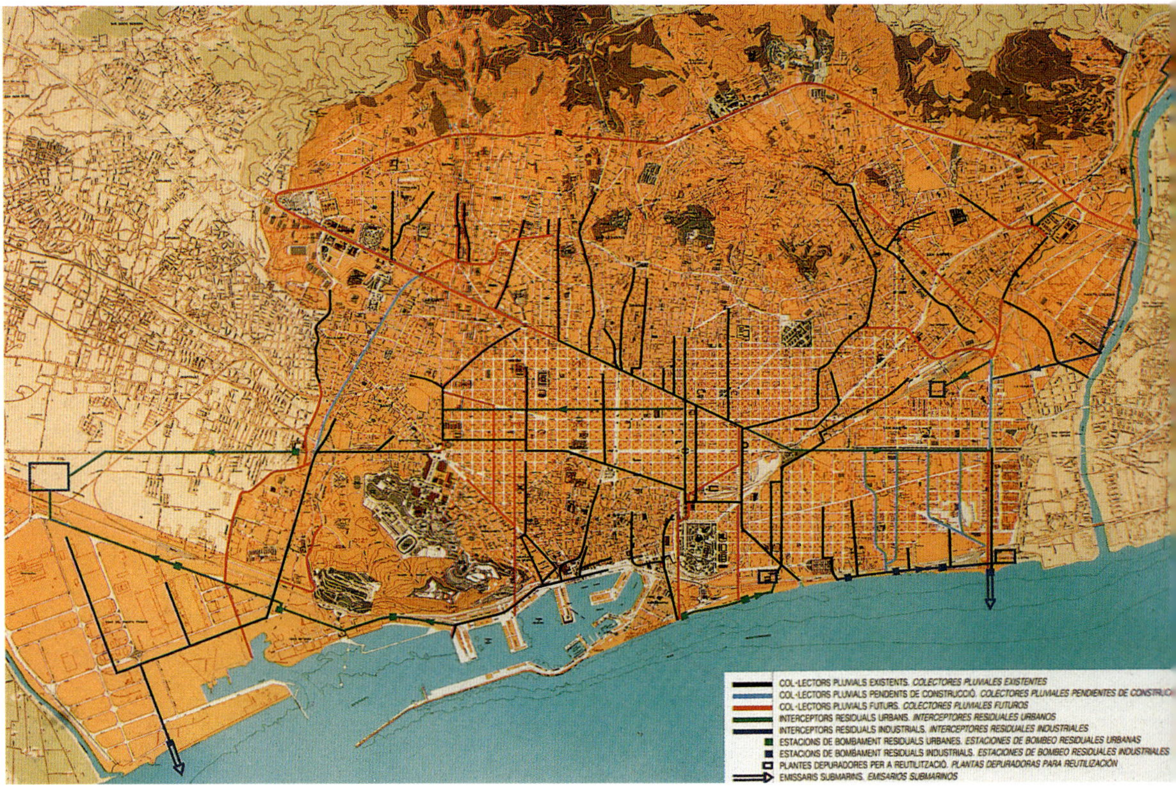

Alignment project for land formerly occupied by the city walls by Ildefons Cerdà. Definitive layout of alignments of the sector, justified by the need to construct the Rondes sewer (1865). Ildefons Cerdà. Source: Municipal Administrative Archive. Barcelona City Council.

1969 Barcelona Drainage Plan. Albert Vilalta. Source: CLABSA.

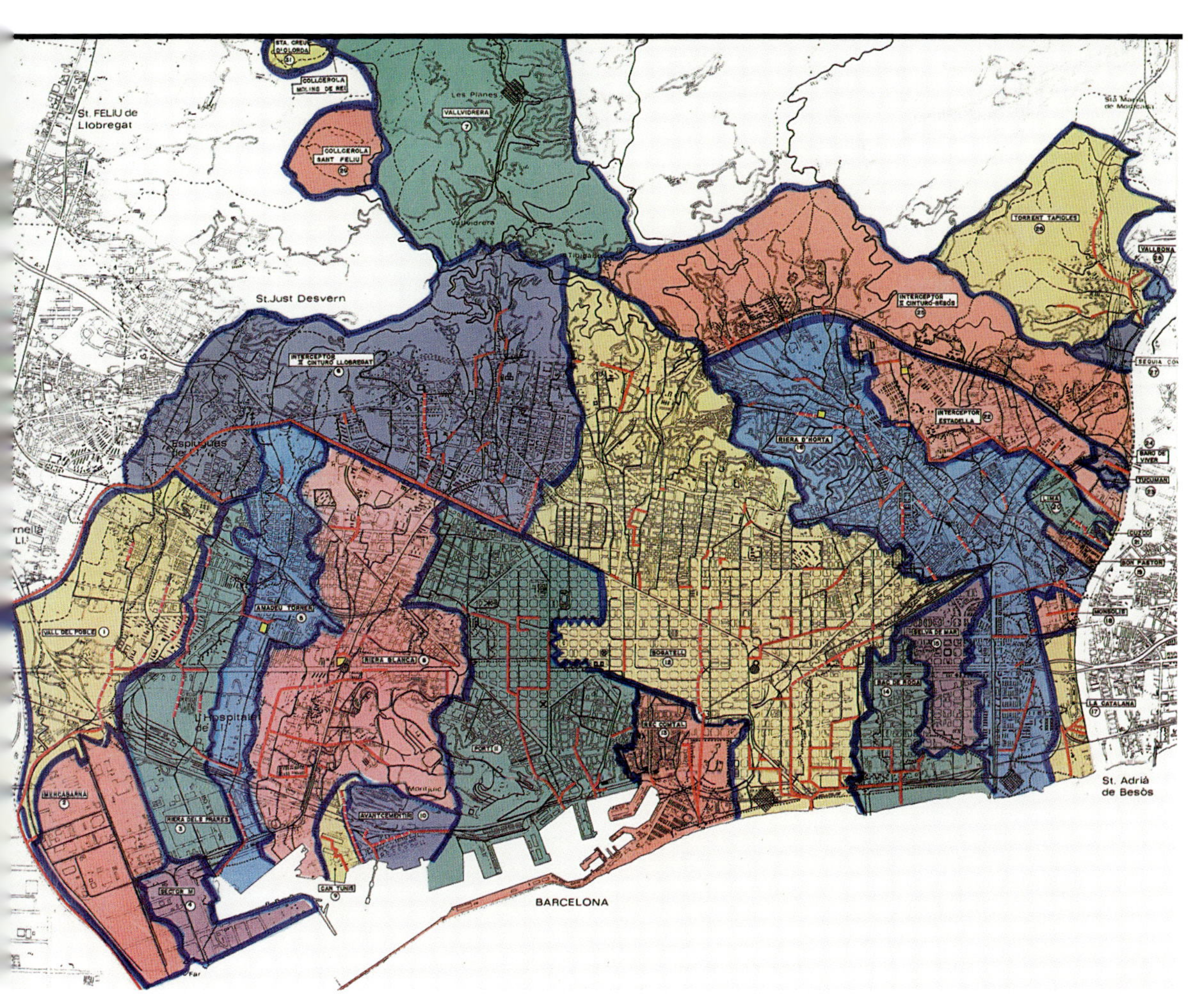

1988 Special Sewerage Plan. Source: CLABSA.

Glòries (1972). Source: Environment. Barcelona City Council.

Sewer under the RENFE railway station. Passeig de Fabra i Puig (1973). Source: Environment. Barcelona City Council.

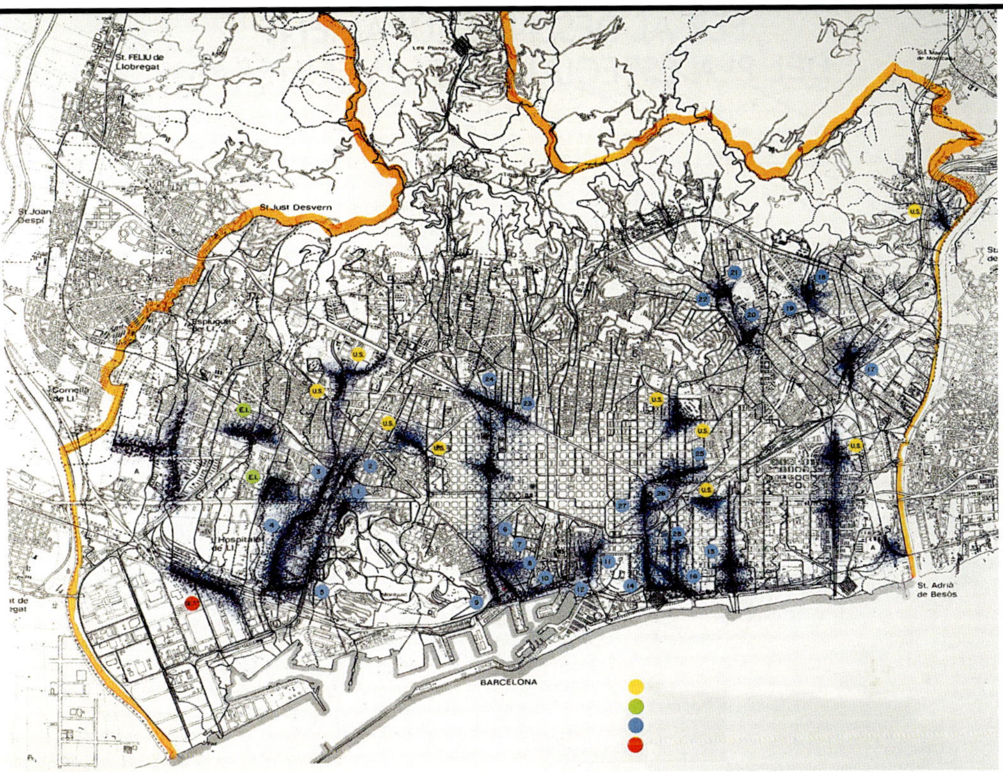

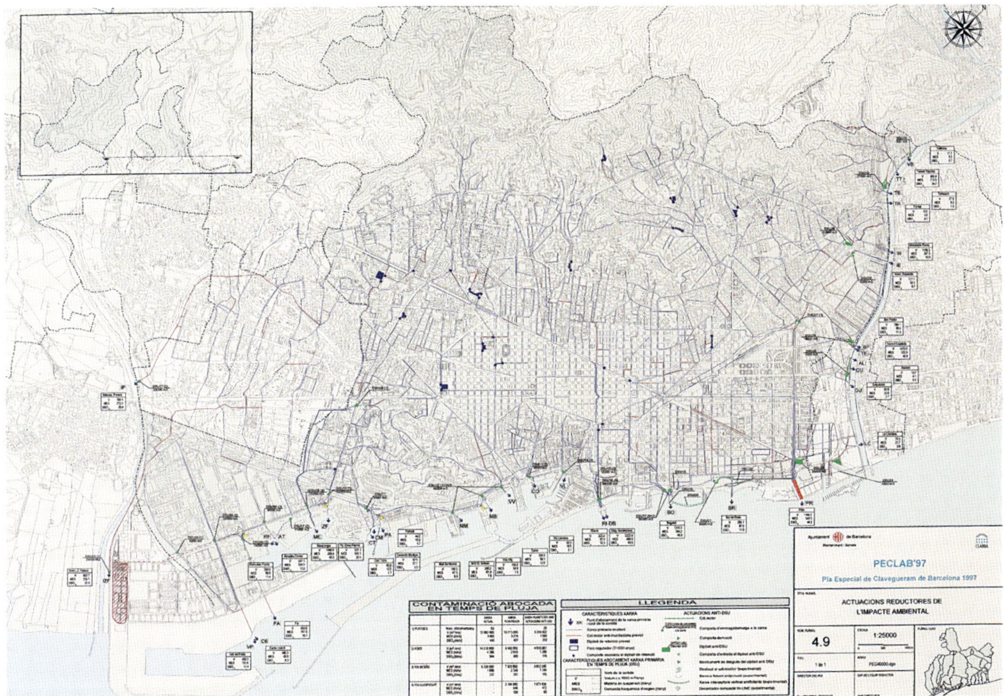

Maps of high-risk flooding areas in the Barcelona of the Olympic Games and after (1997). Fuente: Plan Especial de Alcantarillado (PECLAB). CLABSA.

Barcelona Sewerage Plan indicating flood-control systems (1997). Source: Special Sewerage Plan (PECLAB). CLABSA.

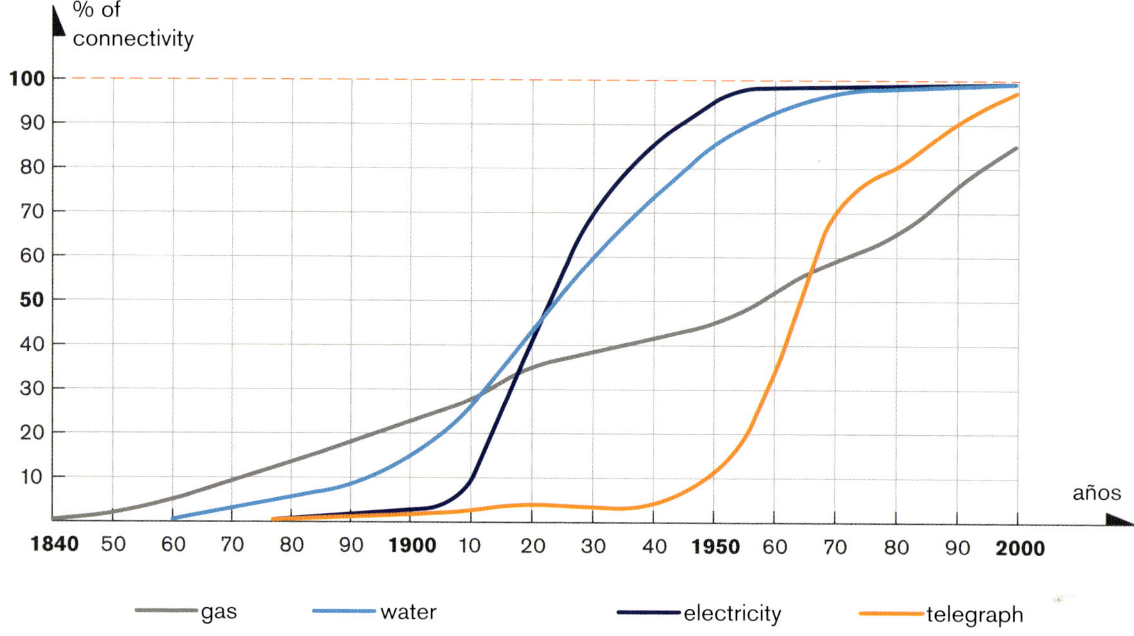

Fig. 1

Developing utility networks

Cities were changing from a local scenario with no networks[1] but with latrines, water wells, coal and wood as energy sources, and transport on foot, to a new situation of connection to urban utility networks characterized by pipes, taps and switches.[2]

The evolution of urban utility networks in the Eixample first took the form of the construction of runoff channels to avoid flooding in urbanized sectors.[3] Then dwellings were connected to the various utility grids (water, gas and telegraph) with Cerdà in 1859, and drainage and urban waste services with Garcia Fària in 1892. Today, it is the turn of telematic networks, for which the 22@ Special Infrastructures Plan is the referent.

[1] See fig. page 149 | [2] See fig. page 150 & 151 | [3] See fig. page 153

Fig. 1_Evolution of territorial coverage of the various urban utility networks in Barcelona. Source: *La construcción de las redes urbanísticas de abastecimiento del área metropolitana de Barcelona: Innovación tecnológica y cobertura espacial.* Daniel Rodríguez Aranda. 2000.

Public washing place in Gran Via de les Corts Catalanes (1917). Photograph: Frederic Ballell. Source: Arxiu Fotogràfic de Barcelona.

Plaça Pedró. *Justo y Emilio García. Fotografías de un siglo* [Justo and Emilio García. Photographs of a century]. 2007. Photograph: Just Garcia Ventosa. Source: Gerardo García-Ventosa Archive.

Joining water supply pipes on the Carretera de les Aigües road (undated). Photograph: unknown author. Source: AGBAR Archive.

Water pipes in Avinguda de Sarrià (undated). Photograph: unknown author. Source: AGBAR Archive.

Installation of water pipes in Carrer del Comte d'Urgell (undated). Photograph: unknown author. Source: AGBAR Archive.

Trench with water pipes in the environs of the Sagrada Família (undated). Photograph: unknown author. Source: AGBAR Archive.

Type of sewerage system used in the municipality of Barcelona (1973). Source: Environment. Barcelona City Council.

Workers in the sewer system (1905). Photograph: Adolf Mas. Source: Fundación Instituto Amatller de Arte Hispánico. Mas Archive.

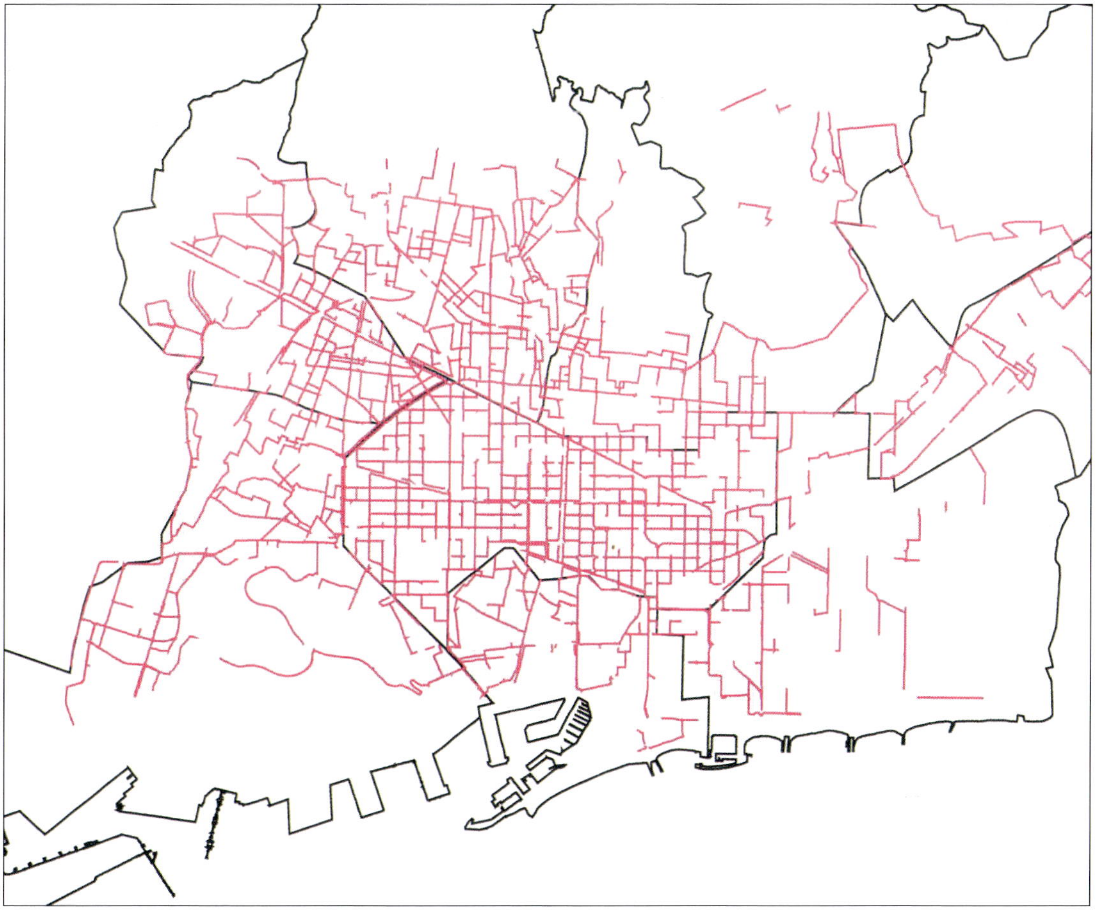

Laying of optic cable in the sewer system (2004). Source: CLABSA.

Plan of optic cabling using the sewer system (2009). Source: CLABSA.

the city block

"In each of these spaces, isolated by urban thoroughfares, there exists a small world, a small city or elementary *urbs.*"

(I. Cerdà: *Teoría General de la Urbanización*, 1867).

Flexibility within order in the city blocks of the Eixample

To the construction of the city blocks, which he termed intervies, Cerdà bought a new instrument: the city block comprising parcels of land built up around a central courtyard.[1]
This structure would be very flexible and evolutive, with each space or city block accommodating homes, shops and industries.[2] In some cases, there would be a predominance of industrial land, forming city blocks with a narrow street through the centre[3]. There were also precarious constructions or dwellings in the central courtyards of some city blocks, known as *passadissos*, or "corridors".[4]
The layout of *vies and intervies*, thoroughfares and the spaces between, and its application to the construction of city blocks were instruments that brought great freedom to the organization of city construction and produced a mix of residential and industrial activities and services, thereby generating economically and environmentally varied fabrics.[5]

Different typologies of fabric in a single layout

One of the most obvious conclusions of the evolution of Cerdà's Eixample in accordance with the 1859 Remodelling and Extension Project is the diversity of solutions and variety of forms used to occupy a single layout of city blocks.
In the city centre, due to high land prices and the building typology, the city block was built on all four sides.[6]
Later, solutions took the form of increasingly built-up city blocks in the left of the Eixample and the district of Sagrada Família, which saw the appearance of city blocks crossed by narrow streets and, in addition to the basement, mezzanine and two penthouse floors, volumes projecting from the façade and the occupation of the inner courtyard. In some cases, dwellings were even built in the courtyard of the city block, in the form of one-storey constructions known as *passadissos*, or "corridors".

[1] See fig. page 156 I [2] See fig. page 168 I [3] See fig. page 169 I [4] See fig. page 170-171
[5] See figs. 1 & 2 page 156 I [6] See fig. page 161

Fig. 1

Fig. 2

Later, in the part of the Eixample extending across the district of Sant Martí, new city block typologies were developed when residential estates emerged between the 1950s and 1970[7]
The conversion of industrial sectors in Vila Olímpica and the areas christened 22@[8] are another example of the transformation of city blocks within the layout designed by Cerdà.

[7] See figs. page 176-177 I [8] See figs. page 186-187

Figs. 1 y 2_Comparison of a city block in the central Eixample and an exclusively residential city block in Poblenou.

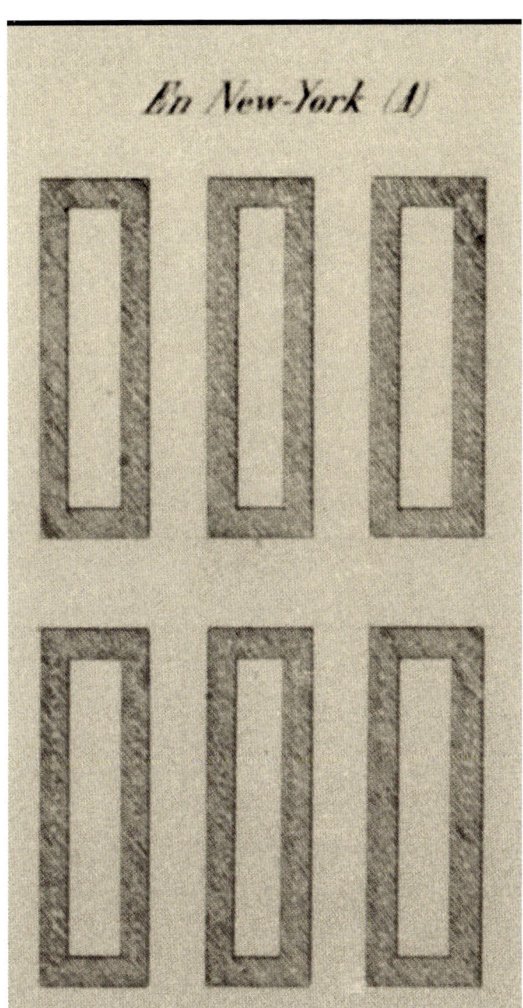

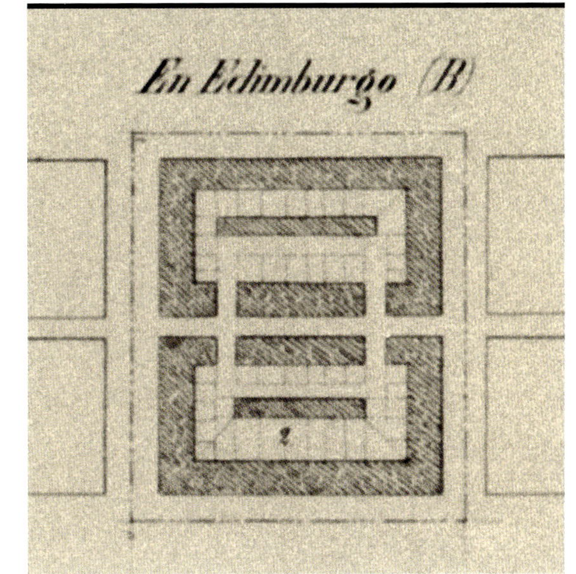

Groupings of city blocks studied by Cerdà. The cases of New York and Edinburgh. Ildefons Cerdà. *Memoria del Anteproyecto del Ensanche de Barcelona*, [Description of the Preliminary Project for the Extension of Barcelona], 1855. Source: Government Archives. Ministry of Culture.

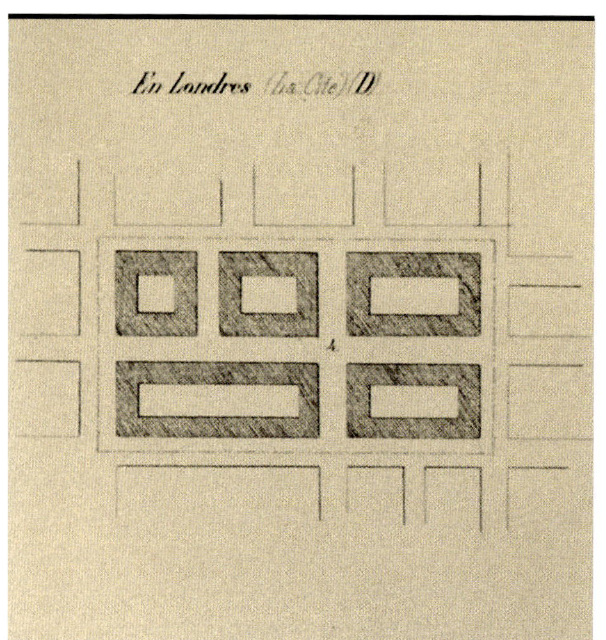

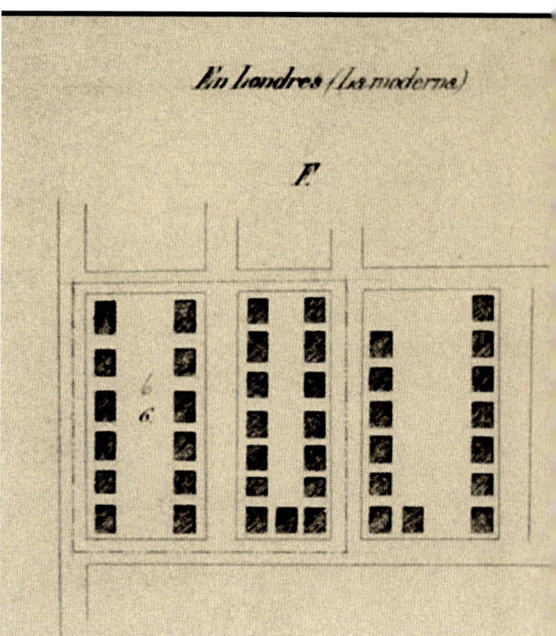

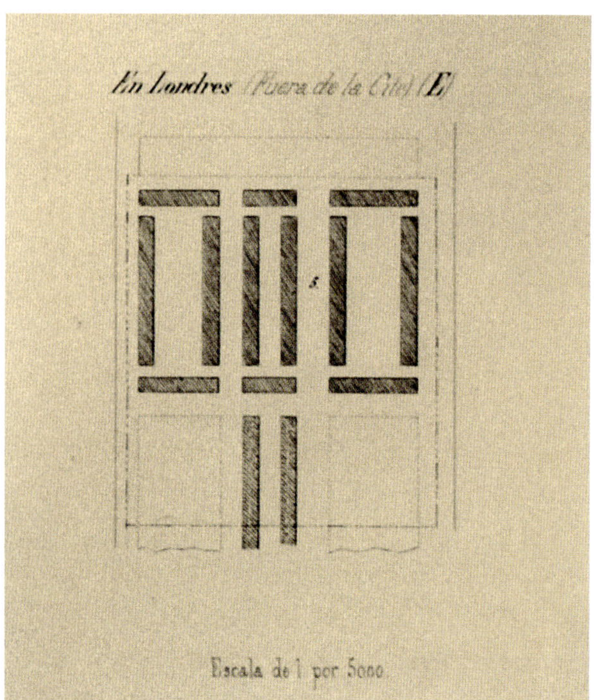

Groupings of city blocks studied by Cerdà. The case of London. Ildefons Cerdà. *Memoria del Anteproyecto del Ensanche de Barcelona*, [Description of the Preliminary Project for the Extension of Barcelona], 1855. Source: Government Archives. Ministry of Culture.

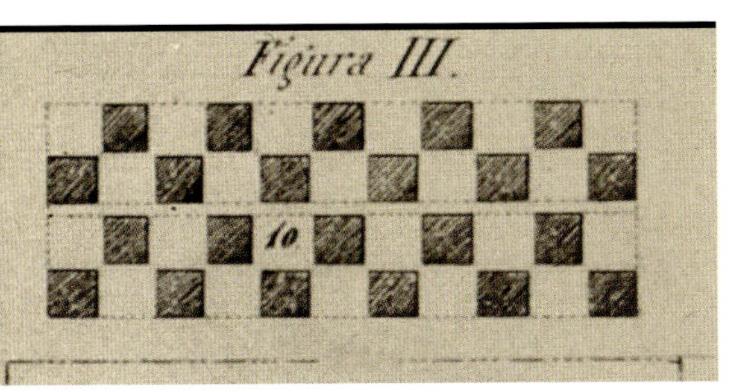

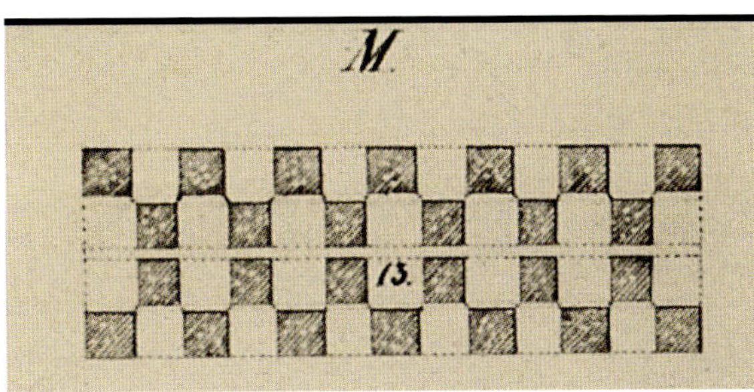

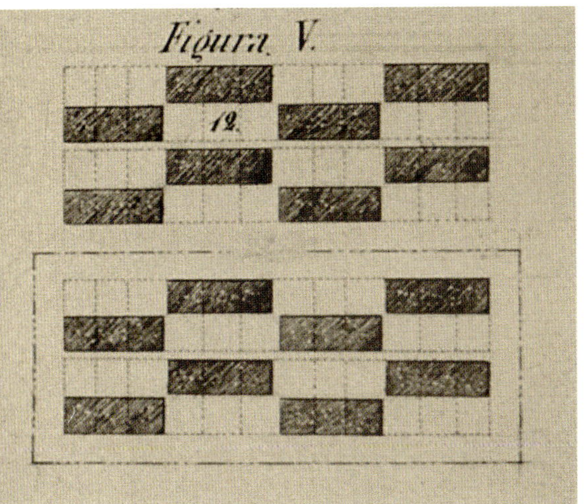

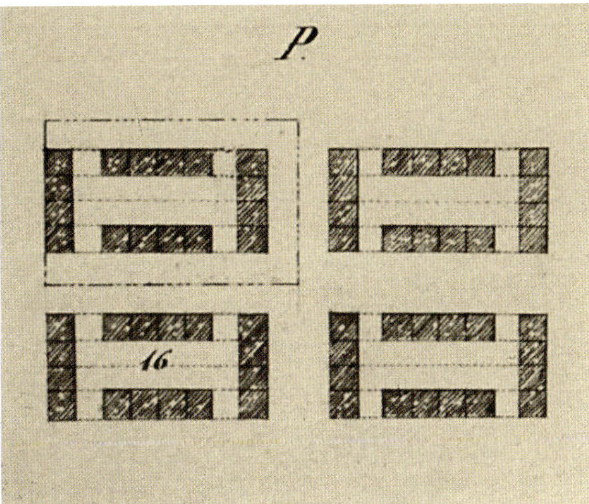

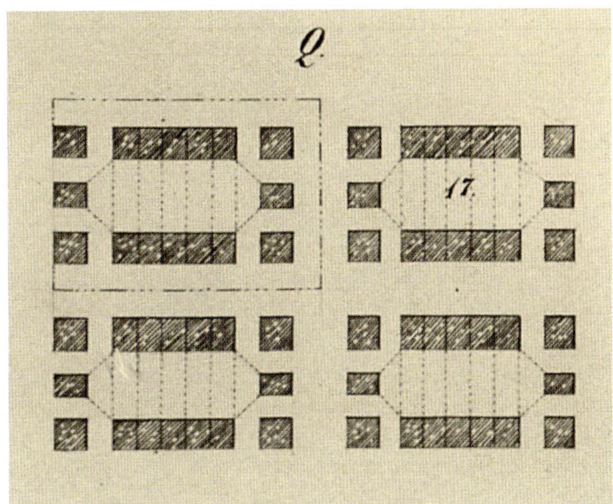

Combinations of city blocks proposed by Cerdà in the Preliminary Project for the Barcelona Extension. Ildefons Cerdà. *Memoria del Anteproyecto del Ensanche de Barcelona*, [Description of the Preliminary Project for the Extension of Barcelona], 1855. Source: Government Archives. Ministry of Culture.

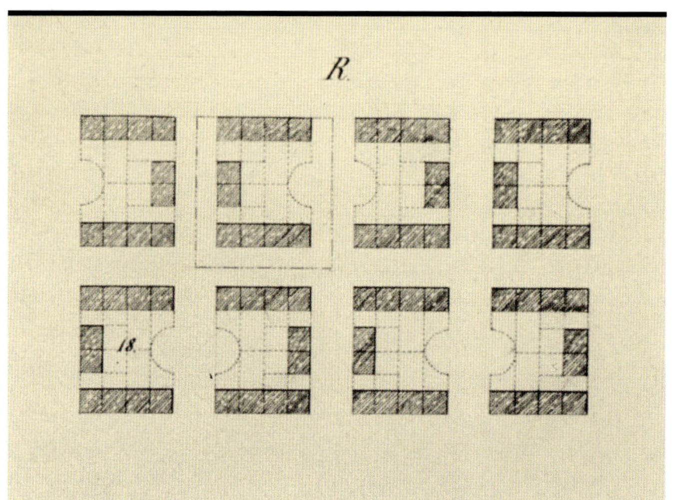

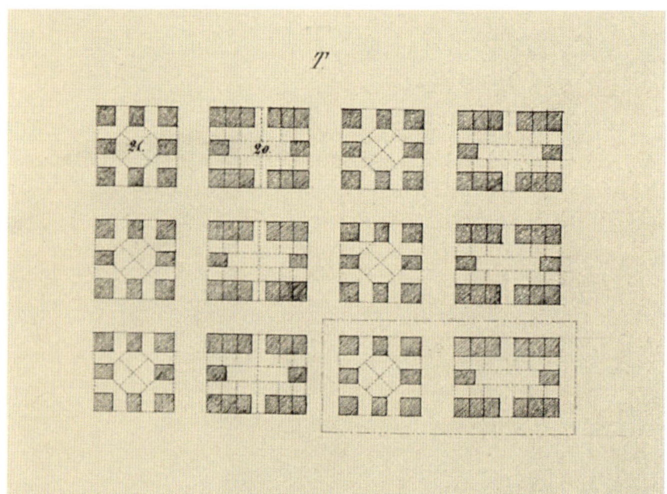

Combinations of city blocks proposed by Cerdà in the Preliminary Project for the Barcelona Extension. Ildefons Cerdà. *Memoria del Anteproyecto del Ensanche de Barcelona*, [Description of the Preliminary Project for the Extension of Barcelona], 1855. Source: Government Archives. Ministry of Culture.

AGRUPACIONS INTERVIÀRIES DEL PROJECTE DE 1859

AGRUPACIONS INTERVIÀRIES DE LA REELABORACIÓ DE 1863

DIFERENTS PROJECTES D'AGRUPACIONS INTERVIÀRIES

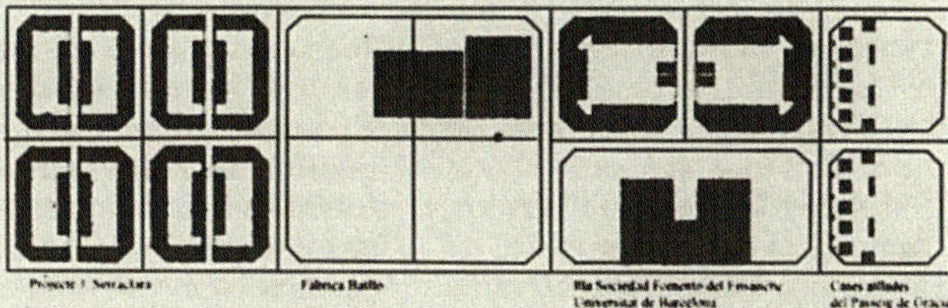

Different groupings of city blocks proposed by Cerdà and city blocks built in the first phase. Conception: Francesc Magrinyà, 1994.

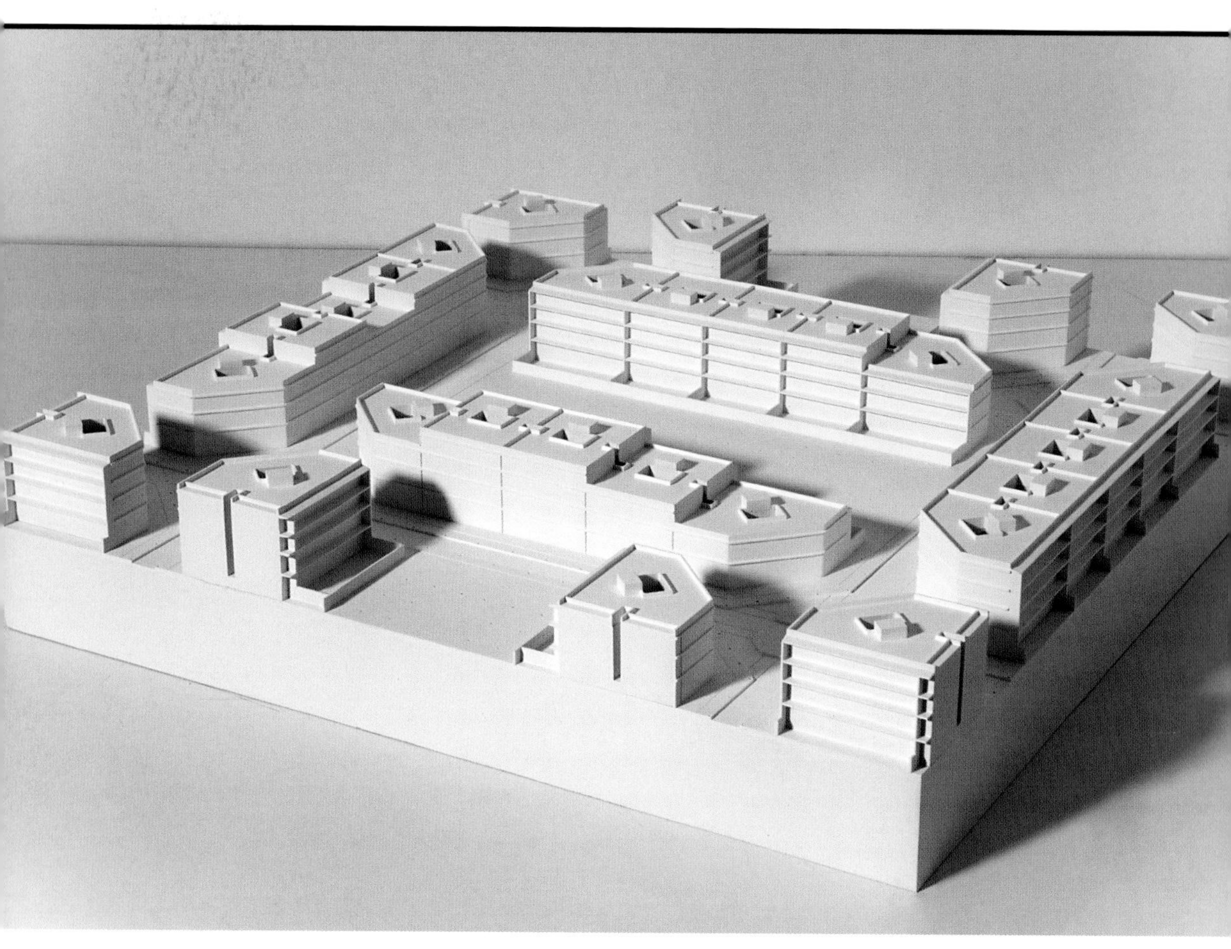

Typical city block of two buildings proposed by Ildefons Cerdà in the 1859 Project for the Remodelling and Extension of Barcelona. Conception: Francesc Magrinyà and Fernando Marzá. Model: ETSAV-UPC model workshop. 2009. Collection of the Fundació Urbs i Territori Ildefons Cerdà.

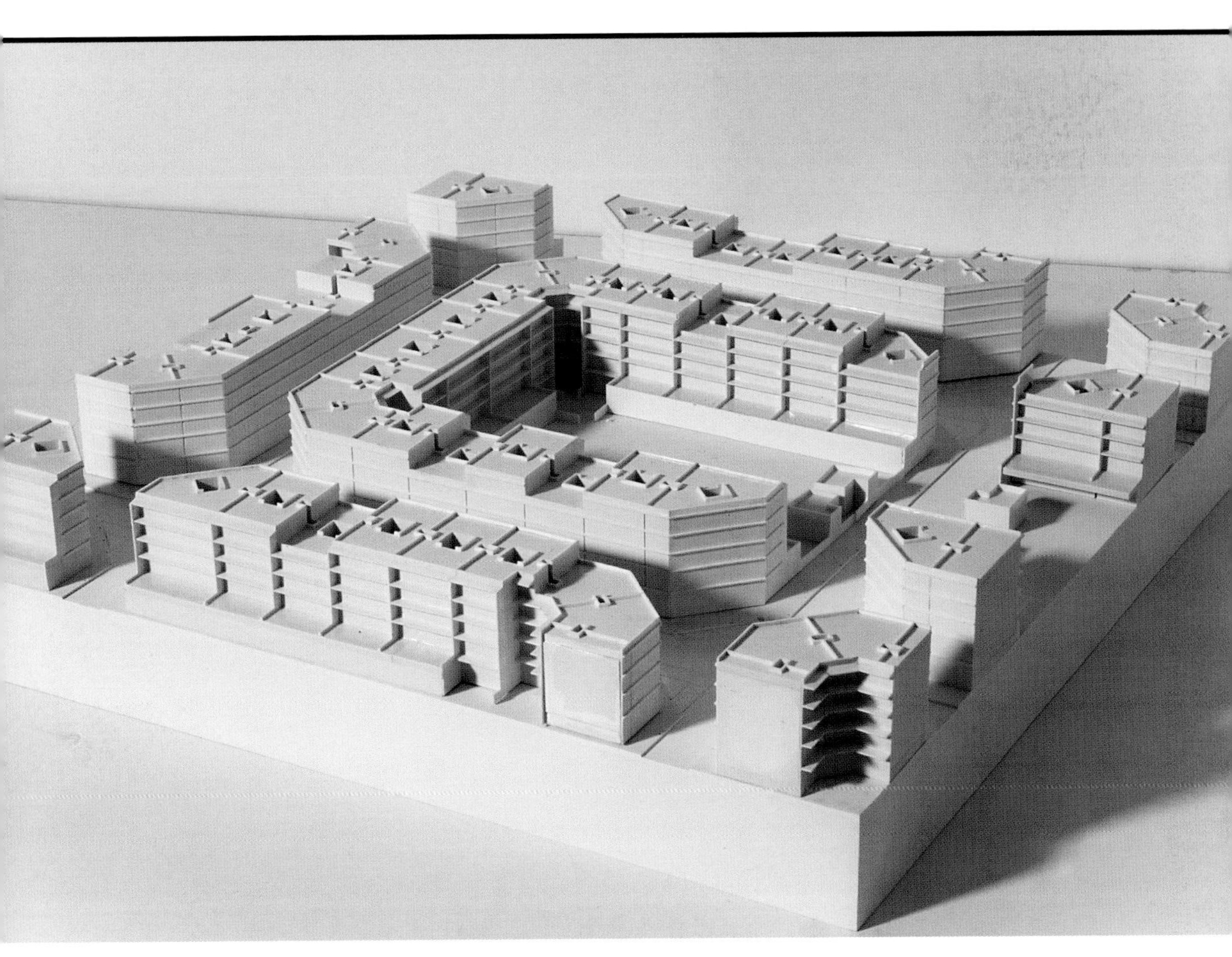

Typical city block of three U-shaped blocks, according to the outlines of the definitive approval of the Project for the Remodelling and extension of Barcelona of 1860, proposed by Ildefons Cerdà with the Sociedad Fomento del Ensanche in 1863. Conception: Francesc Magrinyà and Fernando Marzá. Model: ETSAV-UPC model workshop. 2009. Collection of the Fundació Urbs i Territori Ildefons Cerdà.

A comparison of city blocks: Cerdà and the GATCPAC

The proposals made by the GATCPAC in association with the Macià Plan of 1932 show reflection on the reworking of the city block within the same layout by applying the principles of modern architecture, marking a shift from the block formed by a rental apartment building between party walls to the longer block associated with estates.

The GATCPAC exhibition, "La nova Barcelona" [The New Barcelona] (1934). Architects: GATCPAC. Source: Historical Archive of the Col·legi d'Arquitectes de Catalunya.

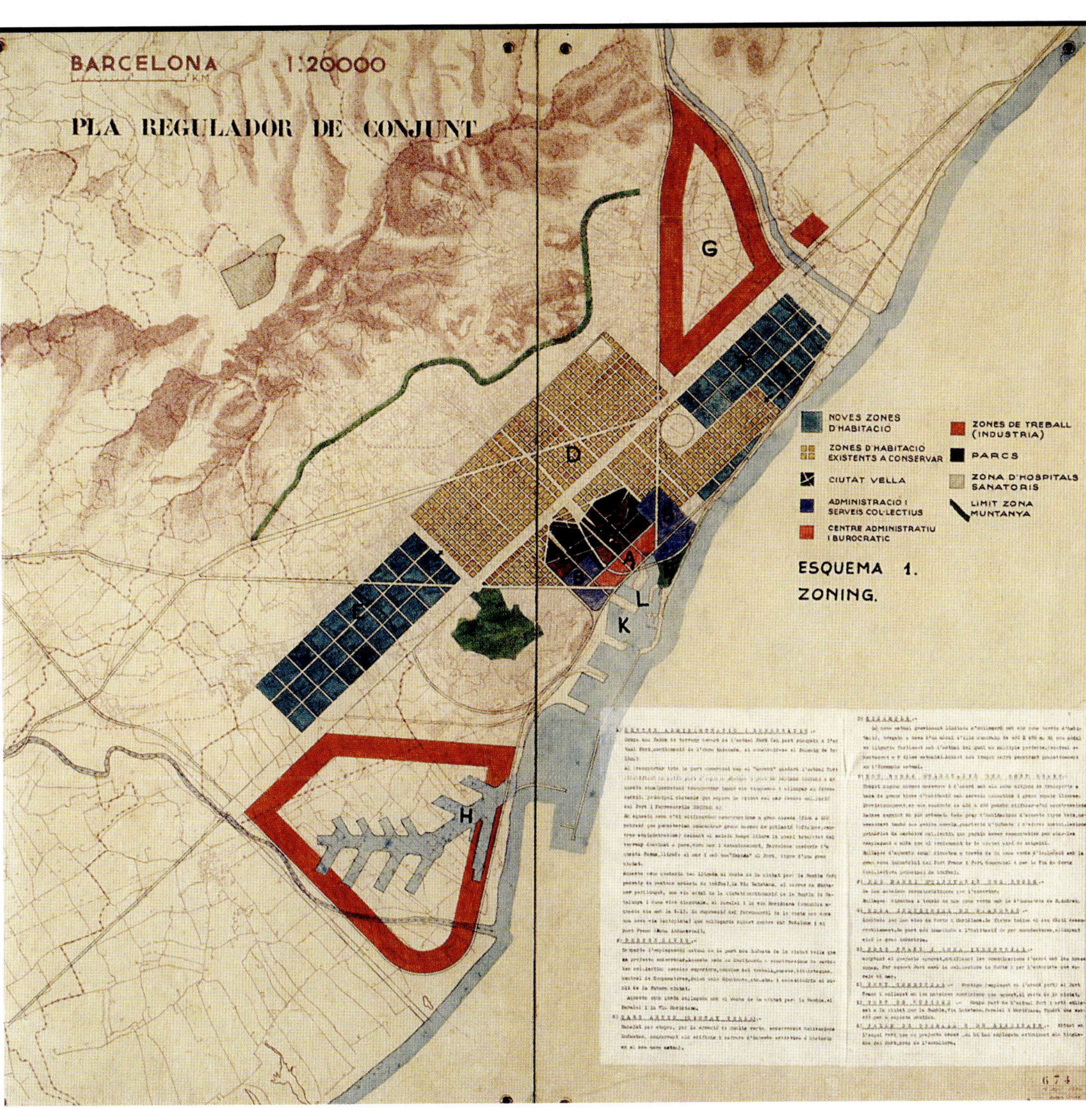

Panel presenting the Macià Plan for Barcelona, 1934: functional zoning. Architects: GATCPAC. Source: CIAM Archives gta-ETH, Zurich.

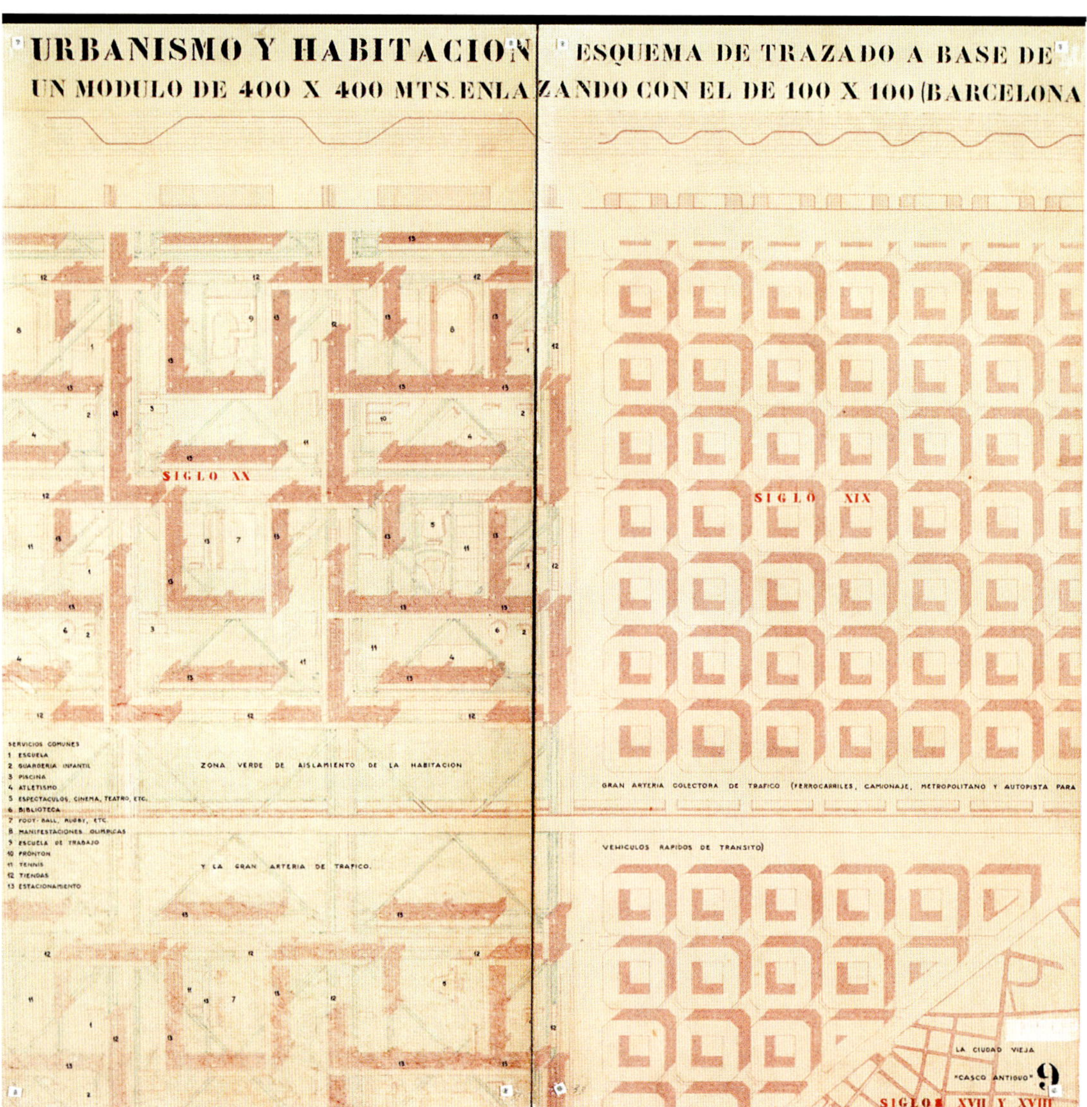

Panel no. 9 from the GATCPAC exhibition, "Urbanismo y Habitación" [Urbanism and Housing], in Buenos Aires (1935). Source: Historical Archive of the Col·legi d'Arquitectes de Catalunya.

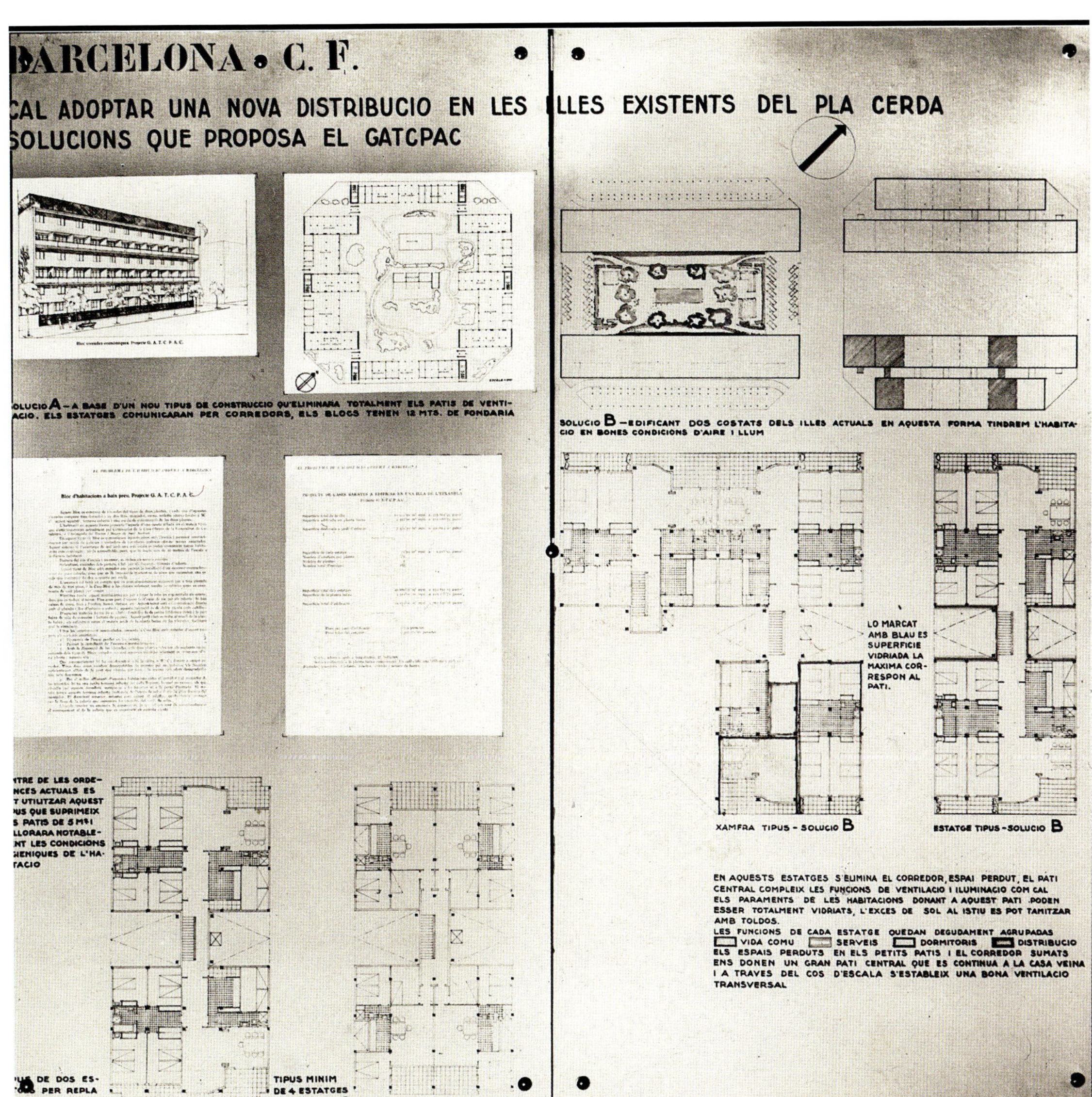

The GATCPAC exhibition, "La nova Barcelona" [The New Barcelona] (1934). Source: Historical Archive of the Col·legi d'Arquitectes de Catalunya.

Aerial view of the central part of the Eixample (1925). Photograph: Josep Gaspar. Source: Arxiu Fotogràfic de Barcelona.

Aerial view of Poblenou from Carrer de Pere IV to the cemetery (c. 1920). Photograph: I. Canals. Source: Photographic Archive of the Centre Excursionista de Catalunya.

Shanties between the railway tracks, to either side of today's Avinguda de Roma, near the Model Prison (1926). Photograph: Josep Maria Segarra i Plana. Source: Josep Maria Segarra i Plana Holdings. Arxiu Nacional de Catalunya.

Model of shanties at the centre of a city block in the 1920s. Conception: Francesc Magrinyà and Fernando Marzá. Model: ETSAV-UPC model workshop. 2009. Collection of the Fundació Urbs i Territori Ildefons Cerdà. (FUTIC).

Model of the "corridor" house located on the plot of land belonging to Tomàs Musqueras in Carrer de Llançà in 1930. Conception: Mercè Tatjer, Francesc Magrinyà and Fernando Marzá. Model: ETSAV-UPC model workshop. 2009. Collection of the Fundació Urbs i Territori Ildefons Cerdà.

Model of the house at Rambla de Catalunya, 121, by the architect Enric Sagnier, in 1898. Conception: Francesc Magrinyà and Fernando Marzá. Model: ETSAV-UPC model workshop. 2009. Collection of the Fundació Urbs i Territori Ildefons Cerdà.

Map of the location of shanties and caves in Barcelona (1949). City map. Source: Municipal Administrative Archive. Barcelona City Council.

Construction of Carrer de Vilamarí and the destruction of shanties. *Memoria de la Comisión de Ensanche* [Report of the City Extension Committee], Barcelona City Council. 1928. Source: Historical Archive of the Col·legi d'Arquitectes de Catalunya.

Destruction of shanties near Avinguda del Paral·lel and Carrer de Vilamarí (1930-1932). Photograph: Josep Domínguez. Source: Arxiu Fotogràfic de Barcelona.

Carrer de Vilamarí shortly after its construction. *Memoria de la Comisión de Ensanche* [Report of the City Extension Committee], Barcelona City Council. 1928. Source: Historical Archive of the Col·legi d'Arquitectes de Catalunya.

PLAN DE ORDENACION DE BARC
GRAFICO DE VTIL
AVENIDA
ANTONIO
PRIMO
DE
RIVERA

Map of land uses in Barcelona and its area of influence (1953). 1953 Barcelona County Plan. Source: Barcelona City Council.

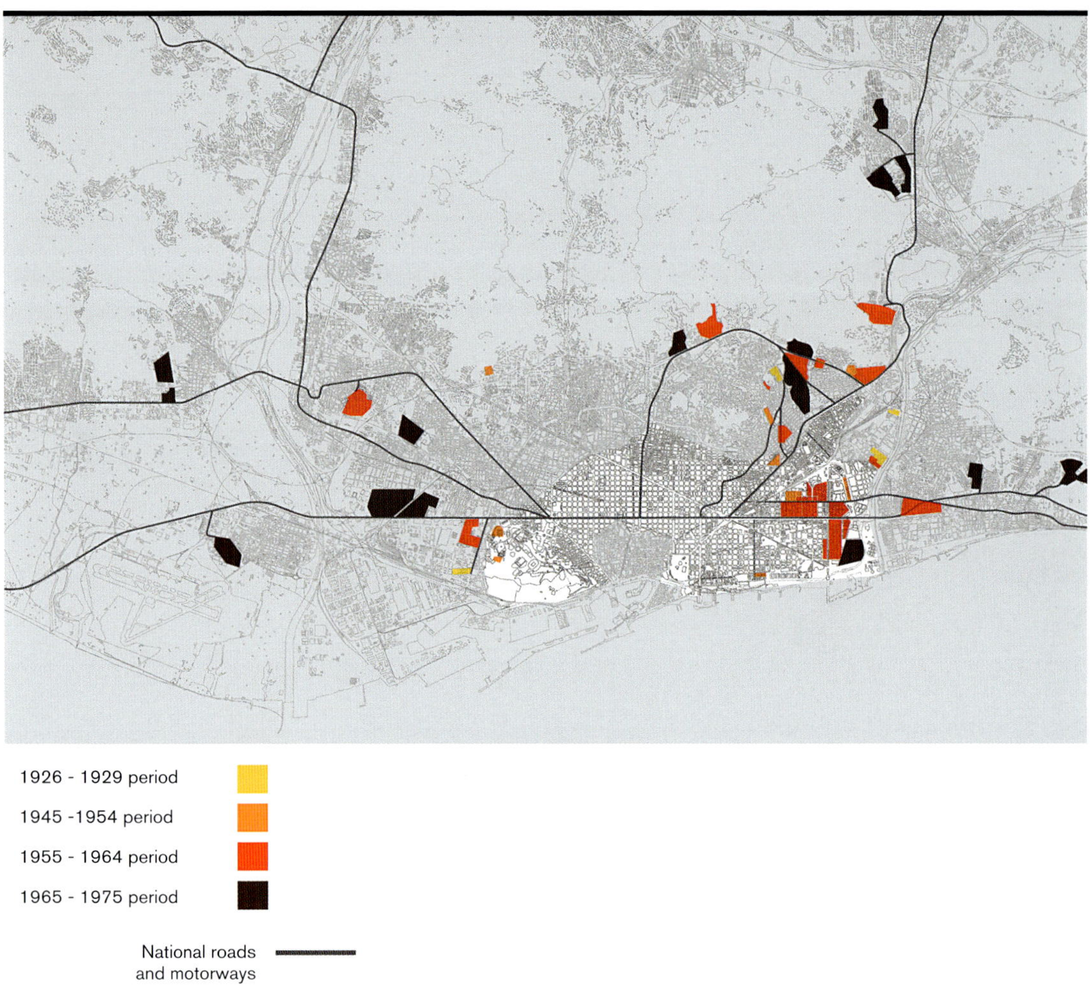

Estates in the Eixample layout

Construction according to the estate model was carried out by the Special Plans that implemented the 1953 County Plan, with particular emphasis on the Levant Sector Plan that served as the basis for the construction of many of the estates in Sant Martí, starting in 1960.

The estates were built in conjunction with the new automobile infrastructures: Carrer Guipúscoa followed the layout of the former national trunk road to France, and Gran Via was built between Plaça de les Glòries and the river Besòs.

Recent years have brought the transformation of Poblenou, first with the extension of Avinguda Diagonal and Fòrum Besòs, and then with the constructions associated with the 22@ Plan. The latter phase represents a new reworking within the city block in the form of tower blocks on Avinguda Diagonal and a combination of existing constructions and new urban projects in the case of 22@.

Barcelona's estates and Cerdà's Eixample (1926-1975). Production: the exhibition.

First development work on Carrer de Guipúscoa in Sant Martí (1958). Photograph: TAF Helicòpters, SA. Source: TAF Holdings. Arxiu Nacional de Catalunya.

Carrer de Guipúscoa and Carrer de Pere IV (1966). Photograph: TAF Helicòpters, SA. Source: TAF Holdings. Arxiu Nacional de Catalunya.

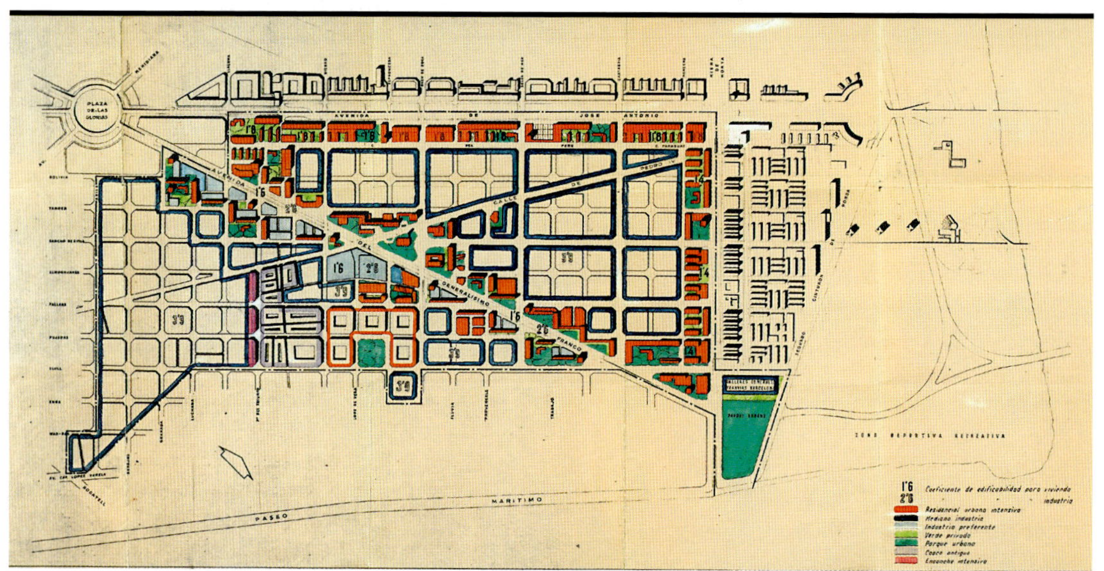

Special Plan of the Levant area. Enlargement of the southern sector (1960). Source: Barcelona City Council.

Special Plan of the Levant area. Enlargement of the southern sector (1960). Source: Barcelona City Council.

Ortho-photomontage of the city block layouts in the special plans for Avinguda Diagonal and the Seafront (1966). Architect: Mercè Berengué.

industry_

“The conditions of public salubriousness in industry are fully met by the orientation, spaciousness and form of the city blocks.”

(I. Cerdà: *Teoría de la Construcción de las Ciudades*, 1859)

Cerdà's Eixample has absorbed residential and industrial fabric alike, largely complying with this principle. The city blocks in the extension are also suitable for housing industry.

Over the last 150 years, industry has been very important in Poblenou, but the residential and industrial functions have also coexisted from the start, first on the left of the Eixample, and later in the districts of Gràcia and Sagrada Família. With the 22@ Special Plan, Poblenou has become an area with a mix of housing and industry.

The transformation of the Batlló factory into the School of Industry in the early 20th century foreshadowed the present-day transformation of industrial tracts of Poblenou into areas where housing coexists with information and communication technology industries at the start of the 21st century. Throughout this whole period, the form and spaciousness of the city blocks have made them perfect venues for these transformations.

The Eixample in Poblenou, near Carrer de Pere IV (1929-1939). Photograph: unknown author. Source: Arxiu Fotogràfic de Barcelona.

Fàbrica Blanch, Carrer de Rocafort, 122-126 (undated). Photograph: unknown author. Source: Historical Archive of the Col·legi d'Arquitectes de Catalunya.

Avinguda del Paral·lel near Portal de la Pau (1915). Photograph: Enric Castellà. Source: Arxiu Fotogràfic de Barcelona.

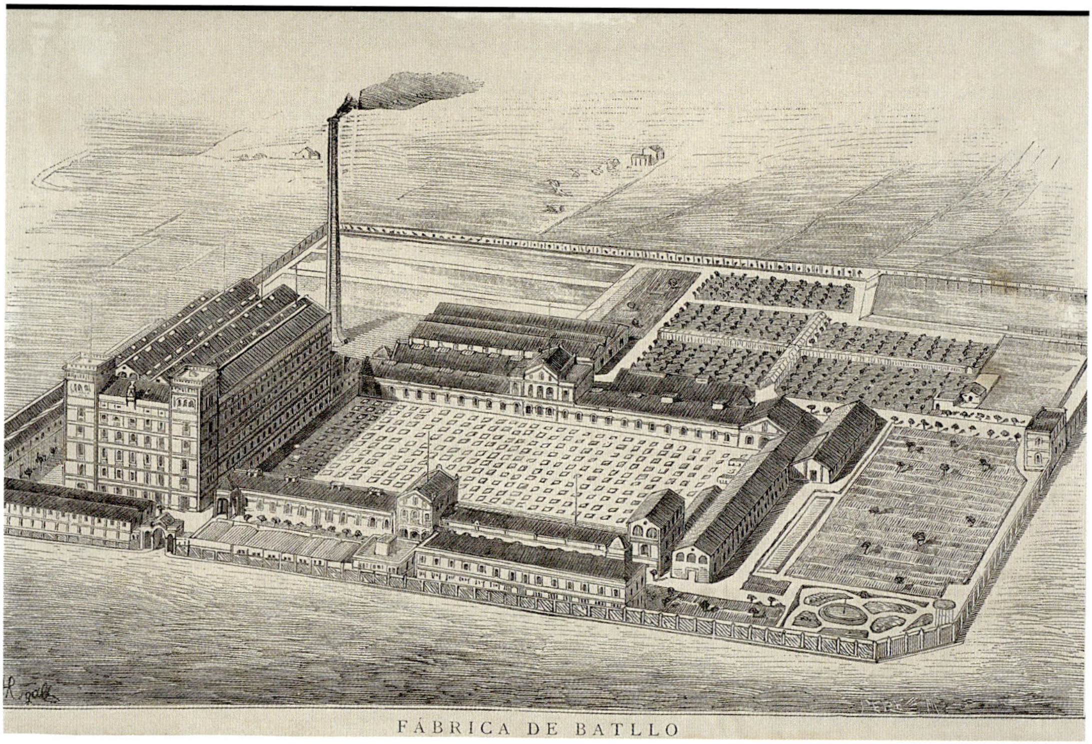

FÁBRICA DE BATLLO

Perspective of Can Batlló factory (1878). Draughtsman: Agustí Rigalt. Source: Arxiu Històric de la Ciutat de Barcelona.

Arial view of the project for the Industrial School (1927). Architect: Joan Rubió i Bellver. Source: Mas Archives. Fundació Institut Amatller d'Art Hispànic.

Laboratory at the Industrial School (undated). Photograph: unknown author. Source: Mas Archive. Fundació Institut Amatller d'Art Hispànic.

Interior of the Can Batlló spinning mill. Weaving room, with looms in operation (before 1875). Photograph: Joan Martí. Source: Galmés Creus Holdings.

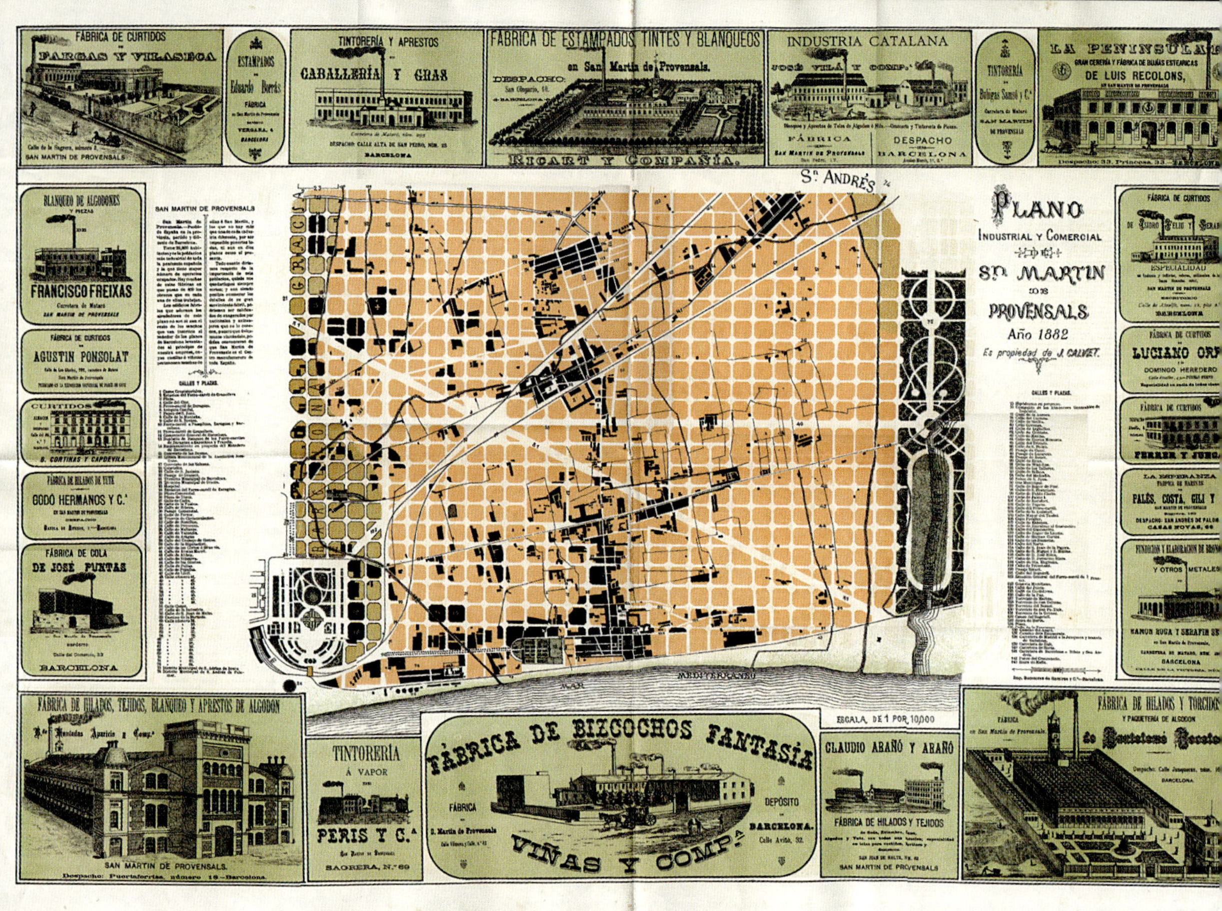

Industrial and commercial map of Sant Martí de Provençals (1872). J. Calvet. Source: Arxiu Històric del Poblenou.

The Espanya Industrial factory (1853-1855). Photograph: Heribert Mariezcurrena. Source: Arxiu Fotogràfic de Barcelona.

Demolition of a factory chimney (1930-1932). Photograph: Josep Domínguez. Source: Arxiu Fotogràfic de Barcelona.

Pompeu Fabra University building (2006-2008). Architects: Josep Benedito, Ramon Valls. Photograph: Lluís Casals.

22@ Audiovisual Campus area (2005). Architects: BB+GG Arquitectes, Beth Galí, Jaume Benavent. Photograph: Andrés Rodríguez.

MEDIA-TIC office building (2009). Architect: Cloud 9. Enric Ruiz-Geli. Photograph: Luís Ros.

MEDIAPRO office building (2008). Architects: Carlos Ferrater, Patrick Genard, Xavier Martí. Photograph: Aleix Bagué.

During the 150 years of the Eixample's evolution, the grid has taken on different styles of city block:

- Blocks structured following ordinances according to the model of plots between sidewalls.
-Blocks structured around buildings, especially with the modernist architectural movement, and with industrial parks.
-Unique blocks usually associated with facilities.

Sample of the range of city blocks in Cerdà's Eixample, grouped by: city blocks closed in on four sides, suburban city blocks with narrow through-streets and city blocks with singular buildings. Conception: Francesc Magrinyà and Fernando Marzá. Model: ETSAV-UPC model workshop. 2009. Collection of the Fundació Urbs i Territori Ildefons Cerdà.

the market_

"In laying out and positioning the markets and other public facilities, we are guided by hygienic doctrine and economic laws."

(I. Cerdà: *Teoría de la Construcción de las Ciudades*, 1859)

Cerdà propone un esquema de equipamientos

Cerdà proposed a series of facilities laid out according to a rational concept that included a social centre for each neighbourhood, a market for each district and a hospital for each sector, plus two urban parks, an abattoir and a cemetery for the city.[1] His proposed outline was followed in the case of the markets[2] and hospitals, but not the social centres.

Equipping the city by phases

During the first phase of extension, the city was served by the facilities that already existed in the historic centre. At this point, the Eixample was occupied primarily by housing and industry.
Then came the facilities: first the markets of the Eixample proper, such as those of Sant Antoni and La Concepció, together with the markets in towns in the Barcelona Plain that were not yet annexed to the city, such as Gràcia, Sants, Hostafrancs, Clot and Poblenou, all built between 1876 and 1892.[3]
Between 1905 and 1925, hospitals and prisons were built on the periphery of the original municipality of Barcelona: Hospital Clínic, Hospital del Mar and the Model prison.[4] It was not until the approval of the 1925 Municipal Statute that the municipality was equipped at the scale of the Barcelona Plain. Facilities were located around the edge of Cerdà's Eixample project, with the hospitals of Sant Pau, L'Aliança and La Creu Roja, and Wad Ras Prison as referents, and, in the 1953-1976 period, they were built on the periphery of the present-day city, with Vall d'Hebron Hospital and Trinitat Prison as significant examples.[5]

[1] See fig. page 193 I [2] See fig. page 194 I [3] See fig. page 195 I [4] See fig. page 196 I [5] See fig. page 196

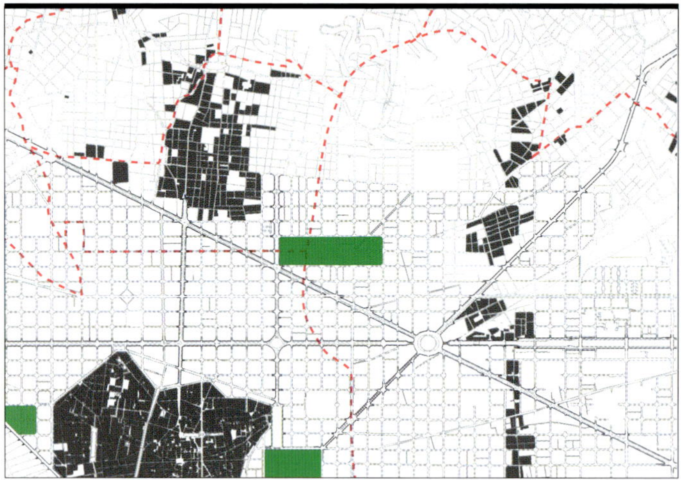

Fig.1

Fig. 2

The interchangeability of facilities and urban parks

The last 150 years have seen ongoing recourse to a mechanism of using park spaces as sites for facilities.

When a new cemetery was designed for the city,[6] it had to be located within the old municipality. The most suitable location was the space envisaged in Cerdà's Plan for the abattoir, which had to be moved to a site earmarked for a park, which did, ultimately, become an urban park, the Parc de Joan Miró (Parc de l'Escorxador). Hospital Clínic and the Ninot market were also built on spaces that Cerdà had envisioned as parks.

The land on which Cerdà planned a racecourse belonged almost entirely to the municipality of Sant Martí. This is probably why the racecourse project was rejected,[7] and the site was gradually occupied first by the construction of the Sagrada Família[8] and then by dwellings.

[6] See fig. page 210 I [7] See fig. 1 I [8] See figs. page 208, 209 & 214

Fig. 1_ Detail of the location of the racecourse on the border between the municipalities of Barcelona and Sant Martí.
Fig. 2_ Detail of the location of the Hospital Clinic.

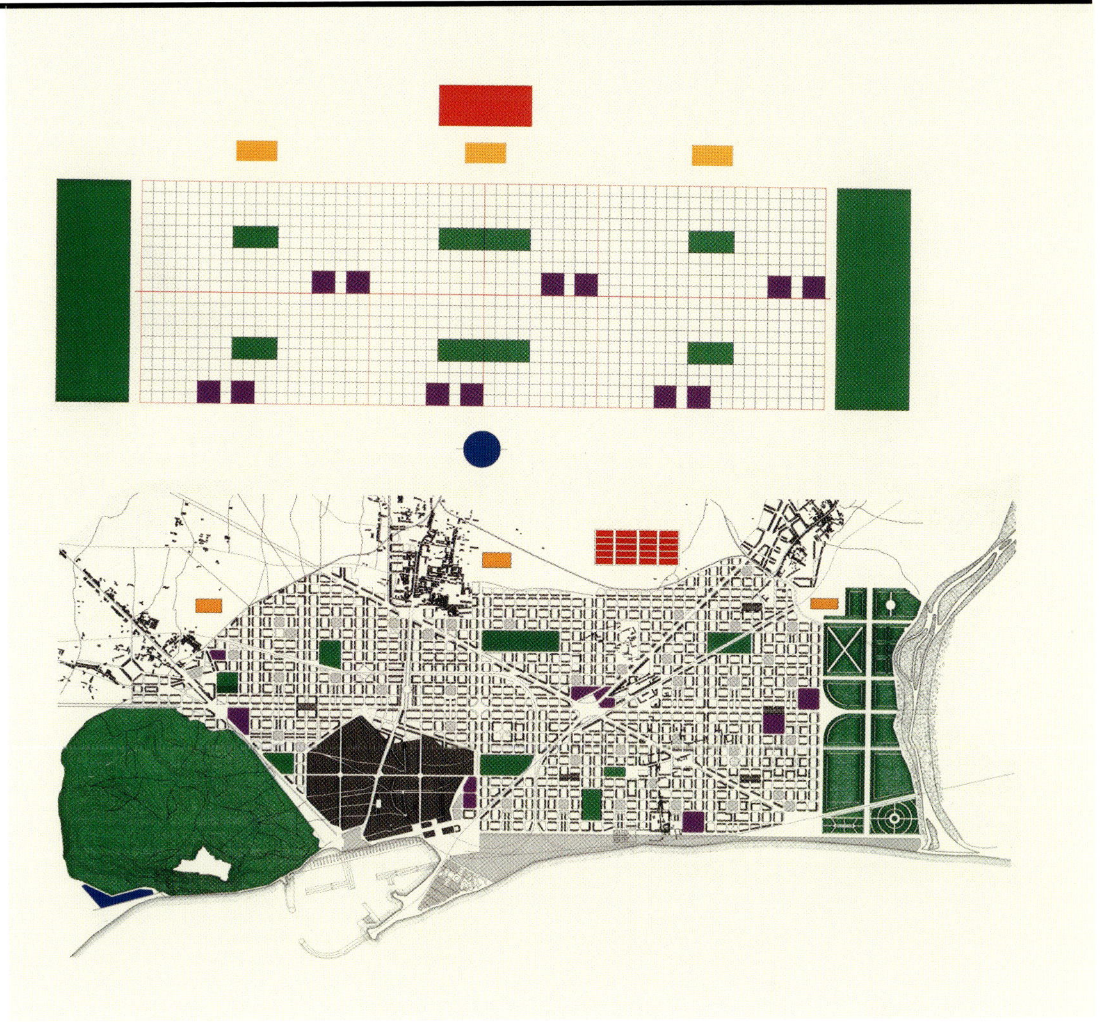

Facilities in the 1859 Remodelling and Extension Project

According to the layout Cerdà envisaged for the 1859 Extension Project, the necessary public facilities would be distributed rationally by neighbourhoods, districts and sectors. Each neighbourhood or arrangement of 25 city blocks (5x5) would have a social centre, each district or arrangement of 100 city blocks (10x10) would have a market, and each sector of 400 city blocks (20x20) would have a hospital, two urban parks and administrative buildings.

Finally, two large suburban parks, an abattoir and a cemetery were to be designed for the overall Eixample with its 1,200 city blocks (60x20).

Diagram of the overall facilities and their application in the 1859 Project for the Remodelling and Extension of Barcelona by Ildefons Cerdà. Conception: Salvador Tarragó. 1994.

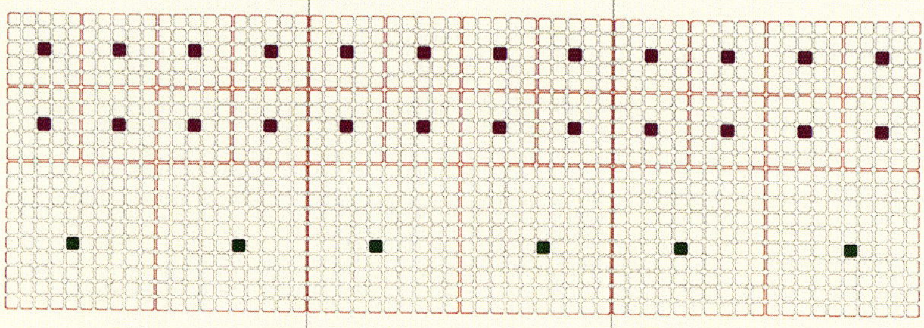

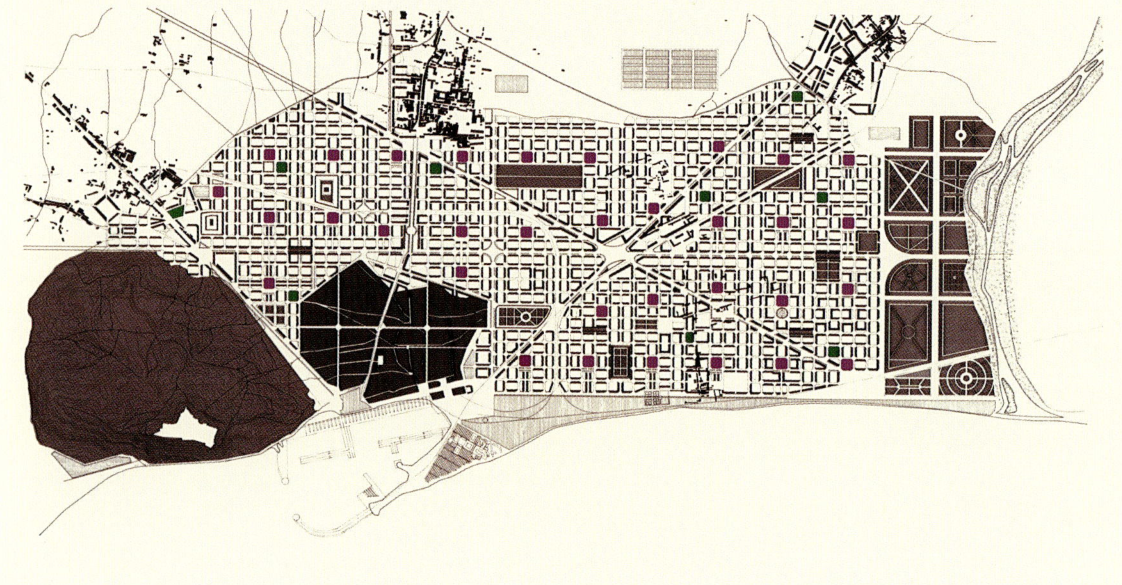

Diagram of the neighbourhoods, districts and sectors, and their application in the 1859 Project for the Remodelling and Extension of Barcelona by Ildefons Cerdà. Conception: Salvador Tarragó. 1994.

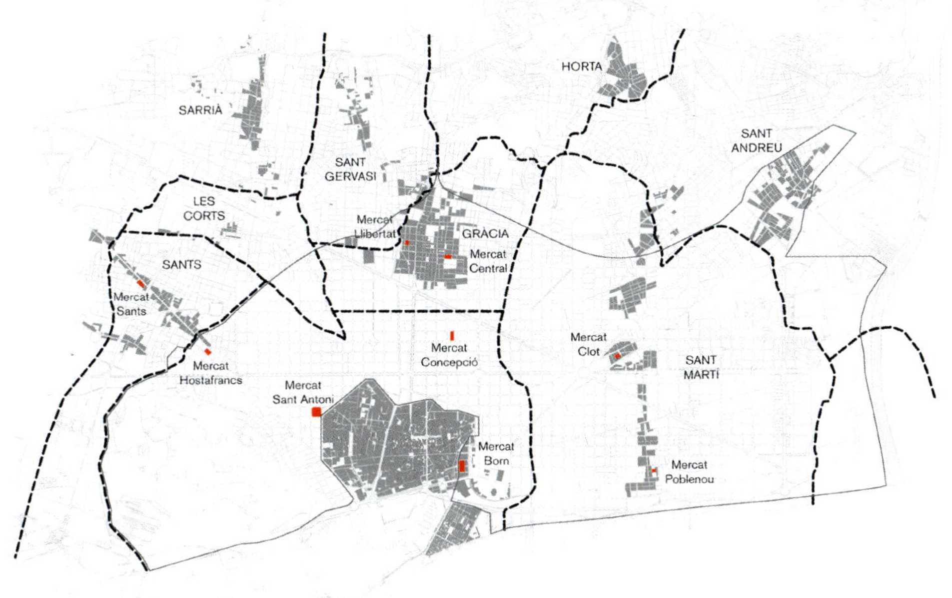

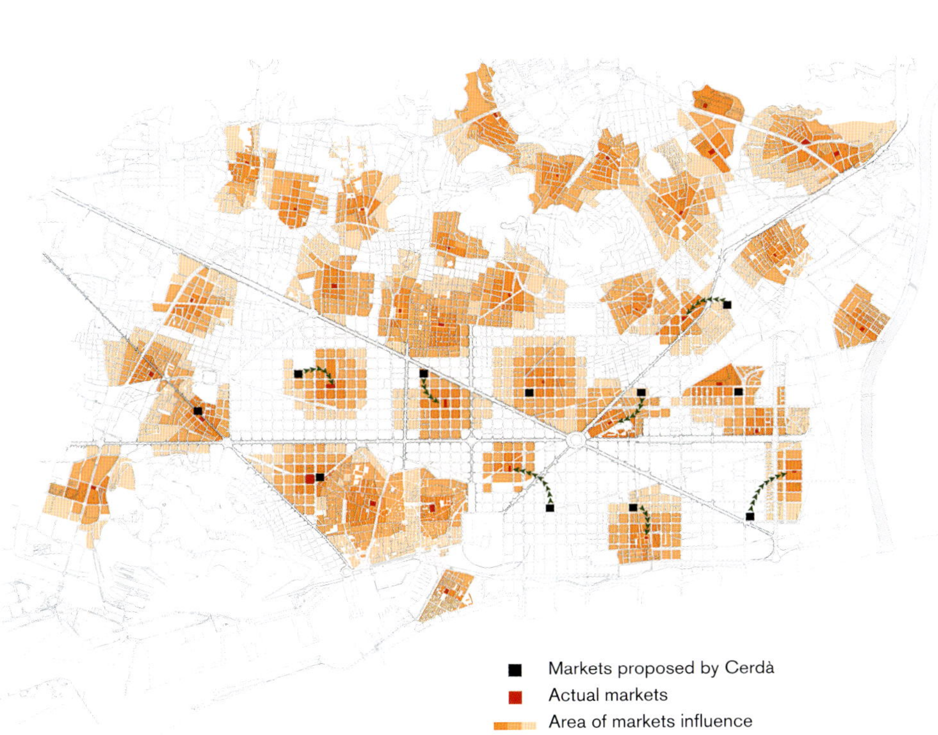

Implantation of markets in the Eixample on the basis of towns in the Barcelona Plain and comparison with Cerdà's model with the present-day distribution of markets. Drawing: for the exhibition.

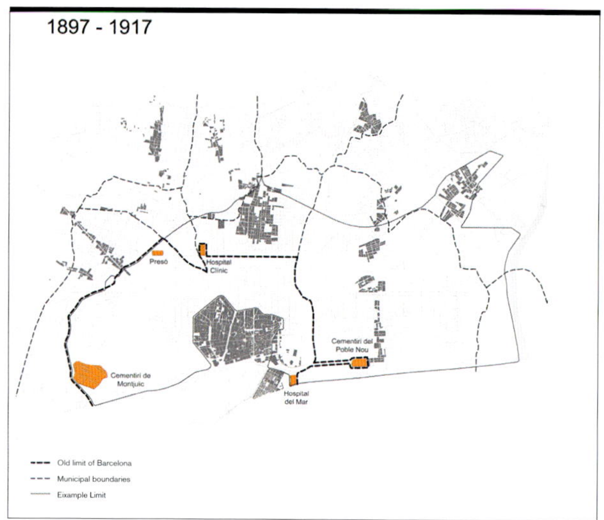

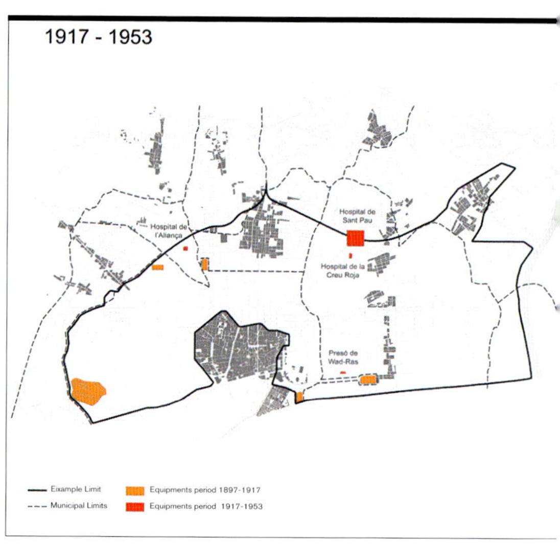

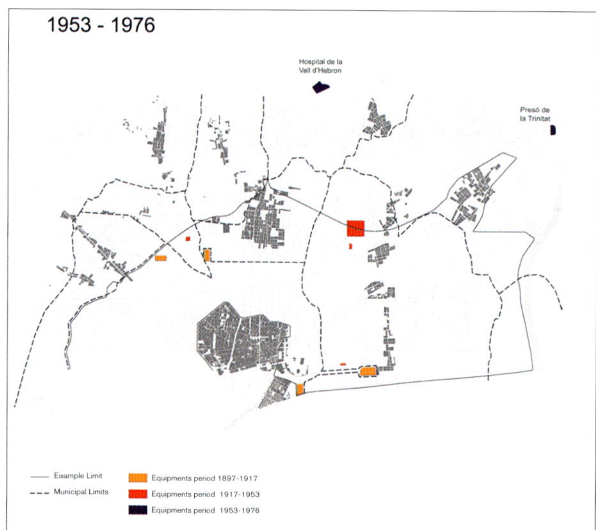

The transformation of the Eixample's markets

Barcelona's markets have undergone a transformation. The market initially comprised traditional stalls covered by a metal framework, with a series of shops around them.

In a second phase, the traditional market was joined by a basement floor for storage space, with its entrance on a different level, and supermarkets and shops were added to create modern shopping centres, as in the case of the markets of La Concepció and Sant Antoni, currently undergoing remodelling.

A third phase of design involves situating various facilities in a city block, as in the case of the Fort Pienc centre, which combines a civic centre, a library and a school, built around a public square.

The hospitals and prisons were situated on the periphery of the city extension, with three leaps of scale: the original city of Barcelona, the limits of the Extension Project and the municipality of Barcelona. Drawing: for the exhibition.

UNIVERSIDAD LITERARIA DE BARCELONA.

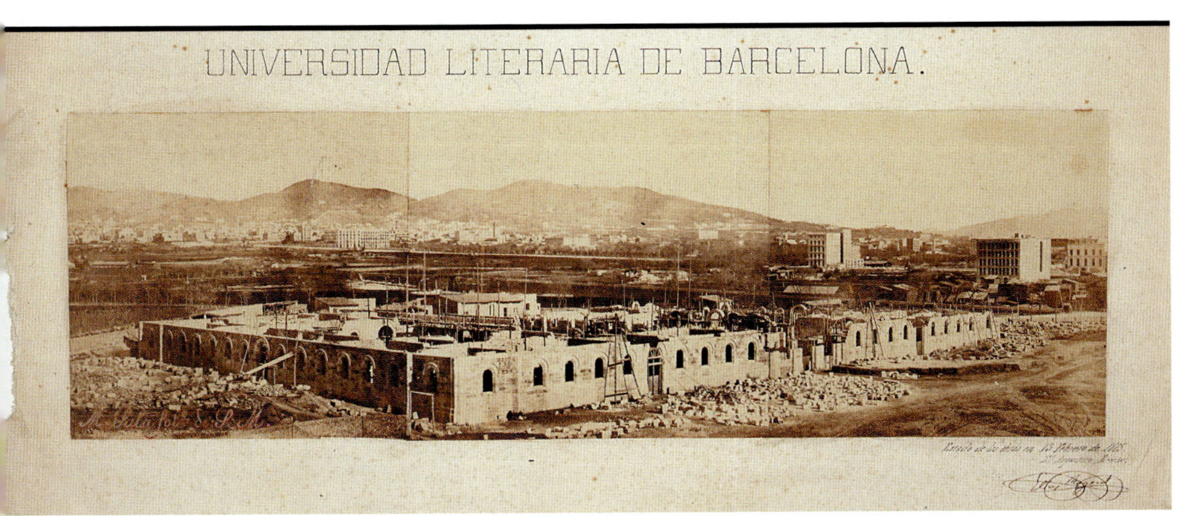

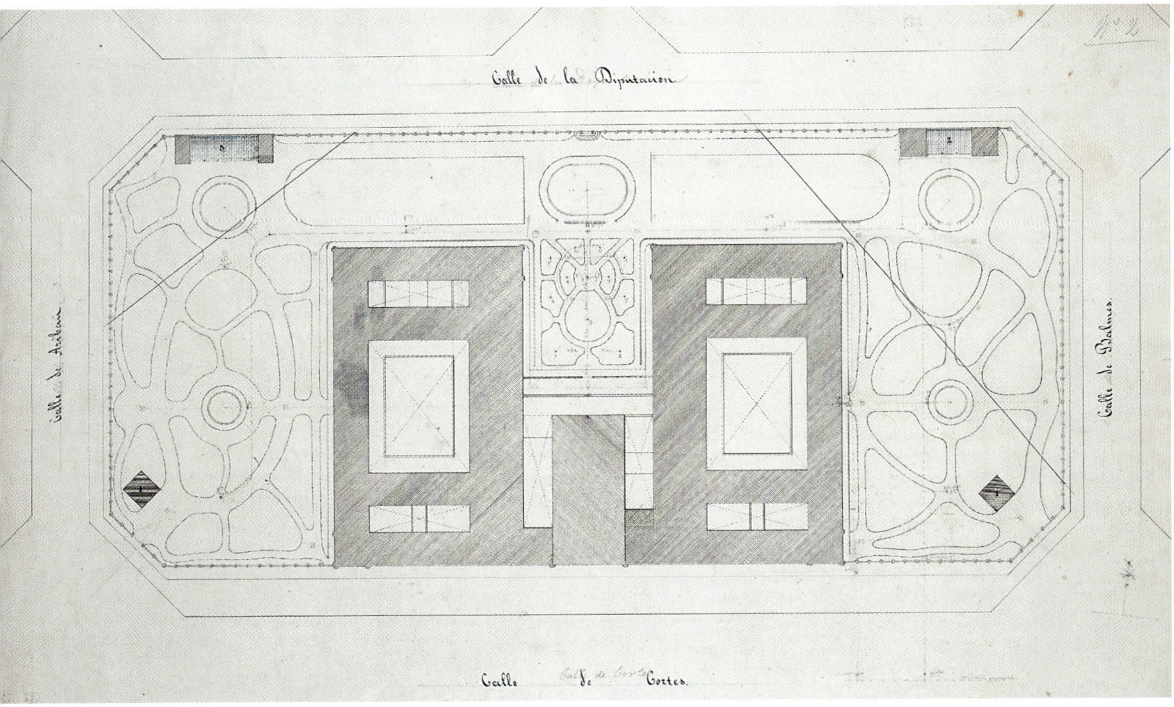
Calle de la Diputacion
Calle de Aribau
Calle de Balmes
Calle de Cortes.

Construction work on the University of Barcelona (1865). Photograph: Marcos Sala. Source: Arxiu Fotogràfic de Barcelona.

University of Barcelona. Gardens and location (1873). Architect: Elies Rogent. Source: Historical Archive of the Col·legi d'Arquitectes de Catalunya.

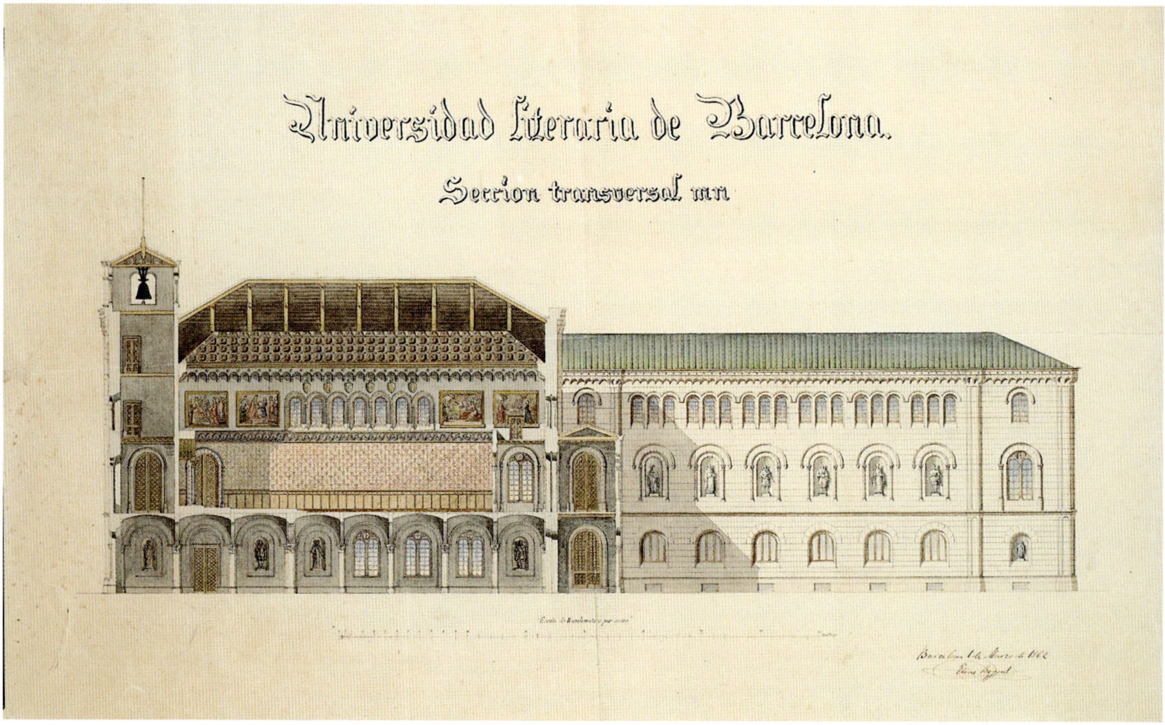

University of Barcelona. Main façade (1862). Architect: Elies Rogent. Source: Historical Archive of the Col·legi d'Arquitectes de Catalunya.

University of Barcelona. Cross-section (1862). Architect: Elies Rogent.Source: Historical Archive of the Col·legi d'Arquitectes de Catalunya.

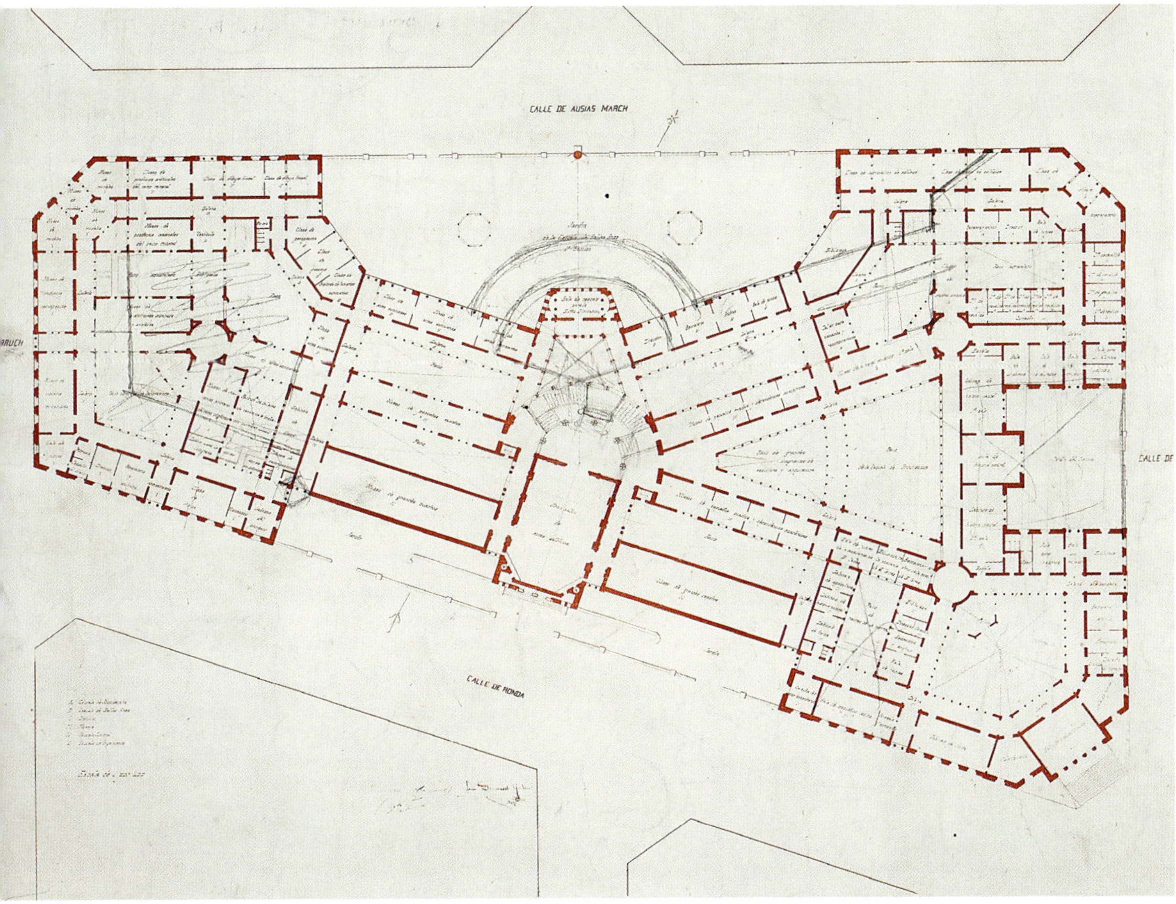

Project for Provincial Institutions of Public Instruction. Elevation (1877-1882). Architect: Lluís Domènech i Montaner. Source: Historical Archive of the Col·legi d'Arquitectes de Catalunya.

Project for Provincial Institutions of Public Instruction. Main floor plan (1877-1882). Architect: Lluís Domènech i Montaner. Source: Historical Archive of the Col·legi d'Arquitectes de Catalunya.

Model Prison (undated). Photograph: unknown author. Source: Historical Archive of the Col·legi d'Arquitectes de Catalunya.

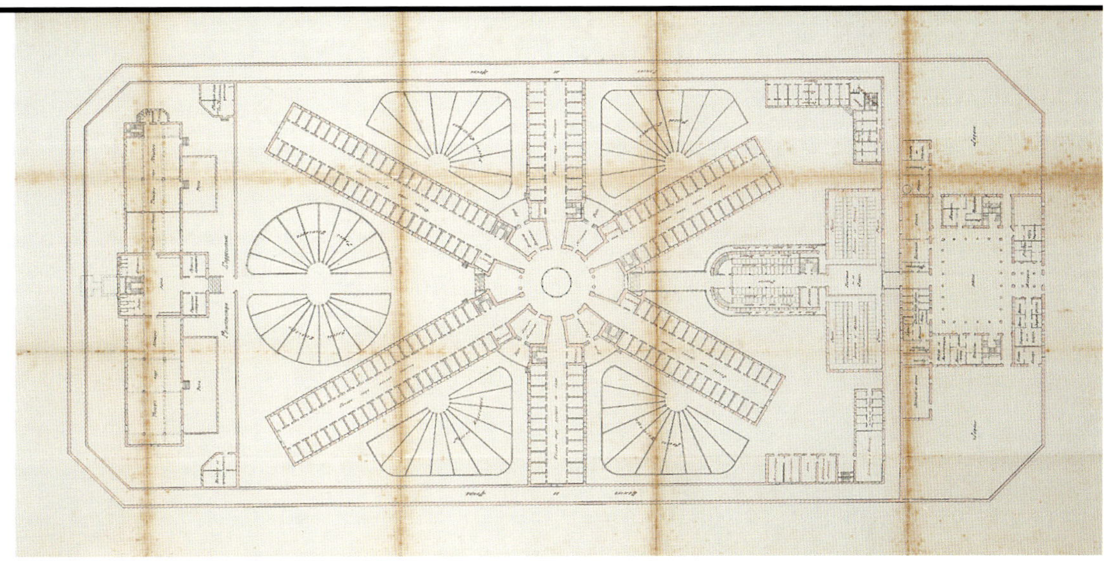

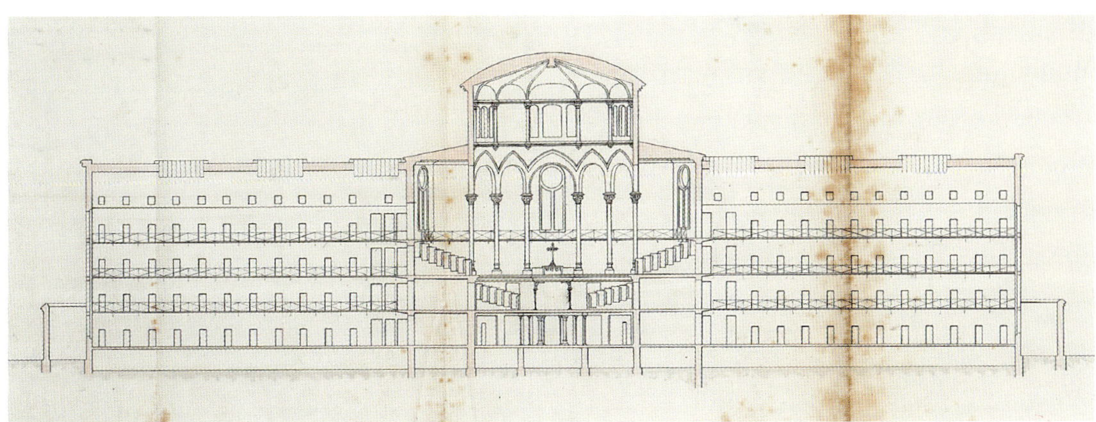

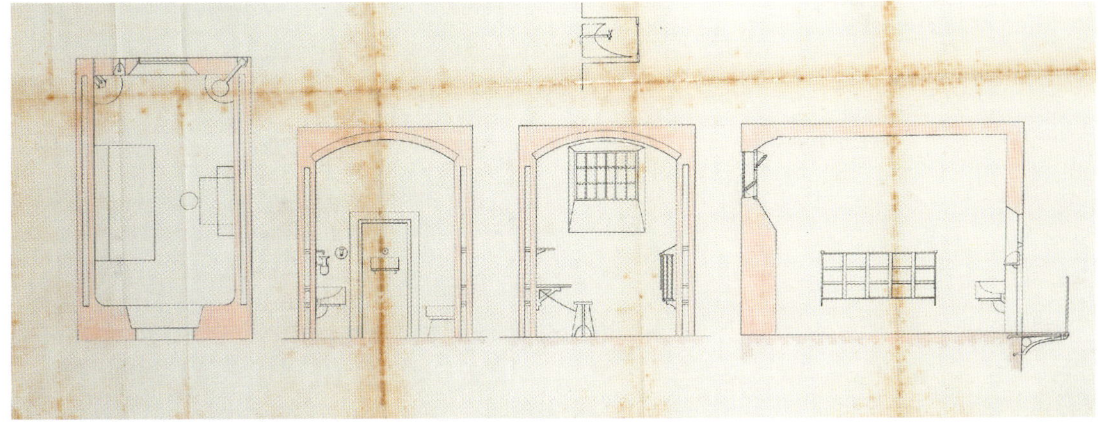

Preliminary project for a prison for Barcelona. Ground floor (1886). Architects: Josep Domènech Estapà - Salvador Viñals. Source: Historical Archive of the Col·legi d'Arquitectes de Catalunya.

Preliminary project for a prison for Barcelona. Section (1886). Architects: Josep Domènech Estapà - Salvador Viñals. Source: Historical Archive of the Col·legi d'Arquitectes de Catalunya.

Preliminary project for a prison for Barcelona. Floor plan and sections of a cell (1886). Architects: Josep Domènech Estapà - Salvador Viñals. Source: Historical Archive of the Col·legi d'Arquitectes de Catalunya.

General view of Barcelona's municipal abattoir (1931-1932). Photograph: Gabriel Casas i Galobardes**.** Source: Gabriel Casas i Galobardes Holdings. Arxiu Nacional de Catalunya.

General floor plan of the abattoir (1880). Architect: Antoni Rovira i Trias. Source: Municipal Administrative Archive. Barcelona City Council.

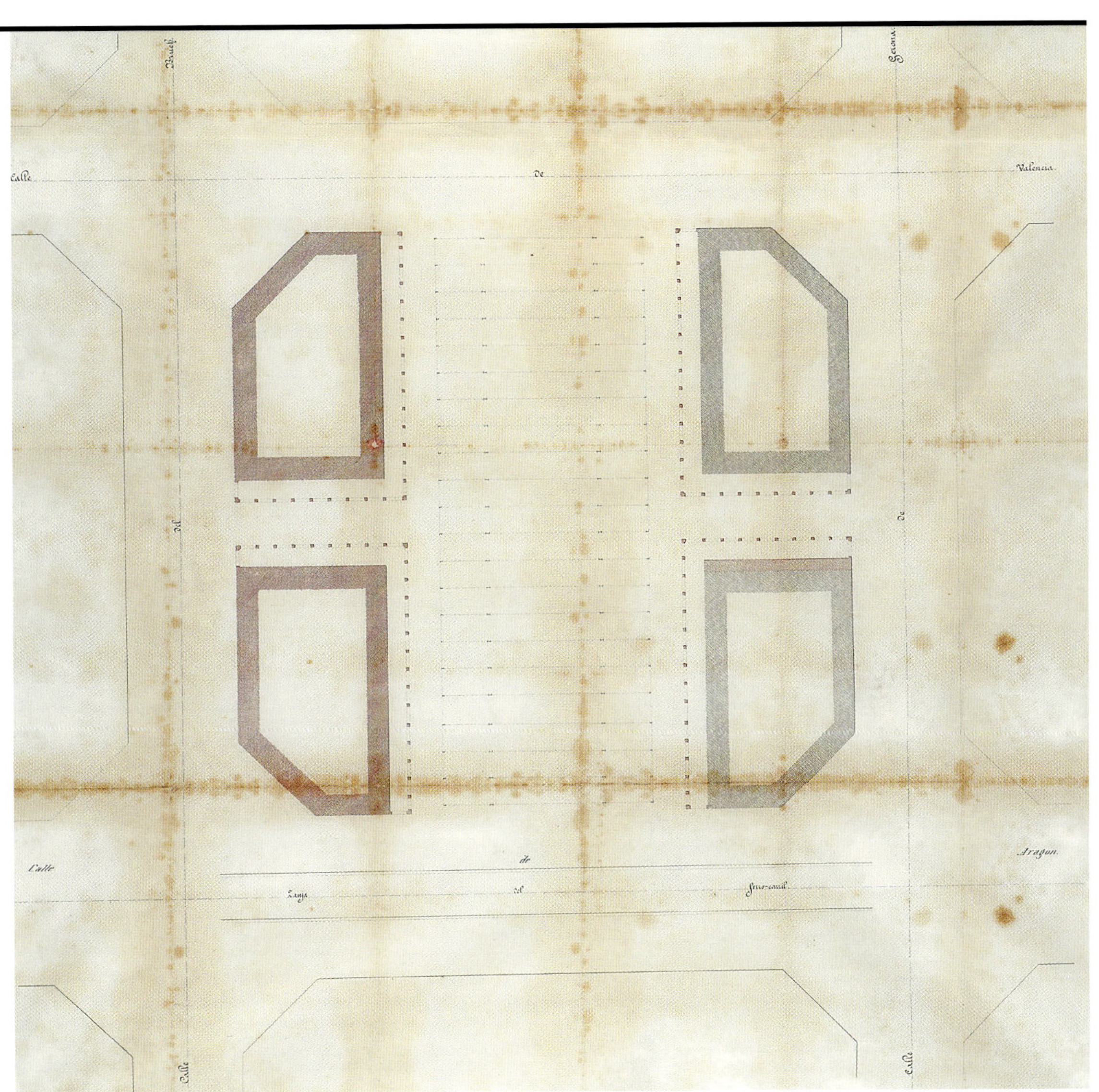

General floor plan of La Concepció market (1885). Architect: Antoni Rovira i Trias. Source: Municipal Administrative Archive. Barcelona City Council.

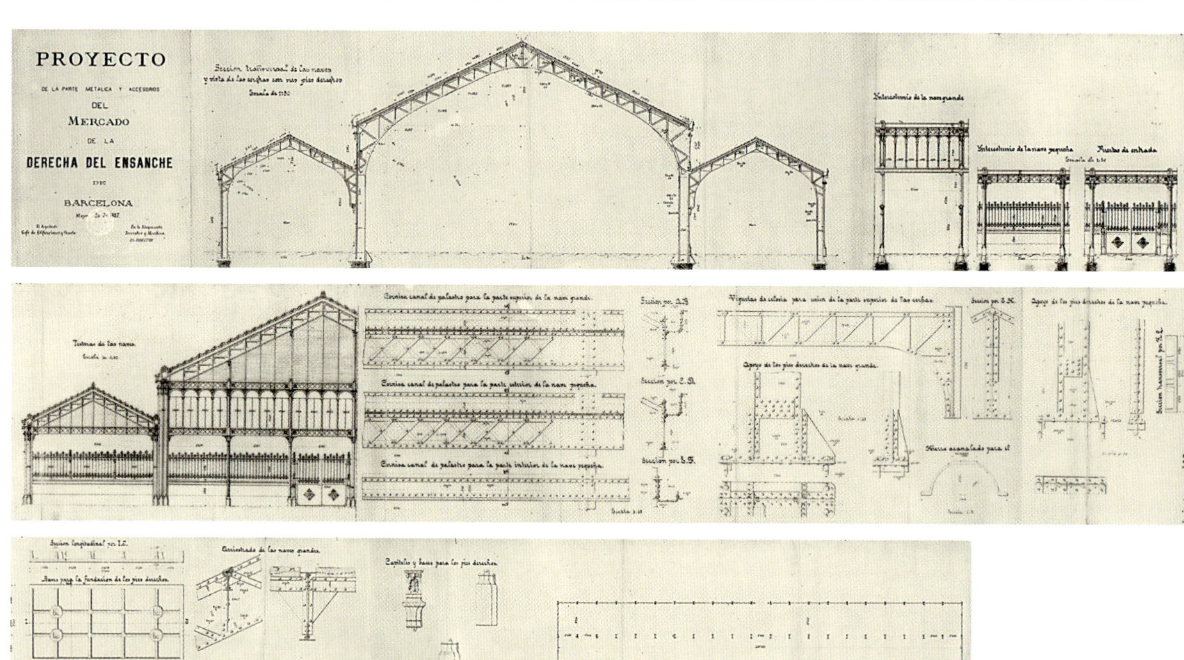

Façade and roof of La Concepció market (undated). Photograph: Josep Maria Sagarra i Plana. Source: Historical Archive of the Col·legi d'Arquitectes de Catalunya.

Project for the metal structure of La Concepció market (1887). Architect: Antoni Rovira i Trias. Source: Municipal Administrative Archive. Barcelona City Council.

Sant Antoni market (1878). Photograph: A. Torija. Source: Holdings of Maquinista Terrestre y Marítima, SA. Arxiu Nacional de Catalunya.

El Ninot market seen from Carrer de Mallorca (undated). Photograph: Josep Maria Sagarra i Torrents and Pau Lluís Torrents. Source: Historical Archive of the Col·legi d'Arquitectes de Catalunya.

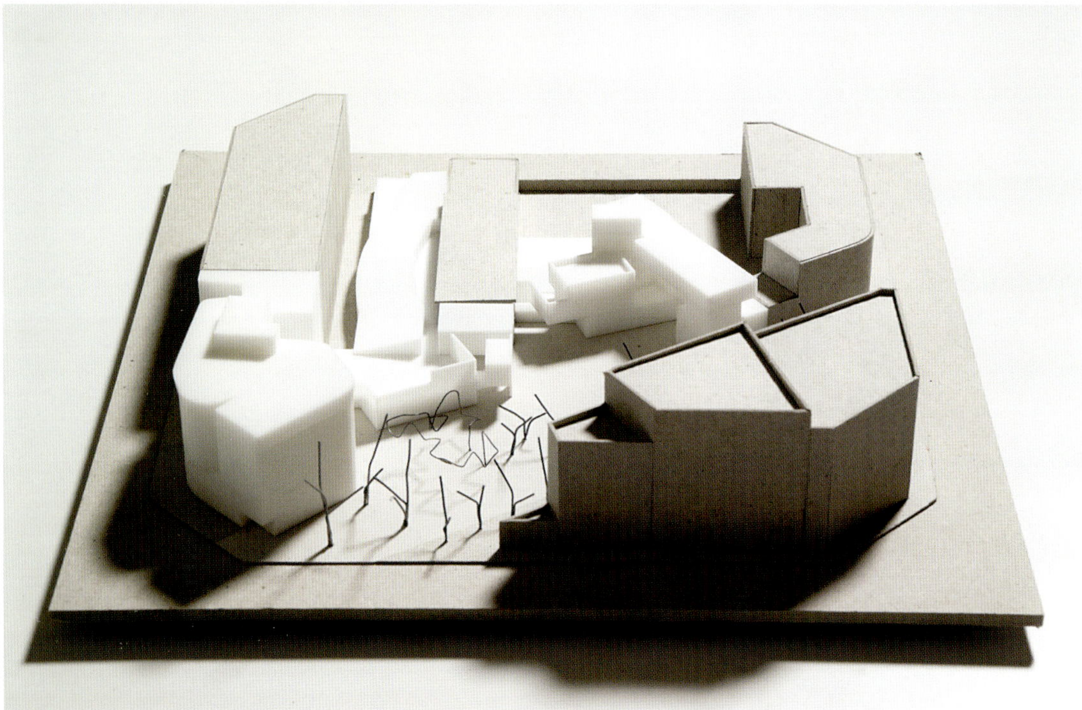

Location of Sant Antoni market. Conception: Pere Joan Ravetllat, Carme Ribas and Olga Schmid. Construction: Ravetllat-Ribas. 2009.

Fort Pienc city block. Conception: Josep Llinàs. Construction: Miquel Lluch. 2008.

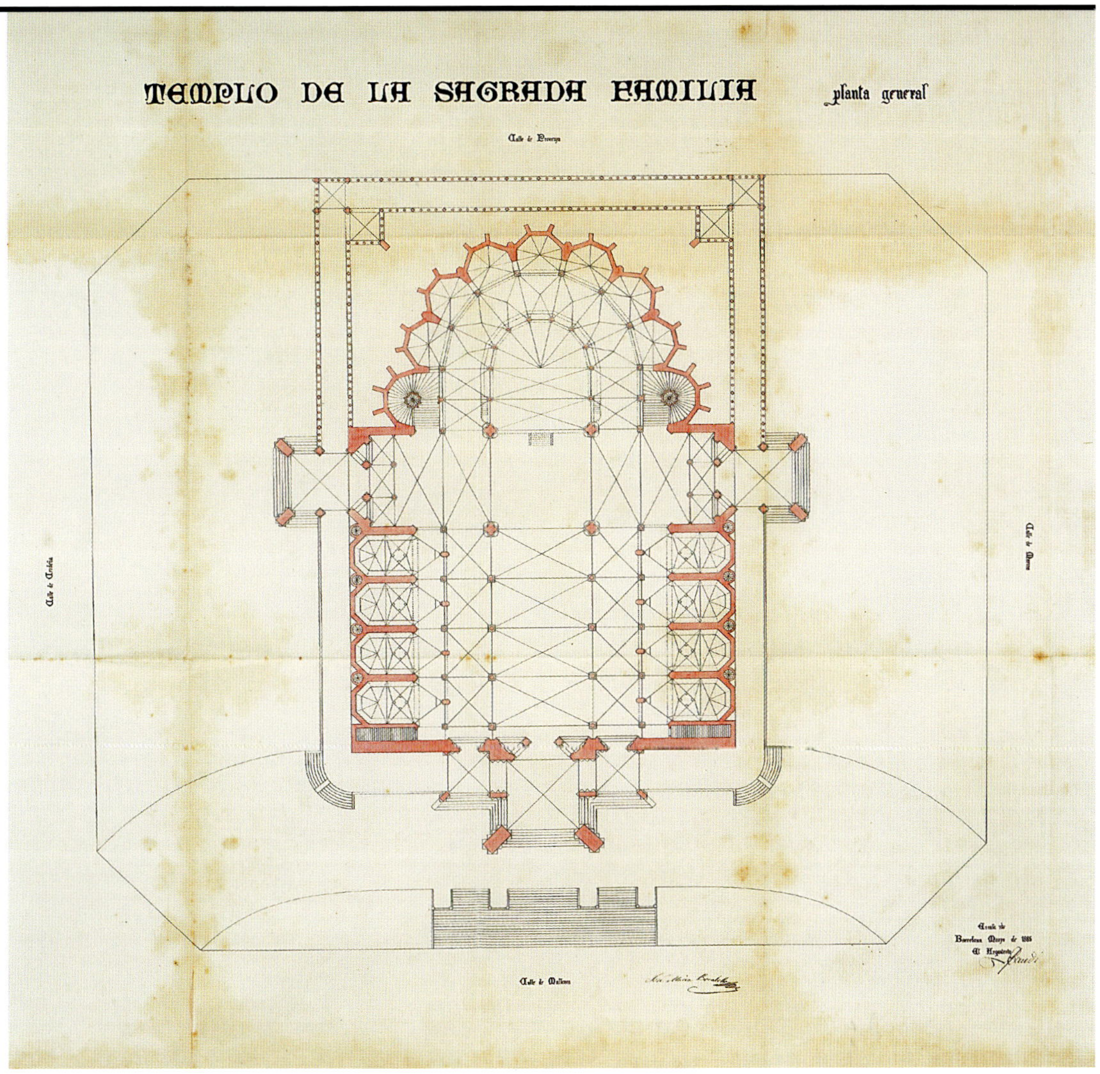

General floor plan of the Church of the Sagrada Família (1885). Architect: Antoni Gaudí. Source: Municipal Archive of the District of Sant Martí.

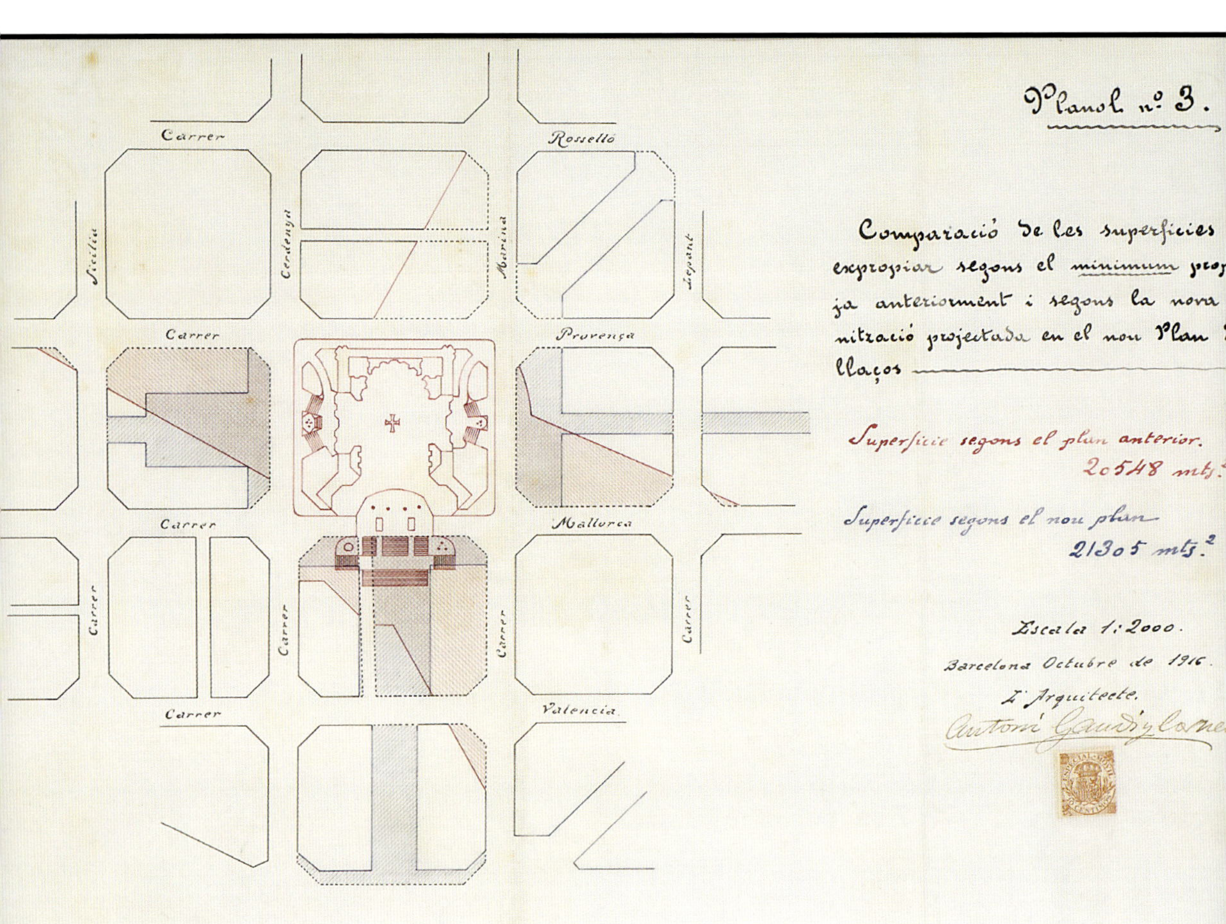

Comparison of the areas for expropriation involved in the urbanization plans outlined in the new Connections Plan (1916). Architect: Antoni Gaudí. Source: Municipal Administrative Archive. Barcelona City Council.

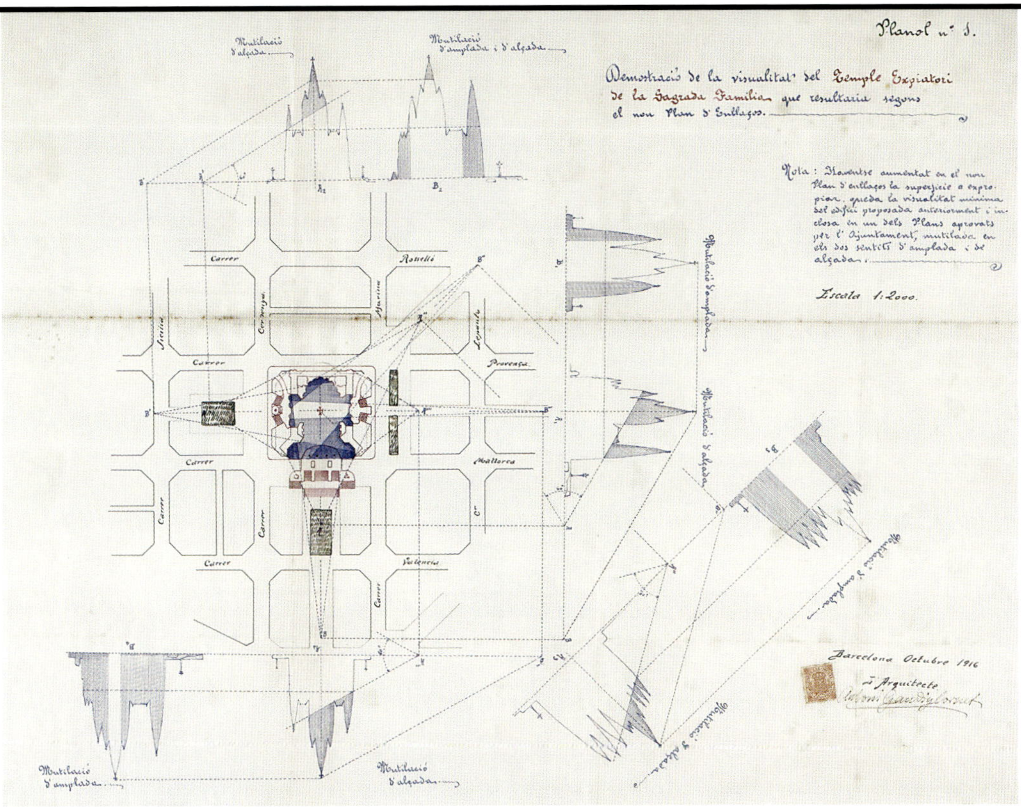

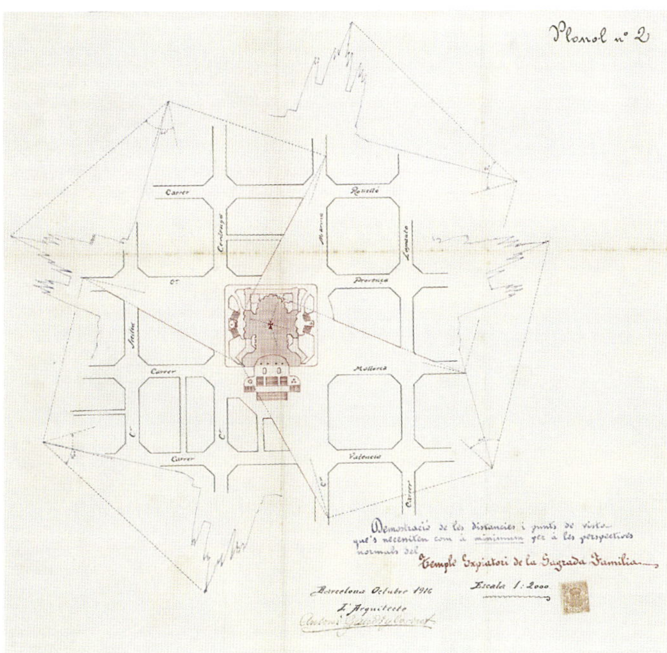

Demonstration of the lines of sight of the Sagrada Família expiatory temple produced by the implementation of the new Connections Plan (1916). Architect: Antoni Gaudí. Source: Municipal Administrative Archive. Barcelona City Council.

Demonstration of the distances and viewpoints required for normal views of the Sagrada Família (1916). Architect: Antoni Gaudí. Source: Municipal Administrative Archive. Barcelona City Council.

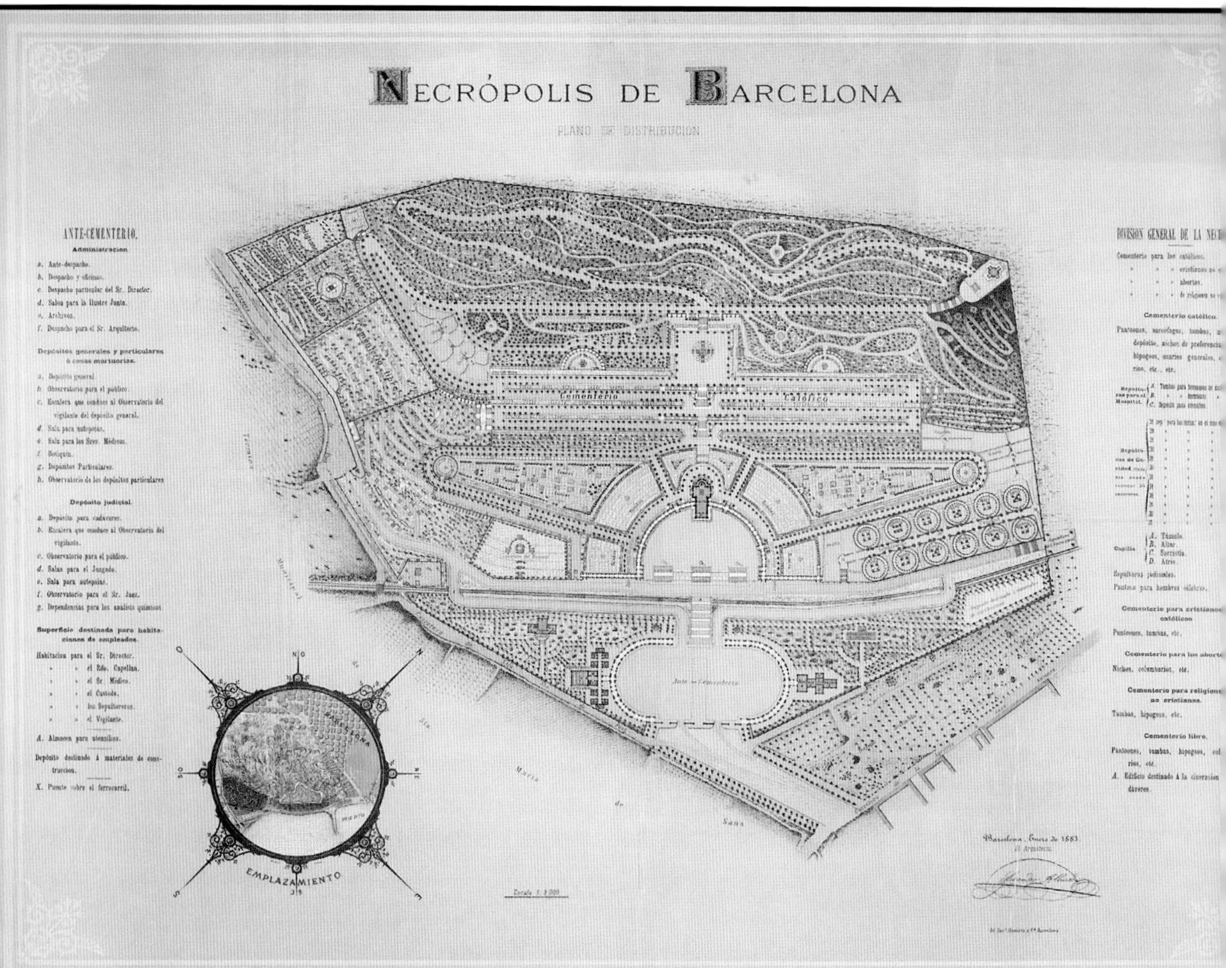

Barcelona's necropolis on the mountain of Montjuïc. Map showing the layout (1883). Architect: Leandre Albareda. Source: Arxiu Històric de la Ciutat de Barcelona.

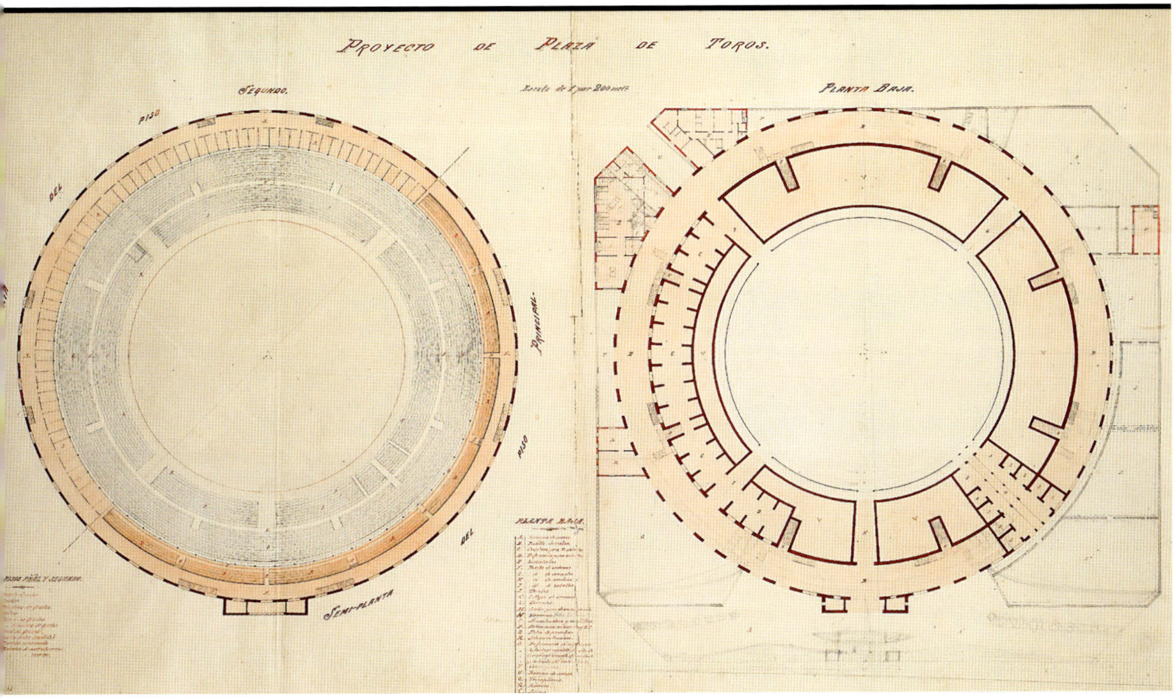

Proyecto de Plaza de Toros.

Segundo. Piso del Principal.

Planta Baja.

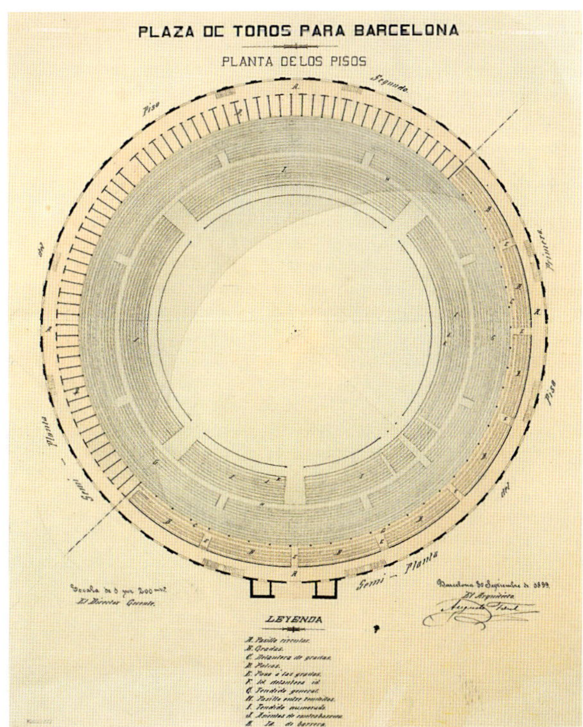

Project for Las Arenas bullring. Ground floor plan and half-floors on the first and second levels (1899-1900). Architect: August Font. Source: Historical Archive of the Col·legi d'Arquitectes de Catalunya.

Las Arenas bullring for Barcelona. Floor plan of upper levels (1899-1900). Architect: August Font. Source: Historical Archive of the Col·legi d'Arquitectes de Catalunya.

Law courts (1914). Photograph: Enric Castellà. Source: Arxiu Fotogràfic de Barcelona

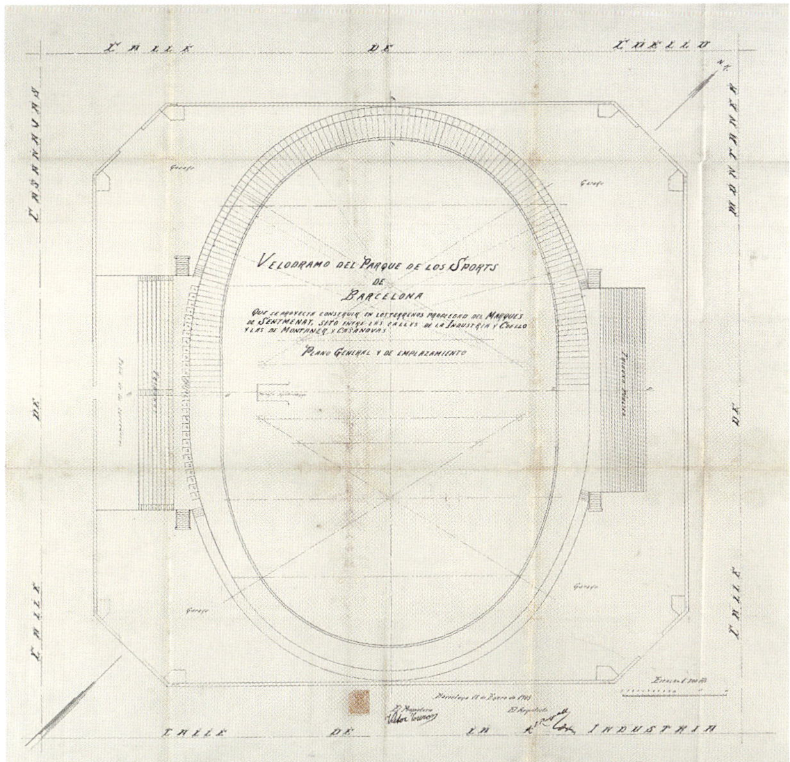

Model of Barcelona's old cycle track by the architect Manel Joaquim Raspall. Conception: model made on the occasion of the exhibition "M.J. Raspall, arquitecte (1887-1938)" [M.J. Raspall, architect (1887-1938)], produced by the Centre Cultural de Granollers (Fundació la Caixa). Model: ETSAV-UPC model workshop. 1997.

Plant and location of the old Barcelona velodrome (1909). Architect: Manuel Joaquim Raspall. Source: Municipal Administrative Archive. Barcelona City Council.

Hospital de la Santa Creu and Sant Pau. In the background, construction of the Sagrada Família (1902)
Photograph: Joaquim Morelló. Source: Photographic Archive of the Centre Excursionista de Catalunya.

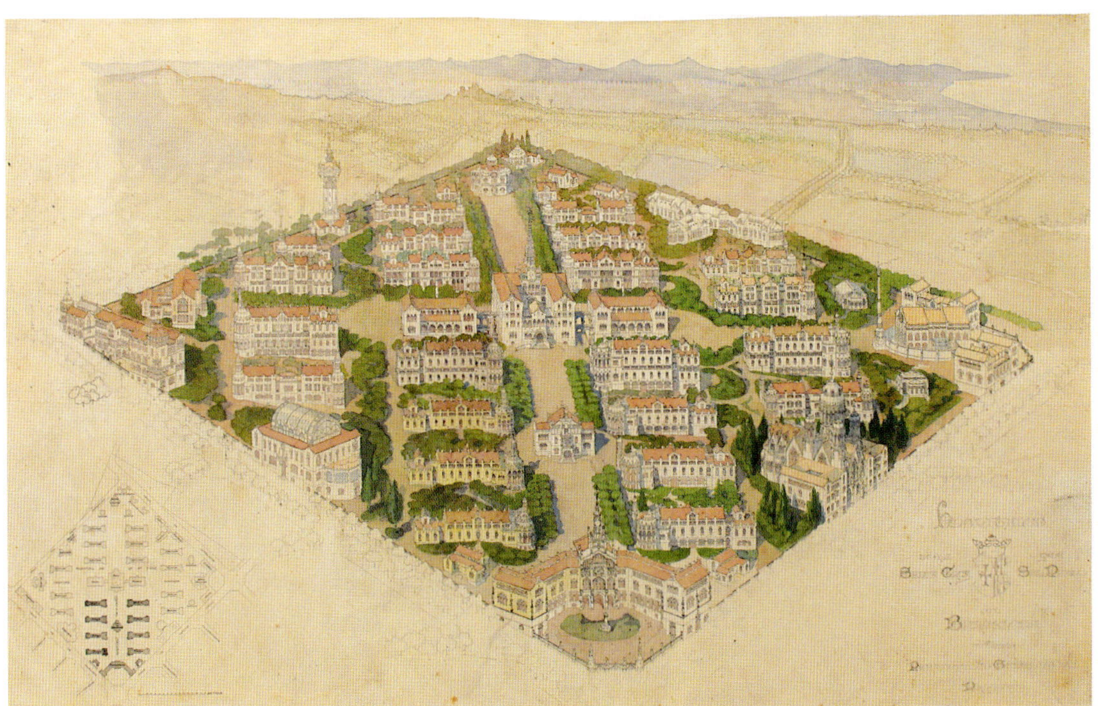

Hospital de la Santa Creu and Sant Pau. Administrative pavilion, rear façade posterior (1901-1903). Architect: Lluís Domènech i Montaner. Source: Historical Archive of the Col·legi d'Arquitectes de Catalunya.

Hospital de la Santa Creu and Sant Pau. Perspective of the complex (1901-1903). Architect: Lluís Domènech i Montaner. Source: Historical Archive of the Col·legi d'Arquitectes de Catalunya.

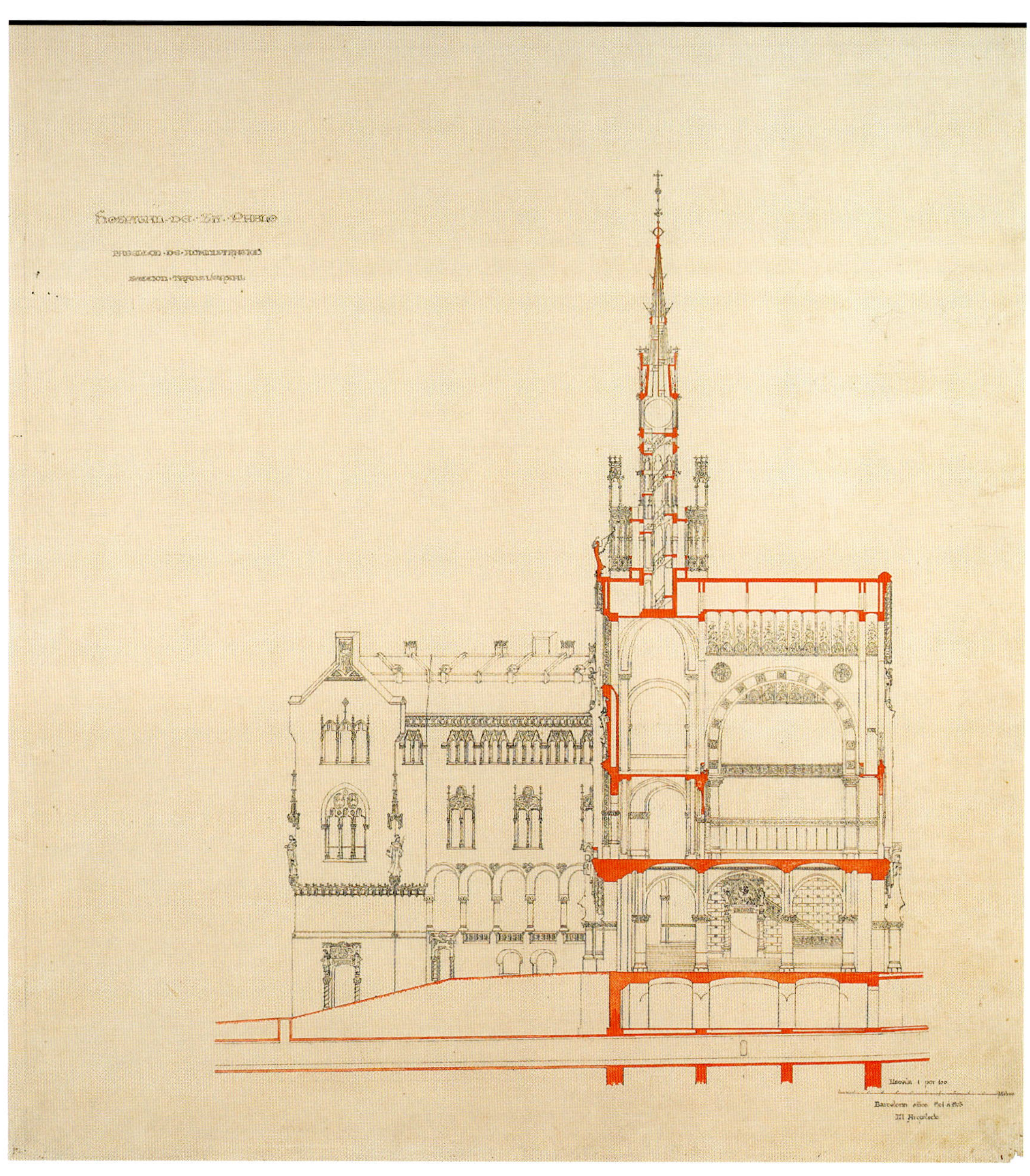

Hospital de la Santa Creu i Sant Pau. Administrative pavilion, cross-section (1901-1903). Architect: Lluís Domènech i Montaner. Source: Historical Archive of the Col·legi d'Arquitectes de Catalunya.

Workshop model of the Hospital de la Santa Creu i Sant Pau and renovation of the complex. Conception: Esteve Bonell, Josep Maria Gil, José Luis Canosa, Quico Rius and Sílvia Barberà. Model: the architects. 1997-1998.

green spaces_

"Urbanize the rural and *rurizing* the urban."

(I. Cerdà: *Teoría General de la Urbanización*, 1867)

Trees and green spaces as vital instruments in the "rurization" of the urban phenomenon

This principle meant, firstly, extending city centres in such a way that the new fabrics were run through by a system of green spaces at all scales. Secondly, it involved designing all streets to have trees[1] and all city blocks to have gardens at their centres.[2]

Over the years, the model of green spaces proposed by Cerdà has seen the occupation of the courtyards at the centre of the city blocks and the loss of large parks such as the one near the river Besòs and on the site of the racetrack, and smaller ones that have been replaced by facilities.

In recent years, the urbanization of the Passeig Marítim seafront, partially substituting the Parc del Besòs,[3] the new design of Avinguda Diagonal as a parkway and the recovery of the courtyards at the centre of city blocks, along with the planting of trees on rooftop terraces and the extension of urban allotments, could mark a return of Cerdà's Eixample to the principle of "rurizing" the urban.

The evolution of green spaces throughout the 150 years of the Eixample

Before Cerdà's Remodelling and Extension Project, recreational spaces were located on the outskirts of the old town. The Esplanade near the Citadel and the gardens to either side of Passeig de Gràcia were the favourite leisure spots for the people of Barcelona.[4] Later, other spaces on the edges of the Extension Project were turned into places for recreation, such as the land at the foot of the mountain of Montjuïc, Turó Park and Tibidabo.

The Parc de la Ciutadella was designed by Josep Fontserè[5] in 1873, and the other spaces that Cerdà had envisaged as parks were preserved until the 1888 International Exhibition.

On the occasion of the 1929 International Exhibition, the mountain of Montjuïc,[6] ceased to be a military sector and was developed, and, under the auspices of Jaussely's Plan, symbolic avenues[7] such as Avinguda Gaudí were created in the Eixample.

The approval of the 1953 County Plan took the planned city beyond the Extension Project to develop a series of parks: Turó de la Peira, Cervantes, El Putget and La Guineueta, among others.

The 1976 Pla General Metropolità de Barcelona [Barcelona Master Plan] salvaged industrial areas for urban parks such as L'Espanya Industrial, Parc del Clot[8] and Parc de la Pegaso. The 1992 Olympic Games brought a new lease of life to the construction of parks, such as La Nova Icària, Les Glòries, La Trinitat[9] and Port Olímpic.

[1] See fig. page 222 | [2] See fig. page 223 | [3] See fig. page 243 | [4] See fig. page 224 | [5] See fig. page 226 | [6] See fig. page 233 [7] See fig. page 220 (1897-1953 period) and page 228 & 236 | [8] See fig. page 240 | [9] See fig. page 242

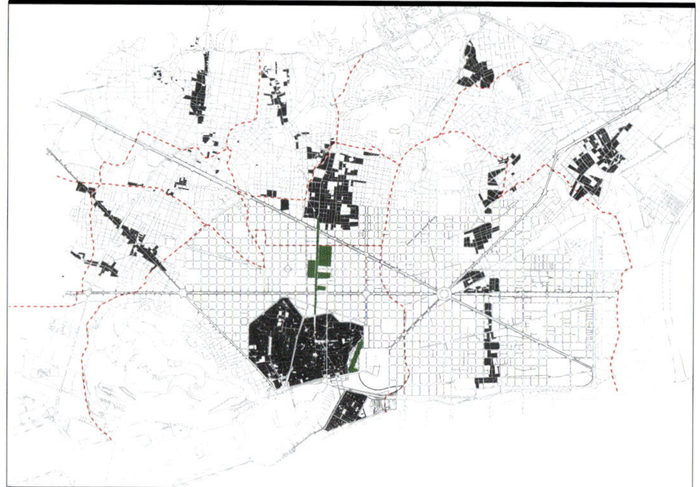

1840 -1859

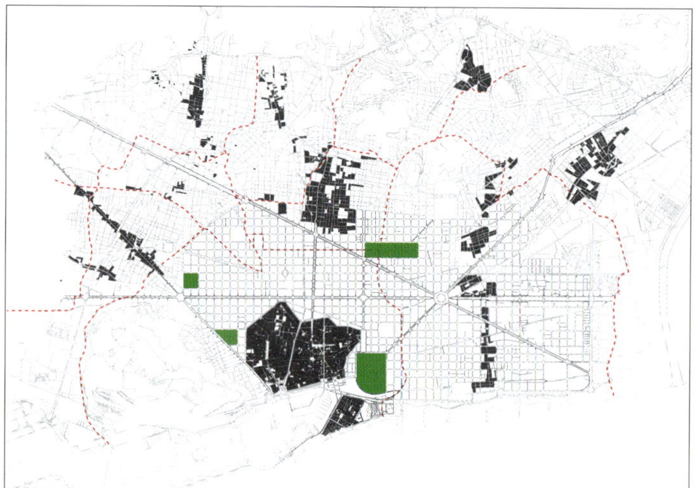

1859-1885

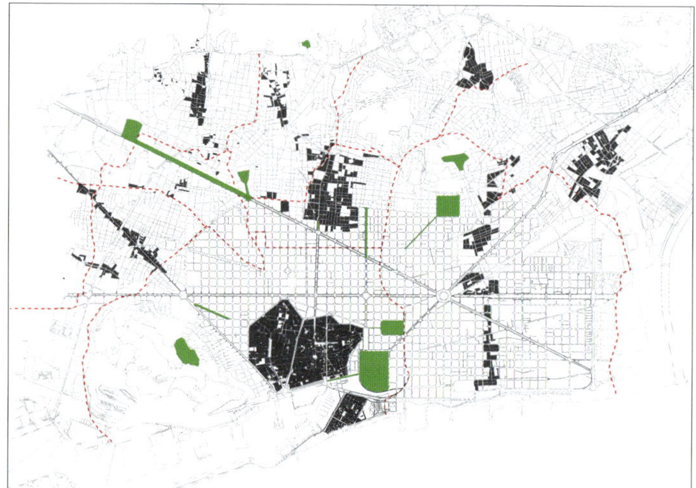

1897-1953

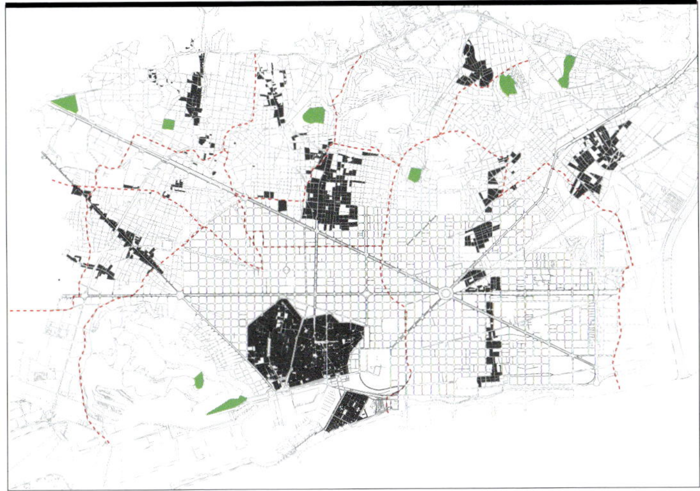

1953-1976

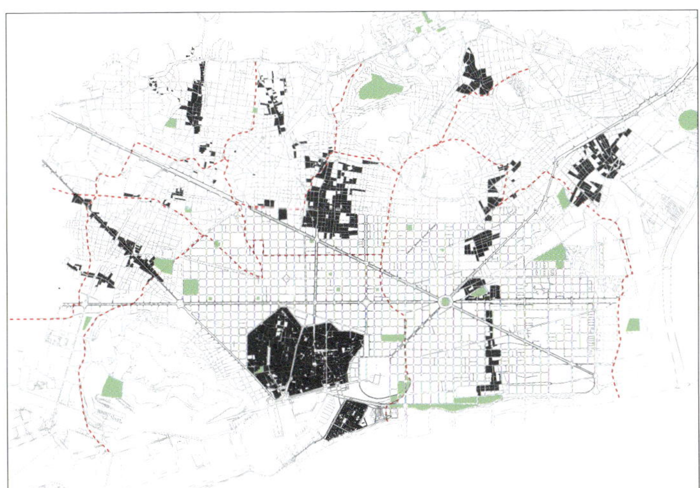

1976-1992

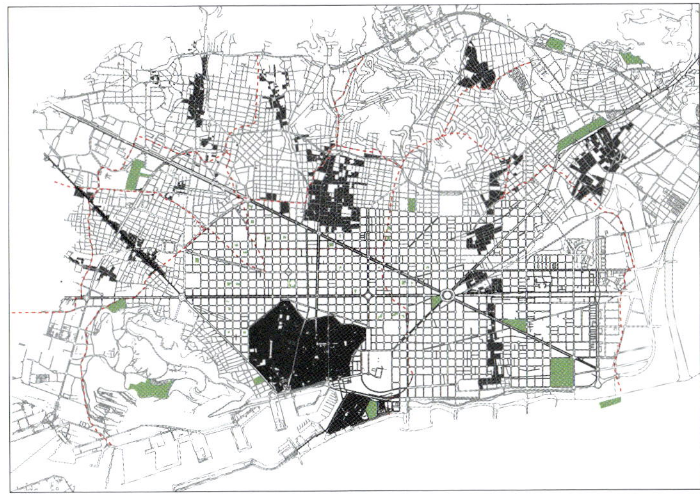

1992-2009

Evolution of green spaces in Barcelona. Produced for the exhibition

Trees and green spaces as vital instruments of "rurization"

Cerdà had a clear conception of the function of trees in green spaces: "Plantations of trees are [...] the most effective way of preventing the infection of the ground, draining the site and even purifying the atmosphere." He considered the use of trees in the street to be an essential element of relation with nature: "Green spaces reduce the density of the population [...] and must be seen as vast deposits of air that represent a powerful contribution to the circulation of air in the streets and houses." Today, the emphasis is on tree-lined streets and parkways.

Cerdà also thought it "vital that each city block should have as its minimum [green space] an area equal to that of the built land". The present-day recovery of the courtyards at the centre of city blocks plays a vital role in complying with the principle of "rurizing" the urban.

Cerdà summed up the principle as follows: "Each street should have a small square, each neighbourhood, a full-sized square, and each quarter, a garden."

Trees in a street in the Eixample. Photograph: Rafael Vargas. 2005. Source: Rafael Vargas Holdings

Trees at the centre of an Eixample city block. Photograph: Rosa Feliu. 2003. Source: Rosa Feliu Holdings

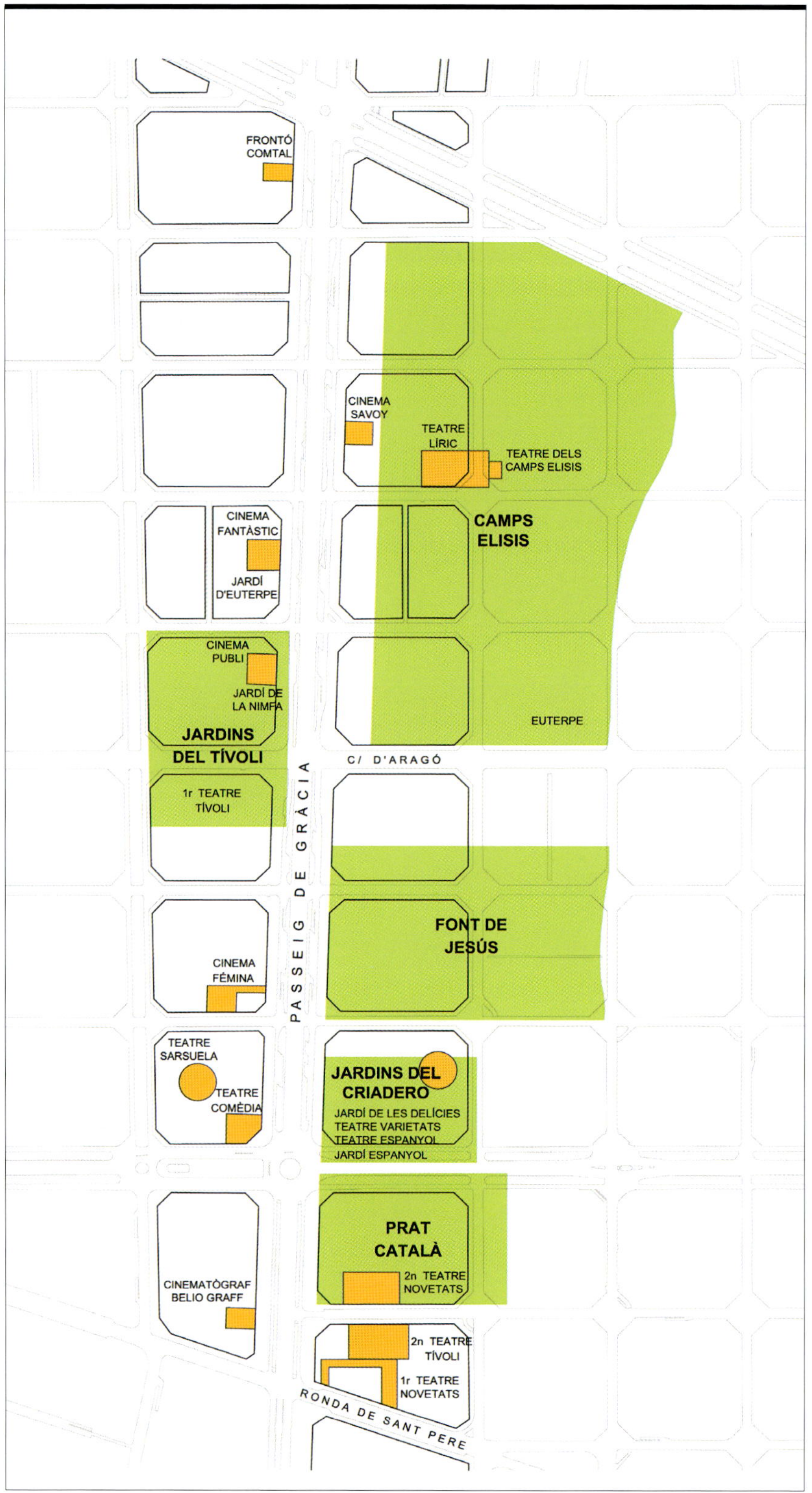

Green spaces and amenities on Passeig de Gràcia in around 1860. Produced for the exhibition.

Parc de la Ciutadella: the first major park in the Eixample

The area originally designated for Parc de la Ciutadella in Cerdà's Project was situated above Avenida Meridiana, which reached all the way to the Port. In the end, the park was built on the grounds of the Ciutadella to take advantage of its developed areas but still occupied the same amount of space as initially provisioned by Cerdà. The project would come to fruition under Josep Fontserè in 1873 and additional structures were built for the 1888 International Exhibition.

Engraving of the demolition of the Citadel (undated). Thomas Pedro. Source: Fernando Marzá-Neus Moyano Collection.

Space occupied by the former military Citadel prior to the park project (1865-1869). Photograph: unknown author. Source: Arxiu Fotogràfic de Barcelona.

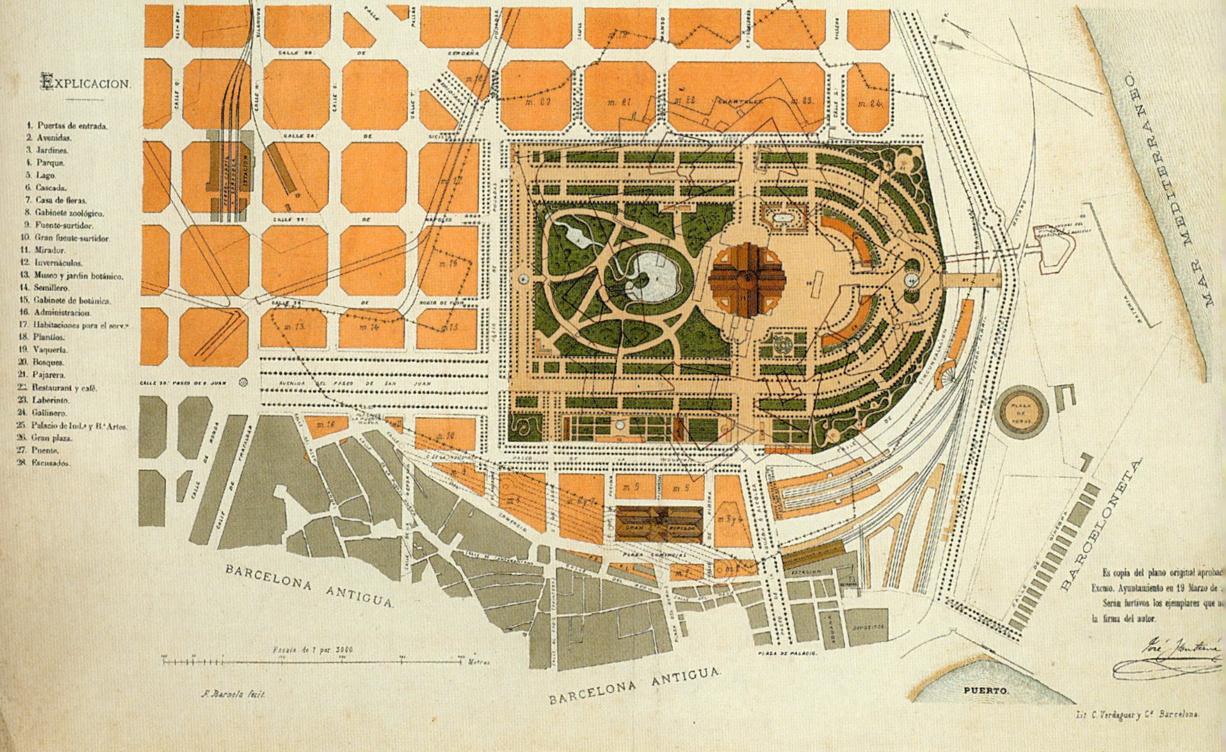

1888 International Exhibition in Barcelona. General plan of the installations (1872). Architect: Josep Fontserè. Source: Historical Archive of the Col·legi d'Arquitectes de Catalunya.

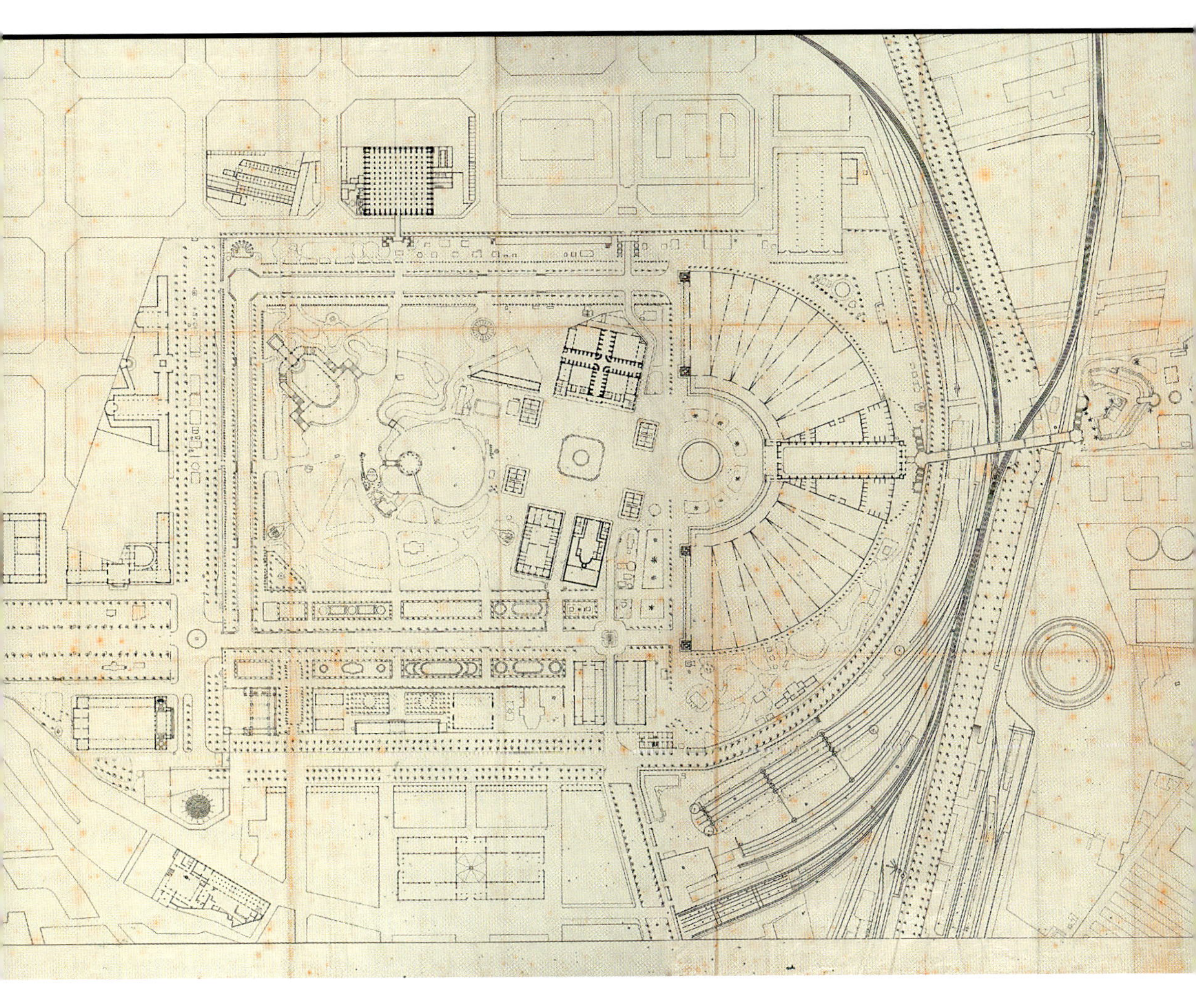

1888 International Exhibition in Barcelona. General plan of the installations (undated). Architect: Elies Rogent. Source: Historical Archive of the Col·legi d'Arquitectes de Catalunya.

Jaussely's Plan of the Preliminary Connections Project and the boulevards

Following the annexation of municipalities around Barcelona, the city was to be planned. To this end, an international competition was assembled for the Plan of the Preliminary Connections which León Jaussely won in 1905. This did not affect Cerdá Project which continued in effect until 1953. Nonetheless Jaussely's preliminary project had a strong influence and for the 1929 Universal Exhibition some of the most symbolic avenues of the Eixample were displayed:

- Avinguda de Gaudí between the Sagrada Familia and Hospital de Sant Pau.
- The *Jardinets de Gràcia*.
- The gardens of Passeig de Sant Joan.
- Avinguda de Mistral.
- Avinguda del Marquès de l'Argentera.
- The axis that connects the Arc de Triomf with the Estació del Nord.
- Avinguda Diagonal between Plaça de Francesc Macià and Parc de Pedralbes.

Project for a boulevard proposed by Jaussely in the Preliminary Connections Project for Barcelona: perspective (1903-1905). Architect: Léon Jaussely. Source: Centre d'archives d'architecture du xxe siècle. Cité de l'architecture et du patrimoine.

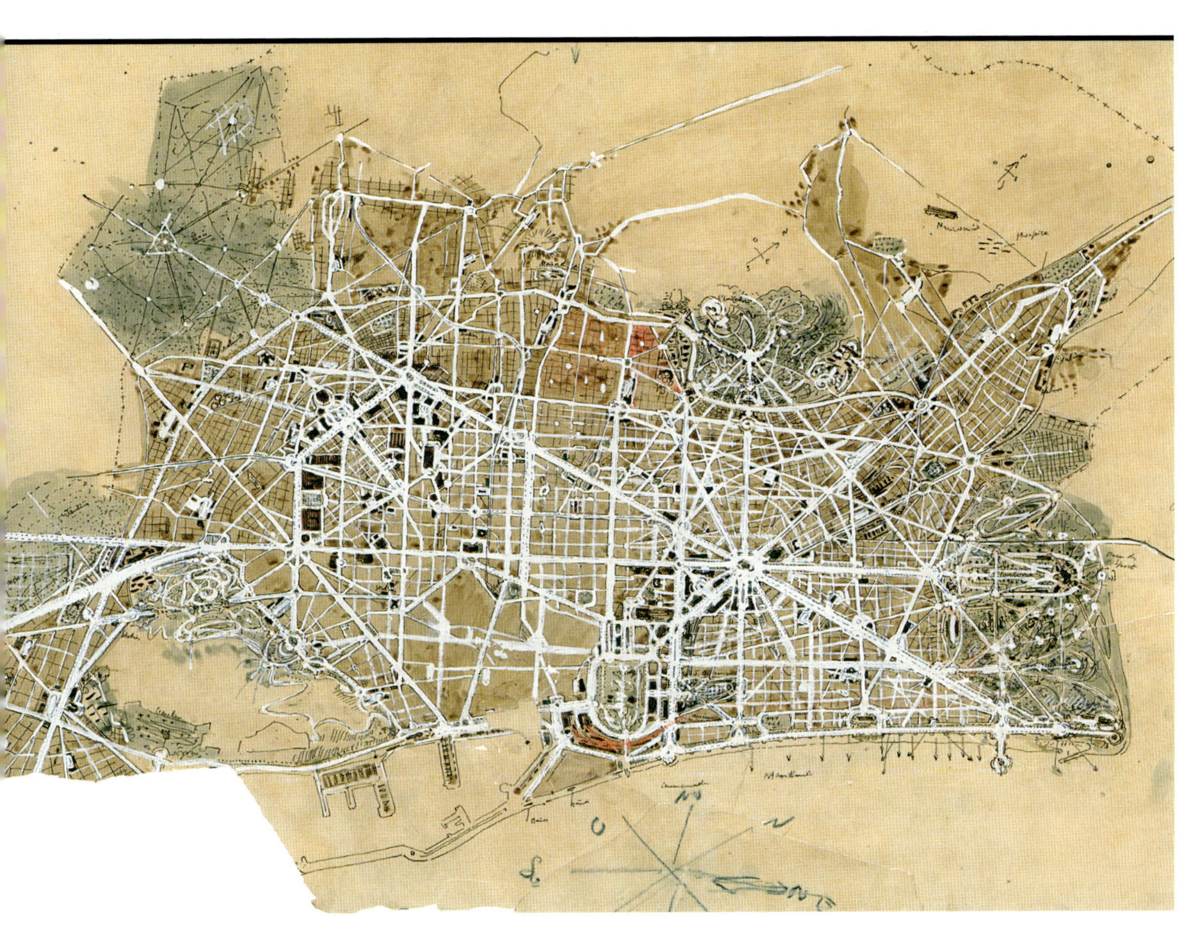

Plan of the Preliminary Connections Project for Barcelona at a scale of 1:20.000 (1903-1907). Architect: Léon Jaussely. Source: Centre d'archives d'architecture du xxe siècle. Cité de l'architecture et du patrimoinees d'architecture du XXe siècle. Cité de l'architecture et du patrimoine.

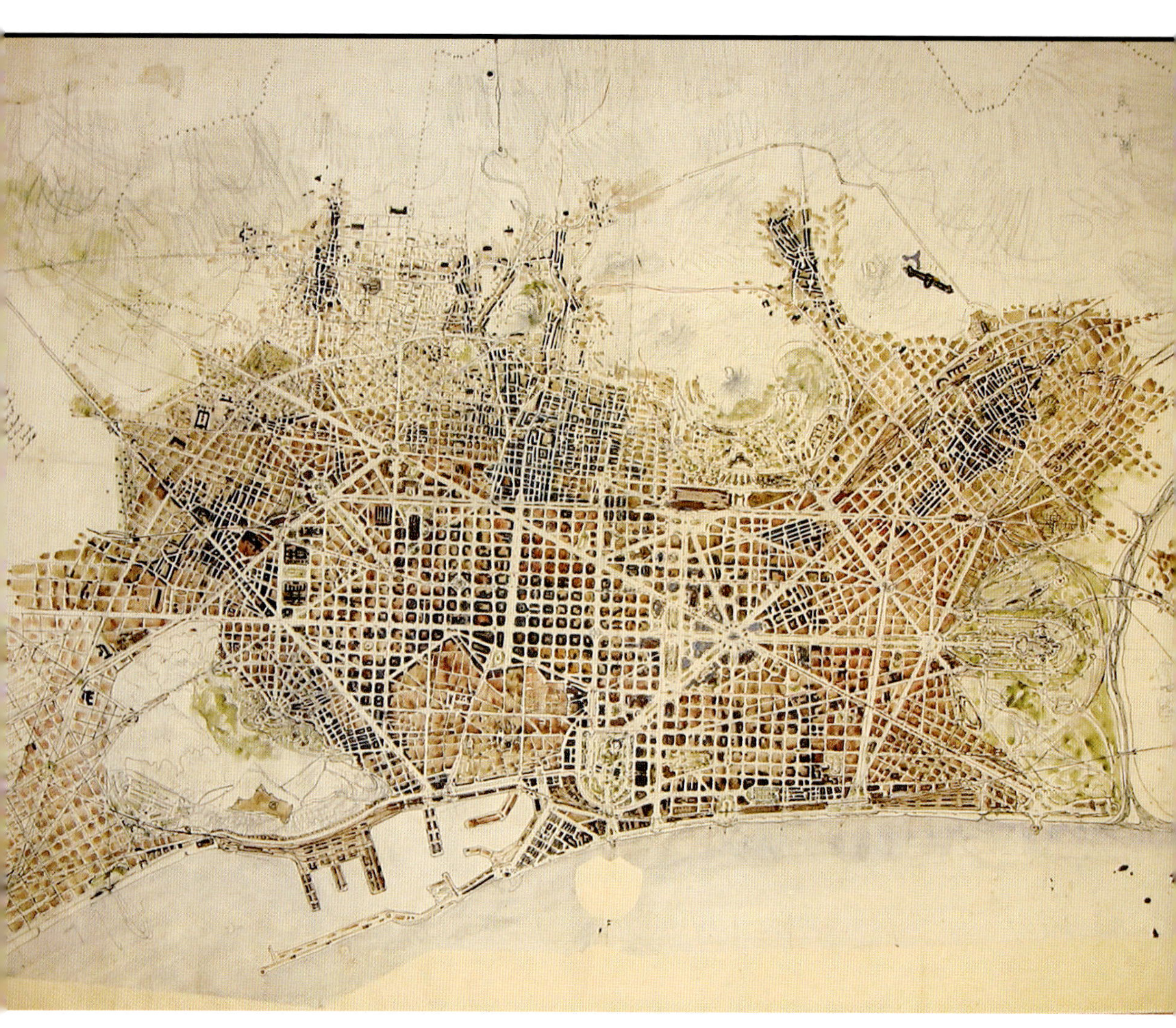

Plan of the Preliminary Connections Project for Barcelona at a scale of 1/10.000 (1903-1907). Architect: Léon Jaussely. Source: Centre d'archives d'architecture du xxe siècle. Cité de l'architecture et du patrimoine.

The parks of Cerdà's Eixample: the tradition of Forestier and Rubió i Tudurí

The designs of J.N.C. Forestier and his student Nicolau Rubió i Tudurí are the main influence on Barcelona's parks. The most important examples are jardins de Laribal in Montjuïc created in 1909, the Teatre Grec (1922) and other parks outside the Eixample such as Parc del Guinardó (1916). This tradition was continued by Rubió i Tudurí with Parc de Pedralbes (1926) and Turó Parc (1934).

Elevation and section of the Font del Gat fountain (1917). Architect: Jean-Claude Nicolas Forestier. Source: Municipal Administrative Archive. Barcelona City Council.

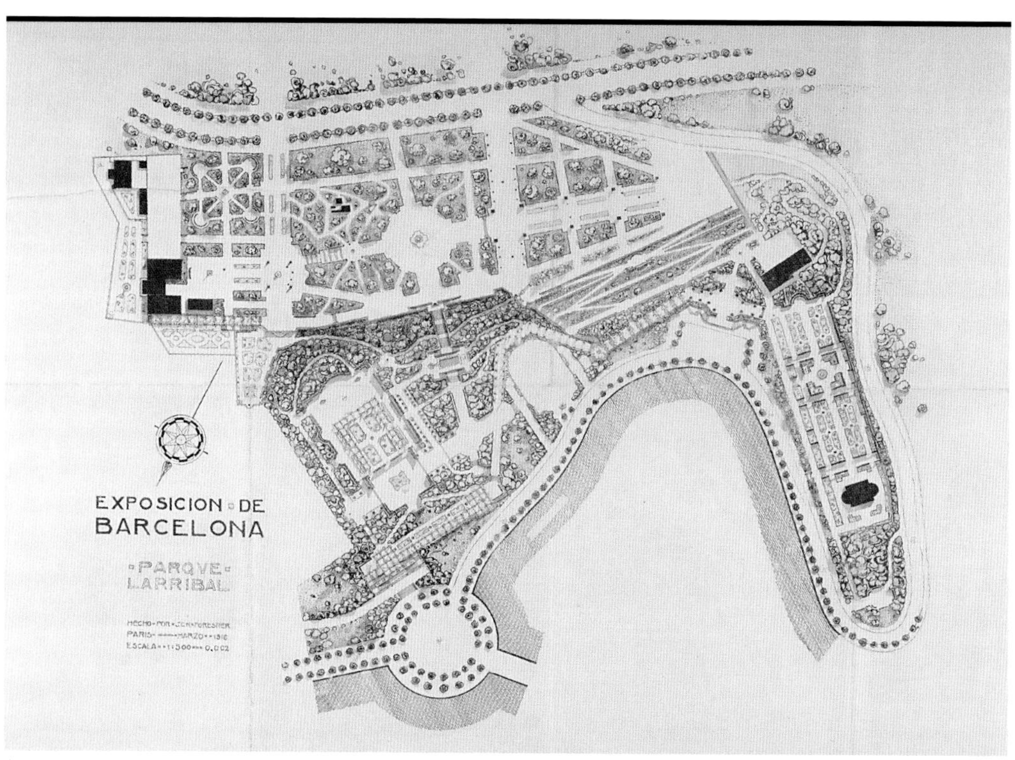

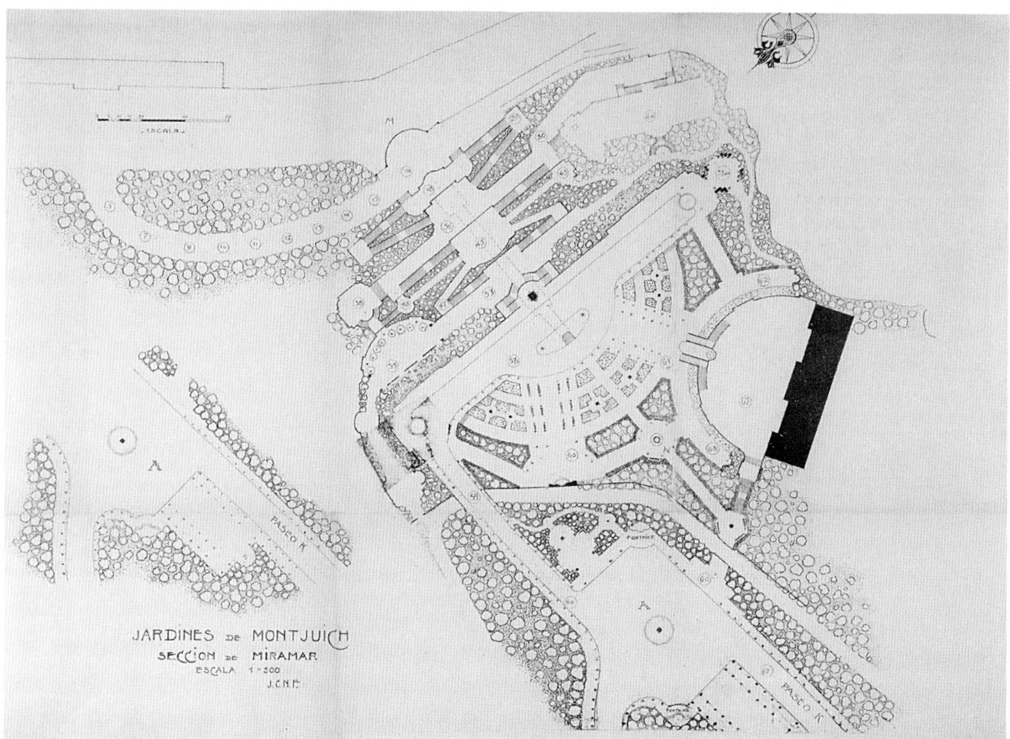

Plan of the location of the Jardins de Laribal (1916). Architect: Jean-Claude Nicolas Forestier. Source: Municipal Administrative Archive. Barcelona City Council.

Plan of the Jardins de Miramar, on Montjuïc (1929). Architect: Jean-Claude Nicolas Forestier. Source: Municipal Administrative Archive. Barcelona City Council.

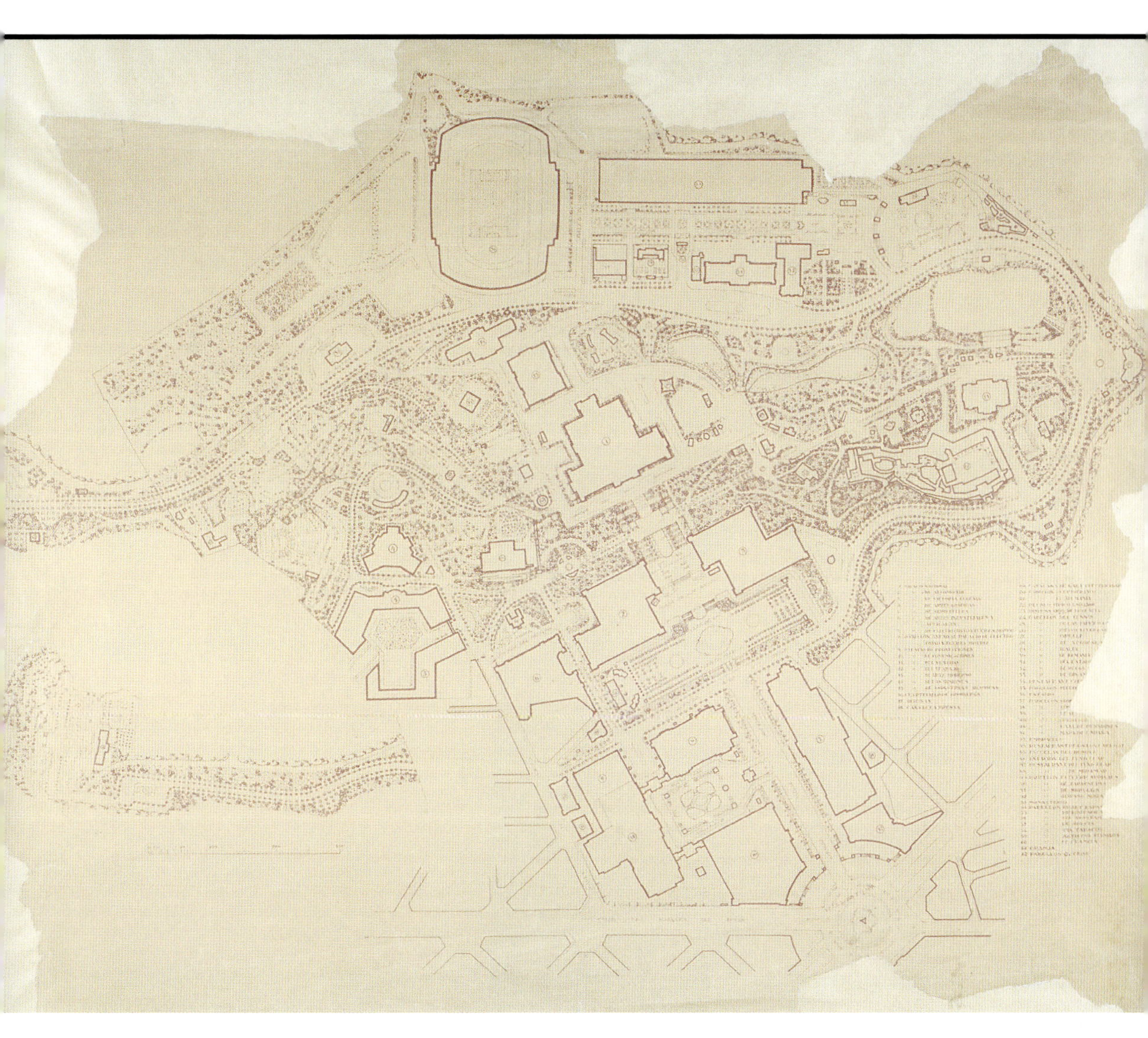

Plan from the Gardens Project for the mountain of Montjuïc designed by Forestier for the 1929 International Exhibition. Architect: Josep Puig i Cadafalch**.** Source: Arxiu Històric de la Ciutat de Barcelona.

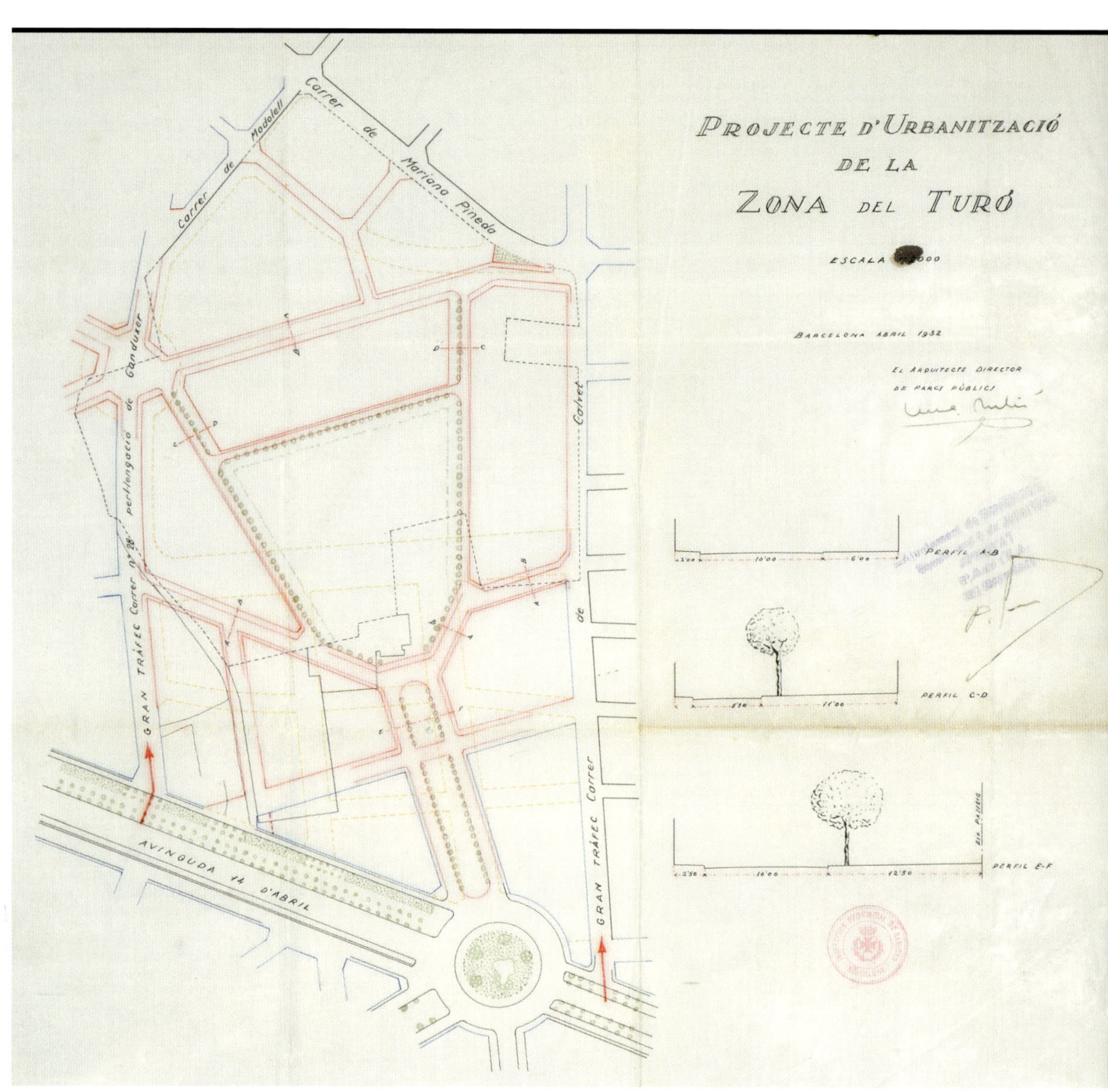

Project for the urbanization of the Turó area (1932). Architect: Nicolau Maria Rubió i Tudurí. Source: Municipal Administrative Archive. Barcelona City Council.

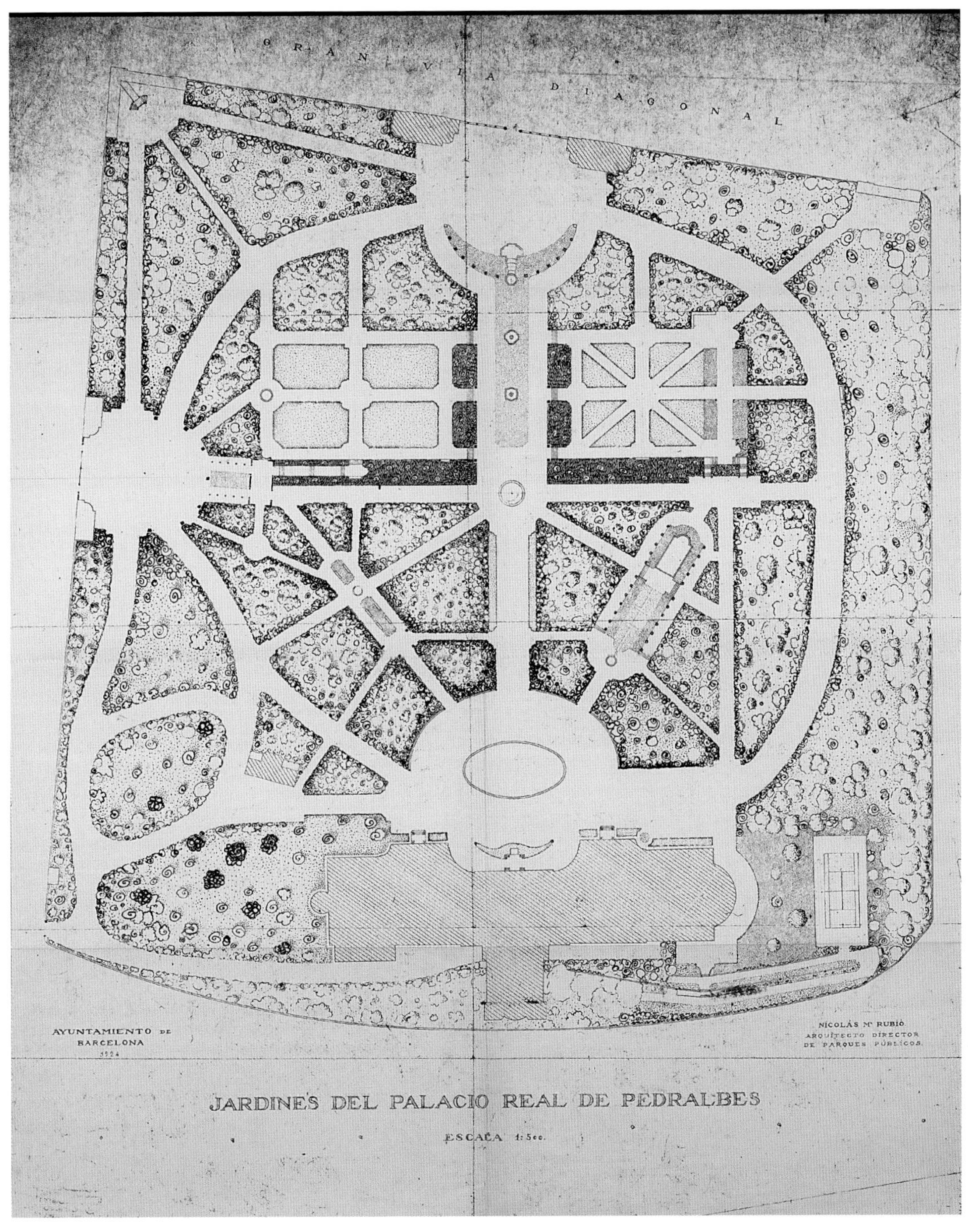

Floor plan of the gardens of Pedralbes Royal Palace (1924). Architect: Nicolau Maria Rubió i Tudurí. Source: Historical archive of the Col·legi d'Arquitectes de Catalunya.

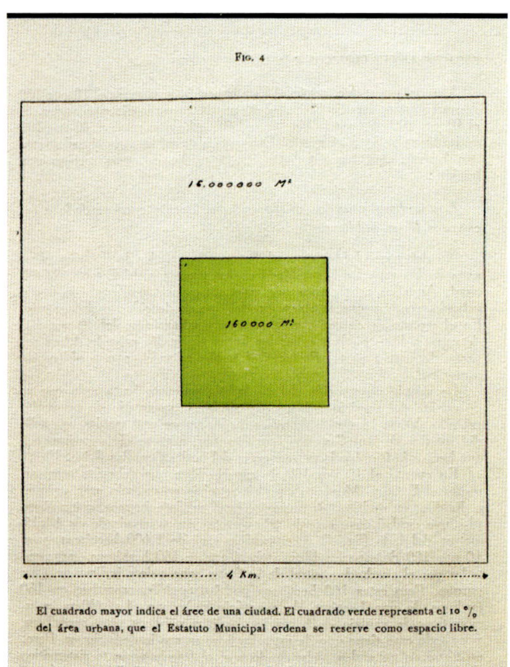

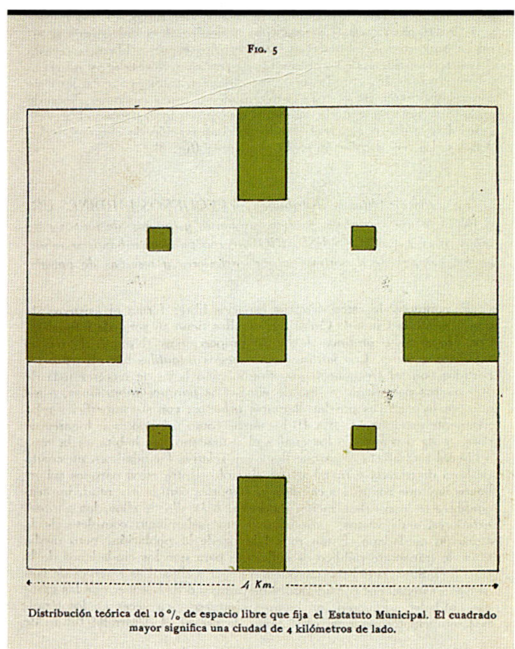

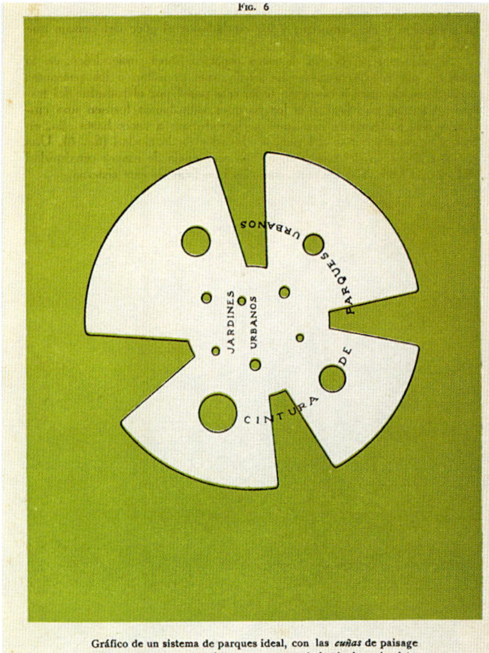

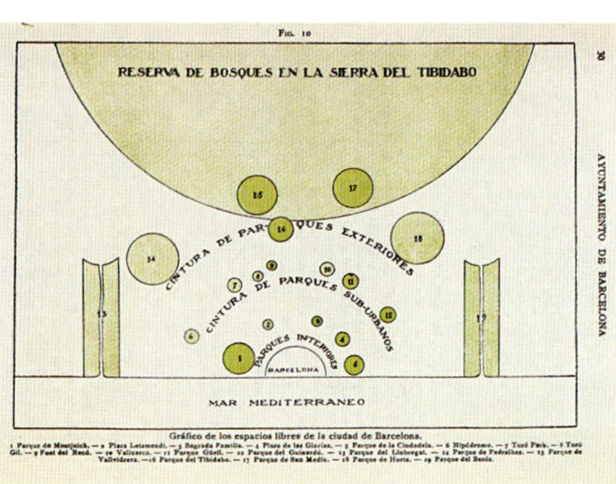

"El problema de los espacios libres: divulgación de su teoría y notas sobre su solución pràctica [The problem of open spaces: dissemination of the theory and notes on practical solutions]." 9th National Congress of Architects (1926). Architect: Nicolau Maria Rubió i Tudurí. Source: Fernando Marzá-Neus Moyano Collection.

Composition of photographs of gardens on the mountain of Montjuïc and for Pedralbes Royal Palace in around 1980. 2009. Produced for the exhibition.

Model of the Olympic Ring Project on the mountain of Montjuïc. Conception: Federico Correa, Alfonso Milà, Joan Margarit and Carles Buxader. Model: Maquetes Malberti. 1984. Source: Correa-Milà.

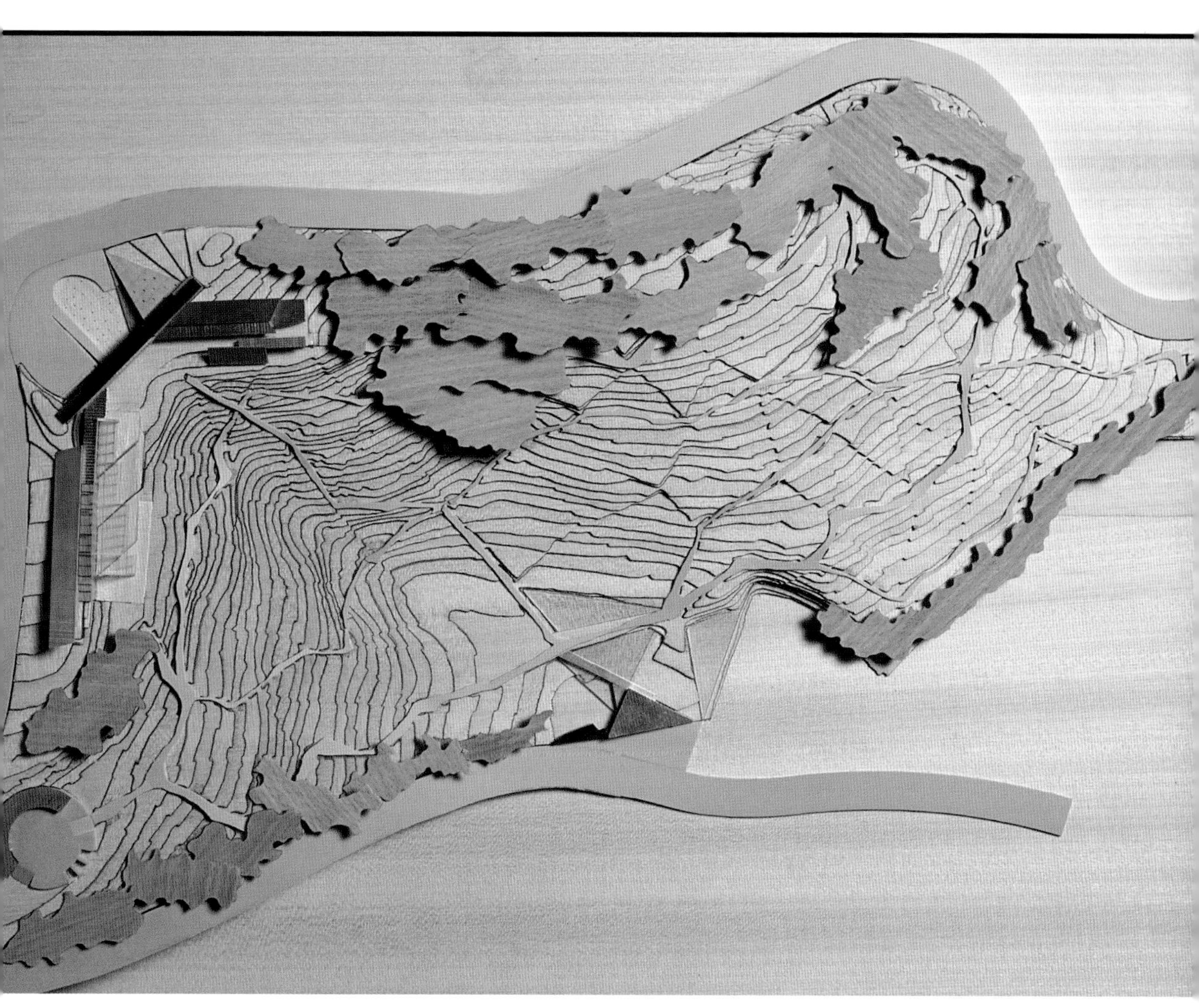

Model of the Botanical Gardens (competition entry). Conception: Carlos Ferrater. Model: Pere Pedrero. 1989. Source: Carlos Ferrater Partnership (OAB).

Parc del Clot. Architects: Dani Freixes and Vicente Miranda. Photograph: Jordi Todó / TAVISA. 1989.

Parc de l'Estació del Nord. Architects: Enric Pericas, Carme Fiol and Andreu Arriola. Photograph: Jordi Todó / TAVISA. 1995.

Park inside the Trinitat intersection. Civil Engineer: Manuel Herce, Architect: Batlle and Roig. Photograph: Jordi Todó / TAVISA. 1995.

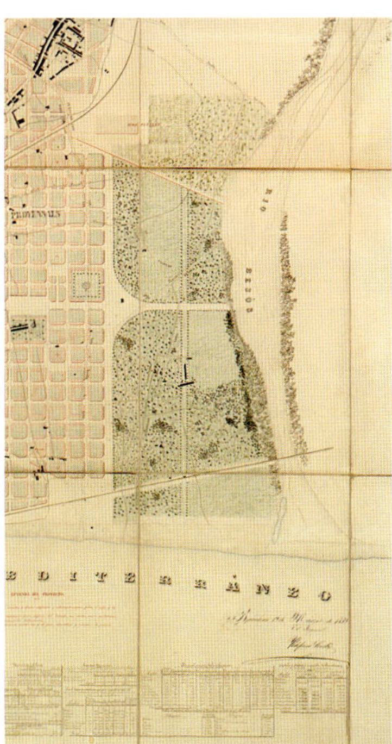

Parc del Litoral which includes the Port Olímpic and the MBM Parc de la Vila Olímpica projects; the Passeig Marítim project for the Icària and Bogatell beaches by Antonio Font and Jon Montero, and the Parc del Poblenou by Manuel Ruisánchez. Fotography: Jordi Todó / TAVISA, 2009.

Detail of Parc del Besòs as proposed by Cerdà in the 1859 Development and Expansion of Barcelona Project. Source Real Academia de Bellas Artes de San Fernando.

transport and city construction_

"Each means of locomotion generates a form of urbanization."

(I. Cerdà: *Teoría General de la Urbanización*, 1867)

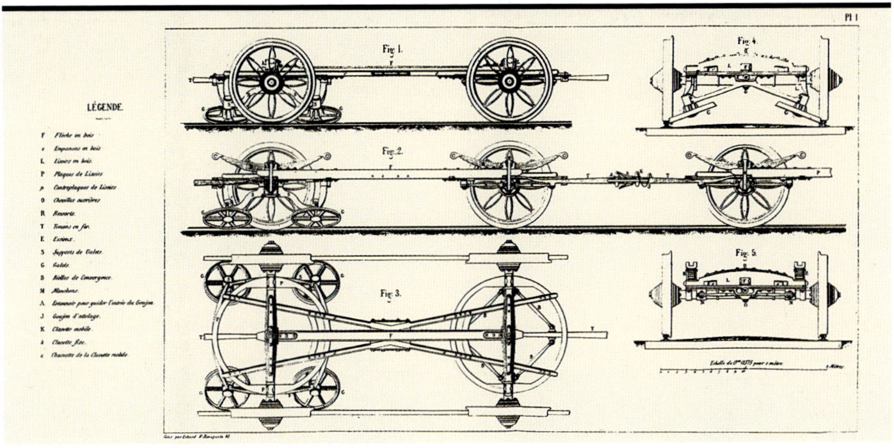

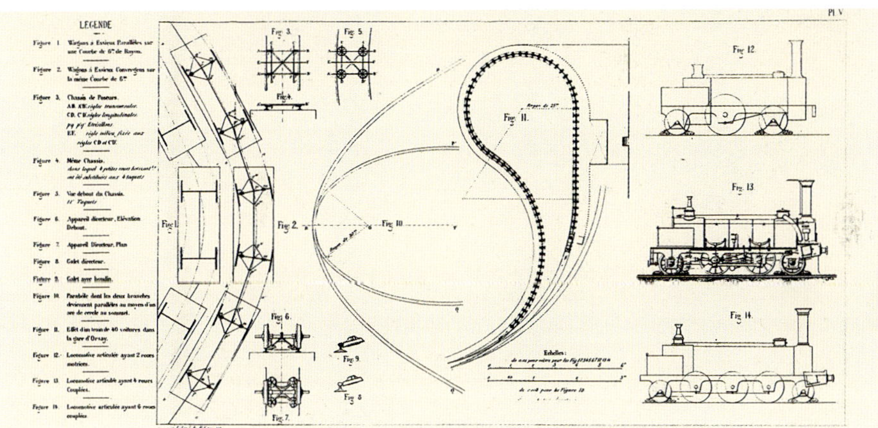

According to Cerdà, each new means of locomotion generates a new form of constructing the city, occupying the streets and new sectors to be urbanized, and therefore giving rise to a new, artificial topography.

During his time in Paris, Cerdà became acquainted with the railway designed using the Arnoux system, which allowed a small turning radius. He decided to introduce it to the Eixample to enable the railway to circulate and turn easily in its streets.

Cerdà used this patent in the 1863 Preliminary Docks Project, proposing his model of city in keeping with the new means of transport that was the railway. He designed a railway layout around the edge of the old town, connecting the various railway stations and maritime transport. He also carried through his maxim that "The railway will become part of the urbanization process", designing a combination of city blocks in the Eixample where the railway, which ran underground, could stop and take on goods every 250 m.

Arnoux's proposal for an articulated train, used by Cerdà in his railway projects. Source: M.C. Arnoux. *De la nécessité des économies*. Paris, 1860.

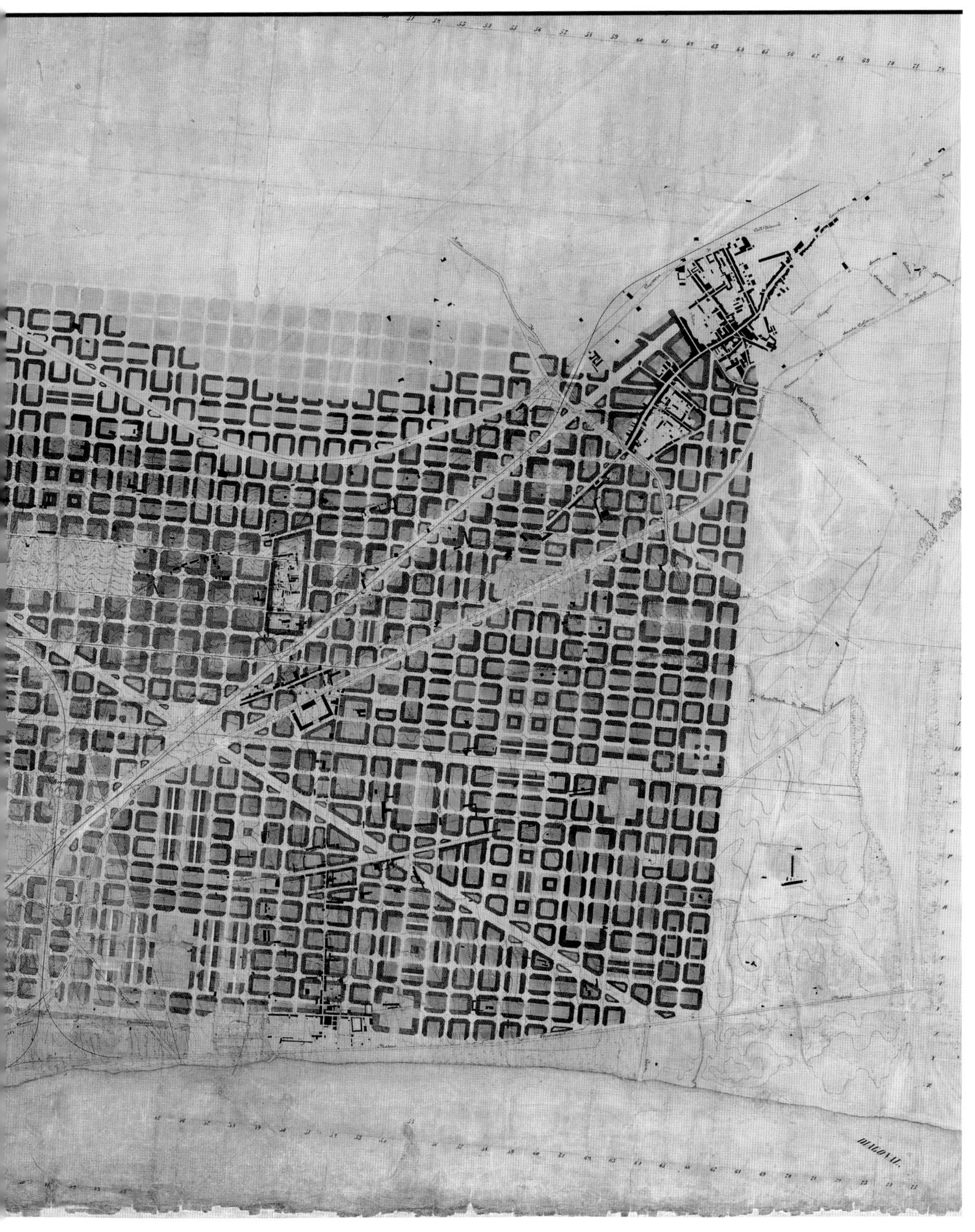

Map of the Barcelona extension of 1863 showing the transcendental connecting railway lines of Ildefons Cerdà. Author: Ildefons Cerdà. Source: Cerdà Legacy. Arxiu Històric de la Ciutat de Barcelona.

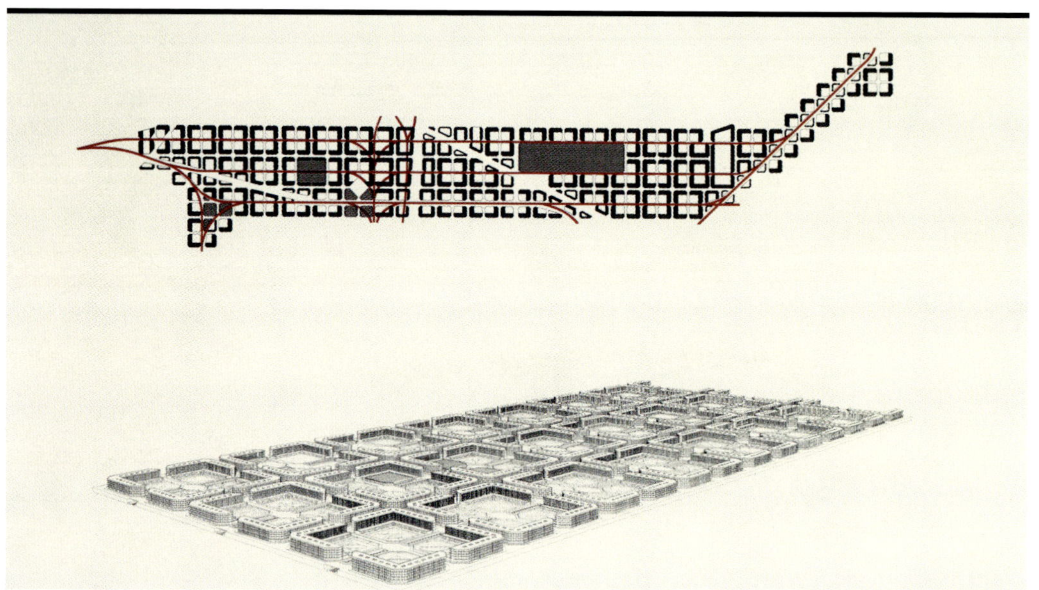

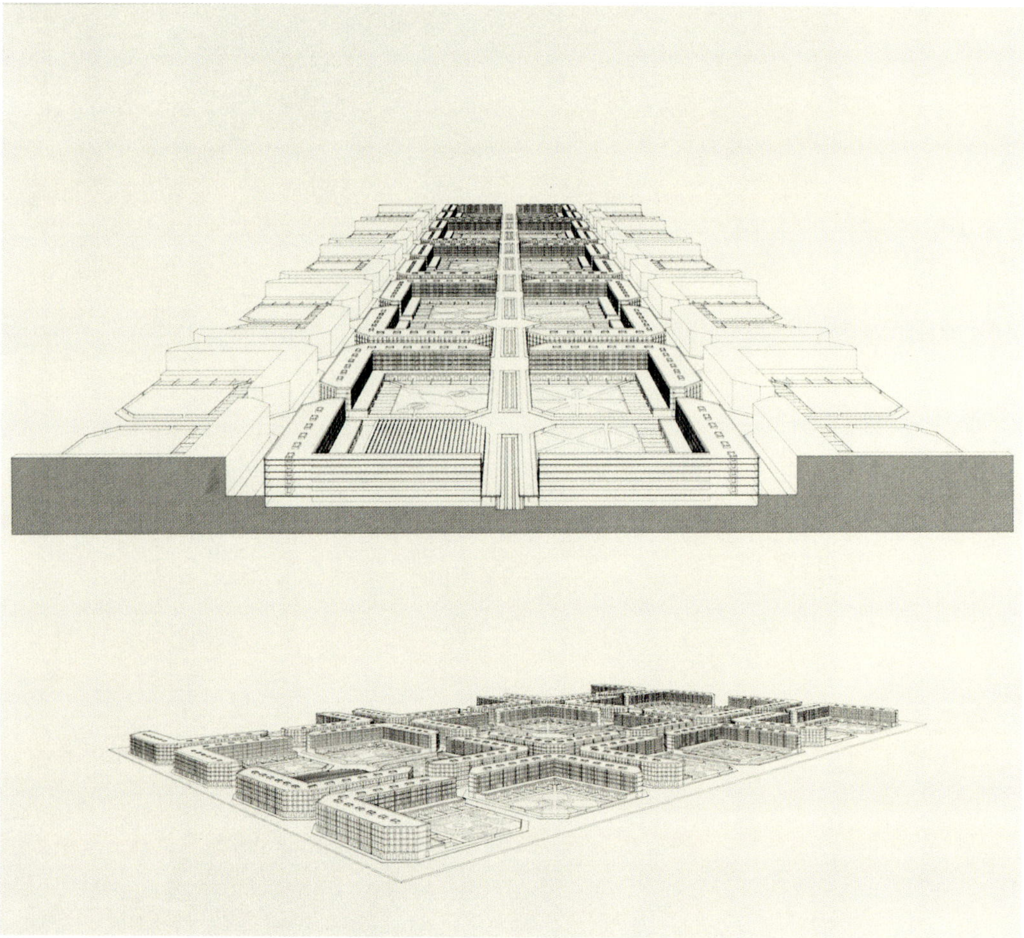

A_Undergrounded trilinear axis proposed by Cerdà for the introduction of the railway into the Eixample.
B_ Grouping of 2x2 city blocks with the superposition of housing, workshops and factories, and the railway.

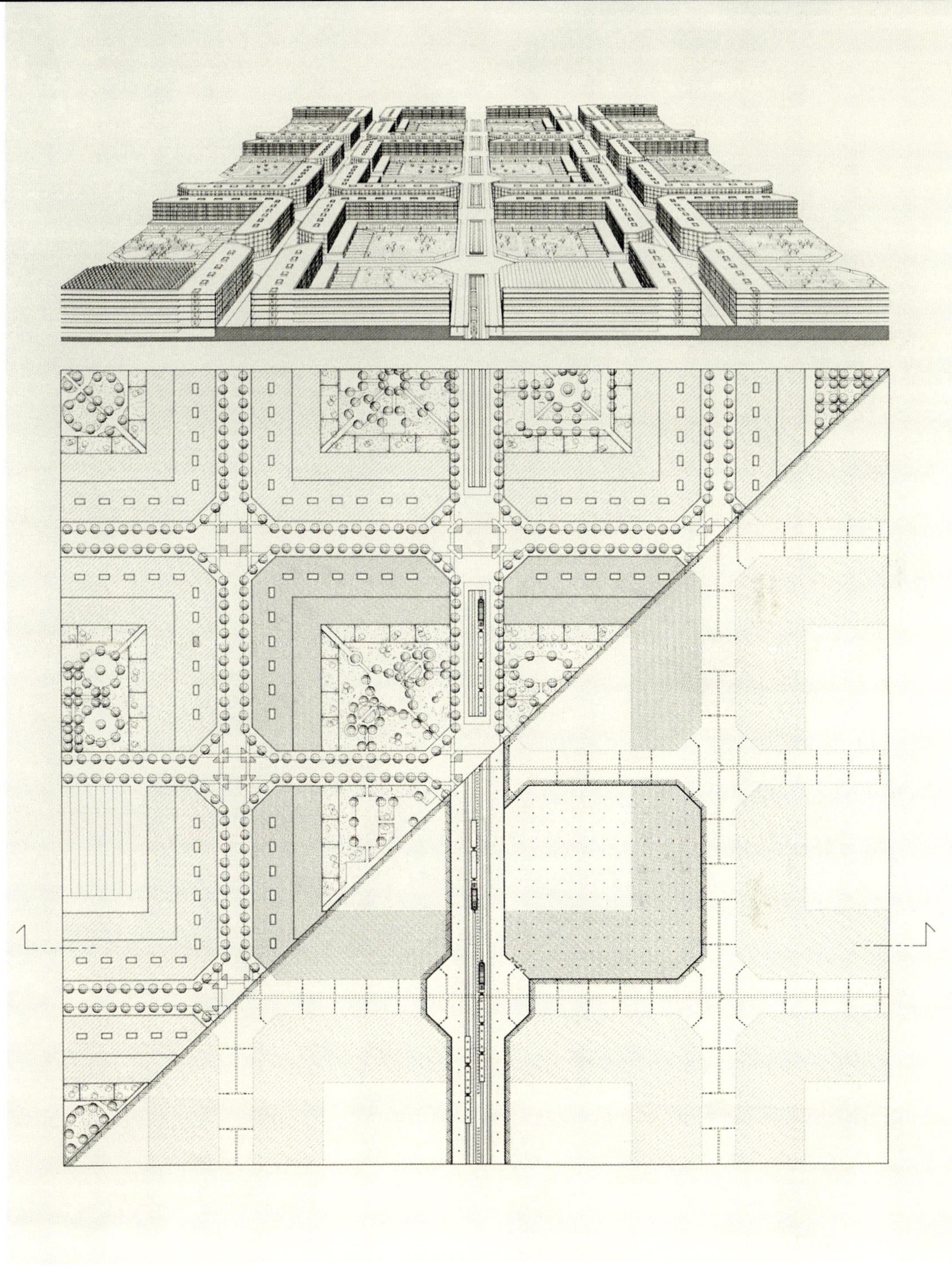

C_Hypothesis of a railway city block connecting the railway and housing, proposed by Cerdà. Conception: Salvador Tarragó and Francesc Magrinyà. 1994.

1st leap of scale: 1860-1878	Railway, stagecoaches and horse-drawn omnibuses.	LThe approval of Cerdà's Project for Remodelling and Extension in 1860 and the leap beyond the walled city centre to land formerly occupied by the walls and to the right of the Eixample extension.
2nd leap of scale: 1878-1897	Horse-drawn trams and interconnection of railway stations.	The preparation of the 1888 International Exhibition and the leap across Carrer d'Aragó to Gràcia and Sant Gervasi.
3rd leap of scale: 1897-1953	Electric trams and the first bus and underground train lines.	The annexing of the towns in the Barcelona Plain in 1897, the preparation of the 1929 International Exhibition and the leap to the towns in the Barcelona Plain, with the Eixample as a nexus.
C4th leap of scale: 1953-1986	Sustitución del tranvía por el autobús, extensión del automóvil y del metro.	The approval of the 1953 Barcelona County Plan, the filling in of Cerdà's Eixample in the direction of Sant Martí and the leap beyond the Eixample and the Barcelona Plain to the Metropolitan Area (26 municipalities).
5th leap of scale: 1986-2009	The metropolitan extension of the road network and bus lines.	The preparation of the 1992 Olympic Games, the definitive occupation of the tracts of land in the Parc del Besòs, the recovery of the seafront and the leap to the Metropolitan Region (166 municipalities).

An interpretation of 150 years of construction of the Eixample based on Cerdà's idea of leaps of scale

The different forms of urbanization associated with the predominant means of transport called for the construction of new infrastructures that served to extend the urbanization process throughout a period of growth and a series of "leaps of scale". The following interpretation of the evolution of Cerdà's Eixample and the Barcelona Plain between 1860 and 2009 proposes five leaps of scale associated with the successive introduction of different means of transport. Within this scheme of city growth, the successive leaps of scale involve a twofold phenomenon. First, the built city was restructured thanks to the construction of infrastructures that organized the urban fabric and prepared the city for the next leap of scale. Then, the further extension of the city was based on the new means of transport associated with this leap

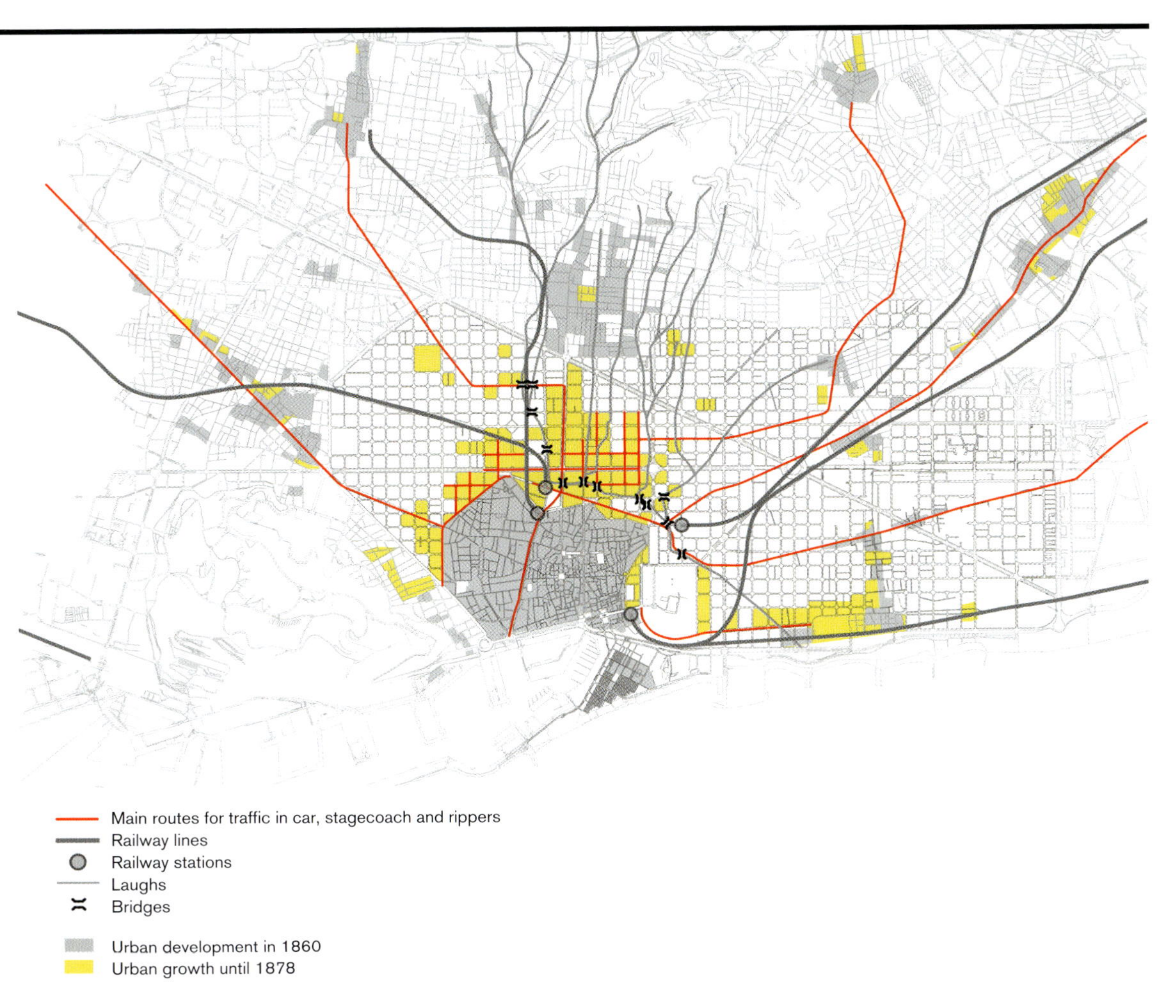

First leap of scale: 1860-1878. Produced for the exhibition.

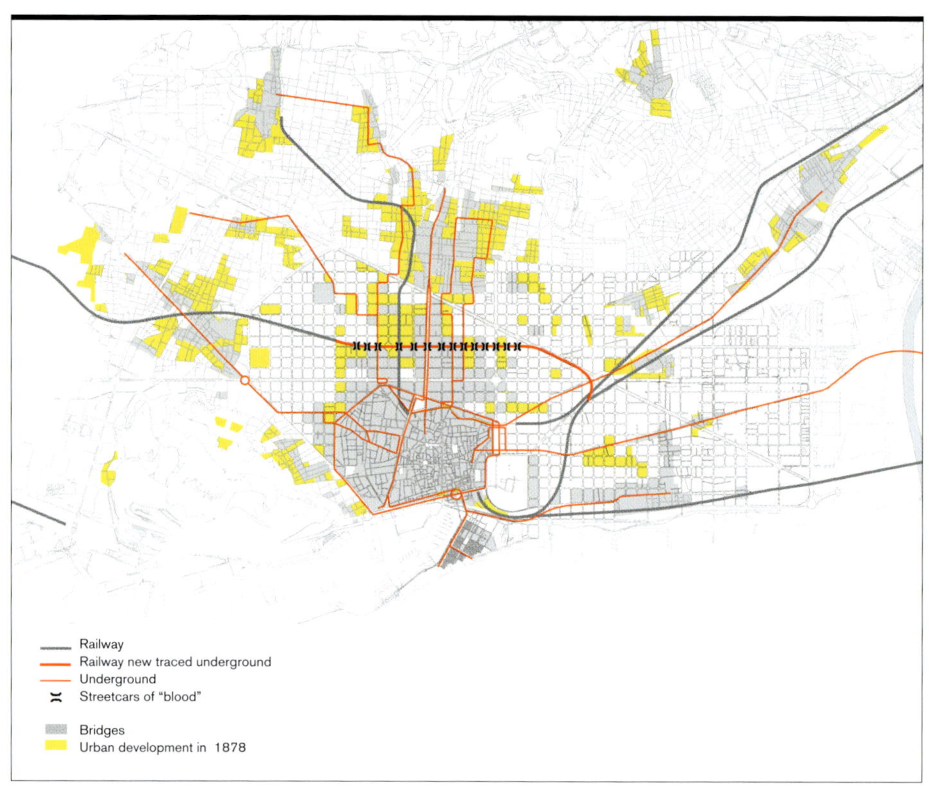

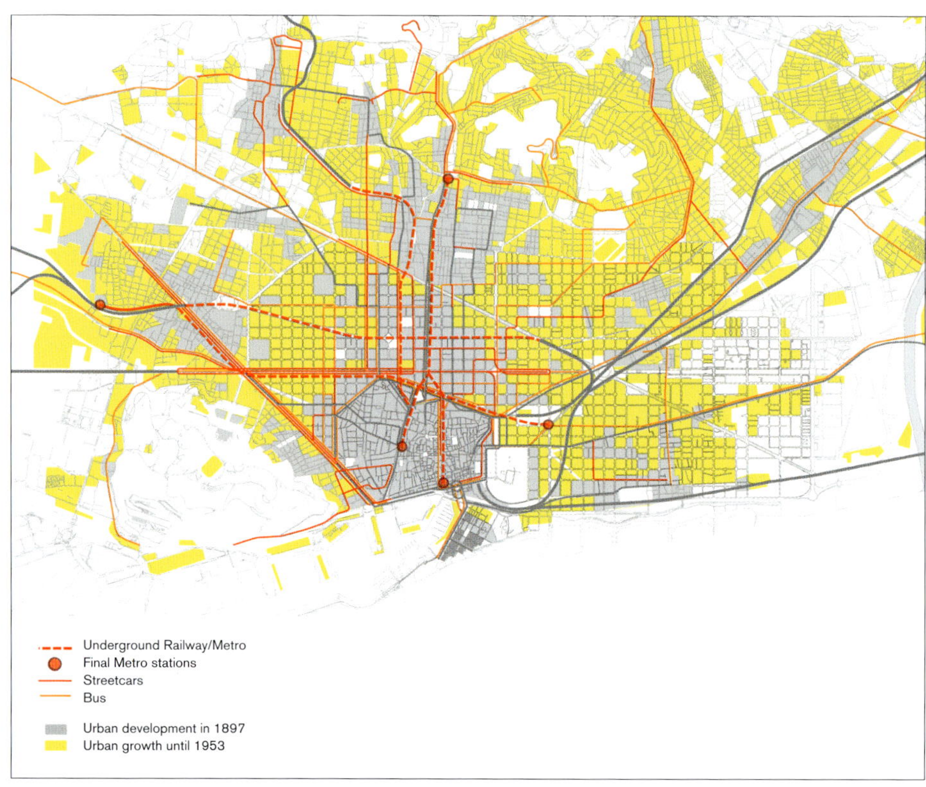

Second leap of scale: 1878-1897. Produced for the exhibition.
Third leap of scale: 1897-1953. Produced for the exhibition.

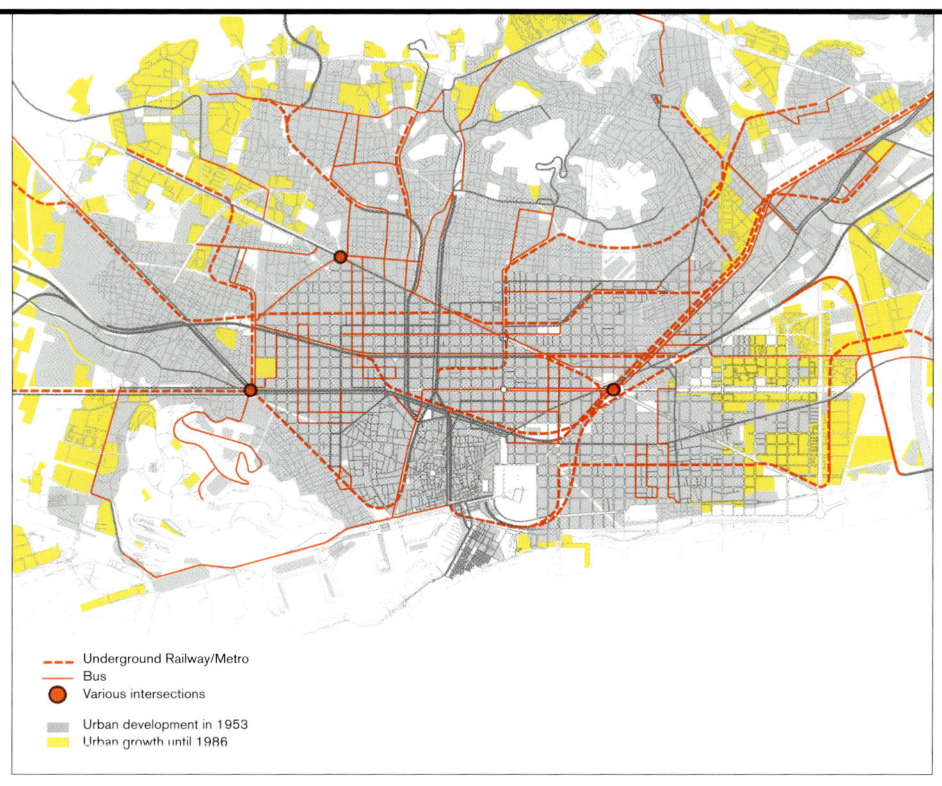

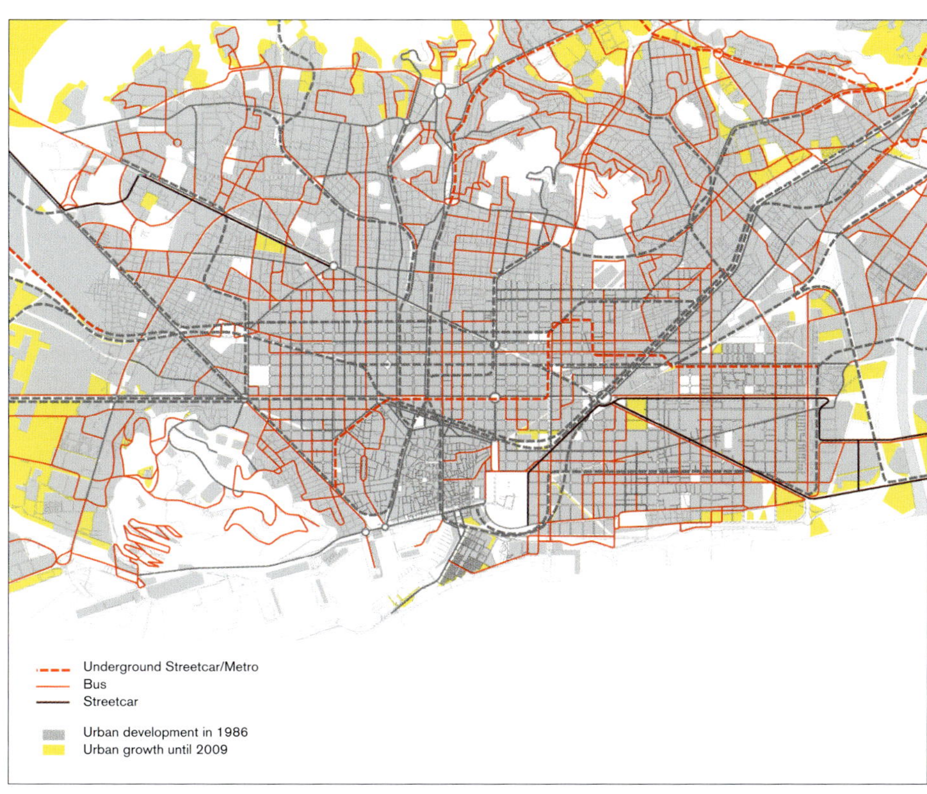

Fourth leap of scale: 1953-1986. Produced for the exhibition.
Fifth leap of scale: 1986-2009. Produced for the exhibition.

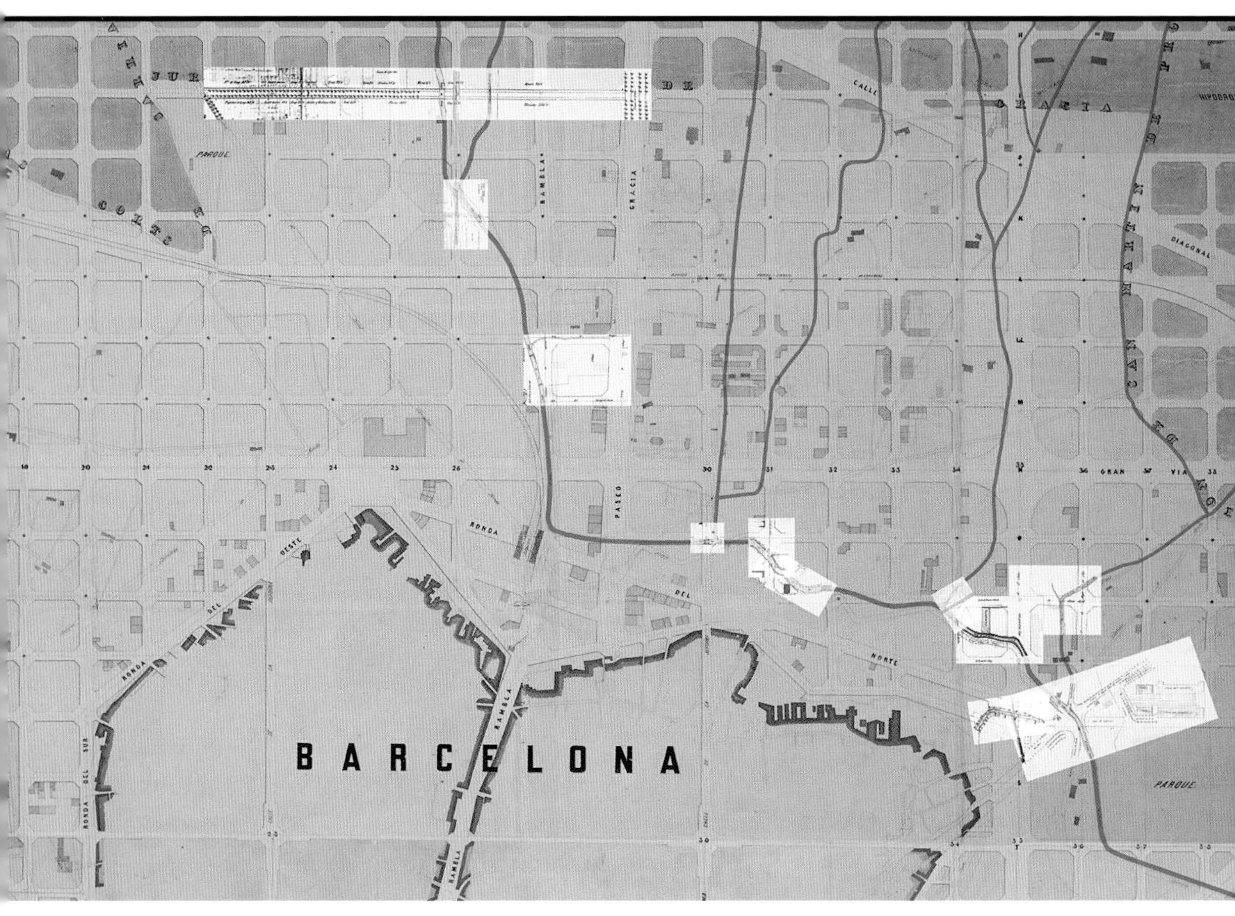

First leap of scale: 1860-1878

The first leap was defined by the adaptation of the natural topography of the Barcelona Plain, its watercourses and the pre-existence of the moat around the city walls to a new "artificial" topography, comprising bridges over the natural watercourses and the empty space produced by the demolition of the city wall.

This new phase of urbanization was underpinned by the circulation of stagecoaches and horse-drawn omnibuses as systems of transport along new streets that followed Cerdà's Alignment Plan.

Map of the bridges on the Malla watercourse that allow urbanization in the grounds of the battlements and on the right of the Eixample. Source: own.

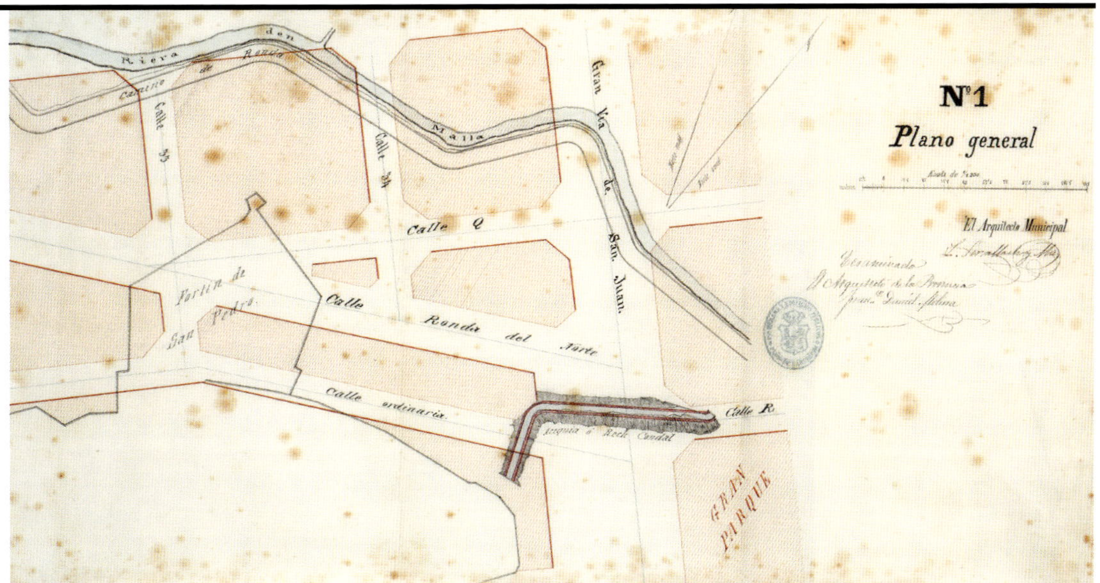

General map no. 1 of the town wall walk along the Malla watercourse (1865). Architects: Leandro Serrallach and Daniel Molina. Source: Municipal Administrative Archive. Barcelona City Council.

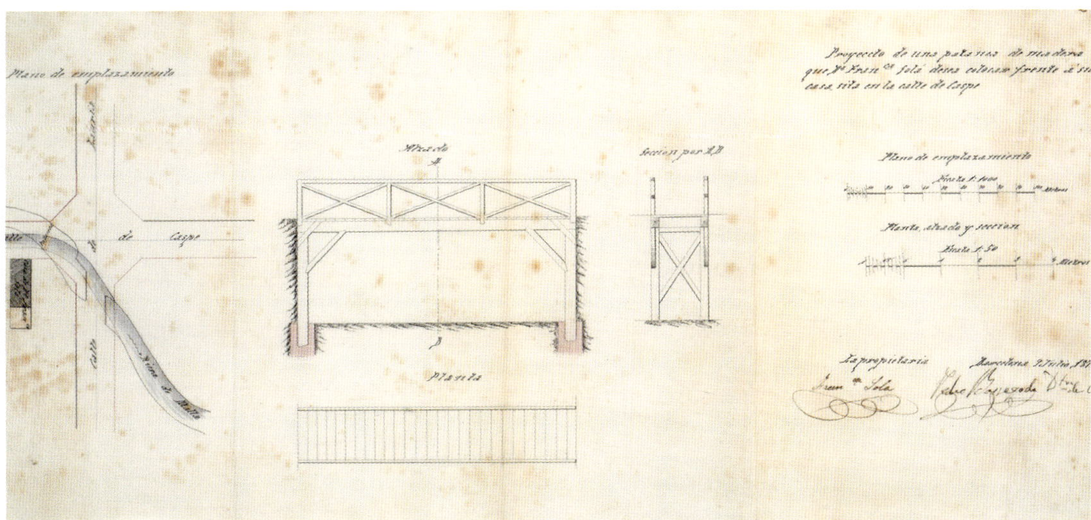

Project for a timber bridge that Mrs Francisca Solà wishes to have constructed in front of her house, on the corner of Carrer de Casp and Carrer Roger de Llúria (1877). Architect: Albert Bassegoda. Source: Municipal Administrative Archive. Barcelona City Council.

Bogatell watercourse (1880-1900). Antonio López, *Barcelona a la vista. Fotografías de la capital y sus alrededores (2ª serie)*. Source: Huertas Archive.

IGLESIA DEL COLEGIO DE JESUITAS

Barcelona á la vista—7.°

Está situada en la calle de Caspe, en uno de los barrios nás ricos y aristocráticos de la ciudad nueva, y figura digıamente entre las más elegantes y suntuosas construcciones, ıo escasas por cierto, que en aquella parte del Ensanche se ıan elevado en pocos años.

Su magestuosa fachada, de acertadas proporciones, consruida con valiosos materiales y adornada, si cabe decirlo así, con toda la sobria explendidez que permite un edificio d carácter religioso, es una concepción artística de mucho alientos y una brillante manifestación del más refinado bue gusto.

La iglesia, cuyo interior corresponde dignamente á l que la fachada deja adivinar, elévase entre dos cuerpos d edificio de extensísima área, destinados á colegio.

Timber bridge over the Malla watercourse in Carrer de Casp. Source: Lluís Permanyer. *Història de l'Eixample.* 199. Library of the Col·legi d'Arquitectes de Catalunya.

Stagecoach at the railway station (early 20th century). Photograph: unknown author. Source: various authors. *Barcelona i el ferrocarril.* 1994.

Horse-drawn omnibus belonging to the Catalana de Ripperts line (1930-1932). Photograph: Josep Brangulí. Source: Arxiu Fotogràfic de Barcelona.

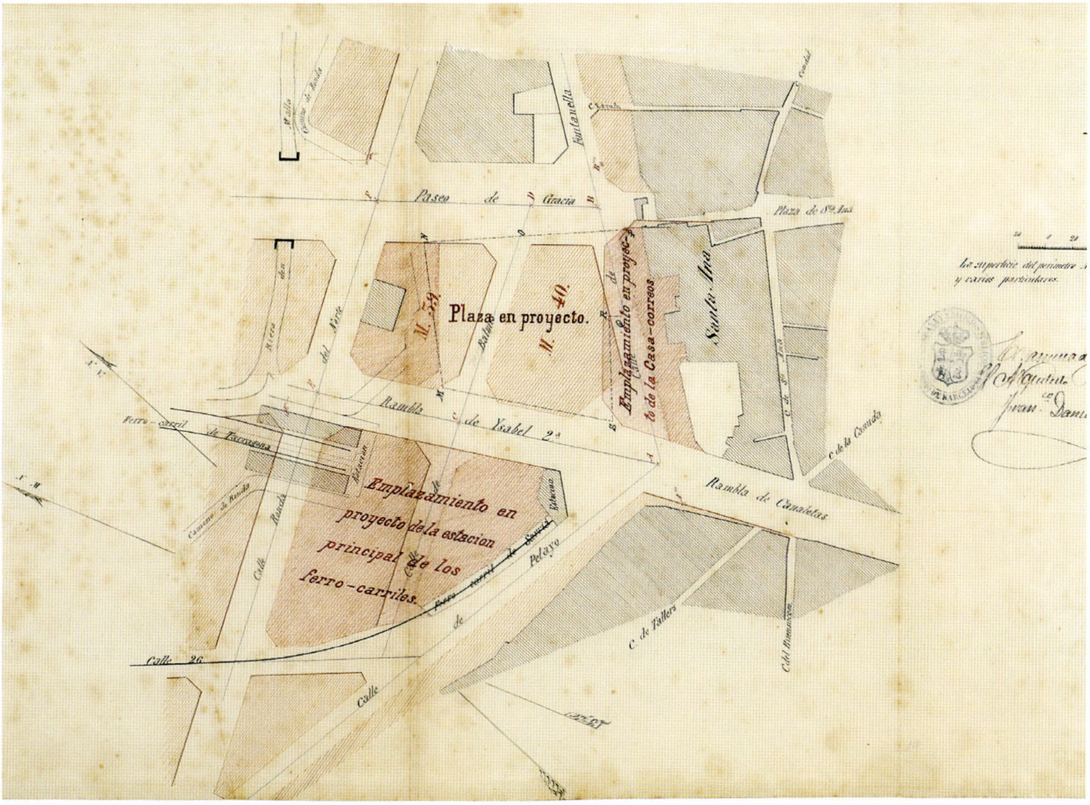

The Barcelona to Sarrià train leaving Plaça de Catalunya (1900-1904). Photograph: unknown author. Source: various authors. *Barcelona i el ferrocarril.* 1994. Gabinet d'Informació i Relacions Externes de RENFE. Barcelona.

Project for a square (today's Plaça de Catalunya) on the large north esplanade, between the former Isabel II and Àngel gateways in the city of Barcelona (1866). Architects: Leandre Serrallach and Daniel Molina. Source: Arxiu Històric de la Ciutat de Barcelona.

Façade of the Sarrià railway station in Plaça de Catalunya (1863). Photograph: unknown author. Source: various authors. *Barcelona i el ferrocarril.* 1994. Arxiu Històric de Sarrià.

Plaça de Catalunya, Gibert House and the railway station for Martorell (1874). Photograph: Joan Martí. Source: Arxiu Fotogràfic de Barcelona.

Estació de França railway station with carriages (undated). Photograph: Photograph Serra. Source: various authors. *Barcelona i el ferrocarril.* 1994. Institut Municipal d'Història.

Plaça de Catalunya, Gibert House and the railway station for Martorell (1874). Photograph: Joan Martí. Source: Arxiu Fotogràfic de Barcelona.

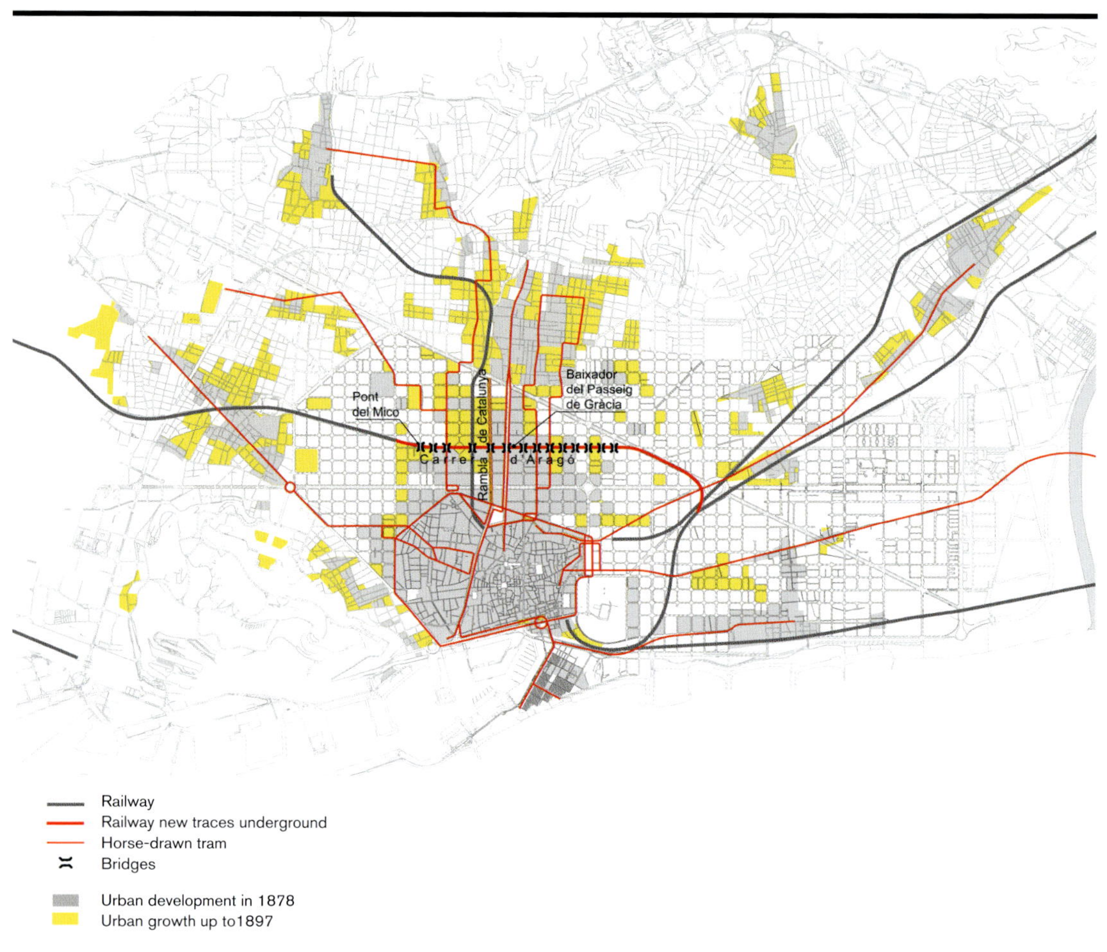

Second leap of scale: 1878-1897

This leap took place after the rerouting of the old Malla watercourse (today's Rambla Catalunya) towards Avinguda Diagonal and the underground connection of railway stations via Carrer d'Aragó, with bridges that spanned it at each vertical street, communicating with land for development above Carrer d'Aragó and connecting the Eixample with the town of Gràcia.

This phase of urbanization was based on the horse-drawn tram, which connected Barcelona and the first stage of the Eixample with other towns in the Barcelona Plain.

Second leap of scale: 1878-1897. Produced for the exhibition.

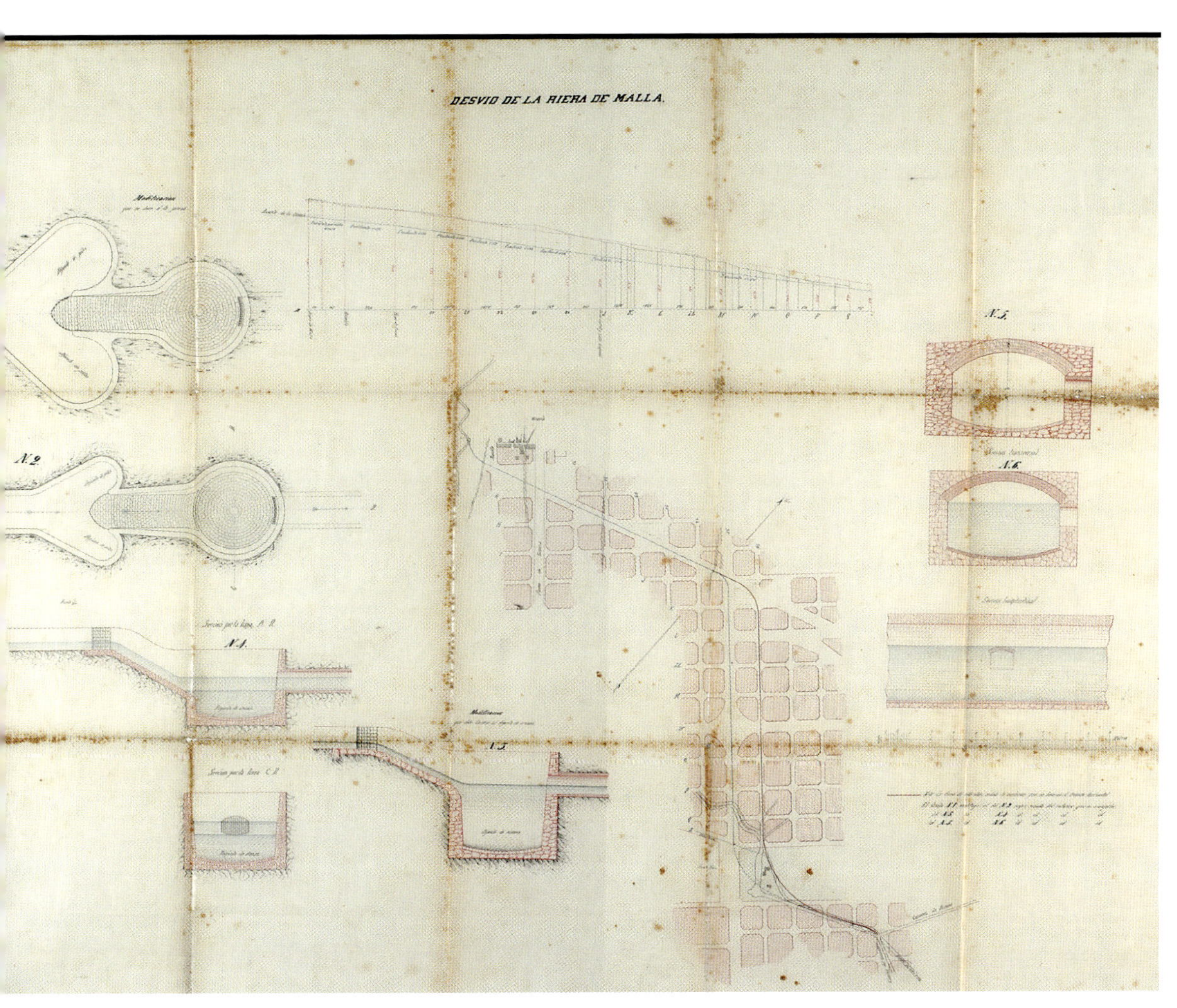

Project to reroute the Malla watercourse presented to Barcelona City Council by the Sociedad Fomento del Ensanche (1865). Author: Sociedad Fomento del Ensanche. Source: Municipal Administrative Archive. Barcelona City Council.

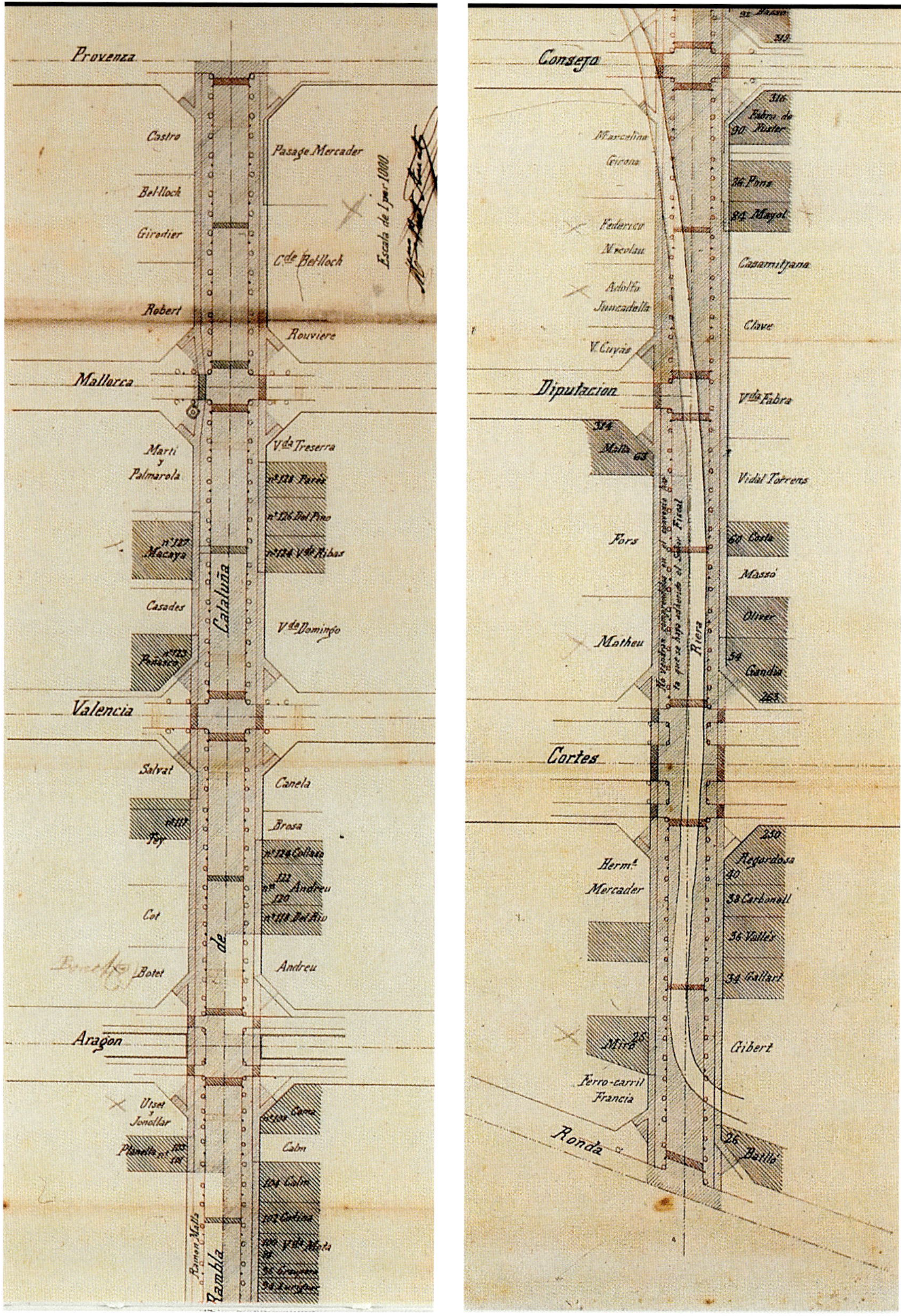

Project for the urbanization of Rambla de Catalunya (1877). Author: M. Prat Amat. Source: Municipal Administrative Archive. Barcelona City Council.

Rambla de Catalunya (1890). Photograph: J.E. Puig. Source: Arxiu Fotogràfic de Barcelona.

Rambla de Catalunya seen from Plaça de Catalunya (1890-1899). Photograph: J.E. Puig. Source: Arxiu Fotogràfic de Barcelona.

Staff of the Barcelona, Eixample and Gràcia tram company (1873). Photograph: unknown author. Source: various authors. *Barcelona i el ferrocarril.* 1994.

Steam train in Carrer de Balmes (undated). Photograph: Branguli fotògrafs. Source: Historical Archive of the Col·legi d'Arquitectes de Catalunya.

Estació de França railway station (1900-1915). Photograph: Brangulí fotògrafs. Source: Holdings of Brangulí fotògrafs. Arxiu Nacional de Catalunya.

Cutting the railway tracks in Carrer d'Aragó (1890-1900). Photograph: unknown author. Source: KLUMPCOL, SL Collection.

People looking at the train in Carrer d'Aragó (1900-1910). Photograph: J. Morelló. Source: Photographic Archive of the Centre Excursionista de Catalunya.

Perspective of the construction of the first phase of the Eixample with the original Plaça del Dr. Letamendi in the foreground (undated). Photograph: unknown author. Source: Fernando Marzá-Neus Moyano Collection.

Train cutting in Carrer d'Aragó (1890-1900). Photograph: unknown author. Source: KLUMPCOL, SL Collection.

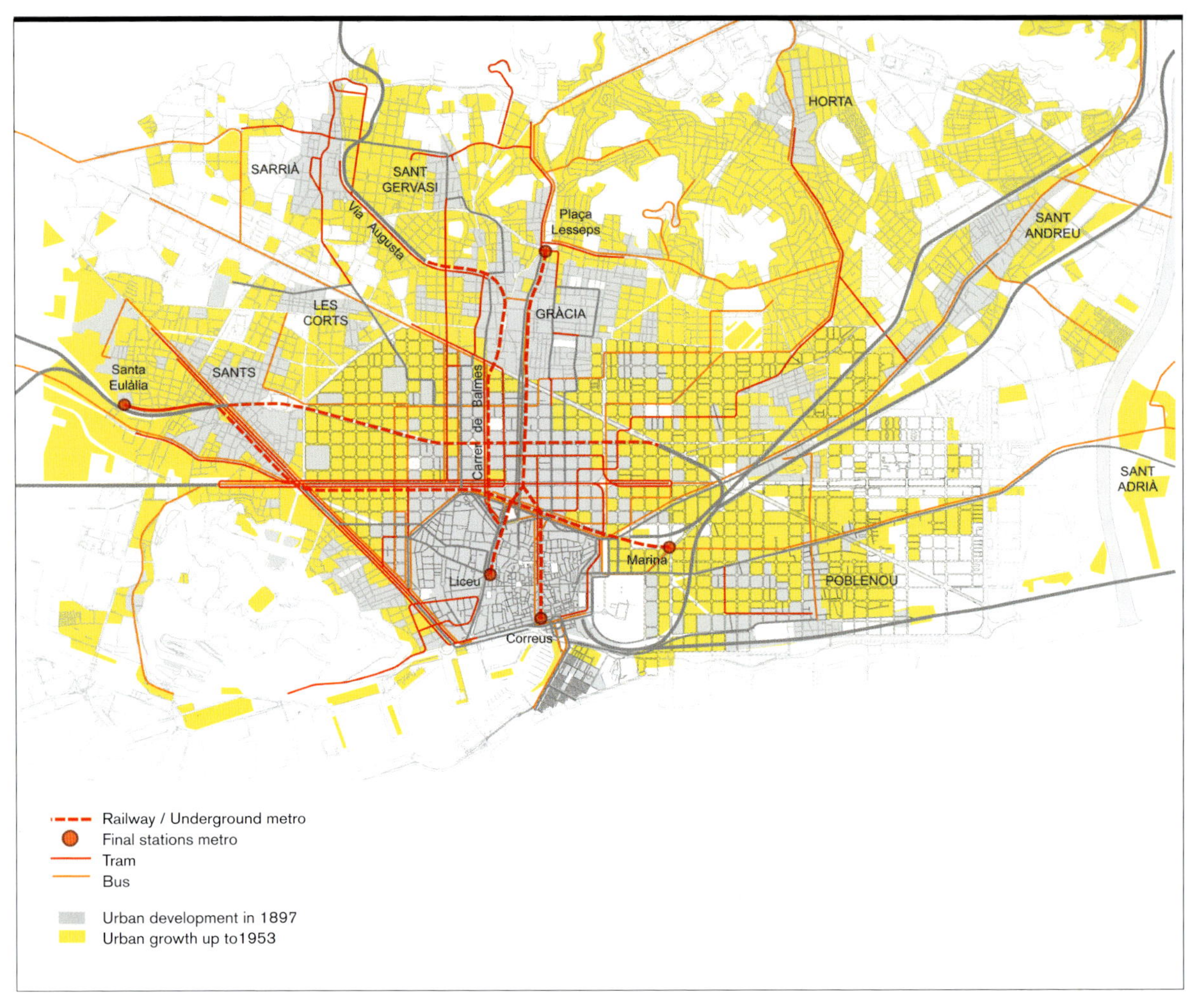

Third leap of scale: 1897-1953

The third leap was represented by the appearance of new Metro lines and the undergrounding of the railway line between Barcelona and Sarrià along the layout of Carrer de Balmes, leading to the disappearance of level crossings for motorized vehicles.

The basis for this latest wave of urbanization was, firstly, the electric trams that by 1915 were affordable for most of the population and, secondly, the bus lines which, after 1921, began to extend where the tram was unable to go due to uneven topography.

Third leap of scale: 1897-1953. Produced for the exhibition

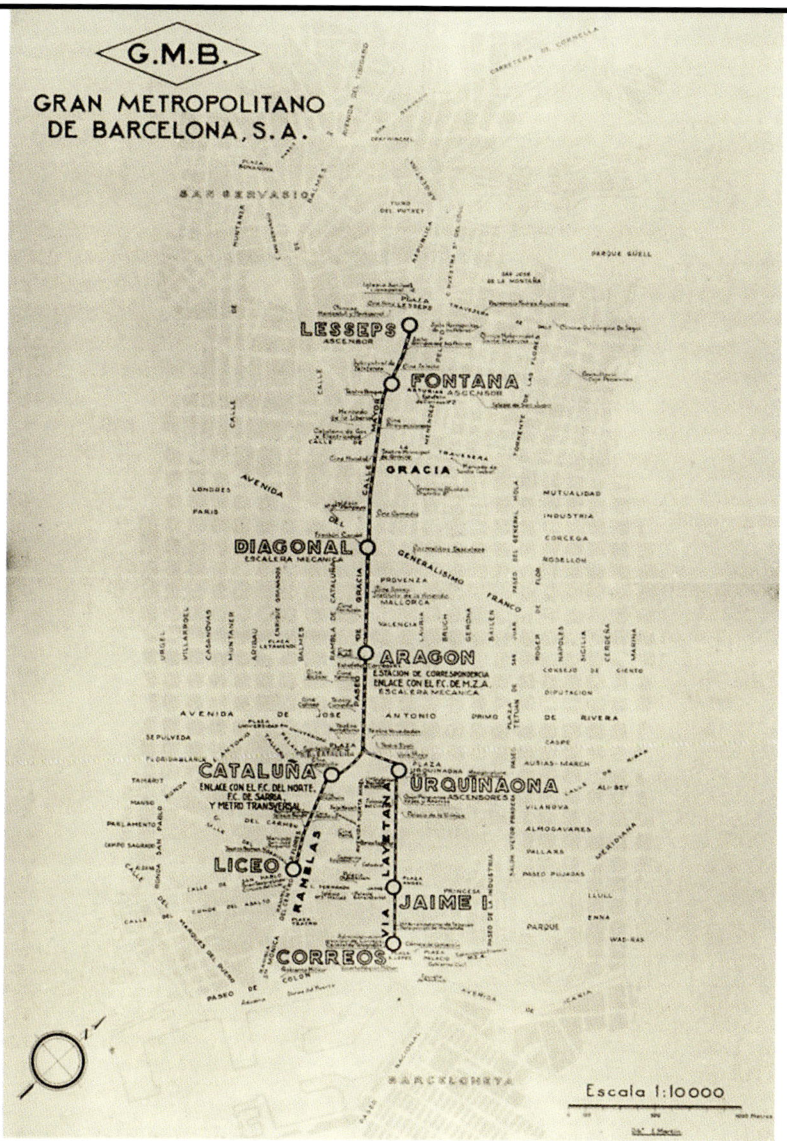

G.M.B.

GRAN METROPOLITANO
DE BARCELONA, S. A.

LESSEPS
FONTANA
GRACIA
DIAGONAL
ARAGON
CATALUÑA
URQUINAONA
LICEO
JAIME I
CORREOS

Escala 1:10000

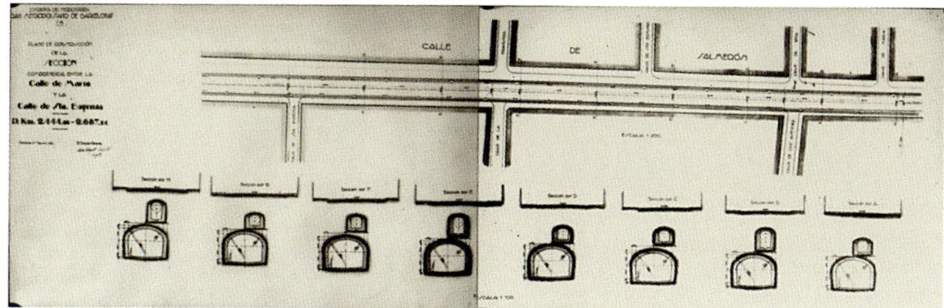

Gran Metropolità de Barcelona underground train line (early 1940s). Source: Carles Salmerón. *El metro de Barcelona*. 1992. Carles Salmerón Archives.

Map of the construction of the section bounded by Carrer de Maria and Carrer de Santa Eugènia (1922) Architect: Santiago Rubió i Tudurí. Source: Historical Archive of the Col·legi d'Arquitectes de Catalunya.

Marquee in Plaça d'Espanya with tram turn-around (1908). Photograph: Frederic Ballell. Source: Arxiu Fotogràfic de Barcelona.

Authorities visiting work on the Metropolità Transversal de Barcelona (1925). Photograph: Brangulí fotògrafs. Source: Holdings of Brangulí fotògrafs. Arxiu Nacional de Catalunya.

Construction work on the Gran Metropolità de Barcelona in La Rambla (1923-1924). Photograph: Brangulí fotògrafs. Source: Holdings of Brangulí fotògrafs. Arxiu Nacional de Catalunya.

Lesseps station on the Gran Metropolità de Barcelona network, shortly before being opened (1924). Photograph: Brangulí fotògrafs. Source: Holdings of Brangulí fotògrafs. Arxiu Nacional de Catalunya.

The Sarrià train at the junction of three streets: Balmes, Pelai and Bergara (undated). Photograph: Brangulí fotògrafs. Source: Historical Archive of the Col·legi d'Arquitectes de Catalunya.

Undergrounding work on the line of the Companyia dels Ferrocarrils Catalans, running between Barcelona and Sarrià. Crossroads of Carrer de Pelai and Carrer de Balmes (1926-1929). Photograph: Brangulí fotògrafs. Source: Holdings of Brangulí fotògrafs. Arxiu Nacional de Catalunya.

Tram in Plaça d'Espanya (1936). Photograph: unknown author. Source: Arxiu Fotogràfic de Barcelona.

The tram over ground in Plaça de la Universitat (1911). Photograph: Frederic Ballell. Source: Arxiu Fotogràfic de Barcelona.

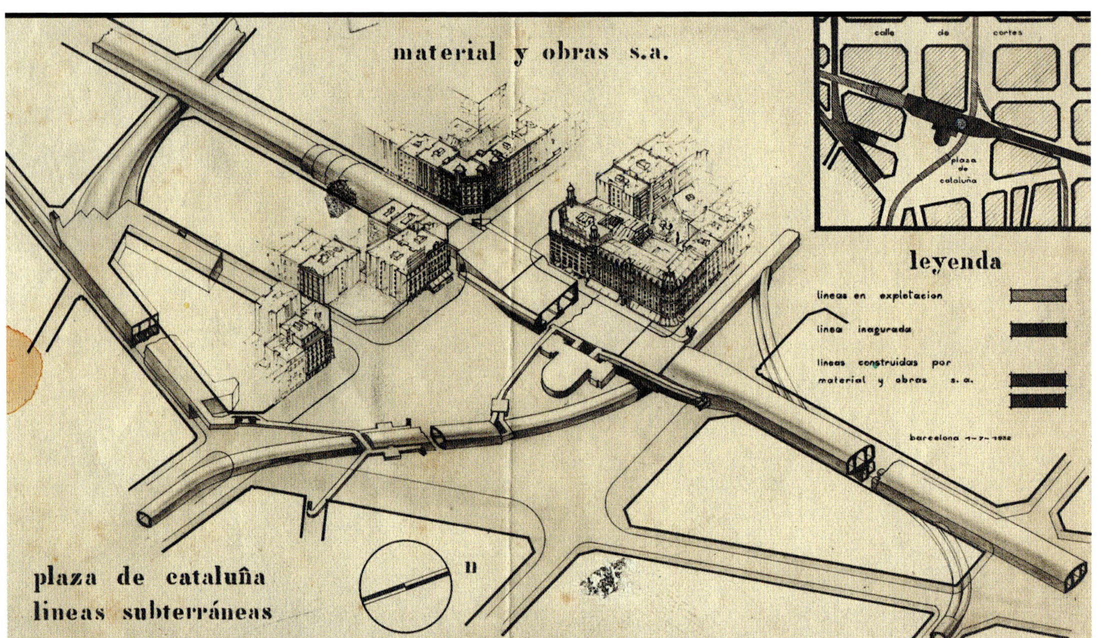

Plaça de Catalunya. Underground lines (1932). Architects: GATCPAC. Source: Historical Archive of the Col·legi d'Arquitectes de Catalunya.

Gran Metro de Barcelona (1925). Photograph: Josep Domínguez. Source: Arxiu Fotogràfic de Barcelona.

Aerial view of Plaça d'Espanya and Avinguda del Paral·lel (1925-1930). Photograph: Josep Gaspar. Source: Arxiu Fotogràfic de Barcelona.

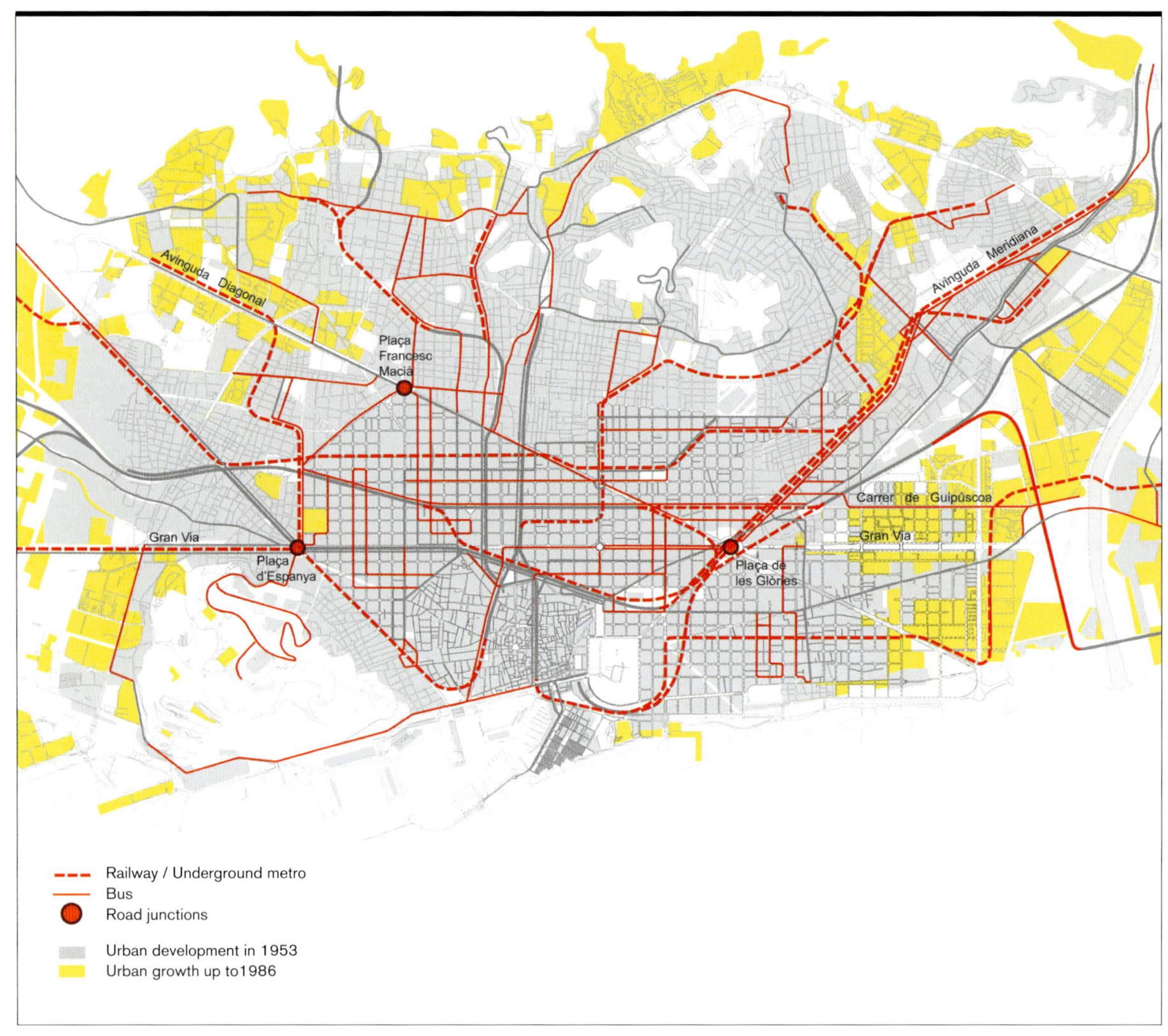

Fourth leap of scale: 1953-1986

The fourth leap is represented by new thoroughfares extending beyond the towns in the Barcelona Plain and throughout the county. Road connections with the territory beyond, which began in 1928-1930 with the construction of Avinguda Diagonal between Plaça de Francesc Macià and Pedralbes Palace, and Gran Via past Plaça d'Espanya, started to extend towards Badalona on one side and Castelldefels on the other. Important new road junctions were Plaça d'Espanya, Plaça de les Glòries and Plaça de Francesc Macià.

The means of transport underlying this phase of urbanization were the automobile and the extension of the Metro and bus lines to districts that had been developed without services, allowing the consolidation of previously occupied areas.

Benediction of Saint Christopher in Avinguda Diagonal (1948). Photograph: Pérez de Rozas. Source: Arxiu Fotogràfic de Barcelona.

Inauguration of a new train, the 251 series, at La Bordeta station on the Gran Metropolità de Barcelona line (1950-1960). Photograph: Branguli fotògrafs. Source: Holdings of Branguli fotògrafs. Arxiu Nacional de Catalunya.

Automobile accident in the cutting made in Carrer d'Aragó (1915). Photograph: Frederic Ballell. Source: Arxiu Fotogràfic de Barcelona.

Covering the cutting in Carrer d'Aragó (1956-1960). Photograph: unknown author. Source: Arxiu Fotogràfic de Barcelona.

Avinguda Meridiana (1950). Photograph: Joan Estorch. Source: Arxiu Fotogràfic de Barcelona.

Traffic on the Castelldefels expressway (1962). Photograph: TAF Helicòpters, SA. Source: TAF Holdings. Arxiu Nacional de Catalunya.

Carrer de Guipúscoa in 1957. Source: Daniel Fernández and Àngels Prats (ed.). *Exposició Universal de Barcelona. Llibre del Centenari 1888-1988.* 1988.

Inauguration of Plaça de les Glòries (1961). Photograph: Pérez de Rozas. Source: Arxiu Fotogràfic de Barcelona.

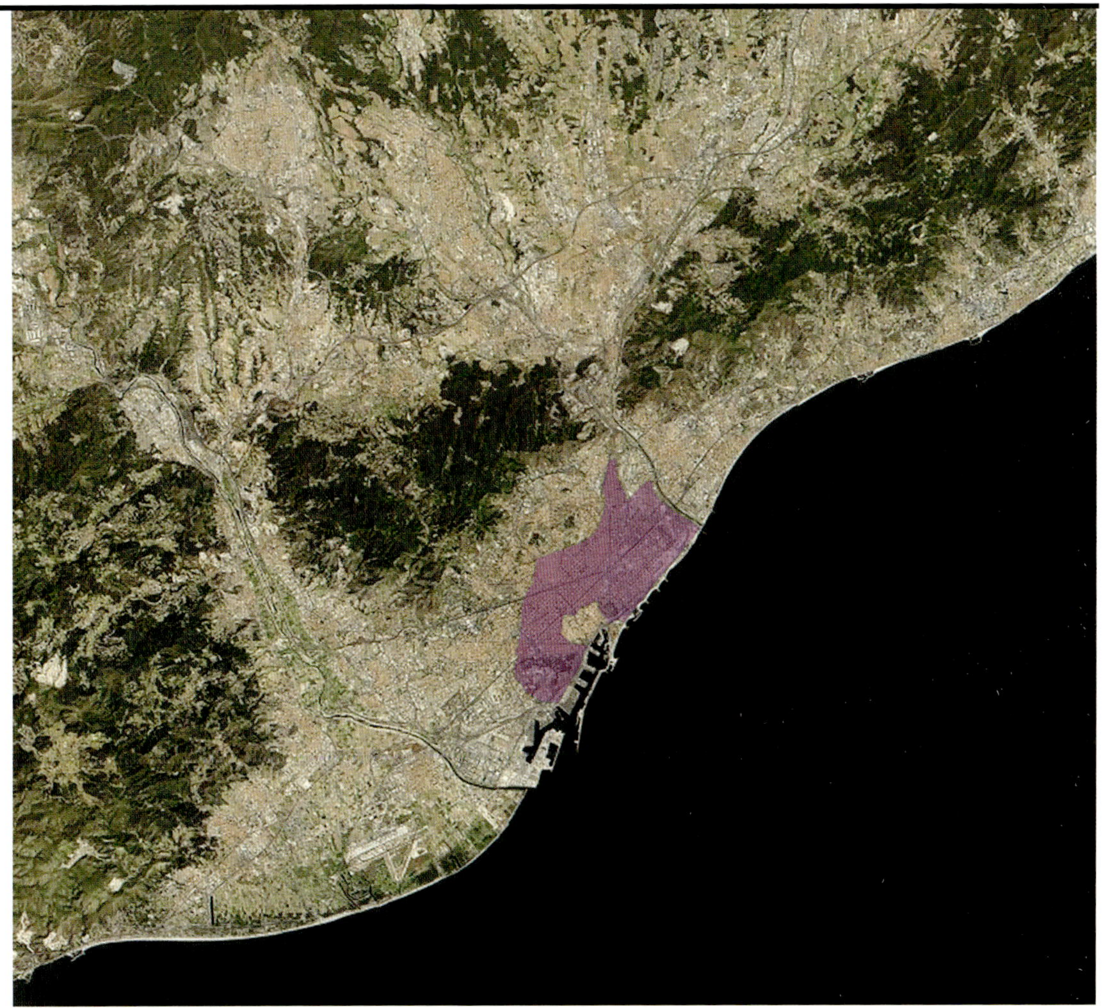

Connection with the world

"The city is merely a more or less imperfect system of interchangers that lie in the path of overall universal road connection."

The High-Speed Train stations of Sants and La Sagrera, terminal T1 at El Prat airport, and the extension of Barcelona's ports are the new interchangers in what Cerdà referred to as universal road connection.

The Eixample has become the great metropolitan interchanger of Barcelona and is the heart that allows the urban system of the metropolis of Barcelona, with three million inhabitants, to function as such. A new structure will have to be designed to be the heart of the new territorial space that is already Catalonia-City.

The Metropolitan Area of Barcelona and Cerdà's Eixample (2009). Produced for the exhibition.

View of the Eixample layout showing Avinguda Gaudí at the centre with the grounds of the Sagrada Família and the Hospital de Sant Pau at either end. Photograph: Jordi Todó / TAVISA. 1990.

View of the Sagrada Família with Avinguda Gaudí in the foreground. Photograph: Jordi Todó / TAVISA. 1990.

View of the Eixample layout showing the Sagrada Família in the foreground, with Avinguda Gaudí to the Leith, Avinguda Diagonal to the right and Avinguda Meridiana in the background. Photograph: Jordi Todó / TAVISA. 1990.

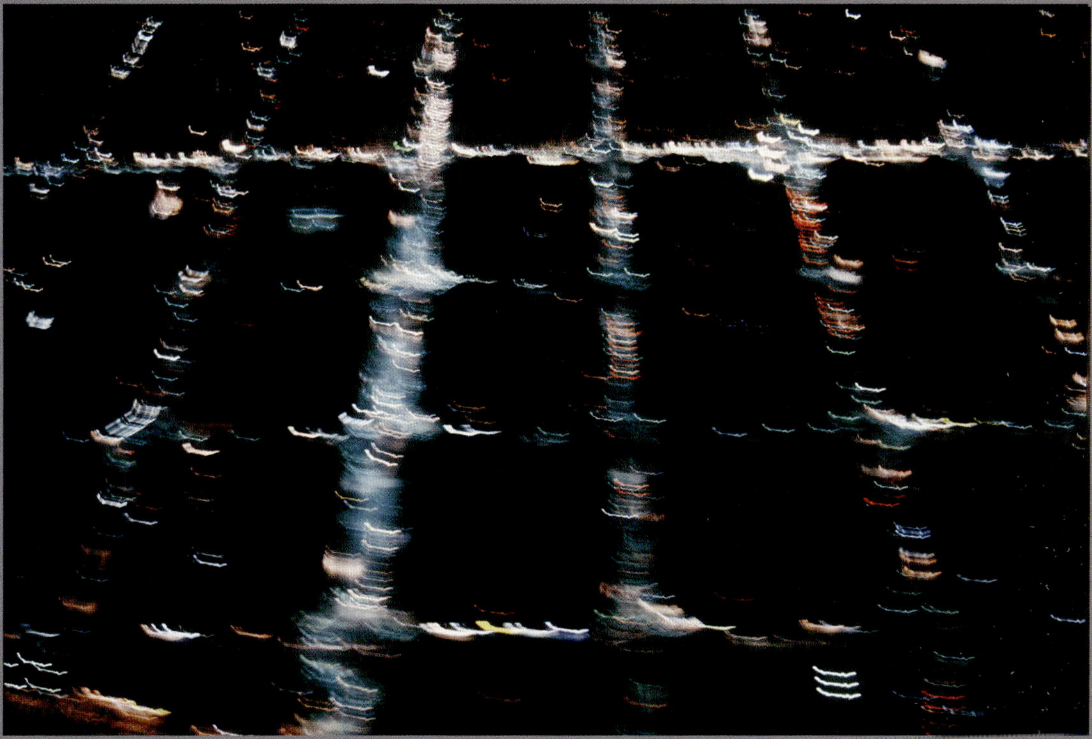

View of the Eixample layout showing Avinguda Diagonal (bottom Leith) and the axes of Passeig de Sant Joan (vertical) and Còrsega (horizontal) with more lighting. Photograph: Jordi Todó / TAVISA. 1990.

Aerial view of Plaça de Catalunya and Passeig de Gràcia. Fotograph: Jordi Todó / TAVISA. 1990.

SARRIÁ
SAN GERVASI
PEDRALBES
PUTXET
CORTS DE SARRIÁ
COLL-BLANCH
SANS
HOSPITAL
BORDETA
HOSTAFRANCHS
ZONA MILITAR
BARCELONA ACTUAL
CASTILLO DE MONJUICH

Project for the Remodelling and Extension of Barcelona. 1859. Ildefons Cerdà. Source: Real Academia de Bellas Artes de San Fernando.

Shortcomings and strengths of the 1859 Cerdà Plan, according to different time perspectives_ Albert Serratosa, Dr. Road Engineer and Urban Planner

1._ The ongoing defence of the "strengths"

When I was a child, my first impressions of the values of the Eixample were shrouded in vague ideas that served to identify it as the ideal of the city. Later, as a newly qualified civil servant, I experienced the centenary of the approval of Cerdà's Plan. The project and site management of Plaça Cerdà, the first sign of public recognition of Cerdà's contribution to Barcelona, brought me into direct contact with this important figure, with an intensity that has only grown until now, the 150th anniversary.

Very soon I began to intuit a murkier atmosphere created by property, political and professional interests: those of owners of plots of land in Ciutat Vella, the old town, faced with the prospect of a fall in value of urban land and insalubrious buildings; of landowners with property outside the town wall, due to the excess of land with collective designs on it; of politicians, due to the alleged "imposition" of a Madrid government, with its approval of the supramunicipal plan; and of professionals in the face of the interference of a technician, of whom it came to be said that he was "not even an architect".

It is quite true that, for over a century, architects were practically the only professionals to take an interest in urbanization (to use the term coined by Cerdà). No other professional group gave any thought to designing higher-level programmes of training in urban development. It is no wonder that the field of urbanism ended up in the hands of those who were actually working on it.

The title of Urban-planning technician granted by the Instituto de Estudios de Administración Local [Institute of Local Government Studies] was the first step to "legal" admission to the field of urbanism for various professions. The team involved in drafting the 1953 Pla Comarcal de Barcelona [Barcelona County Plan] was an incipient multidisciplinary experiment in the field of urban planning. The start of work in 1962 on the anticipated revision of the plan served to consolidate this new trend, and the Pla Director de l'Àrea Metropolitana de Barcelona [Barcelona Metropolitan Area Master Plan] was a landmark, as was the Pla General Metropolità (PGM [Metropolitan Master Plan]) of the 1970s. An Act dated 1983 paved the way in Catalonia for

Regional Plans and, since then, the Pla Territorial General de Catalunya (1995 [Regional Master Plan for Catalonia]) and the successive Plans Territorials Parcials [Detailed Regional Plans] made multidisciplinary collaboration a habitual recourse.

This short historical outline is an attempt to explain a period of transition during which some professionals were second-rate urbanists who felt under an obligation to reinstate the figure of Ildefons Cerdà, who was not only exceptional, but also the veritable founder of a science, with his *Teoría General de la Urbanización* [General Theory of Urbanization]. After 50 years of praise and showcasing its "strengths", the situation has more or less returned to normal. More than 100 of the world's cities have had the occasion to see the travelling exhibition "Urbs i Territori, Ildefons Cerdà" [*Urbs* and Territory, Ildefons Cerdà], and the time has come to close the chapter of panegyrics of this universal figure and embark on a critical phase.

Looking back, the first thing to surprise a planner is the discovery that, over the years, the shortcomings and strengths form part of a circular process in which roles are sometimes reversed. The facts remain the same, but evaluations change according to the historical moment. This article presents some examples that illustrate a series of transfigurations in critical analysis up to the start of the 21st century.

2. A beneficial "shortcoming"

Cerdà foresaw industrialization, a phenomenon which brought humankind out of the Neolithic and into "a new civilization". However, perhaps he did not sufficiently weigh up the consequences of innovation, with its unprecedented territorial and demographic effects. Industry, he thought, could coexist with housing, but he did not take into account the fact that some industry is unhealthy and dangerous. I remember my father taking us to the top of Tibidabo on the very exceptional occasions when it was possible to see the city without its habitual shroud of smog, the contamination that has disappeared over the years despite the combined effects of industry, heating and the increased use of the automobile.

A paradigm example is Poblenou. Situated to the east, it occupies a considerable part of the new city, and the structuring elements (street grid, city blocks, street corners) are the same as in the rest. Cerdà, a civil engineer, did not take into account the marshy land that made it difficult to build tall buildings comprising a ground floor and three upper storeys. As a result, this sector was earmarked for industry, which could be seen as a major shortcoming for the egalitarian city. It was, however, thanks to this error that for over a century Barcelona became "the Manchester of the south", making Catalonia one of the economic driving forces of Europe.

Once the industrial phase was at an end, structural resources (the same throughout the Eixample: sewerage, connection to road infrastructure strengthened by the Ronda Litoral coastal beltway, and the salvaging of the seafront by the 1976 Metropolitan Master Plan) allowed Poblenou to move easily to advanced tertiarization (sectors of 1,450 hectares classified as 22@). Few cities have effected such a smooth transformation to occupy a high position in the world ranking in a short space of time! The Olympic Games provided the bait, but the fishing rod has always been in the firm grasp of Cerdà who, in 1859, planned sufficient urban space to accommodate an unprecedented population growth: from a city of 180,000 inhabitants to one and a half million, and from a metropolitan area of around 250,000 inhabitants to more than 7.5 million.

3. Too low a density?

Another of the plan's often considered shortcomings was low urban density. This is a paradigm example of the bad habit of using an adjective without defining or quantifying it: what are the limits of "low" or "high" density, applied to a city? A baseline consideration of 100 (±40) inhabitants/urban hectare suggests that Cerdà's proposal was based on a "low" density—very low in the 1859 version, and slightly less so in 1863, with the closed city blocks. The rejection of the Construction Bylaws proposed by Cerdà opened the Pandora's box of permitted building levels, with a swing from reasonable values to excesses evidently fuelled by speculation, which involved dividing the ground floor into semi-basement and mezzanine, and adding two storeys in addition to the two existing top floors. In 1972, Mayor Porcioles began a hesitant cutback of building levels after over a century of increases approved by some of the 100 mayors of very different political persuasions. The scandal was ended by the definitive approval in 1976 of the Barcelona Metropolitan Master Plan, which affected 27 municipalities and, based on a real population of 2.7 million, reduced the 9 million inhabitants legally admitted at that time to 4.5 million.

The gradual trend has been to slow down overall density, and today (2009), the 27 municipalities have a combined population of less than 3.1 million. Thanks primarily to Cerdà's Plan, and later to the 1976 Metropolitan Master Plan, densities have remained within reasonable limits, and Barcelona and its 26 surrounding municipalities are now sufficiently flexible to adapt to the quite spectacular changes of unprecedented population growth to affect the whole world in recent centuries. Catalonia (almost an "urban region") has maintained its proportion of one one-thousandth of the world population: today, there are 7.5 million Catalans in a world of 7,500 million earth-dwellers. More surprising is the upward trend in urbanites (inhabitants of cities of over 10,000 inhabitants) who, since 1927, have risen from 20% of the world population to 50%; in absolute terms, this represents an increase from 400 million to over 3,500 million city-dwellers.

The applicability of Cerdà's ideas becomes even plainer in view of the fact (see Manuel Herce) that 80% of urbanites live in shanties—that is, over 2,500 million human beings, in the first decade of the 21st century, live on top of each other in dreadful conditions in marginal districts in Africa, India and Brazil, but also in Europe and other parts of the so-called First World. If any single characteristic stands out from the Pla de Reforma i Eixample [Remodelling and Extension Plan], it is the fact that it laid the bases for a relatively egalitarian city and, except during relatively short periods of upheaval, avoided districts with subhuman living conditions.

One of the main aims of celebrating the 150th anniversary of Cerdà's Plan is to offer the world a series of ideas and a scientifically-based theory that have stood the test of time in Barcelona. The results are highly satisfactory. They have overcome petty differences of the past and now offer contrasted solutions to the over 30% of humankind living in terrible conditions.

Striking a balance between stability and constant change, Cerdà offered the option of smooth transitions, on the basis of which Barcelona's Eixample has prospered for a century and a half.

4. The first transition

One of the great strengths of the 1859 Cerdà Plan lies in long-term planning with a mix of private uses, with industry being situated mainly on marshy land in Poblenou (Sant Martí de Provençals), to the east, and in the Left of the Eixample, to the west. For almost a century, land was relatively cheap in both sectors, and Barcelona was one of Europe's pioneering industrial cities.

An increase in demand for residential land brought about a first transition between 1945 and 2000 in the Left of the Eixample. The entire sector was gradually enlisted for the residential programme, and also offices, as shown in graph number two.

In Poblenou, the transformation process was slower, involving a provisional shift from industry to warehouses and road transport services, which started in 1945, after the (un)civil war and World War II, and continues today.

In both cases, the metamorphosis took place without major conflict, thanks to the structural support of the street grid and to what Cerdà termed the *intervies*, the spaces between the streets, or city blocks, which have not changed in essence, and the improvement of the "transcendent thoroughfares" to link them to the "general road system".

5. A second, parallel transition

In 1953, work began on a new body of supramunicipal planning. An act dated 3 December enforced the Plan de Ordenación Urbana de Barcelona y su zona de influencia [Urban Development Plan for Barcelona and its Area of Influence] (Barcelona and the 26 municipalities immediately surrounding it) and the Comissió d'Urbanisme de Barcelona [Barcelona Urbanism Commission] was set up to administer the deployment of the supramunicipal master plan, which even today remains unique in Spain. In 1960, this Commission (which had been respected by the 1956 Spanish Land Act) was modified, transforming the body into the Comisión de Urbanismo y Servicios Comunes de Barcelona y otros Municipios [Urbanism and Common Services Commission of Barcelona and other Municipalities], though it maintained its scope and other competences.

The first National Urbanism Congress, in 1959, called for a revision of the 1953 Plan, which had lacked in ambition due to the political and economic shortcomings of the years following the two wars. Three years after the Congress, the anticipated revision was authorized. A thoroughly multidisciplinary expert team reached the conclusion that the territory of the 27 municipalities (470 km^2) would not be able to absorb the population growth anticipated by the design year 2010. It proposed an extension of the area, which was authorized as a "field of study". It comprised 162 municipalities (3,250 km^2).

In the face of the magnitude of the new territory, and without prior experience, it was considered reasonable to start with a kind of preliminary urban development plan, entitled Plan Director del Área Metropolitana de Barcelona [Barcelona Metropolitan Area Master Plan] which was completed in 1965 and approved "for internal administrative purposes" in 1968. As of the extension of the field of study, the political direction was undertaken by joint meetings of the Urbanism and Common Services Commission of Barcelona and other Municipalities (27 in total) and the Comissió Provincial d'Urbanisme de Barcelona [Barcelona Provincial Urbanism Commission] (the remaining 135 municipalities).

The problems began as a result of the difference in legal framework between the group of 27 municipalities and the group of 135. The authority to revise the Pla General d'Ordenació Urbana [General Urban Development Plan] of the former corresponded, by law, to the Urbanism and Common Services Commission of Barcelona and other Municipalities (County-level), whereas for the latter group (135), the competence to draft or revise the General Urban Development Plan corresponded, then as now, under the 1956 Spanish Land Act, to the respective councils.

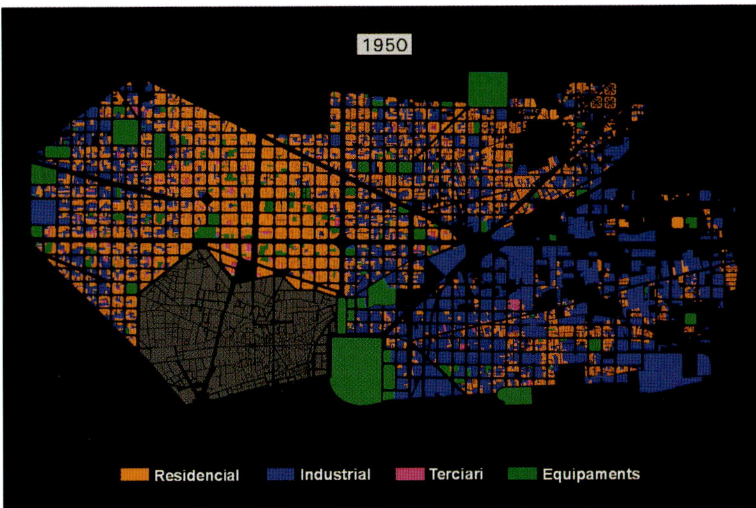

Fig. 1

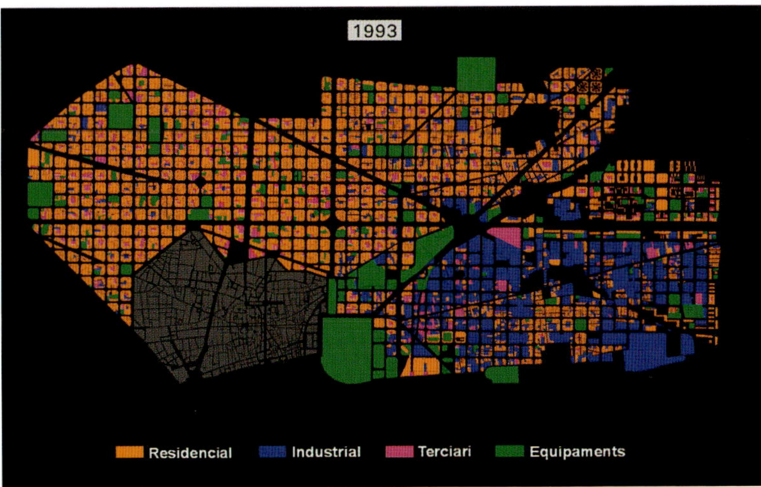

Fig. 2

In 1969, the "County-level" Commission agreed to appoint a technical team to go ahead with the revision of the 1953 Plan, following the basic outline of the Master Plan. The mechanism devised by the joint meeting of the two Urbanism Commissions was more complicated; it proved unable to pass a supramunicipal urban master plan for the group of 135 municipalities.

6. The third transition (supramunicipal urban planning)

In view of the lack of legislative support for continuing revision of the 1953 County Plan covering the 162 municipalities, and faced with the gravity of the situation at the metropolitan centre (27 municipalities), the two Commissions, County and Provincial, with the approval of the Ministerio de la Vivienda [Spanish Ministry of Housing], agreed to pursue two different courses. The County Commission was to continue on its own with finalizing the Revision of the 1953 Plan, and the two Commissions would ensure that the general urban planning of the 135 remaining

Figs. 1 & 2_Evolution of uses in Cerdà's Eixample between 1950 and 1993. (Montse Caldés i Torrent, 1991).

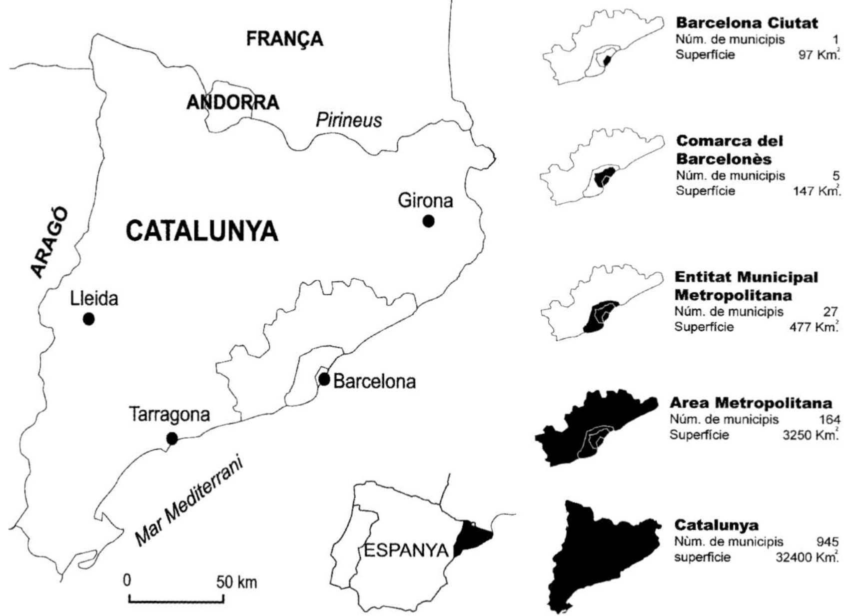

Fig. 3

municipalities was completed, though in both cases guided by the objectives and regulations of the 1968 Master Plan.

The final phase of the Revision of the General Urban Development Plan of the 27 municipalities began in 1970, under the supervision of the county-level Urbanism and Common Services Commission of Barcelona and other Municipalities. This phase might be referred to as the third transition. The fundamental differences between the two courses are quantitative and qualitative.

Firstly, the third transition involved 50% of the metropolitan population in an area of 470 km^2; furthermore, the County Plan of 1953 had undergone serious urbanistic modifications (loss of 50% of urban green areas, increases in density caused by speculation, transformation of spaces of community interest to private interest, and so on).

The impact of the proposed change had a great deal to do with Ildefons Cerdà, whose ideas served to prevent the degradation of Barcelona and its area of influence reaching Third-World levels. In legal terms, the real population of 2.7 million inhabitants could reach nine, and the Plan that was finally approved in 1976 reduced this figure to a maximum of 4.5 million (to date, it is still somewhat short of 3.1 million).

Urban spaces of collective interest (parks, facilities, basic roads, services, etc.) have doubled at least, particularly green areas. Land occupied by woods and farming, and adjacent to rivers, the coast, the port and the airport has been preserved, and the grid of "transcendent thoroughfares" has been completed.

The dictatorial regime would certainly not have approved the Revision of the Plan, but without a proposal based on Cerdà's principles and objectives, it would have been impossible to regener-

Fig. 3_Territorial scopes of Barcelona within Catalonia.

ate Barcelona so quickly during the democratic transition and seize the opportunity of the 1992 Summer Olympic Games.

7. The fourth transition

The approval of a supramunicipal General Urban Development Plan for the 135 municipalities in the second metropolitan ring has not been possible. Work has been ongoing since 1988 on the Pla Territorial de l'Àrea Metropolitana de Barcelona [Regional Plan for the Metropolitan Area of Barcelona], which has not yet received definitive approval, and efforts have ceased on completing a general urban development plan for the now 264 metropolitan municipalities as a whole, including a revision (much needed after 33 years) of the 1976 Metropolitan Master Plan.

Nonetheless, Cerdà's influence has never ceased to make itself felt. The Roman city gave way to the old town of Ciutat Vella and then to Cerdà's Eixample extension with its "transcendent thoroughfares". At the same time, a periphery grew up which never, either before or after being annexed to Barcelona, embraced Cerdà's ideas, just as the 1953 Plan failed to take them into account.

Conversely, both the Metropolitan Area Master Plan of 1968 and the Barcelona Master Plan of 1976 were explicitly developed in keeping with Cerdà's ideas. The clearest way of visualizing their influence is to consider urban densities, the spaces of collective interest and particularly the major infrastructures: the basic road network, international connections and the port (with the addition of the airport).

Cerdà's impact is more evident if we consider the leap the city has taken to its area of influence and to the metropolitan area, by extrapolating the transcendent thoroughfares to Catalonia as a whole (Regional Master Plan of 1995) and across the Pyrenees (plan of the Comunitat de Treball dels Pirineus [Pyrenean Work Community]) to the rest of Europe, clearly highlighting the orthogonal grid of motorways and the classification of the territory into *vies*, or thoroughfares, and *intervies*, the spaces between them.

We can only hope that another of Cerdà's great principles, that "the content (the people)" is more important than "the container (the stones)", will help in the near future to end the anomaly of 80% of urbanites who, instead of having "decent, reasonably priced homes", are struggling to get by in shanties. That would be Cerdà's greatest contribution to the world.

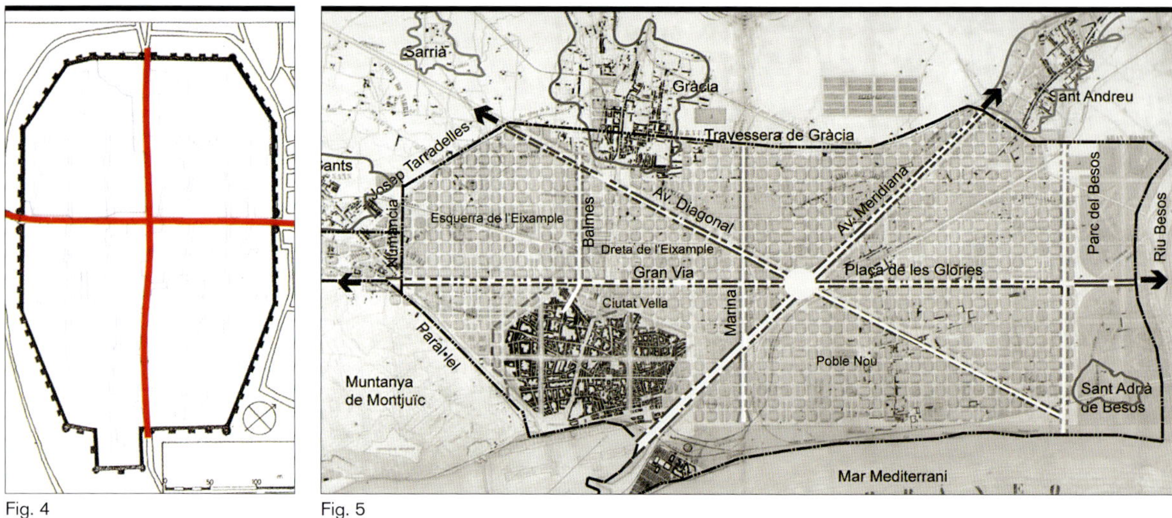

Fig. 4

Fig. 5

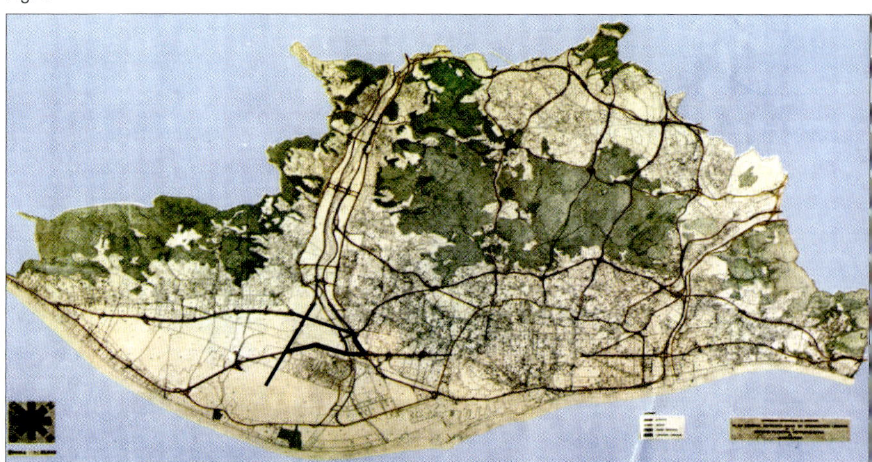

Fig. 6

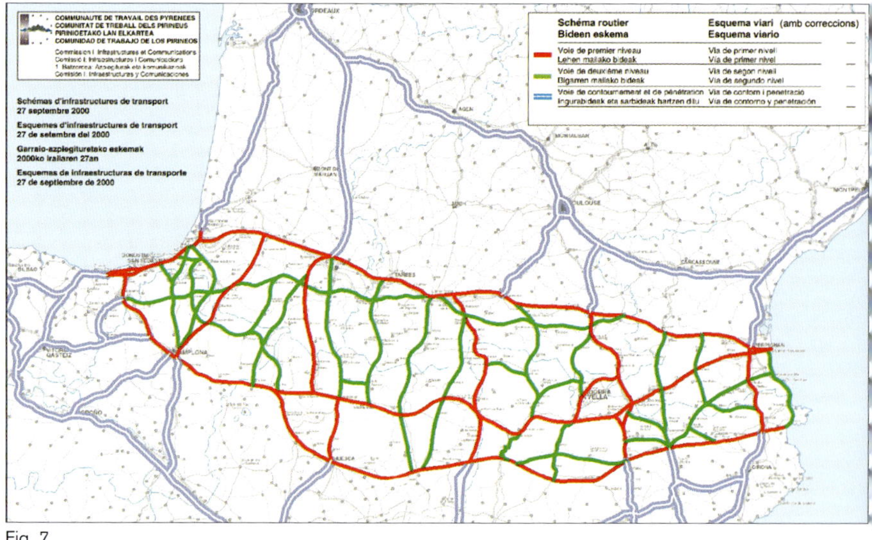

Fig. 7

Fig. 4_ Roman Barcelona (1st century AD): cardo and decumanus.

Fig. 5_Outline for the Remodelling and Extension of Barcelona (Ildefons Cerdà, 1859).

Fig. 6_Pla General Metropolità de Barcelona 1976 [1976 Barcelona Metropolitan Master Plan] (modified).

Fig. 8

Fig. 9

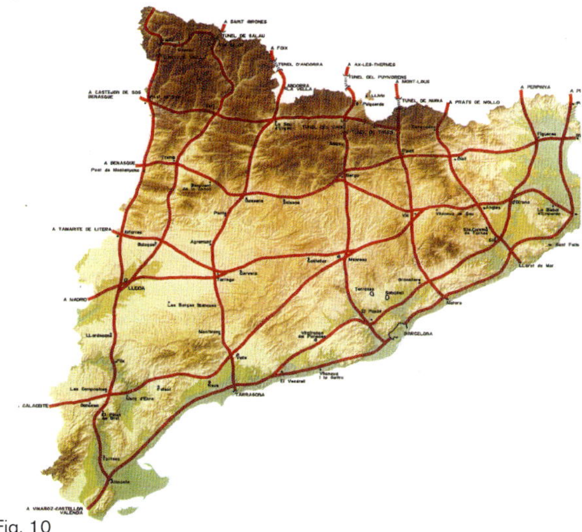

Fig. 10

Fig. 7_ Pyrenees. Proposed road network (Albert Serratosa, 1982).

Fig. 8_ Metropolitan area of Barcelona.

Fig. 9_ Proposed motorway network (Albert Serratosa, 1965/1988).

Fig.10_ Europe. Proposed motorway network (Albert Serratosa, 1982).

0._The following is an entirely free and personal reflection on the significance for urban planning and the territory of the figure of Ildefons Cerdà i Sunyer. It is one of many—indeed, endless—reflections that even today, 150 years after his emergence as the *creator* of Barcelona's Eixample extension, Cerdà continues to excite. It consciously ignores the risk of lapsing into the commonplace or facile repetition. In this respect, I consider that the force of the important figures who, throughout history, have been truly original and innovative lies in their potential for being reinterpreted, reworked and recreated by a new way of seeing. In this case, I am in no doubt that this is very much the situation of Cerdà. It is also the aim of this text: to examine the man in terms of the metaphor represented by the overall import of his contribution and set him in the context of the coordinates of the present day, without forgetting the past, but above all thinking of the future as the optimum time for a positive, tangible projection of his ideas onto the multiple scales of the territory.

In addition to the above aim, this text seeks to remind readers that Cerdà's ideas still have an unsuspected potential—if only in a metaphorical sense—that is worth exploring. By this I mean not simply "applying" his theoretical developments, but embracing, constructively but also imaginatively and openly, his overall legacy: his ideal of territorial balance and harmony, his essential vision of citizenry and the citizen, his way of understanding equity, his integrative view of the territory and of cities, and of the urban world in relation to the rural world, and so on. It is not that I believe, ultimately, that Cerdà contains the key to the future of humankind; I would simply like to highlight the fact that underlying his body of ideas there is an undreamt-of creative potential. This potential is founded on a tremendous dose of rationality, common sense and practice intelligence that I think is perfectly applicable, today, to the management of any territory, any city and any inhabited place on the Earth.

The text is divided into 12 consecutive points in addition to this introduction. Together, these 12 points embrace the entire *chronology* of the history of humankind: from the origin of the universe, with the big bang, to the present day. These 12 points are not tabled as a regular division of this chronology. In some cases, they cover long periods (such as geological time); in others, they focus on moments or epochs that I consider to merit closer consideration, such as the colonization of the territory in Europe and the distribution of the population in the Middle Ages, the impact of the industrial revolution or the challenges presented by the population explosion of the last 100 years, etc. Other important figures also deserve particular consideration, due to a convergence of significance with this examination of Cerdà: the philosopher Kant and the naturalist Darwin. I likewise include some illustrative reflections on Cerdà, by Arturo Soria and Albert Serratosa, which also have a strong power of suggestion. My intention is, ultimately, to present an attractive, thought-provoking view of Cerdà, with a view to stimulating interest and curiosity about the man and emphasising the ongoing value of his contribution, over and above specific events or moments in time. My aim with this text is, within the limits of my possibilities, to cast new light on the eternal Cerdà, the Cerdà who invented, proposed, questioned, imagined and recreated at every scale, from the most everyday to the most universal—in short, the Cerdà who fought to make humankind at least a little better than it was when he had the opportunity of knowing it.

1._It all began some 15 thousand million years ago.

This is not just an anecdote; it is the origin of the universe.

For a long time, a statement of this kind was pure conjecture. Not now. Or, in any case, it is less conjectural. Recent astrophysics has shown that this date is a plausible hypothesis. We now have a milestone, an initial point of reference for tracing our origins. Depending on how you view it, it may not mean much. All things considered, perhaps it is a great deal. Never before has humankind had recourse to this datum. A datum that is a date: universe-time.

As of this moment, humankind has the possibility of *conceiving of itself* that it has never had in its entire existence.

2._The big bang is the zero point, the starting point, but nothing more. So what is the rest? A sequence that brings us up to the present day. Some 4,500 million years ago, the Earth was formed. Some thousand million years later, the first signs of life began to appear in its oceans, and they were signs of a life that gradually organized itself and became more complex...

...On the long road to hominization, there are three key dates: seven million years ago, the last common ancestor of humans and chimpanzees; 3.7 million years ago, the origin of the human species (*Australopithecus afarensis*); 150,000 years ago, the origin of the species *Homo sapiens*.

With the introduction of hominization and *Homo sapiens,* we can no longer speak of the universe in the abstract, or even of the Earth. We are necessarily speaking of Africa. The expression “Africa, the birthplace of humanity” is not just a saying; it is the formulation of an incontrovertible fact that science has brought to the fore in recent decades. On no account should humankind forget that.

3._Recent research into the human genome has allowed us to draw an important conclusion: that two thousand generations before ours—that is, some 55,000 years ago—the first humans left the African continent heading for the Middle East. It was a simple question of survival: the glaciation in northern Europe had produced great droughts in Africa and, with them, the disappearance of pasture and hunting. Famine took the human species to the brink of extinction. It is believed, though, that some two hundred individuals, divided into two groups, managed to reach more propitious lands. The first group, following the coast through Arabia, India and Indonesia, reached Australia, probably not many millennia after leaving the continent of its birth. The other group settled in Central Asia and turned this territory into a major focus of diffusion: it was from this point that humans reached China, 35,000 years ago, Europe, 30,000 years ago and Siberia, 20,000 years ago.

The last glaciation ended 10,000 years ago, and the change of environmental circumstances enabled humans to settle and become farmers. Humankind ceased to be necessarily migrant and embarked on a new cycle.

It is within the bounds of probability that concepts such as culture or urbanism date from this moment.

4._Probably the history of colonization (understood as the process of gradual occupation of the territory by the human species, at multiple scales of space and time) is far more complex and discontinuous than we could ever have imagined before the discoveries of modern paleoanthropology, biochemistry and genomics.

We might think, for example, that the history of colonization has a focus of particular intensity in the Mediterranean (roughly speaking, between the Strait of Gibraltar, the coasts of the Black Sea and the mouth of the Nile). This is a geographical area in which, due to particularly favourable conditions of insolation and temperature, there may, at the time of reference (the last glaciation, 10,000 years ago), have been a relative high density of human occupation.

It is a fact that the oldest cities of which we know are situated in the Mediterranean or in a geographical area adjacent to it. It is also a fact that the colonization of the northern reaches of Europe (the last place in the continent to become free of ice) is relatively recent. By way of example, the Finnish city of Oulu, near the Arctic polar circle, in the European tundra, was founded just 400 years ago. Today, with just 130,000 inhabitants, and despite the rigours of the polar winter, it is one of the leading technological centres in our continent.

5._It initially seems plain, then, that the city is essentially a tangible event (that is, a concrete form of settlement) that is highly conditioned by environmental factors and the shifting circumstances of the historical migrations of human groups, associated with these environmental factors.

Despite this consideration, the history of urbanism has traditionally emphasised the existence of two conceptions of city: one seen as a grouping together of citizens (with the accent on citizenry), the other as a built phenomenon (which can, therefore, be remodelled and planned). The first is associated mainly with Greece, and the second with Rome.

It seems clear that these two conceptions are complementary rather than antithetic. Although it is obvious that each can be envisaged independently, it is perfectly feasible to envisage them from a single, integrated viewpoint—indeed, it would also be more logical and more effective in practical terms.

6._An integrated conception of the history of the urban phenomenon would also serve to address a consideration that is highly debatable in many respects: the dichotomy or specific opposition between city and country, between the urban and the rural world.

The history of Europe, from early human colonization to the present day, highlights the limitations of this dichotomy. It is impossible to understand Europe without its cities, just as these cities cannot be understood without taking into account the deep-seated interdependence they have had since their origins with their respective hinterlands, or the rural world in general.

It has been said that present-day Europe is the product of the network of cities that formed during the Middle Ages, right across the continent. This is partly the case, but it is not the whole truth. Present-day Europe is also the product of the major changes that these cities brought about in their hinterlands and throughout the territory as a whole; of the major processes of deforestation, draining wetlands and marshes, improving pastureland, irrigation and cultivation, and of the incipient network of roads created by the relation between cities and their rural surroundings, which is the basis for the network of overland communications today.

Nor, finally, can the history of Europe be understood without reference to the struggles of the peasant class to free itself of obligations to feudal lords. In an attempt to emphasize the promi nence of urban events in history, it has been said that "city air makes men free". But throughout the medieval centuries, peasants and country people all over Europe defended values that were comparable in many respects. Freedom, as a supreme ideal, has never been the monopoly of either domain, within or without city walls.

7._It is evident that humankind has tended throughout history towards change. "Change—that is, adaptation—or death", we might say, to sum up the general trend in a pithy motto.

But one change stands out from all the others from the viewpoint of the present day. It was a veritable catalyst: it accentuated and took to its conceivable limits the inveterate, persistent tendency towards change. It has been called the "industrial revolution", but it could also be called the "revolution of movement". This revolution, viewed two centuries after it began, has broken all the parameters of time and space that hitherto served human groups as a referent and measure of their existence.

Kant sensed the far-reaching significance of this major change when it was barely making itself felt, and on the basis of this intuition he constructed a new way of thinking. Philosophy is divided into before and after Kant.

Darwin applied the same idea (an intuition, we might call it) to the observation and study of living beings and stated that we are all, without exception, essentially the product of change. His observations marked the start of an inexorable process of demythification of the human species. Science is definitely divided into before and after Darwin.

Cerdà, in turn, aware of the importance of the industrial revolution to urban life and the territory as a whole, envisaged a new idea of city and set out to make it a reality. It was to be the new city of Barcelona, the Eixample of 1859. And his *Teoria general de la urbanització* [General Theory of Urbanization] was the idea made book. He was the first author to conceive of urbanism in terms of theory and practice. The field of urbanism and the science of the territory are also, then, divided into before and after Cerdà.

8._The first condition for designing the city and the territory, today, from a threefold viewpoint of past, present and future, is the ability to rise to a real challenge: accepting the significance of the last century and a half of history of humankind. It may be an insignificant period of time against the scale of the overall history of the universe, yet it is sufficient to radically transmute the rate and the extent of the impact of the human species on its surroundings, both close at hand and more distant.

Today, we might regard Cerdà as the first thinker about the city and the territory to have truly risen to this challenge.

On the one hand, we are dealing with an important figure who was situated chronologically at the point of inflection, at the key moment of change to which we refer. On the other, it is important not to forget that the essence of his thought and the keys to his actions are inseparable from the specific time and geographical context in which this remarkable urban planner lived.

The importance of Cerdà is clearly and succinctly summarised by Albert Serratosa in the following paragraph:

"We have to substantiate the idea of restoring to a pre-eminent place in history an extraordinary man called Ildefons Cerdà, unknown and marginalized by very specific interests of the established order. He is a man who deserves a very high position in the world's history of science ranking. [...] No one, before him, had addressed the theme of the city from so many viewpoints. Indeed, no one had even tried. Cerdà was concerned with 'the hygienic order, the moral order, the economic order', 'the political order, the legal order' and, naturally, with social, functional and aesthetic aspects, logic, rationality, feelings, justice, freedom, equality, internal coherence. No other thinker or treatise-writer has even attempted to grapple with all the complexity of these human artefacts that we call cities. The histories of urbanism feature many people; some, rather few, offered specific, notable contributions; others had important ideas but were dogged by misinterpretation or blatantly overruled by very unfortunate proposals or interventions. They all share the common denominator of the partiality of their analyses, diagnoses and proposals. Cerdà's global, technical and humanistic vision is one of the characteristics that sets him apart from the rest and requires greater attention." (Albert Serratosa, *Una introducció a Ildefons Cerdà*)

9._It has been calculated that in the mid-17th century, the Earth had approximately 250 million inhabitants, a figure reached after a few centuries of very slow growth and some remarkably long intervals and downward fluctuations which, at times, could be quite considerable.

A century later, the figure was nearing 750 million, and after another, by around 1850, it stood at approximately 1,200 million.

From the outset, the revolution of movement had broken all the parameters of the rate and extent of growth of the human population known to date. From 1,200 million, it rose to 1,600 in the early 20th century and then to 6,500 million at the beginning of the 21st century. As regards the coming decades, there is nothing to suggest an interruption of this constant and apparently uncontrollable upward trend.

The emergence and the universal diffusion of the "civilization of movement", in the terms that Cerdà intuited so skilfully, has evidently obliged humankind to rethink itself. And it must do so in many different ways: in scope and in depth. The challenge is unavoidable and is of the utmost complexity because it is based on intrinsically conflicting components. It is, literally, a question of light and shadows. On the one hand, light: the material progress of the last 150 years, served by the exceptional advances of science and technology, is indisputable and has placed levels of creativity at their highest point in the history of humankind. On the other, shadows: this material progress has not been accompanied by the moral and cultural progress that should have correlated. The unfortunate result is that a period that has seen the deployment and development of many of the best and most complete expressions of human genius has also been the period in which ignominy and barbarity, in terms both absolute and relative, reached the highest imaginable level.

10._The civilization of movement, which has been so important to the evolution of humankind in the last century and a half, can also be considered from a more specific viewpoint: that of urbanism and regional planning. In this situation, we now detect a particularly serious problem: the difficulty of reconciling past and present (and also future, in that its seed is contained in the present).

The two are difficult to reconcile because our starting point is a past that has been slowly decanted, laid down over the centuries, and is faced with a present that is, in many respects, the complete opposite: instant, ephemeral, and ruled by constant change and transformation.

They are difficult to reconcile because, in the civilization of movement, the classical ideas of settlement, population and mobility (the latter understood more as "staticness") are reaching an irreversible, inexorable crisis point. The network of villages and cities is the same as ever (indeed, it is a historic legacy). The functions, expectations and needs of these villages and cities are, however, increasingly new ones. The foundations of change have been laid, and change is, in itself, unavoidable.

Reconciliation is, ultimately, difficult because it will never again be possible to look at the city and the territory in the way we used to. From a classical viewpoint, the prevalence of an aesthetics-based conception of urbanism was even, to a point, logical: the city as a work of art, the city as an object of contemplation. Beyond the city, nothing, or almost nothing, existed. Now, this premise has proved completely insufficient: the multifunctionality of the city, its irradiation in space and its serious problems and contradictions call for a broader, better thought-out, more ambitious and operative approach.

In this context, Cerdà and his urbanism, with the figure of the citizen as its epicentre and essential point of reference, once again offer a truly relevant approach, and one with future.

11._Arturo Soria y Puig, a leading theoretician and scholar devoted to Cerdà and his work, suggests that an overall understanding of his legacy has to take into account his progressive achievements in the intellectual sphere. According to Soria, these achievements were the product of an intense personal maturing process, which began its gestation in 1844 and materialized between 1855 and 1876 (the last 21 years of his life). These were not just professional milestones: they were, rather, four successive levels in an intense process of creative reflection that took Cerdà from the scale closest to the individual to the more general, without overlooking the intermediate scales: from the dwelling to the territory as a whole, via circulation and urbanization.

The dwelling is, then, the point of departure. On this head, Cerdà's premises were quite clear: independence and interrelation. Independence of the individual in his or her home, independence of the individual home from the urban whole. Housing problems, according to Cerdà, could only be approached with a determination to breach "this *immoral divorce* that exists between hygiene, art and economy in constructions".

The next level was circulation. It was here that Cerdà stated one of his most innovative achievements: the principle of continuous movement. He applied this principle to different scales of movement, passing from the scale of the pedestrian to that of traffic, and thence to the scale of the railway, all the time considering the compatibility—the continuity—between the various scales. This analysis of the relations between scales produced one of his fundamental theses: "each new means of locomotion determines a new form of urbanization."

The third level is urbanization itself. At this level, Cerdà managed to combine housing and circulation in a single theory. The cornerstone of the theory is his concept of *intervies* (the spaces between the streets, the actual street blocks), another of the planner's great accomplishments. This level also had recourse to relations between scales and a high degree of flexibility of application: this allowed Cerdà to consider housing beyond the limits of the parcel, while promoting an understanding of the street (and of the city) as a network (of a complexity that increases with scale and ultimately constitutes a great grid system).

This brings us to the fourth and final level: the territory. It was the final level in that it marked the "culmination" of Cerdà's overall logic (a logic in which the "culmination" neither invalidates nor excludes the preceding levels, but completes them). It is here that Cerdà's central premise ("Urbanize the rural and rurize[1] the urban") became, in itself, the terse expression of its author's

1_Conceptually, Cerdà made a distinction between "rurize" (from "*rur*") and "ruralize" (from "rural"). He accorded great importance to these themes, which are little known in terms of today's terminology.

thinking. In spite of everything, Cerdà was not ultimately able to apply this premise in the way he had conceived—that is, as a general theory.

Yet this premise has the value of a metaphor. It is a metaphor that allows us to envision new ways of applying, developing and innovatively reinterpreting Cerdà's legacy.

12._In the field of language, a metaphor is a literary figure that serves to trigger off the creative imagination of the reader or receiver of the message, extending beyond the rigid, literal nature of mere words.

The creative imagination is probably one of the most powerful tools to have been developed by the human species, the primitive *Homo sapiens*, in its long (and uneven, and fragmented, and syncopated...) process of adaptation to the constantly changing conditions of its environment. It is a tool the species has developed and now holds in its hands, and will, foreseeably, continue to have in the future.

We might say that the work of Ildefons Cerdà, the notable urbanist, a man who was clear-sighted, controversial and misunderstood in his day, and today known only episodically, tangentially or partially, is, ultimately, a great metaphor hovering over the contradictions, the chiaroscuros, the fortunes and the misfortunes, the sometime inextricable but frequently fascinating magma of our present.

In view of Cerdà's legacy, the point to which the "civilization of movement" has brought us takes the form of an apparently simple, almost ingenuous question: what form should planning take? That is, how can we effectively think ahead, intuit and foresee the situations and needs of tomorrow on the basis of a present which, in itself, is nothing but a fleeting, evasive form?

It may be useful, at this point, to remember the words of Albert Serratosa:

"The need to plan the territory is increasingly peremptory with every passing day. Because the number of agents is increasing exponentially. Because these agents are increasingly qualified and equipped with more possibilities. Because the Earth has imprecise but definite limitations. Because we want to ensure wellbeing (or less ill-being) today, tomorrow and the day after. There is no point planning for a future that is limited and remote in time. The great, unprecedented effort involved must be devoted to preparing presents, the sum of which constitutes that poorly defined entity that we call future." (Albert Serratosa, *Arrels filosòfiques de la planificació territorial.*)

It is not certain, nor is it scientifically demonstrable, that humankind will definitely have what we have come to call, rather abstractly, "the day after". Doubts about its tomorrow hover over the human race today, with almost the same doses of uncertainty as at any moment in the history of *Homo sapiens sapiens*.

But taking as our basis the relativity of things and, most of all, creative human consciousness, we could agree on one quite simple point: that where the metaphor goes, the future will follow.

The Eixample extension of Barcelona and the modernity of Cerdà's urbanistic theories _ Francesc Magrinyà

1._ Barcelona's Eixample: the product of applying Cerdà's urbanistic theories

Cerdà is a controversial figure, but what is unquestionable is the mark left by his Projecte de Reforma i Eixample de Barcelona [Project for the Remodelling and Extension of Barcelona] (CERDÀ, 1859), and the fact that since its approval on 30 May 1860 it has marked the organization of the city of Barcelona for 150 years. By way of example, in 1999 Avinguda Diagonal was extended below Plaça de les Glòries, and Barcelona's great municipal debate in 2009, 150 years later, centres around the remodelling of Avinguda Diagonal using the grid as support for mobility.

Any discussion of Cerdà produces a degree of awkwardness. How can a figure who lived a century and a half ago have had ideas so modern that his planning proposals are still so applicable today? Some have dealt with this dilemma by ignoring the man and centring on his body of work, taking the built Eixample as the object and focus of their research. My aim is the exact opposite: to extract from that body of work a series of urban planning ideas that go beyond Barcelona's Eixample to show how some of his ideas are still very modern today and are, therefore, points of reference in planning and constructing today's cities.

To take this step, it is vital to read *Teoría General de la Urbanización* [General Theory of Urbanization] (henceforth *TGU*) (CERDÀ, 1867). Behind the reiterative, baroque 19th-century forms that are initially rather tedious, a reader who explores the *TGU* in greater detail will discover a precision of approach, an aspiration towards the globality of the urban phenomenon and an impressive coherence in his outlook. A philosopher friend suggested that anyone wishing to learn philosophy should read an author who has dealt with all philosophical issues, and then read other authors to compare and contrast the different responses to the issues arising. While this exercise can be carried out with the few authors to have addressed all philosophical questions, in the case of the urban planning discipline, there are very few urbanists of such depth and breadth, and yet who remain so up-to-date, as Cerdà. It is this that makes him a vital reference point in urbanistic theory.

2. The elements of Cerdà's urbanistic theory

An examination of the elements of urban-planning theory that have been key to the construction of the Eixample as a model produces a list of seven:

_1. The **relation between container and content**. Cerdà carried out a detailed analysis of the population and its activities (CERDÀ, 1868)—that is, the content. He also analysed which would be the best container to adapt to the needs of this content. At that time, the purpose was to provide good housing conditions that met hygienic parameters and responded to new transport needs. His aim was, firstly, for the population to have access to decent housing and, secondly, for cities to adapt to the new transport needs.

_2. The proposal of a territorial distribution that implemented the maxim "**urbanize the rural and 'rurize' the urban"** to go beyond the city-country dialectic. This distribution represents a perfect organization of urban and natural systems, and ensures interpenetration of the two.

_3. The interpretation of urbanization as striking a balance between movement and rest, which corresponds to the dialectic between relation and isolation, society and individual, and streets and housing. The instrument he proposed was the structure of ***vies-intervies*, or thoroughfares and the spaces left between them, which we know as city blocks**.

_4. The decision to **interpret the territory on the basis of a structure of *vies-intervies* that takes as its scale of organization that of the urban nucleus and the *comarca* or county, down to the detailed layout of the rooms and corridors of a dwelling**. This led him to an interpretation of the history of urbanization by means of the successive adaptations of the *vies-intervies*. For Cerdà, urban forms were governed by a successive adaptation to the introduction of each new means of transport and communication. Cerdà saw the introduction of the railway and the telegraph, and designed the **Eixample as an interchanger of relations and activities associated with the railway as a new means of transport**.

_5. The construction of the city using a few simple yet forceful elements, which, in the case of Barcelona's Eixample, were: a model of **street and crossroads** defined at the scale of the urban project, a model of **dwelling** that took the rental apartment building between party walls as a reference, corresponding perfectly to the dimensions of the city block; and the system of **urban utility networks** defined according to the street section. This outline moved the project from street and plot to *via-intervia*. It provides space for movement (the streets) and proposes a balance between the dwelling and the garden in the *intervies*.

_6. Uniform, hierarchical access according to the type of facility for the various **services, in keeping with the economy and the hygienic needs of each community.**

_7. A series of instruments to implement his project, which Arturo Soria calls the five bases of urbanization of the *TGU*: **technical** (which includes the foregoing points), **legal**, **administrative**, **economic** and **political** (SORIA, 1995). In addition to the technical elements deriving from the above points, Cerdà ensured there was legislation to enable the implementation of his proposals. He backed Posada Herrera's 1861 bill on the drainage, remodelling and extension of towns, which finally became the 1864 Extensions Act, for which the *TGU* was to be the application manual, and he introduced the reparcelling system with his document *Cuatro palabras sobre el Ensanche* [A few words about the Extension] (CERDÀ, 1861). Yet it would not be possible to understand his project without the *Ordenanzas de Construcción* [Construction bylaws] (CERDÀ, 1859) and *Pensamiento Económico* [Economic thinking] (CERDÀ, 1860), referents for the administrative and economic bases, which were associated with the implementation of the project. Finally, he proposed the political thinking of transaction to move towards the proposed model.

3._ Some elements of reflection on Cerdà's Eixample

3.1. Construction organized according to the city block and the generation of complex fabric

One of the keys to the success of the Eixample and its modernity lies in the design of city blocks with a side dimension associated with the dimensions of construction. The city block model proposed by Cerdà consisted of a built block on either side, each block with a garden that was as wide as the block. If a city block has a side of 113 m, one metre of which is taken up by the walls of the various constructions, the effective width is 112 m. If this city block is divided into two strips, each of 56 m, and each of these strips is subdivided into 50% construction and 50% garden, the built depth for each block is 28 m. In his *Ordenanzas de Construcción* of 1859, Cerdà limited construction to a maximum depth of 28 m. This figure is an invariable parameter in all the built city blocks in the Eixample.

The approval of the 1860 Extension Project imposed the condition of building on three sides and, later, Cerdà himself designed city blocks that were built on all four sides. What did remain constant, however, was the built depth of 28 m. The shift from a city block with two blocks to one built on four sides meant that the occupation of the city block rose from 50% to 73%, which is the level of occupation recognised by the 1976 Barcelona Metropolitan Master Plan. Maintaining unchanged the maximum depth of grouped buildings led to the formation of a unitary courtyard at the centre of the city block, guaranteeing highly favourable conditions of hygiene and sunlighting. This evolution produced business premises comprising a ground floor and mezzanine that were sufficiently large (between 750 and 2,200 m^2) to allow shops and, later, industrial workshops to coexist with housing. The result is a compact, complex, diverse city that is a present-day point of reference for models of sustainable cities.

3.2. From specialized streets to specialized fabrics

A comparison of the extensions of Sabadell, Terrassa and Vilanova with Barcelona's Eixample reveals a basic distinguishing feature: street width. In the Catalan towns that were extended at the same time (Sabadell, Terrassa, Vilanova), the new streets were between 10 and 12 metres wide, whereas Cerdà proposed streets of 20 metres. This is one of the basic aspects of Barcelona's Eixample, where today it is possible to introduce bus and cycle lanes and parkways, because the streets were designed according to the criterion of the principle of independence of different means of transport.

Any attempt to adapt Cerdà's thinking to the present day has to address the invasion of the Eixample by the car. If a street in the Eixample is opened to vehicles, its average daily traffic (ADT) is over 10,000 vehicles, traffic noise is greater than 65 decibels, and the environmental quality of the streets is poor. This is why, in the Eixample, applying Cerdà's principles, the streets should be specialized, with one in three dedicated to mechanical forms of transport (private vehicles and over-ground public transport), thereby freeing up two other streets with parkways for pedestrians and bicycles, with high environmental quality.

It is also important to point out that the construction of the Eixample has been precarious but consistent, with the owners paying for the reparcelling and transfer of land, and for the initial urbanization, which consisted in the levelling of streets and the definition of a section with a pavement and the introduction of trees. Subsequently, the rates levied on the rents of the apartment building allowed the introduction of the various urban utilities (drainage, water, gas, electricity, telephone and paving) and associated furniture. This system was used during the first period

(1860-1870) of the construction of the Eixample, on land formerly occupied by the city walls and on the right of the Eixample within the original city limits, but it remerged towards the end of the century (1894), when Sant Martí Council published the street typologies according to Cerdà's model. Once this simple yet forceful model was established, the variability was found in the city block solutions.

3.3. The principle of continuity of movement today: the need for nodes as meeting points

Cerdà envisaged each crossroads as a meeting point, a place for interrelation. This is true for sustainable means of transport, but not for private vehicles. The Eixample has been hijacked by the car, which has overtaken other means. Cerdà envisaged 1,200 crossroads for the Eixample, at which he located kiosks to accommodate activities of interrelation and services. In the Eixample today, not one crossroads has become a square, despite the fact that the street junctions are similar in size to all the squares in towns in the Barcelona Plain (Plaça del Sol and Plaça de Rius i Taulet in Gràcia, Plaça del Mercadal in Sant Andreu and Plaça de la Concòrdia in Les Corts, to give some examples).

If, in the future, more sustainable means come to the fore, it will be possible to recover these public spaces that have been taken over by the loading and unloading of private vehicles.

Another paradigm example is that of Plaça de les Glories. Cerdà thought that this node should represent a new centrality, with administrative buildings. Later, in 1905, Jaussely designed a large oval there, with buildings in perspective. That node has never actually become a point of centrality. The decision to construct on the space came with the introduction of urban expressways, after the 1953 County Plan, and the development of the Eastern Sector Special Plan in 1958. Then, a road junction was built using an initial proposal that picked up the large plaza proposed by Cerdà and Jaussely. But two years later, a junction was introduced at a different level and a whole series of slip roads was subsequently built. Evidently, activities shunned the node, because it lacked urbanness and relations, and had just flows of traffic. The city's urban design response on the occasion of the Olympic Games was to turn the road junction into a monument by introducing a park at its centre. This solution has since been perceived as erroneous. The solutions now being proposed are based on the design of an empty space that makes the same mistake. A return to Cerdà's thinking shows that the solution for the junction lies in encouraging the circulation of sustainable means of transport that allow for human interactions and relations, but what are needed above all are activities that generate relations. It is now time to return to the proposals of Cerdà and Jaussely, and design the administrative buildings for the city to make this node a point of metropolitan centrality.

3.4. Facilities that make a city

The model of facilities that Cerdà proposed in the Eixample served to organize housing, shops and industry, but the organization of facilities has not been so successful. The scale of the city block has been good for markets, but not for social centres. It has been insufficient for combining facilities and other activities within a single city block. This may be due, principally, to the lack of action on the part of public services.

A successful recent paradigm case is the Fort Pienc city block, which combines housing with a school, a civic centre and a supermarket, with a square at the centre of the city block that communicates them all.

3.5. The legal basis: reparcelling as a reference

The introduction of a new model of city called for instruments to transform the pre-existing plot system into one defined by *vies-intervies*. This in turn required the introduction of a reparcelling mechanism, outlined by Cerdà in the publication *Cuatro palabras sobre el Ensanche* [A few words about the extension] (CERDÀ, 1861), based on a judicious distribution among the owners of the profits and liabilities produced by turning rural land into regulated urban tracts for development in proportion to the plot in question and adapted to new transport needs. Without this instrument, the Eixample would not have been possible.

3.6. The economic basis: the appearance of the urban planning operator

With his Pla Econòmic de l'Eixample i la Reforma Interior [Economic Plan for the Extension and Remodelling] (CERDÀ, 1860), Cerdà established a system to give physical form to urbanization and rejected the system used by Haussmann in Paris, by means of which the Bank of France paid for the remodelling of the city (CERDÀ, 1861), and which could ultimately be the case of the mammoth task of the remodelling of Madrid and the M-30. Taking as his guide equality and the fair distribution of profits and liabilities, Cerdà established that any urban remodelling was to be financed by the advantages it afforded. If the property owners overlooking the street enjoyed the benefits of the new streets in the form of increased value of their land and buildings, it should be they who provided the financing, thereby interpreting the Roman maxim "*qui sentit commodum et incommodum sentire debet*" (he who receives the advantage ought also to suffer the burden). To his *Teoría de la Viabilidad Urbana y Reforma de la de Madrid* [Theory of urban viability and remodelling of that of Madrid] of 1861 (CERDÀ, 1861), Cerdà added a procedural regulation that involved devising a tendering process comparable to the Contract Specifications of the Railways Tender of 1844. He envisaged financing extensions by levying a tax on plots of land according to their relation to streets, according to the scheme of obligatory free transfer. Cerdà's principle was that landowners were exchanging a rural plot of land for an urban tract, which increased its value fifteen-fold, and that it should therefore be the owners who made over the land for streets and paid for urbanization. This process was administered by the Comissió d'Eixample [City Extension Commission], which was the agency that collected these urban rates and urbanized the streets once the land had been ceded, and became the urban planning operator for the Eixample.

3.7. The political basis: combining what is desirable with what is possible in order to construct proposals, using transaction as a transition to the ideal model

Finally, Cerdà put forward as a guide for intervention the principle of transaction to transition. Realising that the planned solution could not be carried out immediately, he trusted to a transition towards his proposed model, insisting on the imperative of a series of minimums, or transaction, to ensure the constant direction of the trend. The flexibility of the instruments used was to be one of the strong points for his planned development of the city. A comparison of the 1859 Extension and Remodelling Project with the plan for the reparcelling of land formerly occupied by the city walls, passed in 1865, presents a series of essential changes that affected Plaça de Catalunya and represented a high degree of flexibility in Cerdà's work. He had designed a large square on Passeig de Gràcia, next to the old town, but above Gran Via. Cerdà wanted a square near the main streets, Gran Via and Passeig de Gràcia. The owners of plots giving into Passeig de Gràcia realized that their properties would be affected; they brought pressure to bear to modify the 1860 Extension Plan by means of a Royal Order dated 1861, and managed to have the planned square eliminated. Cerdà reacted by locating the square, today's Plaça de Catalunya, below Gran Via, by means of the 1865 Reparcelling Project. One detail to illustrate this change is the fact that the first house to be built was in the present-day Plaça de Catalunya, developed by Gibert, former President of the Diputació provincial council and one of the champions of the Eixample, but who had had his building constructed in 1860-1861 according to the alignments of the Plan passed in May 1860. Where Cerdà would not compromise was on the construction of Gran Via at a tangent to the old town and the construction of the ring roads as major 30-m wide thoroughfares on which the grid was imposed.

4._ The modernity of Cerdà today

To gauge the modernity of Cerdà today, it is necessary to consider whether the principles of his thinking are still relevant and, if so, to what extent.

First, it is important to say that Cerdà's most important contribution was his integrative approach to the urban and territorial issue, similar to other authors who have addressed all urban and territorial issues. Going back to the Renaissance, these include the proposals of Alberti and, more recently, those of Le Corbusier, Wright or Alexander (Choay, 1981).

The key elements of his proposals from a present-day perspective include:

_The **relation between container and content**. This is a vital approach. The contributions of *The Architecture of the City* (Rossi, 1984), interesting at the time, have hijacked urbanism by attempting to mythify the forms of the container, over and above the relations between container and content. Urban planning proposals cannot be merely formal exercises in volume and spatial distribution. It is essential to return to the origins of the relation between container and content.

_The proposal of a territorial layout that implements the maxim "**urbanize the rural and 'rurize' the urban"** to go beyond the city-country dialectic is right up to date. Today we have urban ecology that links urban with natural systems in terms of flows of water, energy and materials. Planning can no longer ignore this approach. Cerdà reminds us that the aim is not to completely separate urban systems and open spaces, but to "rurize" the urban, which he summarised perfectly in the introduction of nature into the city, with the planting of trees in the streets (now known as parkways); the balance between housing and garden in the *intervies*; and the introduction of a system of gardens, parks and woods for the city.

_The interpretation of urbanization as a balance between movement and rest is still very topical. The proposed instrument of ***vies-intervies*** does not yet seem to have been fully assumed. Proof of this is the priority given to the pre-existing plot system, when the most appropriate course of action would be to pick up the pre-existing *vies-intervies*, as applicable, but always to adapt them to the needs of the new *intervies*. Poblenou's carved up Parc Central, instead of a park that draws out new *intervies*, and the city blocks of 22@, which magnify a senseless pre-existing plot division, are proof of a failure to understand that new urban forms must be created in keeping with the new needs of movement and rest, moving beyond the plot division to design at the scale of the *vies-intervies* in each case.

_The decision to **interpret the territory on the basis of a structure of *vies-intervies* that takes as its scale of organization that of the urban nucleus and the *comarca* or county**. Cerdà proposed the **Eixample as an interchanger of relations and activities**

associated with the new means of transport. This is one of the points that calls for a more extensive reworking of his thinking, not so much of the principles as of the solutions put forward. In this respect, the introduction of faster means of transport and the appearance of decentralized means of communication such as the Internet lead to a more fragmented organization of settlements and relations. The associated urban forms can no longer be the 19th-century city extensions, which some people would like to see transferred literally to the 21st century. With a view to producing more sustainable territories, the means of transport, particularly public transport, are dictated by the new territorial topology. That is, urban centrality has to be conceived not at the municipal scale, but at a metropolitan scale defined by a radius of 1,000 m around railway nodes. Each of these metropolitan centralities is an interchanger of relations and associated activities that need to be encouraged. Normally there are two types of centrality: those that are the sum of the traditional urban centre and the central railway station that communicates it, and recently created areas of centrality situated around new railway centralities. The rest of the fabric must be subsidiary to these nodes. The discourse of urban centralities and new areas of centrality has already been introduced, but not so the urban forms they generate. If we base our discourse on compact cities, by which some understand traditional cities with limits, we gradually and indefinitely extend urban fabrics without addressing the issue of a new urban form adapted to the new structure of transport and telecommunications.

_The construction of the city using simple yet forceful elements, which, in the case of Barcelona's Eixample, were: models of **street, dwelling** and garden, and **urban utility networks.** It is necessary to provide the elements with which to construct and remodel the fabrics situated around railway nodes. More than extension, what the city requires is remodelling around nodes of accessibility using public transport or urban axes that connect two neighbouring public transport nodes. We can no longer construct the city piecemeal out of residential fabrics (extension, garden city, estate) (Solà Morales, 1993) and equip it with traditional services and facilities. We have to come up with a new urban form that provides metropolitan services, located in a centrality of metropolitan transport (an interchange station with two suburban train lines), which is also the element that constitutes the urban centrality of the nucleus or town that it has traditionally served.

_Picking up the previous point, so eloquently dealt with by Gabriel Dupuy in his book *Urban Networks—Network Urbanism* (Dupuy, 1991), what is needed is to be able to interpret the territory as a system of three levels of networks. A first level of physical networks of transport and telecommunications; a second level of networks of production, distribution and consumption (the interconnected system of the logistical and shopping centres that also go to make up the city), and a third level defined by the networks of family units which move beyond the limits of a municipality, represented by the organization of the family practices that interconnect the places of work and education of their members, places of consumption and leisure, and facilities. This is a functional territory that leaves behind the municipality to move around a sector of the metropolis. Following Cerdà's principle, access must be provided to the various **services, in keeping with the economy and the hygienic needs of each community, which will be influenced by these three levels of functional networks.** It is rather incoherent to carry on designing cities and territories in which urban and territorial planning is developed independently of the sectoral plan for commercial spaces. Planners set out to create centrality by means of facilities, whereas residents mostly revolve around shopping centres, which, in many cases, have no service or administrative facilities. We need to introduce integrated planning of transport networks and the

nodes associated with the economic networks of production, distribution and consumption, and the traditional structure defined by pre-existing urban systems.
_Cerdà proposed a series of bases: **legal**, **administrative**, **economic and political**. It is now urgent to construct a series of new urban planning bases associated with new means of transport and telecommunications. The master plan/special plan/urban improvement plan approach has become inflexible, principally because urban plans concentrate excessively on housing and traditional facilities (schools, hospitals, libraries). The central elements of transport, shopping centres and business parks function on the fringe and are not integrated with housing and traditional facilities. Municipalities do not have the economic, legal or administrative bases to manage their territory. Cerdà took a leap, stepping from the municipal scale to a scale of seven municipalities. Today, the scale is no longer municipal; it comprises a system of municipalities with a metropolitan dimension.

Barcelona's Eixample is the expression of Cerdà's urbanistic thinking. Cerdà formulated a body of reflection on the dwelling, the street, the crossroads and the sewerage system as instruments for city construction, and organized these elements by means of the concept of *vies-intervies* that took the form of a grid incorporated into the territory by means of "transcendental thoroughfares" (Gran Via, Meridiana, Paral·lel, Diagonal). This grid in turn organized dwelling, street, garden and sewerage by means of the city block, which is occupied by housing, industry and facilities. With this as his basis, he implemented a transport system that connected housing to the world. Understanding this overall organization is an exercise in urban planning of the first order and a point of reference, not as a finished product, but as a way of approaching the design of the territories and cities of our future. This is the great modernity of Cerdà's ideas and urbanistic thinking that goes beyond the Eixample, corroborated by the 150 years of modernity that Barcelona has experienced thanks to its extension.

Bibliography

BASSOLS, Martí. *Génesis y evolución del derecho urbanístico español (1812-1956).* Madrid: Montecorvo, 1973.

CERDÀ, Ildefons. *Monografía estadística de la clase obrera de Barcelona en 1856.* Madrid: Imp. Española, 1868. Appendix in vol. II of the *TGU*, of which Cerdà published one edition. In Fabià ESTAPÉ (1971).

CERDÀ, Ildefons. *Teoría de la construcción de las ciudades aplicada al Proyecto de reforma y ensanche de Barcelona*, April 1859. In *Cerdá y Barcelona* (1991: 107-450).

CERDÀ, Ildefons. *Ordenanzas de Construcción de Barcelona*, 1859. In *Cerdá y Barcelona* (1991: 513-548).

CERDÀ, Ildefons. *Pensamiento económico*, presented to the Spanish Ministry of Public Works on 23 January 1860. In *Cerdá y Barcelona* (1991: 457-471).

CERDÀ, Ildefons. *Teoría de la viabilidad urbana y reforma de la de Madrid, enero de 1861. Memoria del anteproyecto de Reforma Interior de Madrid.* In *Cerdá y Madrid* (1991: 45-280).

CERDÀ, Ildefons. *Cuatro palabras sobre el Ensanche.* Barcelona, Imp. N. Ramírez, 1861. In Fabià ESTAPÉ (1971: 571-589) and *Cerdá y Barcelona* (1991: 577-589).

CERDÀ, Ildefons. *Fomento del Ensanche de Barcelona*, 1863. In *Cerdá y Barcelona* (1991: 591-600).

CERDÀ, Ildefons. *Necesidades de la circulación*, 1863. In *Cerdá y Madrid* (1991: 291-305).

CERDÀ, Ildefons. *Teoría general de la urbanización.* Madrid: Imprenta Española, 1867, 2 vols. In Fabià ESTAPÉ (1971).

Cerdà y Barcelona. Teoría de la construcción de las ciudades, vol. I. Madrid: INAP & Ajuntament de Barcelona, 1991.

Cerdà y Madrid. Teoría de la viabilidad urbana, vol. II. Madrid: INAP & Ayuntamiento de Madrid, 1991.

CHOAY, Françoise. *La règle et le modèle: Sur la théorie de l'architecture et de l'urbanisme.* Paris: Seuil, 1980.

DUPUY, Gabriel. *Urban Networks—Network Urbanism.* Amsterdam: Techne Press, 2008.

ESTAPÉ, Fabià. *Teoría general de la urbanización. Estudio sobre la vida y obra de Ildefonso Cerdá*, vols I, II and III. Madrid: Instituto de Estudios Fiscales, 1971.

GRAU, Ramon (coord.). *Cerdà i els altres. La modernitat de Barcelona 1854-1874.* 2008. (ISSN: 1135-3058).

MAGRINYÀ, Francesc and TARRAGÓ, Salvador (eds.). Exhibition catalogue, *Mostra Cerdà. Urbs i territori*, September 1994-January 1995. Barcelona: Electa 1994.

MAGRINYÀ, Francesc. "Las influencias recibidas y proyectadas por Cerdà", *Ciudad y Territorio. Estudios Territoriales*, vol. XXXI, third period (119-120): 95-117, spring-summer 1999.

MAGRINYÀ, Francesc. "La théorie urbanistique de Cerdà et son application à l'«Ensanche» de Barcelone: une genèse d'urbanisme de réseaux". Doctoral thesis presented at the École Nationale des Ponts et Chaussées (ENPC) & University of Paris I, Paris, 2002.

MAGRINYÀ, Francesc. "Les propostes d'Ildefons Cerdà, 1854-1875: l'expressió urbanística i territorial d'un projecte de modernització", 9th Barcelona History Congress, Ca l'Ardiaca, 2005. Barcelona: *Quaderns d'Historia* (14): 81-116.

MAGRINYÀ, Francesc. "El ensanche y la reforma de Ildefons Cerdà como instrumento urbanístico de referencia en la modernización urbana de Barcelona". *Scripta Nova. Revista Electrónica de Geografía y Ciencias Sociales.* Barcelona: Universitat de Barcelona, 1 August 2009, vol. XIII, no. 296 (3). <http://www.ub.es/geocrit/sn/sn-296-3.htm>. [ISSN: 1138-9788].

ROSSI, Aldo. *The Architecture of the City.* Cambridge MA: MIT Press, 1984.

SOLÀ MORALES, Manuel de. *Les formes de creixement urbanà.* Barcelona: Edicions UPC, 1993. (Spanish edition: 1997).

SORIA, Arturo. *Las cinco bases de la teoría general de la urbanización.* Barcelona: Electa, 1996.

URBS I TERRITORI FOUNDATION ILDEFONS CERDÀ

SPONSORS AND PARTNERS

Ajuntament de Barcelona-Institut de Cultura
Diputació de Barcelona
Generalitat de Catalunya (Departament de Política Territorial i Obres Públiques)
Autoritat Portuària de Barcelona
Cambra de Comerç de Barcelona
Col·legi d'Arquitectes de Catalunya
Col·legi d'Enginyers Agrònoms de Catalunya
Col·legi d'Enginyers de Camins, Canals i Ports
Col·legi de Geògrafs
Consell Comarcal del Barcelonès
Gas Natural
Mancomunitat de Municipis-Àrea Metropolitana de Barcelona
Ministeri d'Habitatge
Obra Social "la Caixa"
Societat General d'Aigües de Barcelona (Grup Agbar)

EXHIBITION

Production
Fundació Urbs i Territori Ildefons Cerdà

Curator
Fernando Marzá

Scientific curator
Francesc Magrinyà

General coordination
Fernando Marzá, arquitecte SLU
Estel Ortega
Guim Català

Documentation
Estel Ortega
Guim Català

With the assistance of:
Alejandro de Guezala
Joan Sanabria

Coordination and preservation consultancy
Neus Moyano

Exhibition design
Fernando Marzá, arquitecto SLU
Marta Balañá

Graphic design of the exhibition
Marga Gibert
David Lorente

Photographic reproductions
Reproducciones Sabaté

Drawings and graphics for the exhibition
Dirección: Francesc Magrinyà
Alejandro de Guezala
Juan Pablo Olabarrieta

Photographs for the exhibition
Rosa Feliu, *Caras del Eixample*
Jordi Todó, *Barcelona de noche*
Rafael Vargas, *Remuntes*

Models for the exhibition
Taller de maquetas de l'Escola Tècnica Superior d'Arquitectura del Vallès - UPC
Angel García
Laura Baringo

Audiovisuals for the exhibition
Realización: Rosa Vergés
Música: Maurici Villavecchia
Fotografias: Quim Boix
Jefe de Producción: Julián Altuna
Atydante de dirección: Sònia Ros
Atrezzo: Vinyet Escobar
Producción ejecutiva: Albert Sagalés
Una producción de Diagonal TV

Lighting
Toni Rueda

Restoration of documents
Estudi B2
Rita Udina
Sophie Lennuyeux

Framing
Marcs Angle
Eric Galliache

Transport
Tti Fine Art Services

Courier
Mensajeros Ciudad

Insurance
AON Gil y Carvajal
Hiscox

INSTALLATION

Coordination
Alberto Calvete

Installation of works
Manubens i associats

Construction of partitions
OPERSIS

Furniture
Sobregrau Project

Metalwork
Lázaro CM

Electricity installation
BCN Servilux
iGuzzini
Instal·lacions i muntatges RST

Audiovisual installations
Codi-AV

Paint
DROPI

Fitted carpet
Alterra

PUBLICATION

Cerdà, 150 years of modernity
Noviembre 2009

Editors
Fernando Marzá
Francesc Magrinyà

Published by
Fundación Agbar

Authors
Rosa Feliu
Francesc Magrinyà
Fernando Marzá
Albert Serratosa
Angel Simón
Joan Tort

Coordination
Laura Parellada

Graphic design and layout
Ramon Prat
Marga Gibert

Translations and corrections
Joaquina Ballarín
Mònica Cabré
Anna Campeny
Elaine Fradley

Digital reproductions
Oriol Rigat

Photography
F. Argila
Pau Audouard
Aleix Bagué
Conxita Balcells
Frederic Ballell
Enric Berenguer
Jordi Blanch
Bordas
Brangulí (fotògrafs)
Josep Brangulí
Ignasi Canals
Martí Cargol
Lluís Casals
Gabriel Casas
Enric Castellà
Francesc Català-Roca
CETFA (Companyia Espanyola de Treballs Fotogramètrics Aeris)
Josep Maria Có de Triola
Colita
Josep Domínguez
Antoni Esplugas
Joan Estorch
Rosa Feliu
Eugeni Forcano
Fotografía Serra
Josep Gaspar
Pau Giralt-Miracle
Ramon Manent
Heribert Mariezcurrena
Joan Martí
Adolf Mas
Juan Mas Guàrdia
Joaquim Morelló
Pep Parer
Pedro Pegenaute
Pérez de Rozas
J.E. Puig
Andrés Rodríguez
Lucien Roisin
Luis Ros
Josep Maria Sagarra i Plana
Marcos Sala
TAF Helicòpters, SA
Jordi Todó
Àngel Toldrà
A. Torija
Pau Lluís Torrents
Rafael Vargas

ISBN: 978-1-945150-35-7

FUNDACIÓ URBS I TERRITORI
ILDEFONS CERDÀ (FUTIC)
Torre Agbar. Avinguda Diagonal, 211
08018 Barcelona

ACTAR Publishers
355 Lexington Avenue, 8th Floor
New York, NY 10017
www.actarpublishers.com

Fundació Urbs i Territori
Ildefons Cerdà

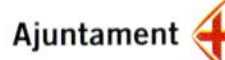

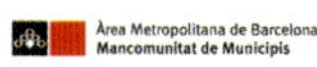

PROVIDERS

22@ Barcelona
Ajuntament de Barcelona
Daniel Aranda
Arxiu Agbar
Arxiu de la Corona d'Aragó. Ministeri de Cultura
Arxiu General de l'Administració. Ministeri de Cultura
Arxiu General Militar de Madrid
Arxiu Fotogràfic de Barcelona
Arxiu Fotogràfic del Centre Excursionista de Catalunya
Arxiu Fotogràfic Ramon Manent
Arxiu Històric de la Ciutat de Barcelona
Arxiu Històric del Col·legi d'Arquitectes de Catalunya
Arxiu Històric del Poblenou
Arxiu Històric de Sarrià
Arxiu Huertas
Arxiu Mas. Fundació Institut Amatller d'Art Hispànic
Arxiu Municipal Administratiu de l'Ajuntament de Barcelona
Arxiu Municipal del Districte de Sant Martí
Arxiu Nacional de Catalunya
Arxiu Carles Salmerón
Associació d'Amics del Ferrocarril de Barcelona
Autoritat del Transport Metropolità
Avery Architectural and Fine Arts Library. Columbia University
BAAS, Jordi Badia, arquitecte
BB+GG, Arquitectes
Beth Galí, Jaume Benavent
Batlle i Roig, arquitectes
Conxita Balcells, arquitecte
Josep Benedito, arquitecte
Mercè Berengué, arquitecte
Biblioteca de l'Ateneu Barcelonès
Biblioteca de Catalunya. Barcelona
Biblioteca del Centre Excursionista de Catalunya
Biblioteca de Ciències Socials. Universitat Autònoma de Barcelona
Biblioteca del Col·legi d'Arquitectes de Catalunya
Biblioteca de l'Escola Tècnica Superior d'Arquitectura de Barcelona. Universitat Politècnica de Catalunya
Biblioteca Pública Episcopal del Seminari de Barcelona
Càtedra Gaudí
Cité de l'architecture et du patrimoine. Centre d'archives d'architecture du xxe siècle
CLABSA
Colección KLUMPCOL, SL
Col·lecció Fernando Marzá - Neus Moyano
Col·lecció Antoni Pujol-Xicoy
Comissió d'Urbanisme i Serveis Comuns de Barcelona. Mancomunitat de Municipis
Federico Correa, arquitecte
CRAI-Biblioteca d'Econòmiques. Universitat de Barcelona
CRAI-Biblioteca de Filosofia, Geografia i Història. Universitat de Barcelona
CRAI-Biblioteca de Lletres. Universitat de Barcelona
Dipòsit temporal del Patronat del Castell de Montjuïc / Museu Militar
Rosa Feliu
Carlos Ferrater Partnership (OAB)
Fons Galmes Creus
Fons Històric de Ciència i Tecnologia. Biblioteca de l'Escola Tècnica Superior d'Enginyeria Industrial de Barcelona. UPC
Eugeni Forcano
Fundació Catalana per a la recerca
Gabinet d'Informació i Relacions Externes de RENFE. Barcelona.
ICIC-Filmoteca de Catalunya
Institut Cartogràfic de Catalunya. Cartoteca de Catalunya
Institut d'Estadística de Catalunya
Institut d'Estudis Fotogràfics de Catalunya (IEFC)
Institut d'Estudis Territorials
Institut Municipal d'Història
Josep Antoni Llinàs, arquitecte
MBM Arquitectes
Medi Ambient. Ajuntament de Barcelona
Museu de Granollers
Museu d'Història de Barcelona. Institut de Cultura de Barcelona
New York Public Library
Obra Social de Caixa Catalunya. Espai Gaudí
Ravetllat-Ribas, arquitectes
Real Academia de Bellas Artes de San Fernando
Enric Ruiz-Geli + Cloud 9, arquitectes
Taller de maquetes de l'Escola Tècnica Superior d'Arquitectura del Vallès. UPC
Tavisa
Televisió de Catalunya. TV3
Ramon Valls, arquitecte
Rafael Vargas
Albert Viaplana / David Viaplana, arquitectes

ACKNOWLEDGMENTS

Araceli Aiguaviva
David Alemany
Daniel Aranda
Elisenda Ardèvol
Joan Ardèvol
Fabián Asunción
Jordi Badia
Esther Bafaluy
Conxita Balcells
Sílvia Barberà
Laura Baringo
Ramon Barnadas
Enric Batlle
Encarna Bayona
Montserrat Beltran
Sergi Benajas
Josep Benedito
Corinne Bélier
Mercè Berengué
Anna Berenguer
Anna Bernárdez
Jordi Bernuz
Mar Berrocal
Oriol Bohigas
Maria Bohigas
Esteve Bonell
Antonio Bonet
Ferran Burguillos
Joan Buxadé
Amaya Caballero
Montserrat Caldés
Montserrat Calvet
Alberto Calvete
Salvador Canas
José Luis Canosa
Cristina Carmona
Andreu Carrascal
Marisa Carrete
Isabel Casas
Montserrat Catafal
CC d'Esplugues
Jordi Cerchs
Carolina Clares
Anna Clavell
Oriol Clos
Carme Clusellas
Manuel Coines
Isabel de Colmenares
Federico Correa
Rosa Cruellas
Lluís Cruz
Mónica Cruz
Albert Cuchí
Alfonso Dávila
Oliva Díaz
Jaume Dols
Mireia Duran
Olga Egea
Imma Espuelas
Josep Maria Farré
Rosa Feliu
Yolanda Fernández
Carlos Ferrater
Carme Ferrer
Laia Foix
Antonio Font
Montserrat Font
Eugeni Forcano
Zoel Forniés
Jordi Fossas
Antonio Gallart
Miquel Galmes
Ángel García
Fernando García Alejo
Jesús Alberto García Riesco
Núria Garcia
Òscar Garcia
Rosó Garcia
Josep Maria Gil
Rafael Giménez
Eva Gimeno
Alicia Gómez
Pilar Gonzalo
Dora Hernández
Guillem Huertas
Josep Jiménez
Toni Killinger
Eugenia Lalanza
Dolors Lamarca
Serafina Lavin
Mercè Lázaro
Josep Antoni Llinàs
Carles Llop
Miquel Lluch
Carlos López
Josep Maria Lucchetti
Núria de Luna
Maquetes Auladell
Maquetes Malberti
Pere Malgrat
Ramon Manent
Xavier Manubens
Joan Margarit
Lourdes Martín
Carme Martínez
Marina Marzá
Ivana Marzá
Josep Masbernat
Núria Masnou
Maria Mena
Alfonso Milà
Jaume Miranda
Anna Molina
Xavier Monteys
Teresa Navas
Josep Obius
Joel Oliver
Jaume Orpinell
Elena Ortueta
Janet Parks
Pere Pedrero
Núria Peiris
Pruden Penedès
Josep Ramon Pérez
Personal de la biblioteca de l'Arxiu Històric de la Ciutat de Barcelona
Conxita Petit
David Peyceré
Carme Piulachs
David Pou
Elena Puigmal
Antoni Pujol-Xicoy
Pere Quílez
Carlos Quirante
Alexandre Ragois
Montserrat Ramon
María José Rancaño
Pere Joan Ravetllat
Carme Ribas
Quico Rius
Dolça Roca
Joan Roca
Joan Roig
Montse Royuela
Enric Ruiz-Geli
María del Carmen Salinero
Jaume Sanmartí
Josep Maria Sans
Berta Santamaria
Maria Jesús Sanz
Carme Sardà
Rosa Saz
Eloïsa Sendra
Jaume Sobregrau Cussó
Jaume Sobregrau Pellicer
Miguel Ángel Sobrino
Xavier Tarraubella
Montserrat Tarrés
Mercè Tatjer
Jordi Todó
Alberto Torra
Rafael Torrella
Emi Turull
Josep Turiel
Gemma Valls
Ramon Valls
Rafael Vargas
Anna Ventura
Albert Viaplana
David Viaplana
Berenguer Vidal
Josep Maria Vilanova
Neus Vilaplana
Sílvia Vilarroya
Juan José Villar
Roc Villas
Rosendo Villaverde
Dolors Visa
Montse Viu
Rosina Vinyes
Gerardo Wadel